Thomas Clark

The Student's Handbook of Comparative Grammar

Thomas Clark

The Student's Handbook of Comparative Grammar

ISBN/EAN: 9783742817594

Manufactured in Europe, USA, Canada, Australia, Japa

Cover: Foto ©Andreas Hilbeck / pixelio.de

Manufactured and distributed by brebook publishing software (www.brebook.com)

Thomas Clark

The Student's Handbook of Comparative Grammar

THE
STUDENT'S HANDBOOK
OF
COMPARATIVE GRAMMAR.

APPLIED TO THE

SANSKRIT, ZEND, GREEK, LATIN,
GOTHIC, ANGLO-SAXON, AND ENGLISH LANGUAGES.

BY

REV. THOMAS CLARK, M.A.

LATE HEAD MASTER OF THE PROPRIETARY SCHOOL, TAUNTON.

LONDON:
LONGMAN, GREEN, LONGMAN, ROBERTS, & GREEN.
1862.

PREFACE.

COMPARATIVE GRAMMAR treats of several languages in conjunction. It explains what has become obscure in one by that which remains intelligible in others. It is thus enabled to trace the origin of grammatical forms, and to illustrate the nature of language itself more fully and satisfactorily than could be done by the investigation of any one language separately.

Lord Bacon judged that to be the noblest form of grammar* which should compare the properties of many tongues, 'both learned and vulgar,' and so attain to a perfect system—as Apelles shaped his Venus, not according to one model, but from the separate beauties of many individuals.

No linguist, however, appeared for centuries to carry out this idea. Little was done until the discovery and study of Sanskrit literature gave the impulse and supplied the materials for those works upon the subject which have appeared in Germany during the last thirty years.

* 'Nobilissima grammaticæ species.'

The results of this study are already considerable. The resources of language have been applied to the elucidation of Roman history,* and have established some important facts which escaped the penetration even of Niebuhr. The same means may reasonably be expected to place in a much clearer light the early social condition of many of the nations of antiquity.

It is also obvious that what makes language itself more intelligible will render important service in philosophical and ethical enquiries.

But it is in the acquisition and teaching of languages that Comparative Grammar will be found most extensively useful. It has been already applied to the Greek and Latin grammars; and it will not long be possible for anyone to teach them satisfactorily who has not at least made himself familiar with its leading principles.

An acquaintance with Comparative Grammar will be equally serviceable to the learner. Hitherto he has had to learn by rote what was never explained. He was told, for instance, that *habes* and *habetis* are the singular and plural of the same word, without being able to see how the one was derived from the other. He had to learn by heart several hundred equally unintelligible symbols, as mysterious to him as the Egyptian hieroglyphics. No doubt a great part of the reproach which has fallen upon the study of languages, as being a mere exercise of memory, is the consequence of so

* See Mommsen's *Römische Geschichte*.

many dead forms having to be learnt. As soon as life is imparted to them by proper explanation, the study of languages will be found to promote a more healthy development of the entire mental constitution than any other study. Many a youth who, under the old system, was glad to give up his Latin in exchange for the physical sciences, or was content to be behind others in a matter which he deemed to depend only upon memory, will then see that his judgment is called into exercise, and will feel as much pleasure in the study of languages as in that of geology or chemistry.

It is, therefore, not only important that the teacher should master this subject, but desirable also that its leading features should be made known to boys in the early part of their studies.

The works hitherto published are too extensive for general use, and one in a smaller compass appeared to be wanting.

In the following pages I have attempted little more than to put into a popular form what has been already established, and thus to meet the wants of those to whom the profounder and more voluminous works upon the subject are inaccessible. The materials have been in a great measure derived from the masterly *Vergleichende Grammatik* of Prof. Franz Bopp, to whom I desire to make the fullest acknowledgment here, as it would have too much broken the continuity of the work to state in every case how far his views have or have not been adopted. I have never differed from him without hesitation; and when his reasons have not appeared to me to be conclusive, if no better solution offered itself, I have stated his views, and have added his name as an authority. In the words of Monsieur Regnier,* 'I shall be glad if my book helps to increase the number of the readers of his great work.'

A larger number of languages could not well have been included in a work of this compass, and fewer would not have sufficed adequately to illustrate the principles of Comparative Grammar, and to give the subject a practical bearing for the English student.

I should have been glad to adopt Dr. Lepsius' admirable alphabetical system, but it would have required too great a departure from English associations for so elementary a treatise.

The employment of Greek characters seemed unavoidable. In other respects I have endeavoured to make the work available for the merely English student.

* *De la Formation des Mots Grecs.*

CONTENTS.

	Sect.
I. INTRODUCTION	1–3
The Indo-European Family of Languages	4, 5
The Indic Branch	6
The Iranic Branch	7
The Letto-Slavic Branch	8, 9
The Græco-Italic Branch	10–12
The Celtic Branch	13
The Teutonic Branch	14, 15
The High German	16
II. ALPHABETS:	
1. Sanskrit	17–19
2. Zend	20
3. Greek	21
4. Latin	22, 23
5. Gothic	24, 25
6. Anglo-Saxon	26, 27
III. SOUNDS	28–31
1. Sanskrit Vowels	32–35
„ Consonants	36–45
2. Zend	46–61
3. Greek	62, 63
4. Latin	64–66
5. Gothic	67–74
6. Anglo-Saxon	75–83
General Remarks	84–92
The Transmutation of Consonants	93–104

CONTENTS

	Sect.
IV. Roots	103–113
Verbal Roots	114, 115
Guna and Vriddhi	116
First Conjugation	117–122
Second Conjugation	123–129
Table of Roots	130
V. Stems	131, 132
Endings of Nominal Stems	133–136
Strong and Weak Stems	137, 138
VI. Formation of the Cases of Nouns	139
In the Singular	140–157
(The Pronominal *sma*)	146, 147
(Latin Names of Places in the Locative Singular)	153
In the Plural	158–169
In the Dual	170–173
VII. Adjectives, Comparison of	174–179
VIII. Numerals, Cardinal	180–195
" Ordinal	196, 197
Numeral Adverbs	198
IX. Pronouns of the First and Second Persons	199–202
" of the Third Person	203–206
Derivative Adjective Pronouns	207
Pronominal Adverbs	208
X. The Verb	209
Formation of the Middle Voice	210–212
Persons: First	213–216
Second	217–219
Third	220–222
The Weight of Personal Endings	223
Conjugations	224–227
The Formation of Tenses	228, 229
Present	230
Imperfect	231, 232
Aorist	233–235
Perfect	236–239
Pluperfect	240
Future	240a

CONTENTS

		Sect.
Moods: Potential, Optative, Conjunctive	.	241, 242
Imperative	.	243
Conditional	.	244, 245
Passive, Causal, Desiderative, and Intensive Verbs	.	246–249
Denominatives	.	250

XI. DERIVATION AND COMPOSITION.

a) Derivatives:

Forms in NT or NTA	251
„ WANS	251*a*
„ MANA	252
„ NDO	253
„ TAR	254–257
„ TA	258
„ NA	259, 260
„ TI, NI	261
„ TU, NU	262
„ SA, SE	263
Germanic Infinitive	264
Greek Infinitives	265, 266
Forms in YA	267–270
Bare Roots	271
Forms in A	272
„ I	273
„ U	274
„ AN	275
„ ANA	276
„ AS	277
„ LA, RA	278
„ WA (VA)	279
„ WAN (VAN) . . .	280
„ NU	281
„ MI	282
„ KA	282*a*
„ TU	283
„ TANA	284
„ SYA	285
b) Compounds: Verbal	286, 287
Nominal	288–296

	Sect.
XII. INDECLINABLE WORDS	297
1. Adverbs	298
2. Conjunctions	299
3. Prepositions	300

The following abbreviations are employed:

a. s. for Anglo-Saxon.	lith. for Lithuanian.
e. ,, English.	o. g. ,, Old German.
ger. ,, German.	o. s. ,, Old Saxon.
go. ,, Gothic.	s. ,, Sanskrit.
gr. ,, Greek.	v. ,, Vêdas.
l. ,, Latin.	z. ,, Zend.
Du. for Dual.	N. for Neuter.
F. ,, Feminine.	Pl. ,, Plural.
M. ,, Masculine.	S. ,, Singular.

THE
STUDENT'S HANDBOOK
OF
COMPARATIVE GRAMMAR

I. INTRODUCTION.

1. LANGUAGE is that which principally distinguishes man from the lower orders of creation. It is inseparable from his mental existence. Thought is internal language, and language is external thought. So distinguishing a quality of human nature could not fail to arrest attention in a reflecting age. Locke and Leibnitz recognised its importance in the philosophy of the human mind. But it was necessary to employ a mode of investigation which was then but little understood, before the essential connection and true relations of mind and speech could be discovered. As the animal economy needed the help of Comparative Anatomy for its elucidation, so the *Comparison of Languages* alone can explain some of the operations of the human mind.

In other respects, also, Comparative Philology was long regarded as of great importance. It was looked upon as serving not only to promote a more exact acquaintance with particular languages, but also as developing *the nature of language itself*, and thus aiding in the solution of the difficult problem of the origin of language.

These and other considerations led to many isolated efforts in this direction at an early period, but it is only in the present century that the subject can be said to have assumed the features, and acquired the proportions of a science. Since then it has had to encounter the fate of every new science. It has been magnified by extravagant pretensions, and assailed by equally extravagant depreciation. Half knowledge on the one hand, and utter ignorance on the other, are equally prejudicial. But meanwhile a large number of works upon the subject have appeared from men of literary eminence, composed in a spirit of moderation, and bearing evidence of great power and deep research. They have placed the science of language upon a secure basis, and furnished the materials for its wide and rapid extension.

2. Though an acquaintance with Comparative Grammar will not do away with all the labour and difficulty of acquiring the knowledge of languages, it will, nevertheless, facilitate their acquisition. Much of the difficulty to a beginner lies in the strangeness of the forms which he meets with in a new language. Whatever diminishes this strangeness will proportionately diminish the difficulty of learning the language. He who is aware, for instance, that in certain cases, German words have *s* where the corresponding words in English have *t*, will more readily acquire a familiarity with the German words *was, das, weiss*, from his previous acquaintance with the English words, *what, that, white*, than another will who begins his study in ignorance of this fact.

The relation of Comparative Philology to history

admits of similar remarks. It has already thrown much light upon historical points which were obscure, and which, but for the scientific study of language, must have remained obscure. Some valuable illustrations of this may be found in the earlier part of Mommsen's 'Römische Geschichte.' But it is specially in regard to the ante-historical period of human existence that the Science of Language promises important results. A nation naturally desires to discover its origin, but history can trace its course only from the time when it had already reached a mature age. Its infancy, boyhood, and youth are hidden in a mysterious obscurity, or coloured by legendary tales. The Divine Record offers but few hints that could serve to connect modern nations with the earliest period; nor were they probably intended to prevent the inquiries of science, any more than the narrative of the fourth day's creation was designed to supersede the investigations of Astronomy.

It is not, however, exclusively nor chiefly on account of its practical utility that Comparative Philology deserves attention. It is worthy of being pursued for its own sake. Even in its present stage it shows that human language deserves no mean place among the objects of nature. It exhibits a growth as wonderful as that of the plants which furnish the materials for the science of botany, and develops laws as subtle as those by which astronomy explains the motions of the planets.

3. The great variety of languages is perhaps referrible to the intimate connection between spirit and speech. The characteristics of the one are expressed in the other. The human mind is exactly the same, probably, in no two individuals. Some peculiarity distinguishes the spiritual nature of every member of the human family. This

variety is reflected in the outward expressions of mind. In proportion as the intellect is cultivated, the countenance assumes a more distinct individuality. In the higher stages of civilisation no two faces contain exactly the same features, whilst a want of culture tends to leave a dead uniformity of expression.

Upon language, also, the mind impresses its own individuality, and but for artificial restraints against multiplication there would be almost as many languages as individuals. A thousand distinct languages are said to be spoken upon the earth. The number of dialects is immensely greater. There are places even in Europe where the inhabitants of each hamlet or small district speak such different dialects of one language, as to be almost unintelligible to each other. The uneducated inhabitants of one county in England, in some cases, deem the language of the next county strange and almost barbarous. The people of Lancashire and those of Hampshire, both speaking genuine English, would be almost unintelligible to each other.

This natural tendency to diversity is checked by artificial means. The use of written and printed characters, the influence of education and social intercourse, impart a certain degree of uniformity to the speech of the same society, or town, or nation.

It is evident that the attempt to form a Comparative Grammar of the entire languages of the human race would be futile. The materials of those languages, even, which have been stereotyped in a classical character are not yet in a sufficiently forward state to be all embraced in the same work.

4. The Indo-European branch of the great family of languages contains the most important literature, is the most easily accessible, and has, to a great extent, been

already examined and classified by eminent men, both of the present and of past generations. This division includes nearly all the languages spoken in Europe, and a large proportion of those spoken in Asia, west of the Ganges. Its range has also been extended in modern times by migration. The English, French, and German languages are spoken in the principal portion of North America, and in isolated parts throughout the rest of the world.

Various terms have been adopted as a collective designation of these languages. Amongst them Indo-European seems the best adapted for our present purpose. It is at once intelligible to English readers, and sufficiently comprehensive; for until these languages were carried abroad by emigration, they were little, if at all, spoken either eastward of India or westward of Europe, whilst at a very early period they stretched in an almost uninterrupted chain from the Ganges to the Atlantic.

This division of languages, however, does not include those commonly called Semitic, and a few other strangers, of minor importance as far as concerns the literature which they possess, or the numbers by whom they are spoken, are mixed among the Indo-European family. Thus the Georgian and Turkish in Asia; the Turkish, Hungarian, Finnish, Lappish, and Basque in Europe, must be left out of account. Probably further investigation will show that some of these are more or less intimately related in origin and development to their neighbours.

5. The languages thus remaining under the designation Indo-European, are numerous and important. They may be conveniently arranged in seven classes, of which two belong to Asia and five to Europe. Another arrangement of them might be made into three divisions, the first including five of the above classes, distinguished by the oldest grammatical forms, the second that which has intermediate forms, and the third that which has the newest forms. The reason for this will appear more fully hereafter. It will be sufficient at present to mention that in the nouns, l. *jugum*, e. *yoke*, ger. *joch*, the letters *g*, *k*, *ch* (for *kh*), distinguish these divisions, and that the same distinction is indicated in the verbs, l. *docet*, e. *teaches*, ger. *zeigt*, by the letters, *d*, *t*, *z* (for *ts*).

1. INDIC or SANSKRIT.

6. In considering the *seven classes*, we begin with the most easterly, and that which also has the most ancient literature, *i.e.* the SANSKRIT. It is a language which, though possessing voluminous and valuable works in prose and verse, has but recently become known to Europe. The Science of Language, as it is now pursued, may, indeed, be looked upon as one of the results of the establishment of British dominion in India. For British residents, Sir William Jones amongst the first, collected and brought over the stores of this ancient literature, which German philologists, with profound research and indomitable perseverance, have made subservient to the elucidation of all the sister languages.

The modern dialects of Northern India, though of the same stock, interest us less in the following inquiry. The elucidation which we seek will be sufficiently supplied by the Sanskrit, under which name, however, we include the *Védas*, as well as the more recent literature specially called Sanskrit.

The *Védas* are not only the most ancient literature of India, but are also the oldest expression of thought in the Indo-European languages altogether. The late Professor H. H. Wilson, reasoning from the later to the earlier compositions, supposed the heroic poems in Sanskrit to have been written about 300 years B.C., the laws of Manu three centuries earlier, the prose *Brahmanas*, which elucidate the Védas, 800 B.C., and the *Védas* themselves about 1300, B.C. This, however, can only be looked upon as an approximation to the chronology of the whole, for the several parts are evidently the work of different authors, and some were manifestly composed at a much earlier period than the time when the whole were collected and arranged together as we now have them.

The Védas thus contain a literature older than the Homeric poems, and, what is more important in a grammatical point of view, it is the literature of a people who had migrated a much shorter distance from the primitive abode of the race, and undergone much fewer political and social changes than the Greeks, the forms of whose language, therefore, for this very reason, must be much nearer to the primitive type than either the Greek or any other branch of the same great family.

The Védas consist of four collections, the last being more recently made than the other three. Their names are: 1, *Rig-Véda*; 2, *Yajur-Véda*; 3, *Sáma-Véda*; and 4, *Atharva-Véda*. Each consists of two divisions, *i. e.* the text, or *Mantras*, and the commentary, or *Brahmanas*. The former comprises principally sacred hymns addressed to various deities. Many of these are representatives of natural objects, *e.g. Agni* ('fire'), to which the first hymn of the Rig-Véda is addressed; the *Maruts* ('winds'), to which the nineteenth is in part addressed. Many are addressed to *Indra*, who presides over the firmament, and sends or withholds the fertilising shower. The valley of the Indus appears to be the locality where these hymns were produced. They reflect simple habits of life, and a primitive state of society. The sacrifices offered are in general not costly, and the blessings implored are principally the material advantages of the present life.

The language of these hymns exhibits a nearer approach than any other to the first forms in which thought must have been expressed by the Indo-European branch of the human family. It serves to clear up many points left in obscurity by the fragmentary state of other languages, and is an essential element in any just appreciation of the questions discussed in Comparative Grammar.

The classical *Sanskrit*, however, though of a later date, contains a richer literature, and more abundant materials for linguistic investigation. The country in which it appears to have been first employed as a spoken language, and to which, as a spoken language in its purity, it was confined, is India. The words preserved by Ctesias, in the time of Artaxerxes-Mnemon, show that the influence of the language had extended over the south as well as the north. The people by whom it was employed are probably the same race as those who, centuries earlier, sang the Véda hymn on the banks of the Indus. Everything shows that they came from the north-west, and gained possession of India by conquest. The simple mythology which they brought with them was soon remodelled under the hands of poets and sages, and, probably in part through contact with the primitive inhabitants whom they found in the country. India thus became the home, and the Sanskrit language the organ, of the Brahman religion.

The literature which is contained in this language extends over a considerable space of time. It must date its commencement, at least, soon after the invasion of the country. The earliest productions have probably perished, and it would be some time before the heroic deeds of the invaders would be made the ground-work of the voluminous epic poems *Mahábhárata* and *Rámáyana*. It ceased to be a spoken language in consequence of the popular agitations in behalf of Buddhism, and the prominence given to the common dialects in opposition to the language of the predominant religion. Sanskrit, however, continued to be the language of the Brahman religion, of learning, and of poetry. It contains numerous works in various branches of knowledge from the earliest to recent times.

The utility of this language in our present inquiry results from the almost perfect preservation of forms which have only a fragmentary and perplexing appearance in modern languages. The English word *came*, for example, is used by us as a past tense, although nothing in its letters indicates past time, unless it be *a* instead of the *o*, of the present *come*. This, however, is not felt to be a tense-sign at all, for it occurs in just the reverse way in the present *break*, as compared with *broke*. Nor is there any termination to the word *came*, except in the almost obsolete second person singular *camest*, to show what person and how many persons came, whilst in Sanskrit a corresponding word not only indicates the tense, but has no less than nine different endings, to show whether it applies to the first, second, or third person, and whether it includes only one or two or more individuals. The enigmatical second person singular, *camest*, is explained by one of them. Again, the same language has eight different endings for as many cases of a noun. One of them presents the form out of which the English possessive 's has come. This termination thus appears to be the remains of a form older than the English language itself, and not to have come from adding *his* to a noun, and then contracting these together as some have assumed; thus taking 'queen's own' to be for 'queen his own,' and 'men's ideas' for 'men his ideas.' That such expressions occur in English writers as 'the king his horse,' only shows that whoever first originated them found the form of the possessive case. obscure, and could not rest without explaining what they did not understand. Thus an appeal to older records supplies the part of the inscription which time had obliterated.

The Sanskrit will generally be appealed to in the following pages; the Védas sometimes as having a few remains of a still older form; but other languages nearly related to them will not come within our scope. They are the following:

1. The *Prâcrit*, or popular dialects assigned to subordinate characters in Sanskrit dramas. They are generally distinguished by a considerable softening of sounds and decay of grammatical forms.

2. The *Pali*, which was conveyed by banished Buddhists to Ceylon. It became, like Sanskrit, from which it differed principally in the loss of grammatical forms, a learned language. It contains theological works on the Buddhist religion as early as the fifth century A. D.

3. The *Kawi*, which was preserved in the Islands of Java and Bali as a literary and poetic language. Its grammatical forms became mutilated, very much

like those of the Pali, by contact with a strange people.

4. The *Gypsy* language belongs to the same class, for after the most varied theories had been adopted respecting their origin, as indicated in the names Gypsies (Egyptians), Bohemiens (Bohemians), it has come to be generally admitted that this singular people came from India. Their language is the old Sanskrit, though very much corrupted and mixed with foreign elements.

The modern languages of India belonging to the same family are reckoned by Pott to be twenty-four in number. The principal is the Hindostanee. They all bear the relation of daughters to the Sanskrit, and not that of sisters, like the four noticed above. They have each a peculiar deviation of features from the primitive type, and have only a subordinate relation to our subject.

2. IRANIC.

7. The *second class* of the Indo-European languages is called *Iranic*, and belongs principally to the country between the Indus and the Tigris. It is so called from the Persian word Iran—another form of the Sanskrit word Aryan—applied to the region which stretches from the chain of the Hindoo Koosh to the Persian Gulf. The term Iranian includes a considerable number of languages.

1. Of these the oldest is the *Zend*, the language of the Zend-Avesta, or sacred writings ascribed to Zoroaster. The country where this language prevailed, and the people by whom it was employed cannot be exactly defined, and the language itself presents many difficulties. Early investigations in it were carried on

principally by means of translations, and presented, therefore, but confused and unsatisfactory results. Of late, however, it has been subjected to more scientific investigation, and much assistance has been derived from the discovery and elucidation of the arrow-headed inscriptions belonging to the time of the Achæmenidæ. The age of Darius, to whom some of these inscriptions owe their existence, is well known, and it lends some help in conjecturing the age of the Zend-Avesta. For on comparing the grammatical forms of the inscriptions with those of the Zend language, the latter are found to be of an older character, and they, therefore, belong to an earlier date. They are thus referred to a period earlier than the fifth century B.C. These writings are loosely spoken of as the writings of Zoroaster, but the date of his existence is a problem not yet satisfactorily solved. Besides, it appears that only a small portion can justly be ascribed to him, and, therefore, if the time when he lived could be fixed, it would leave the chronology of a great part of the Zend-Avesta doubtful.

The great difference between the grammars of the Sanskrit and the Zend might favour the idea that some centuries had elapsed, after the separation of the two peoples, before the Zend acquired the form in which it was written. Such would, undoubtedly, be a reasonable inference if we could assume that the Zend was developed from the Sanskrit. But the two peoples may have spoken very different languages even before they separated, just as in England the people of two counties, or the educated and uneducated in the same county, speak differently one from another. It appears to have been a religious movement which caused the separation of the Iranian from the Indian branch. The oldest

Iranians were fire-worshippers. It is in the nature of things probable that the zeal for this religion would manifest itself chiefly in some particular province, and principally affect some particular class of the community, probably not the most educated. They would, therefore, already have a characteristic—a so-called provincial—language. So that if the Zend-Avesta were written immediately on the separation of the two peoples, its language would differ very much from that of the educated classes whom they left, and whose writings have become known to us as Sanskrit. The word Iranian itself furnishes one illustration out of many which might be adduced. The Sanskrit word Aryan appears in Zend as Airyan, in accordance with a general practice that, when *y* follows a single consonant, *i* is inserted in the preceding syllable. Thus what one (perhaps the educated) called *aryan* (*ar* as in *far*), the other (perhaps the uneducated) called *airyan* (*air* like *ir* in *fire*). Even now, in English, where one says 'are you coming,' another says, 'aire you coming.' Whatever caused the difference, it may have existed before the separation of the peoples, and, therefore, supplies no argument against the antiquity of the Zend-Avesta.

We find here two circumstances which render the Zend valuable in a work on Comparative Grammar. One is that it presents another instance of a very ancient and almost primitive language of the Indo-European family, side by side with the Sanskrit. The second consideration is that it presents grammatical modifications peculiarly its own, and thus serves strikingly to elucidate the genesis of language.

Pott seems inclined to fix its locality in Bactria, and Professor Schleicher calls the language Old Bactrian.

But it is not well to build too much upon what is merely hypothetical.

2. The next Iranian language in historical order is that of the *arrow-headed inscriptions* belonging to the reign of the Achæmenidæ, which therefore belongs to the fifth century B.C., and to the land of Media. The phonetic decay of its form shows that it belongs to a later period than the Zend.

3. The modern *Persian* strikingly illustrates the destructive effect of time upon the framework of language. Like the English it has preserved but few remains of the inflections which are so abundant in the older languages of the same class. It was a hasty generalisation which led to the idea that the Persian was closely related to the modern languages of Germany and England, and that the fuller forms of older dialect were only excrescences which disfigured them. A juster analysis has shown that in regard to grammatical inflection these modern languages are but scanty ruins, whilst the Sanskrit presents a grand and almost complete edifice.

4. To the east of Iran there are a few scattered populations, which have issued from the same stock, and speak languages belonging to the same class as those mentioned above. They have thus far rendered but little service to Comparative Grammar, and here require but a brief notice.

The *Pushtoo*, in Affghanistan, is nearly related to the Persian, but exhibits some peculiar grammatical forms and has a large admixture of foreign words. The *Beloochee*, of which but little is known, is spoken at the mouth of the Indus, and the *Parsee* by the Parsees in Guzerat and elsewhere.

5. To the westward we meet with three other mem-

bers of the same family. The language of the *Koords* in Koordistan; the *Ossetic*, spoken by a small mountain tribe on the Caucasus, who call themselves Iron, and their country Iron-sag, thus preserving the tradition of their origin; and the *Armenian*, which possesses an important literature, including a translation of the Septuagint, made at the beginning of the fifth century, and of the works of some of the Greek fathers. It seems likely, when further examined, to render more extensive service upon questions of Comparative Grammar than any other language of this class, except the Zend.

Almost all the modern literature of this class of languages contains a considerable admixture of Semitic words, in consequence of their geographical position, and of the spread of Mohamedanism.

The Iranian class of languages is remarkable for the number of characters employed in writing them, the Zend, the Arrow-headed inscriptions, and the Armenian, having characters quite distinct one from the other.

3. LETTO-SLAVIC.

8. The *third class* consists of the Lettic and Slavic languages.

1. The *Lettic* includes the Lettish, the Lithuanian, and Old Prussian. The Lettish is spoken in Kurland and Livonia, but has been much corrupted by the influence of other languages.

The *Lithuanian* is now spoken by only a small population in the north-east of Prussia and in the neighbouring districts of Russia. Its literary store is very circumscribed and of recent date. It has, however, considerable value on account of its almost perfect preservation of some of the original grammatical forms. The *Old Prussian*, which has now ceased to be a spoken language, bore a very close resemblance to the Lithuanian. They were neither of them much exposed to the influence of those external causes which generally modify the language of a people. The Lithuanians occupied a flat and marshy country, and never attained a very high state of civilisation. The character of their home, together with the inactive political life which they have led, will help to account for the unaltered state of their language. The Sanskrit, for instance, has probably preserved the interrogative pronoun in its primitive state. It there appears as *kas*, so written three thousand years ago. In the Lithuanian, as spoken at the present day, it is likewise *kas*, whilst the Greek almost three thousand years ago had changed it to *kos*, the Latin above two thousand years ago, to *quis*, the Gothic, fifteen hundred years ago, to *hvas*, and we have it in the still further reduced form of *hwo* (*who*). The Lithuanian *katras*, again, is almost identical with the Sans. *kátaras*, whilst the Greek is *poteros*, the Lat. *uter*, the Go. *hvathra*, and Eng. *whether*. There is perhaps no other people who have spoken the original Indo-European language with so little alteration in many of its grammatical forms for the same length of time.

9. 2. The *second branch* includes a large number of languages stretching from the Adriatic to the Gulf of Finland, and from the coast of the North Sea to the Ural mountains. They are condensed together, however, principally in Russia and Austria. History cannot trace the Slavic population back to their original abode in Asia, but it finds them at a very early period in the extreme East of Europe. Herodotus, in the fifth century B.C., speaks of the Βουδίνοι, iv. 21, and Larcher, in his note upon the passage says, 'The opinion of Rennel and Heeren, who assign the *Budini* to the vicinity of Voroniej near the southern border of the government of Tambof, is entitled to preference.' The description of them accords with the idea of their being a part of the Slavic people, and Shafarik, in his important work upon the antiquities of the Slavic race, does not hesitate to claim them. This people, therefore, who probably left the primitive abode at about the same time as the Iranians, are found on the north of the Caspian at the time when the Medes under Darius were leaving a written memorial of their presence on the south of the Caspian in the arrow-headed inscriptions. They appear in Dacia, north-west of the Black Sea, in contact with the Romans under Trajan, at the beginning of the second century of the Christian era. We find the evidence of their presence later in Pannonia, for *Buda* is one of the names of Pesth, the capital of Hungary, and in more recent times they gave its name to the town of Bunzlau, more properly Budissin, in the Prussian province of Lusatia. Thus, as time passes on, we find them proceeding further westward.

The Slavonians began to attain political consolidation and importance after the death of Attila, who with his Huns had held them in terror and subjection. The Bohemian nation appears as early as 650; the Bulgarian about the same time, but in greater power under Boris in 850; the Moravian under Rastislaw and the farfamed Swatopluk during the ninth century; the Polish as early as the seventh century; the Russian under Rurik in 862; and the Servian in the eleventh century. Some of these states for a short time extended their dominion along the south coast of the Baltic and westward to the mouth of the Elbe. The only independent Slavic nation at present is Russia, the rest being under foreign dominion, and the imperial family even of Russia is of German origin.

The literature of the Slavonians is modern. The earliest remains go no further back than the ninth century. The first impulse was given to it by the two brothers Methodius and Cyrillus (Constantine), who came from Constantinople as Christian missionaries to labour among the Slavonians, as Ulfilas had done four or five centuries before among the Goths. They made an alphabet founded upon the Greek character, which, with some modifications, is still employed in Russia and Servia. They translated the Gospels into the language of the people among whom they dwelt, who were probably the Bulgarians. The language is therefore sometimes called Old Bulgarian as well as Old Slavic and Church Slavic. The last name is employed in consequence of the language in which the missionaries made their translation being still employed in the services of the Greek Church; so that, like the Latin in the Roman Catholic Church, it has acquired an ecclesiastical character. Nestorius in the eleventh century also wrote his Chronicles of Russia in the same language.

No less than fifteen languages are enumerated as belonging to this class. Several of them, however, have had but little literary development. Those which contain the most important literature are—1, the *Bohemian*, whose remains begin with a collection of national poems belonging to the thirteenth century; 2, the *Polish*, which begins with the Psalter of Florian, belonging to the thirteenth and fourteenth centuries; and 3, the *Russian*, which has made rapid progress since the time of Peter the Great, and now possesses an extensive literature, especially upon scientific subjects.

The Old or Church Slavic is the most serviceable of this branch for the purpose of Comparative Grammar, but this entire class is not quoted in the following work because the Sanskrit and Zend elucidate the points to which it would apply, sufficiently for our purpose.

4. GRÆCO-ITALIC.

10. The *fourth class* is the *Græco-Italic*, spoken principally in the two great peninsulas which run southwards into the Mediterranean, and in the neighbouring islands. That neither the Greek nor the Latin owes its origin to the other, but that they are related together as sister-languages becomes obvious on an examination of their grammatical forms and the roots of words. Their resemblance to one another is somewhat disguised by their being written in different characters, and by the circumstance that different means are resorted to in expressing the analogous changes which time has produced in both. The defective analysis of former years caused the Latin to be spoken of as *derived* from the Greek, whereas recent investigations have shown that, in some instances at least, the Latin has older forms than the Greek. Such, for example, is the preservation of the ablative singular which is wanting in Greek, and the fuller ending *-bus* in the dative plural. Greek, on the other hand, undoubtedly has many older forms than the corresponding Latin ones. Evidence also supports the theory that the Italic tribes did not enter Italy by sea from Greece, but by land from the north. The Hellenic and Italic races seem to have parted company in the neighbourhood of the Danube and to have taken a southerly direction previously to the approach of the Slavic race, which we have seen in the same region.

The first three classes probably left the original abode of the family at the same time, the Indian taking a south-eastern direction, the Iranian a south-western, whilst the Slavic went directly westward. We now come to those classes which, from their more westerly position and from the greater deviation of their languages from the original type, seem to have left the common home at an earlier time. Their history also exhibits them in a more adventurous and victorious character, which agrees with the idea that they were the first to break off the associations of home and dare to invade distant lands.

11. 1. The *Greek* language claims our first attention from its occupying a more easterly position and possessing an older literature than the Latin. It flourished principally in the eastern peninsula of the Mediterranean, in the islands of the Archipelago, and on the western coast of Asia Minor. It there produced the most perfect literature in the world — a literature which continues greatly to influence the opinions, the character, and the institutions of all the members of the Indo-European family throughout Europe and America.

The variety with which Greek was spoken as a living language is illustrated in three principal *dialects*, the Æolic, Doric, and Ionic. The last differs considerably from the other two. This difference is illustrated in the national legend by Æolus and Dorus being represented as sons and Ion as a grandson of Hellen. The Ionic grew up in a foreign land, Asia Minor; a fact represented in the legend by the name of Ion's father, Xuthus, meaning 'banished.'

The *Ionic* far surpasses the other dialects in the abundance and perfection of its literary remains. The oldest form in which it appears is the *Epic* dialect of

'Homer and Hesiod, whose date is variously fixed from the twelfth to the ninth century B.C. It next appears in the *New Ionic* of Herodotus, which belongs to the middle of the fifth century. But its richest productions are in the *Attic* dialect, brought to marvellous perfection by dramatists, historians, philosophers and orators, from the middle of the fifth to the middle of the fourth centuries.

The *Æolic* was spoken chiefly in Asia Minor, Bœotia and Thessaly, and includes the celebrated names of Alcæus, Sappho and Corinna. The range of its literature is very limited, but it preserves some very old forms in its grammatical construction, and has a special interest from its close resemblance in several points to the Latin language.

The *Doric* was spoken chiefly in the north of Greece, in the Peloponnese, in Crete, and in Sicily. Its principal representatives are Pindar and Theocritus.

The Greek furnishes us with striking examples illustrative of the effect accomplished in a certain length of time by the influences which are continually producing phonetic decay in living languages. The language of Homer may be regarded as five hundred years later than that of the Védas; and this difference of time corresponds with the difference of form in the one language as compared with the other. For instance, the genitive case singular of the *a* stems in Sanskrit ends in *a-sya*. In Homer it is *o-io*, in which we see that every element has undergone a change; for *a* the lighter vowel *o* is substituted in both cases, for *y* the vowel *i*, and *s* is lost altogether. Five hundred years later, again, the Attic dialect presents to us the same form reduced to *ou*; that is, *oo* is reduced to the weaker form *ou*, and *i* is lost altogether. These changes are not sporadic instances which might be owing to accident. They affect the entire mass of the language to which they belong, and rest upon general principles. There is no example of the older *a-sya* in the language of Homer, nor any instance of the Homeric *o-io* in the Attic dialect. These effects appear as if they were accomplished at once and therefore artificially, but this only results from our not possessing literary records during the time which intervened between these epochs to illustrate the gradual approaches towards the final result. Any one will see how gradually such modifications are effected who examines the change which is going on from *th* to *s*, from *hath* to *has*, for instance, in the third person singular of the present tense in English verbs. It is long since it began, and it is not yet completed; but if when *hath* is exterminated and *has* is universal, all the intervening literature between the first employment of *s* and the last use of *th* were to disappear, we should have an instance similar to those noticed above.

12. 2. The *Italic* branch of this class of languages belongs almost exclusively to the western peninsula of the Mediterranean. The Latin tribe gradually gained the upper hand in the political constitution of the country, and the Latin language became the organ of public life, of education, and of literature. It was not, however, the only language spoken by the Indo-European population who entered the peninsula from the north. It is evident that before their arrival, or soon after their settlement, their speech was marked by varieties as distinct as the Greek dialects, and though only one has become embodied in a considerable literature, yet some important remains belonging to others have recently been discovered.

The science of language has thrown considerable

light upon the character of the ancient population of Italy. It seems to have been invaded in succession by very different races. Some of them probably were not Indo-Europeans. But several tribes of which remains have been preserved evidently belong to the same family as the Latin. In the extreme south-east of the country inscriptions have been discovered composed in a language which, for want of a better name, has been called *Iapygian*. It appears at one time to have prevailed more or less throughout Apulia and Calabria. The remains of this language have not yet been sufficiently deciphered to determine the exact ethnological position of the people by whom it was spoken, and they appear to have presented but little if any resistance to the superior civilisation of Greece; for Apulia, which is spoken of in the time of Timæus the historian (400 A.C.C.) as inhabited by barbarous Iapygians, in less than two centuries appears to be an entirely Greek district.

Clearer evidence is supplied of the relation of two other peoples, or branches of the same people, who early occupied the middle of the peninsula, *i.e.* the *Latin* and the *Umbrian* branches. The latter, including the Marsians and Samnites in the south, comprised a considerable population. The dialects which prevailed amongst them have a close resemblance to one another, but in many points they form a contrast to the Latin. Distinctions appear which are also found in other classes of the Indo-European languages. Thus, where the Roman employed *q*, as in the interrogative pronoun, the Samnite and Umbrian employed *p*, sounds which also distinguish the Ionic from the Attic dialects in Greek, and the Celtic languages in Bretagne and Wales from the Gaelic and Irish. The Latin language has, upon the whole, some such relation to the Umbro-Samnite, as the Ionic has to the Doric, whilst the varieties in the Oscan and Umbrian, as well as other dialects related to them, in distinction from the Latin, are similar to those of the Doric in Sicily and in Sparta.

Of all the Italic languages, the *Latin* only has furnished us with any considerable literature, and from it, therefore, our examples for this branch of languages will be principally derived. It presents no great literary works in a perfect state earlier than the second century, B.C. What precedes that period is fragmentary or only brief. These older remains exhibit some archaic forms which are of great value. But Roman literature is several centuries later than that of Greece, which, of itself, is sufficient to account for the terminations of Latin words being, upon the whole, much more curtailed than the corresponding Greek ones. Thus the genitive singular, which appears in Sanskrit as *a-sya*, in Homer as *o-io*, and in Attic Greek as *ou* (from *oo*), is in Latin, two or three centuries later, reduced to *i* (from *oi*). The classic literature of the Latin language is not only of a later date, but is also far inferior in extent and variety to the literature of Greece. The style of the two differs materially. The Latin is distinguished rather by a sonorous majesty and exactness of expression than by the graceful elegance and endless versatility of her Grecian sister. But their close relationship to one another is, nevertheless, undeniable. This is rendered evident by an examination of their grammatical structure, and it would be unnecessary to quote two languages so nearly allied in order to illustrate Comparative Grammar, but for the circumstance that they supply each other's defects in a remarkable manner. Thus, for instance, the letters *s*, *w*, *y*, are generally either lost or disguised in certain positions in Greek, but are more or less fully preserved in Latin. On the other hand, the aspirates, which are numerously represented in Greek, are generally lost or altered in Latin. Again, the Greek preserves short vowels when final, but the Latin drops them, whilst final consonants, lost in Greek, are preserved in Latin. So, also, the Greek distinctly preserves the important aorist forms, but has greatly obscured the reflexive pronoun in verbs, whilst in Latin the latter is unmistakable and the former almost absent.

5. CELTIC.

13. The *fifth class* consists of the *Celtic* languages. This name appears, variously modified, in application to the *Galatians* of Asia Minor, the *Gauls* (Galli) of northern Italy and France, the *Celt*-Iberi of Spain, and the *Gael* of Scotland. The earliest notices of the people represent them as occupying a considerable part of the south-west of Europe and the British Isles, but we have no historical evidence to connect them with the original abode of the family in Asia. The settlement in Asia Minor appears to have been the result of a migration eastward from Europe. Bohemia owes its name to them, for the Boii were one of their tribes. The Celtic languages are now spoken in Ireland, the Isle of Man, the Highlands of Scotland, Wales, and Bretagne. Some remains also are preserved of the language of Cornwall and of the ancient Gauls. The principal literature of the Celts belongs to a recent period, and the inflections of the language have, consequently, become greatly abridged. No doubt, however, remains of the fact that the Celtic belongs to the Indo-European family, and that it is very nearly related to the Italic languages. The effect which time has had in abridging or destroying the grammatical inflections will be seen on comparing the Irish *ech*, 'horse,' with the Latin *equ-us*, and the Sanskrit *açw-as*; ir. *deich*, 'ten,' l. *dec-em*, s. *daz-an*.

The Celtic languages are also subject to some peculiar phonetic changes. One of them is the 'assimilation of vowels,' by which a weak or strong vowel causes the insertion of one of its own class in the preceding syllable if there be not one there already, as in *echaire*, *echire* ('mulio,' 'muleteer'), which requires for its full explanation the help of the corresponding Latin word, *equarius*, 'groom.' The *i* after *r* has caused *i* to be inserted before *r*, which then ultimately causes *a* to disappear. A similar influence is exerted in other cases upon a subsequent syllable; for example, the *a* of labra in *labra-tar* (l. *loquu-n-tur*) requires the ending to be *tar*, whilst the *i* of labri in *labri-tir* (l. *loqua-n-tur*) requires *tir*.

Another striking peculiarity is the 'aspiration' of initial consonants, that is, *h* is added to an initial consonant in connection with certain changes of inflection or derivation, thus, *gair* is 'voice,' and *fo-ghur*, 'sound.'

These and other peculiarities render it difficult to introduce the Celtic languages into a work like the present. The necessary explanations would greatly increase its bulk, and the peculiar phenomena of this class of languages would render the subject more complex than is desirable for an elementary work.

6. TEUTONIC.

14. The *sixth class* is the Teutonic, including three principal branches, the Gothic, the Low German, and the Scandinavian. It is distinguished from the *Germanic*, which comprises the High German language. These terms are employed not as being scientifically accurate, for that would be difficult at the present stage of the subject, but as being intelligible and definite.

The sixth and seventh classes form the second and third divisions mentioned in section **5**, and are distinguished from the classes of languages previously enumerated by a remarkable feature. The operation of what is called Grimm's Law of Consonant Changes separates the sixth and seventh classes from the other five, as well as from one another. At present the cause of these changes is hidden. Why should the sounds k, t, p have been changed by the Teutons for the aspirates kh (*ch, gh*), *th* (*dh*), *ph* (*f, v*)? Not from any preference for aspirates, for the original aspirates at the same time were changed to g, d, b. Nor are these latter special favourites, for in their turn they have to give place to k, t, p. All the languages of the sixth class have undergone this change, though in many respects they differ greatly from each other, and many of them, as long as history has known them, have been entirely independent one of the other. Of course, however, the presumption is that when the change was made they all formed but one language. We will take the following instance, illustrating the effect upon letters belonging to both the labial and dental organs: the Icelandic word *fotr*, Swedish *fot*, Gothic *fotus*, Anglo-

Saxon *fot*, English *foot*, Old Saxon *fot*, Friesian *fot*, Dutch *voet*, all have the aspirate (*f*, *v*) for the first consonant, and the mute (*t*) for the last, the final *r* and *s* in two cases being the nominative sign. Now the classes of languages which we have considered before, agree in having a mute (*p*) for the first consonant, and a vocal (*d*) for the last, e.g. Sanskrit *pad-as*, Greek *pous* for *pods*, gen. *pod-os*, Latin, *pés* for *peds*, gen. *ped-is*.

It is, moreover, singular, that from the sixth class, as a starting point, a perfectly analogous change is made in producing the seventh class, or the High German language. Thus the word mentioned above is in High German *fuss*, which does not preserve the final *t* of the sixth class, nor return to the original *d* of the other classes, but changes the mute into an aspirate. The aspirate, however, has become *s* in modern German generally, as it has in modern English, in the third person singular present of verbs, e.g. *has* for *hath*. It was also the practice to preserve the characteristic *t* of the sixth class, when final, thus producing *ts*; hence, by assimilation is formed *ss*. In other cases, the compound is written *z* and pronounced *ts*. Initial aspirates appear to have resisted the change, and, therefore, *f* remains in the above word instead of becoming *b*. But the regular change is seen in the word *leib*, as compared with the English, *loaf*.

The time when these changes took place cannot be exactly determined, but Grimm identifies the *Goths* and *Getæ*, and the latter, as far as their language is known to us, seem to have retained the original consonants. Indeed, the names indicate the difference, for Getæ has the mute (*t*) in place of which Goths has the aspirate (*th*). The consonant changes generally, therefore,

probably accompanied this change of name, and took
place as the Getæ disappeared, and the Goths acquired
importance, that is, a short time before the beginning
of the Christian era.

Not only the Getæ, but also the Thracians, are
identified by Grimm as belonging to the same race of
people with the Goths. We have thus the means of
tracing them to an early period, and to a remote
easterly position. The Thracians are mentioned by
Homer, and are described by Herodotus as being more
numerous than all others except the Indians. He
mentions also that Darius encountered the Getæ on his
march to Scythia. We thus find evidence of the
presence of the Teutons in considerable numbers on the
north-west of the Black Sea, at a time when a large
body of the Slavonians were north of the Caspian, and
the Celts were in the west of Europe, whilst the Græco-
Italic race already possessed the north coast of the Mediterranean. The order in which they entered Europe
appears, therefore, to have been the following : 1. The
Celts; 2. The Græco-Itali; 3. The Teutons and Ger-
mans; 4. The Slavonians.

15. 1. *Gothic.* A remarkable passage in Strabo confirms the view taken by Grimm as to the relation of
the Getæ, Thracians, and Goths; for he states that in
the time of Augustus, 'Ælius Catus brought from
beyond the Ister (Danube) 50,000 persons of the
Getæ, a people speaking the same language with the
Thracians, into Thrace, and they now live there under
the name of Mœsians.' Now, it was for the inhabitants
of Mœsia, that Ulfilas, 300 years later, made his translation of the Scriptures, which is hence called the
Mœso-Gothic. This work, though preserved only in
fragments, is, in some respects, the most important of

all the literary remains of the Teutons for the purposes of Comparative Grammar. It belongs to the years 360—380, A.D., but preserves many traces of the language of a much earlier period especially in the use of the short vowels, *a, i, u*. It exhibits, however, the effect of time in wasting away the grammatical inflections of words. It preserves two of the four letters mentioned in Sect. **11** as originally belonging to the genitive case singular, but this is probably in consequence of *s* being one of the two. The Gothic form vulf-*i*-s appears fuller than the earlier Latin equ-í (for equ-*o-i*), but *m*, the sign of the accusative singular, which is still preserved very fully in Greek and Latin, is almost entirely lost in Gothic.

2. The *Low German* branch includes: (*a*) The Old Saxon, spoken on the continent, and supplying a valuable poem of the 9th century, called the Heljand ('Saviour'). (*b*) The Friesic, spoken by a numerous population who occupied the coasts of the North Sea from Flanders to Jutland in the 13th century. It contains some remains of the 13th and 14th centuries, which strikingly resemble the language of the Angles. (*c*) The Dutch. (*d*) The Flemish; and (*e*) the *Anglo-Saxon*. This last is the most important of the Low German branch, both in regard to the compass of its literature, and its near relation to our own language. The poem of Beowulf exhibits the ante-christian ideas of the 6th and 7th centuries, and contains many reminiscences brought over from the continent, although in its present form it is of a much later date, and greatly christianised. The oldest Anglo-Saxon remains are three or four centuries later than the Gothic of Ulfilas, and the grammatical forms are correspondingly diminished. The sign of the nominative

singular *s*, for instance, retained in the Gothic, as well as in the older languages, is lost in Anglo-Saxon. Thus the Anglo-Saxon, *gaest*, ' guest,' suffers in comparison with the Gothic *gasts*, and the Latin *hostis*. Some vestiges of the ancient heritage remain, but it only required another step aided by the political convulsions of the country, to reduce the language in 600 years more to the denuded state of modern English.

3. The *Scandinavian* branch includes: (*a*) The Icelandic, which possesses an extensive and valuable literature, some of it dating as far back as the 9th century. (*b*) The Swedish, which, especially in the earliest periods, nearly resembles the Icelandic. Its literary remains begin at about the 10th century. (*c*) The Danish, whose literature begins with the latter part of the 12th century. It has suffered great changes from the original type, especially in the loss of its grammatical forms, and also in its roots.

7. GERMANIC.

16. The *High German* forms the last class. Its relation to the other languages has been already pointed out. Its literary remains date from the 9th century. As they thus begin 500 years after the time when the Gothic translation was made, they naturally exhibit a still greater falling off in the grammatical forms. In some cases, however, the High German preserves a fuller form than the Gothic. For instance, the first person plural of verbs ends in -*més*, where Gothic has only *m*, as in *bair-a-m*, whilst the Latin has -*mus*, as in *fer-i-mus*.

The grammatical forms of the High German are sufficiently represented for the purposes of this work.

by the sixth class, whilst the peculiarity which distinguishes it from that class is treated of in the sections referring to Grimm's law. See Sect. **93—104.**

The object of the above outline is not to supply a full description of the Indo-European family of languages, but merely to furnish a general classification which may aid the reader to bear in mind the relative position, chronologically and geographically, of the languages principally referred to in the following pages.

II. ALPHABETS.

a) THE SANSKRIT ALPHABET.

17. The Sanskrit Alphabet consists of the following characters:

Form.	Characters employed in the following pages.	Power.	Example.
अ	a	a	had
आ	â	â	far
इ	i	i	bid
ई	î	ê (ee)	heed
उ	u	oo	hood
ऊ	û	ȯȯ	food
ऋ	ṛ	ri	rid
ॠ	ṝ	ree	reed
ऌ	lṛ	lri	wheelrim
ॡ	lṝ	lree	all reed
ए	ê	â	made
ऐ	ai	î	hide
ओ	ô	ô	bode

ALPHABETS

Form.	Characters employed in the following pages.	Power.	Example.
औ	au	ou	loud
क	k	k	bake
ख	kh	kh	bakehouse
ग	g	g	log
घ	gh	gh	loghouse
ङ	ng	ng	ring
च	ch	ch	reach
छ	chh	chh	reach here
ज	j	j (dg)	judge
झ	jh	jh (dgh)	judge him
ञ	ṅ	ṅ	injure
त	t	t	right
थ	th	th	right hand
द	d	d	red
ध	dh	dh	red hand
न	n	n	then
ट	ṭ	ṭ	———
ठ	ṭh	ṭh	———
ड	ḍ	ḍ	———
ढ	ḍh	ḍh	———

THE SANSKRIT ALPHABET

Form.	Characters employed in the following pages.	Power.	Example.
ऄ	ṇ	ṇ	———
प	p	p	loop
फ	ph	ph	loophole
ब	b	b	job
भ	bh	bh	job-horse
म	m	m	room
य	y	y	yea
र	r	r	ray
ल	l	l	lay
व	w, v	w	way
श	ż	ż (s)	pleasure
ष	sh	sh	shed
स	s	s	said
ह	h	h	head
ळ	l	ll (in Welsh)	———

Remarks.

18. In the examples given a vowel is to be considered short when not marked long; e. g., in *rájan*, the first vowel is long and the second short.

The *pronunciation* of the letters is that given under 'power.' It will be seen that the vowels are employed rather with the Continental than the English sounds.

Judging from modern pronunciation in India, the Sanskrit *a* seems to have had the sound of *u* in *but*, or *a* in the second syllable of *readable*. In pronouncing the aspirates it will be seen by the examples that the aspiration (*h*) must be sounded separately from the mutes after which it is written. I have not attempted to supply examples of the pronunciation of the fourth class of consonants, because the sound of them is so utterly different from anything in our own language that it seems impossible to convey a notion of it by written characters. The peculiar modification of sound is produced by bending the tongue upwards and as far back as possible. A hollow sound is then produced, which seems as if it proceeded from the upper part of the head. The letters are, therefore, in Sanskrit grammars, called *múrdhanya* (capitalis), from *múrdhan*, 'head.' By Bopp the term 'cerebral' is employed, as being of similar meaning.

19. It is supposed that the palatal consonants, *ch*, *j*, acquired the sounds thus indicated at a later period, and that there intervened between the pure guttural pronunciation, *k*, *g*, from which they sprang, and the palatal pronunciation, such sounds as those of *k* and *g* in the English words *kind*, *guard*, that is, *ky* and *gy*. See Schleicher, *Compendium*, pp. 13, 14.

b) THE ZEND ALPHABET.

20. The Zend Alphabet consists of the following characters:

Form.	Characters employed in the following pages.	Power.	Example.
ʌɪ	a	a	had
ʌɯ	â	â	fâr
ϵ	è	è	après (Fr.)
ϵ	'è	è	très (Fr.)
ƿ	ê	â	mâde
ð	i	i	hid
ϙ	î	ê (ee)	heed
ɩ	u	oo	hood
ʅ	û	óo	food
↧	o	o	hod
↧	ô	ô	bôde
ɞ	k	k	bake
ɑ	kh	kh	bakehouse
ʅɔ	qh	qh	———
ϵ	g	g	log
ʅ	gh	gh	loghouse
ɟɕ	ng	ng	ring
ɾ	ch	ch	reach
ɯ	j	j	judge
ɾ	t	t	right
ɕ	th	th	right hand
ɟ	d	d	red
ɘ	dh	dh	red baad

Form.	Characters employed in the following pages.	Power.	Example.
⟨n-char⟩	n	n	then
⟨p-char⟩	p	p	loop
⟨f-char⟩	f	f	roof
⟨b-char⟩	b	b	job
⟨m-char⟩	m	m	room
⟨y-char⟩ initial / medial	y	y	yea
⟨r-char⟩	r	r	ray
⟨w-char⟩ initial / medial	w	w	way
⟨w-char⟩ after *th*	w, v	w, v	way, vane
⟨z-char⟩	z	z	haze
⟨ż-char⟩	ż	ż (s)	pleasure
⟨sh-char⟩	sh	sh	shed
⟨s-char⟩	s	s	said
⟨h-char⟩	h	h	head
⟨d-char⟩	ḍ	ḍ, dh (th)	then

Remarks.

qh represents a deep guttural sound, somewhat rougher than the German *ch*. Of the two characters for *ng*, the second is only employed after *i* or *é*.

Further remarks upon the Zend alphabet will be found in III.

c) THE GREEK ALPHABET.

21. The Greek Alphabet consists of the following characters:

Form. Large. Small.		Power.	Example
A	α	a â	had, made
B	β	b	bad
Γ	γ	g	gate
Δ	δ	d	red
E	ε	e	led
Z	ζ	z	haze
H	η	ê	hêre
Θ	ϑ	th	thin
I	ι	i î	hid, hide
K	κ	k	take
Λ	λ	l	lay
M	μ	m	room
N	ν	n, ng	then, ring
Ξ	ξ	x (ks)	box
O	ο	o	hod
Π	π	p	loop
P	ρ	r	ray
Σ	σ ς	s	said
T	τ	t	right
Υ	υ	u, û	bud, bude
Φ	φ	f	roof
X	χ	k (kh)	take
Ψ	ψ	ps	lips
Ω	ω	ô	abode

d) THE LATIN ALPHABET.

22. The Latin Alphabet consists of the following characters:

Large: A B C D E F G H I J K L M N O P Q R S T U V X Y Z.

Small: a b c d e f g h i j k l m n o p q r s t u v x y z

23. They are pronounced by us as in the English language. It must, however, be borne in mind that the Romans probably uttered the vowels with the Continental and not the English sounds of those letters. *j* represents the half-vowel *y*, and was doubtless pronounced like *y* in *yea*; whereas the Latin *y*, being in fact the Greek *υ*, is always a vowel, and was probably pronounced something like the French *u* in *une*. The Latin *u*, in some positions, stands for the half-vowel *w*, as, for instance, in *sanguis*, where it is pronounced just as in the English word sanguine. In *c* and *g*, only the sounds in *cot* and *got* should be employed for the examples adduced in the following pages. The soft sounds of these consonants were of later introduction, and are of less service for the purpose of comparison with the other languages here treated of.

e) THE GOTHIC ALPHABET.

24. The Gothic Alphabet consists of the following characters:

Form.	Power.	Example.
𐌀	a	had
𐌁	b	bad
𐌂	g	log

THE GOTHIC ALPHABET

Form.	Power.	Example.
d	d	red
є	â	mâde
ϝ	f	roof
ɡ	j, y	judge, yea
h	h	head
ï I	i	hid
єI	ee	heed
к	k	bake
λ	l	lay
м	m	room
N	n	then
ᚱ	ô	bôde
π	p	loop
⊙	hw	when (hwen)
к	r	ray
s	s	said
т	t	right
ψ	th	then, thin
n	u	hood
u	cw	quantity (cwantity)
v	w	way
x	kh (ch)	(ger.) lachen
z	z	haze
λI	e â	led, mâde
λn	o ô	hod, bôde
гг	(gg) ng	ring

Remarks.

25. The characters employed are the same as those which express the powers of the letters in the above table, except that *y* is represented by *j*, *w* by *v*, and *ee* by *i* or *ei*. The same character was probably pronounced *w* in some instances, and *v* in others.

26. The pronunciation of the Anglo-Saxon letters, especially of the vowels, is very uncertain, but the following list is sufficient for comparing the grammatical forms and roots with other languages.

f) THE ANGLO-SAXON ALPHABET.

27. The Anglo-Saxon Alphabet consists of the following characters:

Form.	Power.	Example.
A	a	bad
B	b	bad
C	ch	chide
D	d	red
E	e	red
F	f	roof
G	j	judge
H	h	head
I	i	hid
K	k	work
L	l	lay
M	m	room
N	n	then
O	o	hod

THE ANGLO-SAXON ALPHABET

Form	Power	Example
P	p	loop
R	r	ray
S	s	said
T	t	right
Ð	dh (th)	then
þ	th	thin
U	oo	hood
ƿ	w	way
X	x	box
Y	y	yes
Z	z	haze

III. SOUNDS.

28. The articulate *sounds* which can be produced by the human voice are very numerous, and merge one in the other by almost imperceptible degrees. In the original construction, however, of the Indo-European languages, only a limited number of these sounds were employed, and they are such as are clearly distinguishable from one another. The system on which they are arranged is remarkably simple, and they may be traced with surprising distinctness through a great variety of languages during a period of more than three thousand years.

29. On comparing the Alphabets now in use with those of the oldest Indo-European languages, we find that the vowels have undergone greater modifications than the consonants. They are of a feebler construction, and less able to resist the violence of impetuous utterance or overcome the hindrance occasioned by climate etc. in the organs of speech. Hence, in some countries they preserve a free open sound, but in others are compressed and indistinct. In one language they are few and simple, in another numerous and difficult to distinguish.

There was probably, at first, only one vowel *sound*, and this, being considered the natural accompaniment of the consonant, had no written character assigned to it. Before writing came into use it doubtless acquired some variety of pronunciation, and as speech came to be fixed in written forms, it was increasingly found necessary to adopt a corresponding variety of characters to represent these modifications in the vowel sound. In course of time more complex sounds were formed by combining and contracting together the simpler ones already in use.

30. The original vowel sound is that represented by *a* in *had*. In organic formation it corresponds to the guttural consonants, being a simple sound emitted from the throat. The first modification to which it was subject was probably the development of *i* as in *hid*, which corresponds in organic formation to the dental consonants. There was then produced *u*, sounded as *oo* in *hood*, which corresponds in organic formation to the labial consonants.

31. These three sounds we find represented in ancient as well as modern alphabets. The sounds, however, represented in different languages by the same letter, are not identical. The *a*, for instance, has a perceptible difference in German, Italian, and English pronunciation. This has probably resulted from varieties of social habits, climate, etc., after the various races had separated. New modifications afterwards arose, which must be considered in connection with the individual alphabets.

1. SANSKRIT.

a) VOWELS.

32. In *Sanskrit* the original vowel *a* combines with the derived ones *i* and *u*, making with the former *é*, as in *neigh*, and, with the latter, *ó*, as in *nó*.

These, as simple sounds, are still represented in the French language by the original letters, *ai* and *au*, as in *mais*, *maux*; whilst their originally diphthongal character is indicated not only by this circumstance, but also by the fact that in Greek they appear not as ι and ο, nor as η and ω, but as ει and ευ, or as οι and ου.

By prefixing another *a* to *é* and *ó*, the diphthongs *ai* and *au* are formed, having the vowels *a-i*, *a-u*, pronounced separately, with the principal stress on the first vowel, and resembling *i* and *ou* in *hide* and *loud*.

The short vowels *e* and *o* seem not to have been part of the primitive alphabet, but to be later modifications of the original sound, for they are wanting alike in the Sanskrit and Gothic alphabets, and appear in Greek and Latin as representatives of the Sanskrit *a*. For example:

Sanskrit	Greek	Latin	
ashtau	ὀκτώ	octo	'eight'
navan	ἐννέα	novem	'nine'
navas	νέος	novus	'new'

33. The following three characters also occur in Sanskrit. 1. *Anuswára*. It is represented by a point over the preceding letter, and is pronounced like the final *n* in French. At the end of a word it stands in place of an original *m*, and in the middle of words in place of an original *n* before sibilants, e.g. *tá sunum* for *tam sunum*, 'the son;' *hása* for *hansa*, 'goose.' 2. *Anunásika*. It is represented by a point over a curve above the preceding letter, and denotes that a final nasal has been assimilated to *l*, *y*, or *w*, at the beginning of the following word, e. g. *pakshál lunáti* for *pakshán lunáti*, 'cuts off the wings.'[*] The Lithuanian and Old Slavic retain the sign of a nasal in the preceding vowel, the former without, the latter with, the corresponding sound. 3. *Visarga*. It is represented by two points at

---

[*] Bopp, *Kritische Gram.* 2nd ed. 66, 70.

the end of a word, and stands in place of final *s* or *r*, which then is pronounced as a soft aspiration, e.g. *puna:* for *punar*, 'again;' *du:kha* for *duṣkha*, 'pain.'

The modifications of sound represented by these three characters are euphonic, and are generally occasioned by the consonants which follow them.

34. ṛ and ḷ, as vowel sounds, seem to have grown out of the syllables *ar* and *al* (cf. Greek ἄ-φερτος with Sanskrit *bhṛtas*, and Latin **art** for *cart* with Sanskrit *kṛtis*). ḷ occurs only in one root, *kḷp* for *kalp*.

35. We may here introduce a reference to the COMPARATIVE WEIGHT OF VOWEL SOUNDS. In his second edition Bopp has given a detailed account and fuller illustrations of this subject.

Of the original vowels *a* is the heaviest, *i* the lightest, and *u* intermediate. The principle on which this point is determined is that when a preceding or following syllable, on account of its own weight, requires the one next to it to be lightened, the vowel introduced for this purpose is considered lighter than the one for which it is substituted. For instance, the termination of the first person plural in verbs, *-mas*, is heavier than the termination of the first person singular, *-mi*; therefore the syllable preceding the former must be lighter than the syllable preceding the latter. Now the last syllable but one in *yunâ'mi*, 'I bind,' contains *â*, whilst the corresponding syllable in *yunî'mas* contains *î*. Hence *î* is lighter than *â*. Similarly, in *ê'mi*, 'I go,' and *îmas*, 'we go,' *i* is lighter than *ê*; in εἶμι and ἴμεν, *ι* is lighter than *ει*. A similar result is occasioned in Latin by prefixing prepositions, or by reduplication. Thus, *jacio*, 'I throw,' becomes *abjicio*, 'I throw off,' and *cano*, 'I sing,' becomes *cecini*, 'I sang.' *i* is therefore lighter than *a*. The concurrence of two consonants has the effect of partly (*abjectus*, 'thrown off') or wholly (*contactus*, 'touched') preventing the lightening of the root vowel. The same phenomenon appears in the past and present tenses in the strong verbs of the Germanic languages. In Gothic the *heavier* terminations of the present tense are affixed to the *lighter* stem, as *sit*, whilst the *lighter* terminations of the past tense are connected with the *heavier* stem *sat*. In English, where the inflections which originally caused the difference have disappeared, the distinction itself is retained, as in *sit, sat*. Another illustration is derived from a comparison of older and later forms of languages. The effect of time is to render grammatical forms lighter and easier of enunciation.* Hence the older Sanskrit *a* (*dádámi*, 'I give') becomes *i* in the later Greek (δίδωμι). We have *a* in the older Sanskrit *chatwá'ras*, 'four,' and *i* in the later Greek πίσυρες, and Gothic *fidvor*. The Latin *quatuor* is in this respect of an older character than the Greek. From similar facts it is inferred that *u* is lighter than *a*, e.g. s. *karó'mi*, 'I make,' *kúrmas*, 'we make;' l. *calco*, 'I tread upon,' and *conculco*, 'I crush;' e. *came* and *come*. In this last word the older pronunciation has now become provincial. *Coom* has changed to *cum*, for in *come*, though *o* is written, the *u* sound is preserved. For older s. *náktam*, 'night,' we have later gr. νύκτα. That *i* is lighter than *u* appears from such cases as, s. *aundídam*, a later form for *aundudam*, and L. *fructífer*, 'bearing fruit,' for *fructufer*.

b) CONSONANTS.

36. Sanskrit grammarians arrange the consonants in *five classes*; an arrangement which it will be convenient

* See *Diversions of Purley*.

to follow here, though we shall afterwards see that a more accurate division for the purposes of Comparative Grammar would be into *three principal* and *two subordinate* classes. There are also four half-vowels, three sibilants, and *h.* This arrangement is determined by the organs used in pronunciation. Each of the Five Classes contains five letters—a mute, a vocal, the corresponding aspirate of each, and a nasal. In the aspirates the aspiration is pronounced distinctly from the letter to which it belongs; e.g. the aspirated *p* is pronounced as *ph* in *haphazard*, and the aspirated *b* as *bh* in *abhor*. The later substitution of a single sound and character, as *f* and *v*, is analogous to the change of the diphthongs *a+i* and *a+u* to ê and ô.

37. The *first* class of consonants, the GUTTURALS, contains the letters *k, kh, g, gh, ng*. They occur in most of the cognate languages with great regularity, and require little elucidation. The aspirates, however, especially *kh*, are rare. Yet the following examples are met with:

'nail'	s. nakha	gr. ὄνυχ-	l. ——
'light'	laghús	ἐλαχύς	levis
'warm'	gharmás	θέρμη	(uro)

In the last example there is a change of aspirates, the Dental θ (for *dh*) being used in Greek for the Guttural *gh* in Sanskrit. That the Guttural was the original appears likely from the evidences of it in other languages. In Latin, although the Guttural is lost from *uro*, as it is in many other Latin words, yet the *u* indicates its previous presence. The same may be said of the *w* in the Germanic languages, e.g. go. **varm**, a. s. **wearm**, e. **warm**, ger. **warm**. For these letters are usually developed from a Guttural, e.g. s. *ka-s*, l. *qui*, e. *who* (for hwo). In the second example above there is another variation of aspirates, *v* (for *bh*) being used in the Latin for the Sanskrit *gh*. Indeed, we shall find that such variations in the aspirates are not unfrequent.

36. The *second* class, the PALATALS, contains the letters *ch, chh, j, jh, ṅ*. A modification in the sound is produced by pressing the tongue against the palate, whence the class obtains its name. These letters are derived from the first class, and are used only before vowels, half-vowels, and nasals. They were probably originated after the separation of languages, which would account for their being entirely absent from some alphabets. The following examples illustrate their absence from the Greek and Latin alphabets:

| 'four' | s. *chatwāras* | gr. τίσυρες | l. *quatuor* |
| 'cut' | *chhid* | σχίζω | *scindo* |

Instances illustrating the use of these letters can therefore be found in only a small number of languages. They serve, however, to exemplify the development of sounds one from another; and analogous phenomena, independently produced, may be seen in the Slavic languages, as well as in the Romance languages as compared with the Latin.

In the first of the examples given above, the Greek τίσυρες has the Labial π for the original Guttural out of which the Sanskrit Palatal has been developed, and which, with the usual development of *u*, is preserved in the Latin *quatuor*. This deviation from the original form is common in Greek, and sometimes distinguishes one dialect from another, e.g. Ionic κότερος, 'which,' and Attic πότερος. Letters from all the three organs are in different cases employed in the Greek language to represent the original Guttural sounds, for the Dental τ appears in Attic τέσσαρες for the above Æolic πίσυρες. In the second example the Guttural is not aspirated in Latin, and in both Greek and Latin an initial s appears, which may have been originally in Sanskrit.

39. The *third* class, the DENTALS, contains the letters *t, th, d, dh, n*. The *dh* is represented in Greek by ϑ, whilst *th* appears as τ, from which it is probable that ϑ represents the former as well as the latter *sound*. The Latin sometimes omits the aspiration, and sometimes substitutes the aspirated letters of other organs. These letters are often inserted inorganically in Greek after similar letters of another class, e. g. πτόλις for πόλις, and χϑές for χές. Instead of *d* in Sanskrit, we often find in other languages *l* or *r*.

Examples:

s.	gr.	l.	
dhûmás	ϑυμός	fumus	'smoke'
madhya	—	{ medius { meridies	'middle' 'mid-day'
purî	πτόλις	—	'city'
hyas	χϑές	heri	'yesterday'
daḷ	λιγνύς	lignum	'firewood'

40. The *fourth* class, the CEREBRALS, contains the letters *ṭ, ṭh, ḍ, ḍh, ṇ*. They are derived from the Dentals, and are similar in sound, except that in pronouncing them the tongue touches the roof of the mouth, pointing perpendicularly towards the brain, from which they take their name. They seldom begin a word, *ṇ* never; and they rarely appear in the cognate languages. They are substituted for Dentals after *sh*, and are very common in Prâcrit, probably as the result of local influences.

41. The *fifth* class, the LABIALS, contains the letters *p, ph, b, bh, m*; *ph* rarely occurs. *bh* is represented in Greek by φ or β, and in Latin by *f* or *b*. The Greek φ may have represented both aspirates in sound. Final *m* generally becomes *Anuswára* in Sanskrit, is preserved unchanged in Latin, and appears as ν in Greek; in Gothic it is sometimes *m* and sometimes *n*.
Examples:

s. phéna	gr. ——	l. ——	——
lubh	λαβον	——	——
pánchan	πιντε	quinque	'five'
bháran	φιρων	ferens	'bearing'
déwám	θιον	deum	'god'

As Labials are used in Greek for Sanskrit Gutturals, so we have the converse in the Latin *quinque*, i.e. a Guttural *qu* for a Sanskrit Labial *p*.

42. The HALF-VOWELS are *y, l, r, w*. They are more frequently interchanged with one another than the consonants, and are therefore less easily traceable in the sister languages. This is more especially the case with *l* and *r*, which correspond to the class of Dental consonants, and differ from each other only in the circumstance that in pronouncing *l* the tongue touches the roof of the mouth once only, while it does so more than once in pronouncing *r*. Hence only one of them is found in some languages. *y* corresponds to the Guttural consonants in organic formation. In Prâcrit it has become *j*, as it has also in the transition from Latin to Italian; e.g. in L *Jugum*, 'yoke,' the *j* answers to English *y*, and in it. *giogo, gi* answers to English *j*. In Greek it becomes ζ or ', or is assimilated to a preceding letter. *w* corresponds, in organic formation, to the Labial consonants. In Prâcrit it is often assimilated to a preceding consonant. In Sanskrit it seems to have become *v*, except after a consonant. In Greek it is either assimilated or changed to a vowel, or appears as φ (from the digamma), or is lost. In Latin it is changed to a vowel or is lost. It assumes the character of a mute Guttural in l. *victum, factum*, and in e. quick. The following list will serve to illustrate most of the above statements :

'shine'	s. *ruh*	gr. λευκός	L. *luceo*
'leave'	*rik*	λείπω	*linquo*
'another'	*anyas*	ἄλλος	*alius*
'join'	*yuj*	ζεύγνυμι	*jungo*
'liver'	*yakṛt*	ἧπαρ	*jecur*
'four'	*chatwá'ras*	τέσσαρις	*quatuor*
'horse'	*áswa*	ἴππος	*equus*
'thou'	*twam*	τύ, σύ	*tu*
'his'	*swas*	σφός	*suus*
'sail'	*plávámi*	πλέω (πλεΓω)	——
'sheep'	*avis*	ὄις	*ovis*

43. The SIBILANTS are *ẕ, s, sh*. *ẕ* corresponds, in organic formation, to the Guttural consonants, and has, in fact, in almost all cases sprung from an original *k*. Hence it is generally represented by a Guttural in the sister languages. In Lithuanian, however, it appears as *sh*, and in Slavic as *s*. Its sound resembles that of *s* in the word *pleasure*. *s* corresponds, in organic formation, to the Dental consonants. It seldom remains unchanged at the end of a word. Final *as* followed by a word beginning with a vocal letter becomes *o*; probably through the changes *as, ar, au, o*. Instead of this

54   SOUNDS

letter we frequently find *r* in other languages. *sh* corresponds in organic formation to the Labial consonants. It takes the place of *s* in certain cases where the latter is not admissible in Sanskrit.

44. *h* is a feeble aspirate. It appears in Greek as χ, and in Latin as *h*. Sometimes it is only the aspiration of another letter which has been dropped, as *han* for *dhan*. The above statements are illustrated in the following list of words:

'dog'	s. *śvan*	gr. κύων	l. *canis*
'ten'	*daśan*	δέκα	*decem*
'right'	*dakshinas*	δεξιός for ἐκσίος	*dexter* for *dec-ster*
'winter'	*himám*	χεῖμα	*hiems*
'kill'	*han-*	θάνον	*nex*

In the Latin word *funus* the Labial aspirate *bh* (f) is used instead of the Dental aspirate *dh*.

45. The following table exhibits the relation of the letters in the Sanskrit alphabet. The larger characters represent the three older classes, viz. Gutturals, Dentals, Labials; the smaller characters represent the two later derived classes, viz. Palatals and Cerebrals.

	Mute.		Vocal.		Nasal.	Half-vowels.	Sibilants.	Vowels.
Gutturals	k	kh	g	gh	ng	y	ż	ă
Palatals	ch	chh	j	jh	ñ	—	(h)	ĕ ai
Dentals	t	th	d	dh	n	l r	s	ĭ
Cerebrals	ṭ	ṭh	ḍ	ḍh	ṇ	l ṛ		ŏ au
Labials	p	ph	b	bh	m	w	sh	ŭ

2. ZEND.

46. The *Zend* has a close relation to the Sanskrit, and from its grammatical forms, as well as from remains of the two subordinate classes of consonants, it may be supposed to have been separated from Sanskrit at a later stage of development than was the case with Greek and Latin. The same conclusion is also supported by the local proximity of the peoples by whom Sanskrit and Zend were spoken.

a) VOWELS.

47. *a*, and in some cases, through the influence of particular consonants, *è* (resembling the French *è* in *après*), occupy the place of *a* in Sanskrit. *â, i, î, u, û,* generally answer to the same letters in Sanskrit. Sometimes, however, *ô* occurs for Sanskrit *u*, as in *kèrènaôt* for a. *akṛnaut*, which is written *akṛnôt*. This form probably arose when the original diphthong was pronounced *a + u,* not *ô*. The vowel *ô* or the diphthong *eu* answers to the Sanskrit *ô*, *eu* having arisen probably out of the original *au*. Generally *âo*, but sometimes also *âu*, stand in place of the Sanskrit *au*. Thus *gâus* for a. *gaus*. Generally Sanskrit *ê* is represented by *è*, but by *ôi* after *y* or before final *s* or *ḍ*, e. g. *yôi* for a. *yê*, 'who.' At the beginning and in the middle of words the combination *aê* occurs, which Bopp regards as containing a gunaed form of *i* in the original diphthong *ai*. Thus *a + è* would be for *a + a + i*, and this instead of *a + i* or *ê*. The sound, however, remains the same as that of the original diphthong. Thus there occur in the same word *rathwê* and *rathwaêcha*.

b) CONSONANTS.

48. Of the GUTTURALS, Sanskrit *k* remains *k* before vowels and *v*, but becomes *kh* in other cases. Sans. *kh* remains unchanged. *qh* is in sound nearly the same as *kh*, but of different origin. It has grown out of *qw*, and answers to Sans. *sw*, e.g. **qh**a-*dhâta* = s. **sw**a-*dhâta*, 'self-made;' **qh**a*fna* = s. **sw**a*pna*, 'sleep.' *g* and *gh* correspond to the same Sanskrit letters.

49. The PALATALS have in some cases become sibilants, but there remain the two unaspirated Palatals *ch* and *j*.

50. The DENTALS are *t*, *th*, *d*, *dh*, and correspond to the Sanskrit letters of the same organ. *t*, however, sometimes stands in place of Sans. *th* or *ţh*, e.g. *stâ* for s. *sthâ*; *ishta* for a. *ishtha*. The aspiration in such cases seems to be prevented by the preceding sibilant. At the beginning of words *d* sometimes stands for s. *dh*, e.g. *dâ* for s. *dhâ*, gr. ϑη.

51. Sanskrit CEREBRALS are represented by Dentals in Zend. On the other hand, *ḍ* is used for Sans. *t* at the end of words and before case-endings beginning with *b*.

52. The LABIAL *p* corresponds to Sans. *p*, except that when immediately followed by *r*, *s*, or *n*, it becomes *f*, e.g. *fra* for s. *pra*, gr. πρό. *f* corresponds in other cases to Sans. *ph*, and *b* to Sans. *b*.

53. The HALF-VOWELS are *y*, *r*, *w*. *y* is represented by the three characters given in the table, of which the last shows by its form that it has arisen out of the vowel *i*. *y* and *i* as well as *é* have an assimilating power, which causes the insertion of an additional *i* in the preceding syllable, e.g. *maidhya* = s. *mádhya*, 'middle;' *túirya* = s. *tú'rya*, 'fourth.' The combination of two consonants, however (except *nt*), and sometimes a single consonant, prevents this assimilation from taking place. Hence we have *aiti* and not *aiżti* for a. *asti*, 'is.' Bopp also ascribes a like assimilating power to *y* over a *succeeding* syllable, in changing *a* to *é* (= *ai*). In all the cases adduced, however, there is an *i* in the syllable which follows the *é*, and this will account for the change without introducing any new principle.

54. *r* is usually followed by *è*, in order to separate it from other consonants, e.g. *dadarèża* for s. *dádarśa*, gr. δέδορκα, 'I saw.'

55. *w* is represented by three characters, as in the table. Of these the first occurs only at the beginning, and the second only in the middle of words, e. g. ϛℛωϛ *waém* for a. *wayam*, 'we;' ℳℳϣϙ *tawa* for a. *tava*, 'of thee.' The form of the second shows that it originated from the vowel *u*, being, like the English letter, a 'double *u*.' The third character occurs after *th*, and sometimes after *dh*. Bopp puts all three together under the designation of Half-vowels, but represents the first two by *v*, and the last by *w*. Now *v* is not in any sense a half-vowel, any more than *f*, *v* having the same relation to *b*, both in origin and sound, as *f* has to *p*. The combinations, also, which are given of the last character, with *y* and *r*, in *wyo*, *wra*, *aiwyô*, 'aquis,' *żuwrá*, 'sword,' supposing the first letter = e. *w*, if not phonetically impossible, at least are strange. These terminations correspond to the s. *bhyas* and *bhra*, and would therefore be more correctly represented by *vyo* and *vra*, seeing that *v* is the aspirated *b*, just as *f* is the aspirated *p*. We should be inclined to follow Rask in giving the sound *w* to the first two characters; while the difference between Rask and Anquetil in regard to the last — the one assigning to it the sound *w*, and the other the sound *v* — would lead us to the conclusion that it had either the one or the other sound, according as it arose from a consonant or a vowel. *w* and *u*, like *y* and *i*, have an assimilating power over the preceding syllable, e.g. *haurva* = s. *sarva*, 'whole.'

56. *y, r, w, m, n*, and the sibilants, cause a mute before them to become an aspirate; e.g. *merèthya, ughra, kaśethwaṅm, takhma, pathní*, correspond to the Sanskrit *mṛtyu, ugra, kas-twam, taṅk, patní*.

57. The SIBILANTS are *ż, sh, z, s. ż* has the two characters given in the table, which differ little in sound, but are not of the same origin. The *first* answers generally to the Sanskrit *ż*. In some cases, however, it stands in place of Sanskrit *s*, e.g. *żtáró* for s. *stáras*, 'stars.' It has the effect of changing *w*, immediately after it, to *p*, e.g. *żpá* = s. *żwan*, gr. *κύων*, 'dog' (hound). The *second* character for *ż* answers to Sanskrit *y* and *j* (a Latin *y* becomes *j* (*ż*) in French— Lat. *jocus*, Fr. *jeu*), e.g. *yúżem* = s. *yúyáṃ*, 'you;' *żènu* = s. *jánu*, 'knee.'

sh is represented by two characters, which, however, are of the same origin. The second is used before vowels and the half-vowels *y, w*. They both answer to Sanskrit *sh*, e.g. *ashta* = s. *áshṭa*, 'eight;' *aitaishwa* = s. *été'shu*, 'in these.'

z answers etymologically to Sanskrit *h*, e.g. *azèm* = s. *aham*, gr. *ἐγών*, 'I.' In some cases it stands in place of Sanskrit *j*, e.g. *yaz-* = s. *yaj-* 'worship;' and in a few cases for Sanskrit *g*, e.g. *záo* = s. *gáus*, gr. *γῆ*, 'earth.'

58. *h* answers etymologically to Sanskrit *s*, e.g. *há* = s. *sá*, gr. *ἡ*, 'she.' *n* is prefixed to *hr* for s. *sr*. *nhr* = s. *sr*.

59. The NASALS are numerous. *ng* has two characters, of which the second is evidently only a modification of the first, and is used only after *é* or *i*. They answer to Sanskrit *ng*, e.g. *yénghê*, 'who;' *anghāo*, 'of this.' *n* has two characters, of which the second is used before strong consonants. They correspond to Sanskrit *n*. *m* also is the same as the Sanskrit letter. *ṅ* is represented in two characters, of which the second = *aṅ*.

60. The Zend Alphabet, as compared with the Sanskrit, has already sustained considerable loss. The Cerebrals are entirely wanting except *ḍ*, which, however, answers to Sanskrit Dentals and not Cerebrals. There are no Palatal aspirates. *bh* and *l* are also missing. On the other hand, the sibilants and diphthongs are more numerous than in Sanskrit.

61. The following table exhibits the Zend Alphabet:

	Muta.	Voeal.	Nasal.	Half-vowels.	Sibilants.	Vowels.
Gutturals	k kh (qh)	g gh	ng	y	ź	ĕ
Palatals	ch —	j —	ń	—	z	ě ê äi
Dentals	t th	d dh	n	r	s	ī
Cerebrals	— —	ḍ —	—	—	—	ŏ äu ăo ŏi
Labials	p f	b —	m	w	sh	ŭ

3. GREEK.

62. The following list of *Greek* letters consists mainly of what was called the Cadmus Alphabet, traditionally derived from Phœnicia.

The aspirates were at first represented by the unaspirated letters. χ, ϑ, φ, however, are found on the earliest monuments. There appears to be no aspirated κ or τ, unless, like the English *th*, χ and ϑ represent two sounds each. The two subordinate classes of Sanskrit consonants are altogether wanting. The long vowels η and ω, which usually answer to the Sanskrit *á*, were represented by ε and o. The formation of the diphthongs is easily understood. As ε, o stand for Sanskrit a, so ευ, οι answer to ai, and ευ, ου to au, which in Sanskrit appear as é, ô. Similarly αυ, ου, being formed of aai, aau, correspond to Sanskrit ai, au. The improper diphthongs introduce no new elementary sound. ξ and ψ are merely later inventions, used in place of mutes combined with a Sibilant: ξ for κσ, which represents κ, γ, or χ followed by σ; and ψ for πσ, which represents π, β, or φ followed by σ. ζ is in some cases used for σδ, as in 'Αθήναζε for 'Αθήνασδε; in other cases it was probably a simple sound similar to the English z, and was produced by the combination of y (in Gr. ι) with a preceding Guttural, as in Ionic μέζων, Attic μείζων, 'greater,' for μεγιων. But it seems never to be used for τσ (δσ, θσ). The Dental is dropped before σ instead of being combined with it. τρίβω, 'I rub,' forms τρίψω in the future; but σπεύδω, 'I hasten,' forms σπεύσω.

63. Six consonants are wanting in the three classes of the Greek as compared with the Sanskrit, viz.: Gutturals, kh, y, ż; Dental, th; Labials, w, sh. The w, however, may have been represented by ου in οὐαί = go. vai, e. woe.

	Mute.	Vocal.	Nasal.	Half-vowels.	Sibilants.	Vowels.
Gutturals	κ (χ)	γ χ	γ	(ι)	—	ᾰ η ε
				ʽ(h)		ει οι
						αι
Dentals	τ (θ)	δ θ	ν	λ ρ	σ	ῐ
						ευ ου
						αυ
Labials	π φ	β (F)	μ	—	—	ŏ ω

4. LATIN.

64. In the *Latin* Alphabet there are no Palatal or Cerebral letters. It is also very deficient in aspirates. *c* and *q* are identical in origin. They occur in different words where the Sanskrit has but one and the same letter (*k*). There is no distinct character for the Guttural nasal (*ng*), though the sound may have occurred in such words as *concors*. Compare also *concha* with the gr. κόγχη. The Labial half-vowel is not represented, though it may have been heard in such words as *sanguis*. The English character ('double *u* ') *w* is nothing more than *u* (v) written twice. There is but one sibilant character. It may, however, have represented different sounds, as the English *s* represents three in *pleasure, soon, sure*. The vowels and diphthongs are nearly the same as in Sanskrit and Greek. The *i*, however, of *ai, oi* (gr. ει, οι) is represented by *e* in *ae, oe*. *x* is merely a compound letter substituted for *cs* etc.

65. Final *d* often appears in place of *t*, and *b* for *p*, e. g. the old Ablative *facillumed* etc., as compared with the Sanskrit Abl. in -*t*, the preposition *pród* in several compounds, e. g. *pród-eo* etc., compared with the s. *práti*, gr. προτί, e. *forth*, and *ab* compared with s. *ápa*, gr. ἀπό, e. *off*. Probably the Latin language was averse to final mutes. In Greek, when the final vowel was dropped from προτί, τ was changed to ς in προς. Possibly the final *b* and *d* in these cases in Latin were pronounced *p* and *t*, as is done in the German language.

66. There are eight of the Sanskrit consonant characters wanting, viz.: Gutturals, *kh, gh, ng, ź*; Dentals, *th, dh*; Labials, *w, sh*.

	Mute.	Vocal.	Nasal.	Half-vowels.	Sibilants.	Vowels.
Gutturals	c q --	g —	(n)	j	(s) h	ä (ê) o
Dentals	t —	d —	n	l r	s	æ œ i au eu
Labials	p f	b v	m	(u)	(s)	ŭ (ó) o

5. GOTHIC.

67. The examples to be obtained from the Gothic are not very numerous, because the remains of that language are almost confined to fragments of one book and to one period of history. What there is, however, possesses great value, from its presenting an intermediate step between the oldest languages and the High German, with regard to the change of consonants. At the same time it has a peculiar interest from being closely connected with the Low German dialects and the English language.

a) VOWELS.

68. Sanskrit *a* is generally represented by *a*, but sometimes, especially before final *s* in polysyllables and frequently before *th*, we find *i*. Sometimes this vowel is dropped, e. g. *wulfis*, 'wolf's,' for s. *vṛkasya*; *wulfs*, 'wolf,' for s. *vṛkas*; *bairith*, 'beareth,' for s. *bhárati*; but *magath*, 'maid.' Sanskrit *á* becomes *ó* or *é*. The former is more general; and this again, by abbreviation, becomes *a*, e. g. *airthôs*, 'earth's,' *airtha*, 'earth.' Final *ó*, however, remains where a consonant has been dropped, e. g. *whathrô*, 'from whence,' answering to the Sanskrit Ablative which ends in -ât; airthrô Gen. Pl., which in Sanskrit ends in âm. When a syllable requires to be lengthened, a becomes ô, e. g. fidurdôgs, 'every four days,' from daga, 'day.' The contraction of a+a or of a+ô also produces ô. We have an instance of ê for â in slêpu, 'I sleep,' for s. svâ'paydmi.

Sanskrit i and î are respectively represented by i and ei (=î), e. g. víduvón, 'widow,' for s. vidavá; bairandein, 'bearer,' for s. bhárantî. Final i is suppressed except when it stands for ja, e. g. im, 'am,' for s. ásmi; ufar, 'over,' for s. upári; but hari, 'army,' from harja.

Sanskrit u and û are represented by u without any distinction in Gothic. u is often preceded by the guna vowel i, e. g. tiuha, 'I draw,' L. dûco.

Sanskrit ê, ô, formed from ai, au, are represented by ai, au, e. g. bait, 'bit,' for s. bibhê'da; baug, 'bent,' for s. bubhô'ja.

69. h and r cause a to be prefixed to a preceding i or u, e. g. tauhum, 'we drew,' for s. duduhimá; daur, 'door,' for s. dwâ'ra; getalhum, 'we told,' for s. didlzimá; aihtrô, 'I beg,' connected with s. íchh. A similar phenomenon appears in Latin. Thus we have peperi (e approaching to the value of a+i) where we might have expected pepiri like cecini. The connecting vowel also in the third conjugation is e before r, but i in other cases, e. g. veheris, vehis. And though a preposition generally causes the Sanskrit root-vowel a to become i, yet before h and r we have e in adveho, affero.

b) CONSONANTS.

70. The GUTTURALS are k, q, h, g, ng. k and q are equal in phonetic value, and correspond to Sanskrit g, whilst h and g correspond respectively to Sanskrit k and *gh*, e. g. **qv**iva, 'living,' 'quick,' for s. **jîv**, where *j* is for an original *g*; **hv**as, 'who,' for s. **kas**; **gards**, 'yard,' for Latin **hortus**; **gistra**, 'yesterday,' for gr. χθὶs, l. **hesternus**, **heri**. The nasal, in imitation of the Greek, is written *g* before Gutturals, e. g. *tuggó*, 'tongue;' *juggs*, 'young.' The half-vowel (*w*) *v* which appears after all the Gutturals, viz. *qv*, *hv*, *gv*, sometimes answers to the same letter in the older languages, as in **hv**eita, 'white,' s. żwêtá for kwaitá. In other cases it was perhaps developed after the languages had become distinct. A similar process seems to have taken place in Latin — **hv**a, 'who,' l. **qu**i. In many instances the original Guttural is dropped, as in **v**urm, 'worm,' l. **v**ermis. The half-vowel, when thus left alone, is pronounced as the consonant *v* in some languages, the German for instance. In English *who* (for *hwo*), the order of the letters is inverted in writing, though not in pronunciation.

71. The DENTALS are *t*, *th*, *d*, *n*, corresponding severally to Sanskrit *d*, *t*, *dh*, *n*, e. g. **ta**gr, 'tear,' for gr. δάκρυ; **than**, 'then,' for l. **tunc**; **daur**, 'door,' for gr. θύρα; **namo**, 'name,' for l. **nomen**. Final *t* in the older languages is dropped in Gothic as it is also in Greek, e. g. *bairai*, 'he may bear,' gr. φέροι, for s. *bháret*; but where *t* was originally followed by a vowel *th* is preserved in go., e g. *bairith*, 'he bears,' for s. *bháratl*.

72. The LABIALS are *p*, *f*, *b*, *m*, answering severally to the Sanskrit *b*, *p*, *bh*, *m*, e. g. *thorp*, 'thorp,' for l. *turba*, 'crowd;' *fulls*, 'full,' for gr. πλέος; *bairan*, 'bear,' for gr. φέρειν; *mikils*, 'great,' for gr. μέγας.

73. The HALF-VOWELS *j* (pronounced as *y*), *l*, *r*, *v*, are frequently interchanged, but their general correspondence with the same letters in older languages is clearly

established: e. g. juk, 'yoke,' for l. jugum; leiban,
'leave,' for l. linquere, gr. λείπω; raihts, 'right,' for
l. rectus; vai, 'woe,' for gr. οὐαί.

74. The SIBILANTS are *s, z*. The latter is used in
place of the former between vocal letters. Thus *mais*,
'more,' becomes *maiza*. This is a step in the progress
from *s* to *r*, which takes place so extensively in Latin,
and of which the English word compared with the Gothic furnishes a striking instance (i. e. in go. *mais*,
maiza, e. *more*), e. g. **s**ibun, 'seven,' for s. **s**aptam;
thizê, 'of these,' for s. *tê'*sh*âm*. In this last word *s* is
changed to *sh* by the preceding vowel.

75. The Gothic Alphabet, therefore, comprises the
following letters:

	Mute.	Vocal.	Nasal.	Half-vowels.	Sibilants.	Vowels.
Gutturals	k h	g —	ng (ʀ)	j	—	a
						ai â
Dentals	t th	d —	n	l r	s z	i ei
						au ô
Labials	p f	b —	m	v	—	u

6. ANGLO-SAXON.

76. The Anglo-Saxon has a still nearer relation to
the English than the Gothic has. It supplies also an
abundant and valuable literature.

a) VOWELS.

The *vowel sounds* are very numerous, and their relation to the Gothic and Sanskrit vowels not easily defined and classified. Notwithstanding the labours of
Grimm and Rask, much remains to be done before the
relation of the Anglo-Saxon vowels to those of the older

languages can be satisfactorily established. The investigation, as the former states, must encounter 'no small difficulties.'

77. There are no less than seven short vowels, *a*, *æ*, *e*, *i*, *o*, *u*, *y*, with their corresponding long ones, besides several diphthongs. It is obvious that these must have resulted from a much wider and freer action than we have seen in the development of the vowels of the older languages. The variety of dialects in the Anglo-Saxon literature also increases the difficulty of classifying its forms, since they result not from one law, but from different and conflicting tendencies. The vowels *a*, *i*, *u*, often correspond to the same in Gothic, e.g. *fram*, go. *fram*, 'from;' *dim*, go. *dim*, 'dim;' *sum*, go. *sums*, 'some:' but *i* also, in some cases, takes the place of *a*, e.g. *scippan*, 'shape,' for go. *skapjan*, and sometimes that of *u*, e.g. *cin*, 'kind,' for go. *kuni*; whilst *u* sometimes supplies the place of *i*, e.g. *swustor*, 'sister,' go. *svistar*. *æ* is a modification of *a*, principally under the influence of inflection, e.g. *wær*, 'wary,' go. *vars*. *e* occurs for *a*, when *e* or *i* has been dropped in the following syllable, e.g. *hel* for *hele*, go. *hali*, 'hell.' It also stands for *i*, e.g. *he*, for go. *hi*, 'he.' The fact that in Anglo-Saxon *e* is thus written for an older *i* is probably the reason that in English *é* is pronounced like a Continental *i*. *o* stands for *u* or *a*, e.g. *dol*, 'dulness;' *cwom*, 'came.' *y* is pronounced like French *u*, and developed from *u*, e.g. *cyn* as well as *cin*, 'kind;' go. *kuni*. *â*, originally a diphthong, answers to Gothic *ai*, e.g. *âv*, 'age;' go. *aivs*; l. *ævum*. *ǽ* stands for Gothic *ai* or *ê*, e.g. *sǽ*, 'sea;' go. *sal*. *é*, also, sometimes stands for Gothic *é*, as *cwén*, 'queen,' 'woman;' go. *quêns*. *í* stands in place of Gothic *ei*, e.g. *swín*, 'swine;' go. *svein*. *ô* stands generally in place of Gothic ó, e. g. dôm, 'doom;' go. dôms. ú, for Gothic ú, e. g. rûm, 'room;' go. rûms. For this latter ý is often substituted: cý for cú, 'cows.'

b) CONSONANTS.

78. The GUTTURALS are c, h, g, ng, which correspond to Gothic k, h, g, ng, and to Sanskrit g, k, gh, ng, e.g. cwic, go. qvius, 'living,' 'quick;' hwæt, go. hvat, 'what;' geard, go. gards, 'yard.'

79. The DENTALS are t, th, d, dh, n, answering to the same Gothic letters, and to Sanskrit d, t, dh, n, e. g. tear, go. tagr, 'tear;' thorn, go. thaurns, 'thorn;' duru, go. daur, 'door;' nama, go. namô, 'name.'

80. The LABIALS are p, f, b, m, as in Gothic, and answer to Sanskrit b, p, bh, m, e.g. thorp, go. thaurp, 'thorp,' 'village;' full, go. fulls, 'full;' beran, go. bairan, 'bear;' mycel, go. mikils, 'great.'

81. The HALF-VOWELS are e or g, l, r, w, as j, l, r, v in Gothic. e and g are pronounced as y in certain cases, e. g. geoc, go. juk, 'yoke;' lýfan, 'allow,' 'leave;' riht, 'right;' wâ, 'woe.'

82. The only SIBILANTS are s (which is not, as in Gothic, softened between two vowels, but always preserves the hard sound, e.g. seófon, 'seven;' thissa, 'of these') and z.

83. The Anglo-Saxon Alphabet is as follows:

	Mute.	Vocal.	Nasal.	Half-vowels.	Sibilants.	Vowels.
Gutturals	k h	g —	ng	y	—	a, e æ
Dentals	t th	d dh	n	l r	s z	i, o
Labials	p f	b —	m	w	—	u ý

The Guttural and Labial vocal aspirates (*gh* and *bh*) are wanting. The sibilants are very defective, but the vowels numerous.

84. On comparing the above alphabets, we obtain the following

RESULTS.

The *Cerebral* consonants, which are so distinctly and fully developed in Sanskrit, do not appear at all in the other alphabets. To a careful observer, it is manifest that the Dental consonants, out of which the Cerebrals arose, are pronounced differently in different positions in the living languages of Europe; and, although the alphabets of those languages have no characters to represent the distinction, it is clear that in pronouncing those letters there is the same tendency as that which caused an entire class of consonants to be adopted in the Sanskrit alphabet.

85. The *Palatals* have disappeared from Greek, Latin, Gothic, and Anglo-Saxon, but in Zend and English there are *ch* and *j*. The English Palatals, however, are not etymologically traceable to Sanskrit, but are later and independent developments. They are, in fact, compound characters, *ch* being equal to $t + sh$, and $j = d +$ French *j*. In German, z is a similar compound, being equal to $t + s$.

86. The Sanskrit alphabet contains ten *aspirates*; Zend, four, besides *gh* and *ḍ*; Greek, three; Latin, two; Gothic has three; Anglo-Saxon, four; and English and German three each. It is possible that some of the characters represent two aspirates each, the mute and vocal, as is the case with the English *th*. But even if this be so, the other alphabets are much less fully provided with aspirates than the Sanskrit.

87. The *nasals* and *half-vowels* have suffered little diminution, though the Zend has no *l*, the Greek no *y*, and the German no *w*.

88. The Zend and English have each four *sibilants*; Sanskrit and German, three; Greek, Gothic, and Anglo-Saxon, two; and Latin only one.

89. The *vowels* are abundantly represented, and have acquired many new combinations in modern alphabets.

90. The survey which we have thus taken of the alphabets of some of the principal languages of the Indo-European family shows that the effect of change has not been to perfect, but to mutilate, the system of consonants, and not to simplify the vowels, but to render them more complex. Both consonants and vowels in their earliest condition appear perfectly symmetrical. Those which are formed principally by the throat, the Gutturals, have exactly the same number, corresponding to them in all respects, formed in the centre of the mouth, the Dentals; and analogous to both are those formed by the lips, the Labials.

91. The distinction between the three classes becomes more obvious if we follow the arrangement adopted by Lepsius, and founded upon the order of the letters in the Hebrew alphabet,— Guttural, Labial, Dental. On pronouncing a letter from each organ in this order, the difference between them becomes more obvious, and the principle of arrangement more distinct. No one can fail to recognise the organic relation of such a series of letters as the following, if the Consonants be pronounced with the sound of *a* in *had* before or after them: g, b, d; k, p, t; ng, m, n; y, w, l; z, sh, s; a, u, i.

92. All the modern languages of this family, however cultivated the literature, and however civilised the nation, present only mutilated and fragmentary alphabets compared with what we find in use at the earliest period, and in immediate proximity to the primitive abode from which the different tribes diverged. The Indo-European family, therefore, did not begin with a defective instrument of speech which required to be filled up and polished by subsequent use in order to attain its perfection. The earliest is its most perfect form. It appears to us at once in vigorous maturity, and fully equipped for the service which it has to perform. This circumstance deserves consideration in endeavouring to decide the much vexed question of the origin of language.

THE TRANSMUTATION OF CONSONANTS.

93. A remarkable modification of some of the consonants distinguishes three different divisions of the Indo-European languages. We owe the discovery, establishment, and full illustration of this fact to Rask and Grimm. The variation thus brought to light is not confined to a few isolated instances, but affects the mass of the languages. It appears as a general law regulating the development of later out of earlier languages.

94. The terms *later* and *earlier*, however, in this connection are not used in a chronological sense; for a language which is here said to belong to a later stage may have existed and had a literature centuries before one which belongs to an earlier stage. If, for instance, A and B be two languages which both have the same consonants in words etymologically the same — e. g. gr. ζυγόν and L *jugum*, which both have *g* in the middle of the word — and if C and D be two other languages which are like each other in this respect, but both differ alike

from A and B—e. g. go. *juk* and e. *yoke*, which both
have *k* in place of the *g* in the former languages — then
C and D are in the second stage of development, and are
later in this respect than A and B, though not in any
sense derived from them. It does not, however, follow,
because A and B both belong to the first class of
languages, that they were therefore both spoken and
written contemporaneously; nor, because C and D both
belong to the second class, that they were therefore both
spoken and written at the same time; nor does it follow
that A and B were spoken and written before C and D.
So that this arrangement of languages has no necessary
connection with the chronological order in which we
find their literature. Still a language of the second
division must have sprung from some language of the
first division, and must therefore have come into use
later than that particular language of the first division.

95. To the *first* of these three divisions belong the
Sanskrit, Zend, Greek, Latin, as well as many others.
To the *second* belong Gothic, Anglo-Saxon, and English, with several besides. The *third* division consists
only of the High German.

96. This distinction has nothing to do with grammatical inflections; for Anglo-Saxon and English, though
they belong to the same division, differ more widely in
their grammatical forms than English and German,
which belong to different divisions. The difference affects
almost exclusively the lexicography of the languages
— the consonants employed in the Roots and Stems of
words. Thus, s. *pitṛ́*, gr. πατήρ, L *pater*, belong to the
first division. They all have *p* at the beginning and *t*
in the middle of the word. But go. *fadar*, a. s. *fader*,
e. *father*, belong to the second division, all having *f*
instead of *p* of the first division, whilst the first two

have *d* (possibly pronounced *dh*), and the last *th* (pronounced *dh*), for *t* of the first division. Again, we have s. *twam*, gr. (Doric) τύ, L *tu*, in the first division; go. *thu*, a. s. *thu*, e. *thou*, of the second; and ger. *du*, of the third, where *t*, *th*, and *d* respectively distinguish the three divisions.

97. This law does not, however, extend to all the consonants. It has no influence upon the nasals, half-vowels, and sibilants, but is confined to the mute and vocal consonants, with their aspirates. These in the oldest alphabet were *k*, *kh*, *g*, *gh*; *t*, *th*, *d*, *dh*; *p*, *ph*, *b*, *bh*. The two series of aspirates have to be reduced to one, so that there will then be in each organ three classes of consonants answering to the above division of languages. Their relation to one another requires that they should be arranged in the following order: Vocals, *g*, *d*, *b*; Mutes, *k*, *t*, *p*; Aspirates, *gh*, *kh*, *dh*, *th*, *bh*, *ph*. Thus, when a word has a Vocal consonant in any of the first division of languages, the same word has a Mute in the second, and an Aspirate in the third. Again, if in the first division the word has a Mute consonant, it has an Aspirate in the second, and a Vocal in the third. And, further, if in the first division the word has an Aspirate, it has a Vocal in the second, and a Mute in the third. The order of succession is always the same.

98. Many words seem irreconcilable with this law, merely because the same sound is represented by different characters in different languages, e.g. *ph* in Sanskrit, *f* in Latin and English, *f* and *v* in German. It must be remembered that these letters are identical, as far as the present law is concerned, which has to do with *sounds*, and not with the characters in which they are written. Another circumstance requires to be

borne in mind, i. e. that, in their cultivated or 'classical'
state, languages often contain an extensive admixture
of heterogeneous elements. The modern High German
contains many Low German forms, and oftentimes the
same word fluctuates between the two systems. The
intimate intercourse of the people, who, in the heart of
Germany, spoke languages which belonged to two of
the above divisions, and the influence of Luther and
his contemporaries upon the popular literature, have
indelibly stamped this mixed character upon the language of the country. Thus, for l. *frater*, e. *brother*,
we have ger. *bruder*, where the *b* is characteristic of
Low German, and *d* of the High German. In old
High German we find *pruodar*, where both consonants
belong to the High German character. Again, for
l. *fui*, e. *be*, we have ger. *bin*, but in old High German *pim*.

99. The consonants, thus viewed, fall into nine series
of three each, and each series of three represents the
three divisions of languages, viz. G, K, GH; D, T, DH; B,
P, BH, where words in the first division of languages
have Vocal consonants;—K, GH, G; T, DH, D; P, BN, B,
where words in languages of the first division have
Mute consonants;—GH, G, K; DH, D, T; BN, B, P, where
words in languages of the first division have Aspirates.

100. It may fairly be presumed that such was the
original relation of these letters in the Indo-European
languages. But long before these languages were fixed
in writing, and before the documents were secured from
which our illustrations must be derived, they had all
undergone great changes. Language is of delicate
construction and has nevertheless been exposed to all the
vicissitudes which have affected the history of mankind.
For all thoughts, feelings, and experiences leave their

impress upon the language in which they are communicated. There must therefore be many apparent exceptions and deviations from the original law of development. These exceptions and deviations, however, further discoveries may, by correcting our conceptions of the laws themselves, show to be the normal results of an unerring force.

101. The following list contains an illustration of each series:

g k gh	l. jugum	e. yoke	ger. joch
d t dh	odi	hate	hassen
b p bh	labium	lip	lefze (o.g.)
k gh g	doceo	teach	zeigen
t dh d	frater	brother	pruodar (o.g.)
p bh b	septem	seven	sieben
gh g k	trabero	drag	trahan (o.g.)
dh d t	θυγάτηρ	daughter	tochter
bh b p	fagus	beech	puocha (o.g.)

102. The Guttural aspirate is lost in the pronunciation of modern English. The letters in some cases are written, but not pronounced, as *gh* in *bough*; sometimes they are not written, as in *bow*; but in the above word, *teach*, *ch* is preserved in writing, but with an altered pronunciation. In German the sound of the Dental aspirates is lost, and its place supplied by the sibilant *s*, as in the above example *hassen*. A similar change has taken place in English, and is even now hardly completed, that is, in the ending of the 3rd Sing. Pres., *th* becoming *s*, e.g. *hates*, *hateth*. In Latin the Guttural aspirates are represented by *h*, as in *trahere*, and the Dental aspirates are changed to Labial aspirates, e.g. Θυμός, fumus; Θήρ, fera; Θύρα, fores.

103. A singular fact is observable in German, which illustrates the dependence of the later upon the earlier classes of languages. When Dental or Labial aspirates occur, the mutes out of which they have arisen, and which characterise an earlier class of languages, are also preserved, e.g. *pfeffer, zehn* ($z = ts$), for English *pepper, ten*, where *p* and *t* of the second class are preserved, and *f* and *s* of the third added. Sometimes the preceding letter is assimilated, and the aspirate becomes doubled, e.g. *hoffen, hassen*, for English *hope, hate*, from *hopfen, hatsen*.

104. For a fuller discussion of this law, the reader is referred to Grimm, *Geschichte der Deutschen Sprache*, i. pp. 392—434, 1st ed.

IV. ROOTS.

105. The Latin word *dicitur*, 'it is said,' is found, on examination, to consist of several parts of different origin. It may be thus divided, *dic-i-t-u-r*. The letter *r* is in Latin distinctive of the Passive voice, and the *u* by which it is here preceded is a connecting vowel which has no effect on the meaning of the word. When these two letters are removed, there remains *dicit*, 'it says.' Again, *t* expresses the Third Person Singular, answering to the English pronoun 'he,' 'she,' or 'it;' and *i* is another connecting vowel. When these are removed, we have the monosyllable *dic*, which is called the 'root' of the word.

106. All primitive verbs in the Indo-European languages may be similarly reduced to monosyllabic *roots*. These *roots*, however, have no meaning, and, as far as we know, were never thus used in ordinary speech. Such words as the Imperatives *dic*, *fac*, etc. form no real exception, seeing that this is not their original form, but the result of abbreviation. For the sake of rapid utterance the endings of the Imperative have been dropped, and the words have retained the meanings which the terminations gave them. The *roots*, not having had such terminations, have acquired no distinctive meaning, and are therefore incapable of being used in such languages as those of the Indo-European family.

THEIR DISTINCTIVE CHARACTER 77

107. It has sometimes been assumed that before terminations were used the *roots* were placed one after another, as in Chinese, and acquired a meaning from their position. The system of affixes is supposed to be of a later date. No doubt modern languages of the Indo-European family tend towards the state of the Chinese. For instance, the phrases 'I have seen,' 'you have seen,' 'they have seen,' express three different meanings, not from any change in the terminations, but from the use of different words. In Latin, 'vidi,' 'vidistis,' 'viderunt,' by a mere change in the terminations of one word, express the same three meanings. We have historical proof, therefore, of a system of affixes changing to monosyllabic words. But within the range of the Indo-European family we have no historical evidence, and no literary remains, to show that languages once consisting of monosyllabic *roots* changed to a system of affixes. The oldest remains which we have of these languages exhibit them in the possession of grammatical forms, and the older the remains the more perfect are the terminations.

108. The fact that in these languages each *root* consists of one syllable has caused them to be called 'Monosyllabic,' in distinction from the Semitic languages, which are also inflected, but their roots, for the most part, consist of three consonants or two syllables. They are therefore called 'triliteral' or 'dissyllabic.' The evidence as to whether or not these dissyllabic roots are derivatives from monosyllables, is not yet sufficient to prove that the two classes of languages do, or do not, in this respect, belong to one system.

109. There is a singular contrast between the grammatical system of the Indo-European and that of the Semitic languages, the one being dependent chiefly upon *external*, the other upon *internal* changes. The modification of meaning in Semitic verbs is brought about chiefly by a change in the vowels between the root consonants. The variation of verbs in the Indo-European languages results mainly from the syllables prefixed or added to the roots. Hence the vowels are much more numerous and complex in the former than in the latter class of languages, e. g. Arabic, *katala*, 'he killed;' *kutila*, 'he was killed;' Hebrew, *kôtêl*, 'killing;' *kâtûl*, 'killed.' In corresponding forms of the Latin the *root* remains unchanged: *lau*d*a*vit, 'he praised;' *lau*d*a*tus est, 'he was praised;' *laudans*, 'praising;' *laudatus*, 'praised.'

110. In the Chinese system the primary elements of language follow one another without undergoing any of those changes of form which characterise the above two families of inflected languages. The meaning of words is the result of their relative position, and not of grammatical forms. Thus *shŭi*, 'water,' and *sheù*, 'hand,' when placed together, *shŭi sheù*, mean 'helmsman;' *jhĭ*, 'sun,' and *tsè*, 'son,' form *jhĭ tsè*, 'day.'

111. The Roots, therefore, of the Indo-European languages are the primary elements of words which, by internal modification or external addition, acquire an almost endless variety of meanings. They may consist of any number of letters, forming but one syllable, e. g. *i*, as in s. *i-más*, gr. *l-μεν*, l. *i-mus*; and *skand*, as in l. *scand-o*. At the end of *verbal roots*, however, *a* and *ău* do not occur. Almost every other combination is admissible.

112. It is not possible at present to say with certainty on what principle these elementary parts of speech were formed. Nor is there any clear connection between sound and sense in most of them. That πέτ-ομαι should mean 'fly,' and κεῖ-μαι 'lie,' is not indicated in the character of the letters of which these words consist, nor very obviously in the sounds with which they are uttered. Various theories have been adopted, but none of them appear quite satisfactory. Further discoveries in the science of language will probably render the solution of the problem easier.

113. The *roots* of verbs and those of pronouns are distinct and independent of one another. Verbal roots usually express some state or action, as in *es*-se, 'to be;' *da*-re, 'to give.' Pronominal roots do not express any fact or name any object, but denote some relation generally to the speaker, as in *ay*-am, 'this,' the nearer; *id*-am, 'that,' the remoter. In accordance with this difference of meaning, they are also distinguished as Roots Predicative and Roots Demonstrative; the one serving to predicate or apply some fact or phenomenon to a subject, as l. *laud-ant*, 'they *praise*;' whilst the other point out (*demonstrant*) the subject, as l. laud-*ant*, '*they* praise.' The latter are generally employed in the external inflections of the former. For example, in *as-mi*, 'I am;' *as-si*, 'thou art;' *as-ti*, 'he is;' *as* is the *verbal root*, and *mi*, *si*, *ti* are weakened forms of the *pronominal roots ma, sa, ta.*

114. The VERBAL ROOTS in Sanskrit are divided into *ten classes*, amongst which the primitive verbs of the language are distributed as follows: the *first* class contains about 1,000; the *second*, 70; the *third*, 20; the *fourth*, 130; the *fifth*, 30; the *sixth*, 150; the *seventh*, 25; the *eighth*, 10; the *ninth*, 52; the *tenth*, a large number of primitive verbs as well as the Causative and Denominative verbs.

115. This is the order followed by Indian grammarians, but the whole are also arranged in two divisions, or *Conjugations*. The first of these contains classes 1, 4, 6, and 10. The second contains classes 2, 3, 5, 7, 8, and 9. The distinguishing *characteristics* of the different classes, except in the tenth, appear only in what are called the Special Tenses, viz. the Present Indicative, the Potential, the Imperative, and the single-formed Preterite. The other parts of the verbs are without these distinguishing marks. These two divisions in Sanskrit correspond to the two conjugations of Greek verbs; the first to verbs in -ω, the second to verbs in -μι. The first conjugation inserts *a* between the root and the ending, e. g. a *bódh-â-mas*, 'we know;' gr. τύπτ-ο-μεν, 'we strike:' the second appends the termination immediately to the root, e. g. a. *dwésh-mi*, 'I hate;' gr. φή-μι, 'I say.'

116. The processes of GUNA and VRIDDHI need here to be noticed. The former, GUNA, in Sanskrit, consists in prefixing *a* to another vowel, thus changing *i* or *î* to *ê* (a+i), *u* or *û* to *ô* (a+u), and *r* or *ṝ* to *ar* (a+r). The latter, VRIDDHI, prefixes *â* in a similar way, and changes *a* or *â* to *â* (â+a); *i* or *î* to *âi* (â+i); *u* or *û* to *âu* (â+u), and *r* or *ṝ* to *âr* (â+r).

117. The FIRST CONJUGATION inserts *a* between the root and the ending. The four classes of which it consists are distinguished principally by the use or omission of *guna* and the position of the *accent*. The *First Class* both gunaes and accents the *root* vowel. Thus *budh* becomes *bó'dh-a-ti*, 'he knows.' The *Sixth Class* does not guna the *root* vowel, and places the accent on the connecting vowel: *tud* becomes *tud-á-ti*, 'he strikes.' Those verbs which have *a* as their *root* vowel, since it is not affected by guna, can of course be known as belonging to the first or sixth class only by the position of the accent. *Lup, vid,* etc. of the sixth class have no

guna, but insert a nasal in the root, e. g. s. *lump-á-ti,*
'he splits,' l. *rump-i-t*; s. *vind-á-ti,* 'he finds.'

118. In Greek the connecting vowel has become ε
(before nasals ο): λείπ-ε-τε, 'you leave;' φεύγ-ε-τε, 'you
flee;' λείπ-ο-μεν, 'we leave;' φεύγ-ο-μεν, 'we flee.' The
guna-vowel has also become ε, as is seen by comparing
the above forms with ἔ-λιπ-ον, 'I left;' ἔ-φυγ-ον, 'I fled.'
These being gunaed belong to the first, but γλίχ-ο-μαι,
without guna, to the sixth class. There is not the same
distinction of accent between these two classes in Greek
as in Sanskrit. The third conjugation in Latin furnishes analogous examples. The connecting vowel has
become *i* (before *nt* it has become *u*), e. g. *leg-i-mus,*
'we read;' *leg-u-nt,* 'they read.' In Gothic the connecting vowel is *a* or *i.* Thus *haitan,* 'to be named,'
has in the Sing. *hait-a, hait-i-s, hait-i-th,* and in the
Pl. *hait-a-m, hait-i-th, hait-a-nd,* where the *a* appears
before a nasal, like *o* in Greek, *u* in Latin, and *â* in
Sanskrit. The guna-vowel appears as *i.* Thus *kin*
becomes *keina,* 'I germinate' (*ei* being for i+i), and
bug becomes *biuga,* 'I bend.' A radical *a,* being incapable of guna, as in Sanskrit, either remains unchanged,
e. g. *far-i-th,* 'he wanders,' for s. *chár-a-ti*; or it becomes *i, qvim-i-th,* 'he comes,' for s. *gám-a-ti.* In
some cases this derived *i,* being looked upon as primitive, is gunaed, e. g. *greipa,* 'I grasp,' for s. *grabh-á-mi.*
Almost all the Germanic Strong Verbs belong to the
first class in Sanskrit.

119. It is interesting to observe analogous deviations
from general rules in different languages. One of these
consists in the radical vowel being *lengthened* instead
of being gunaed, e. g. s. *gû'h-a-ti,* 'he covers,' from
guh; gr. τρίβω, 'I rub,' from τριβ-; L. *dúco,* 'I lead,'
from *duc-*; go. *us-lúk-i-th,* 'he unlocks,' from *luk.*

G

Each language avails itself of this liberty, without any dependence upon the rest for the individual instances which occur.

120. The analogy in the influence of the *nasal consonants* upon the connecting vowel in different languages is also remarkable. In Sanskrit the vowel *a* becomes strengthened to *â*, in Greek *ε* is strengthened to *o*, in Latin *i* is strengthened to *u*, and in Gothic *i* is strengthened to *a*. We observe here the operation of the same law in having stronger vowels to connect *nasal* consonants than to connect others with the *root*. At the same time the individual modifications appear to have been independently chosen. In Latin the 1st Plural has again reduced the stronger to the weaker vowel: comp. *leg-i-mus* with *leg-u-nt*. The *u* is irregular in the substantive verb, *s-u-m*, 'I am,' *s-u-mus*, 'we are,' *s-u-nt*, 'they are,' because this verb belongs to the second conjugation, which admits no connecting vowel, e. g. s. *as-mi*, *s-mas* (but *s-a-nti*), gr. ἐι-μί (for ἐσ-μι), ἐσ-μέν, εἰ-σί. The *u*, however, is preserved in the Latin *vol-u-mus*, 'we will,' if this word is etymologically connected with the Greek βούλ-ο-μεν.

121. The *Fourth Class* agrees with the first in accenting, and with the sixth in not gunaing, the root-vowel. It is further distinguished from both by prefixing *y* (or *i*) before the connecting vowel; that is, it inserts *ya* between the *root* and the ending. The verbs of this class, therefore, resemble the Passive voice in form, and are generally intransitive in meaning, e.g. *náz-ya-ti*, 'he perishes,' from *naz*; *kúp-ya-ti*, 'he is angry,' from *kup*. The *y* appears in Greek as ζ, e. g. in βύζω, βλύζω, βρίζω, σχίζω. So also πίζω for πί-yω, which furnishes some of the tenses of πι-πί-σκω, corresponds to a. *pí'-yê* (Mid.), 'I drink.' After a liquid the *y*, in the form of ι, is sometimes thrown back into the root, just as ἀμείνων, 'better,' is for ἀμενγων, and χείρων, 'worse,' for χερχων: e. g. χαίρ-ω, 'I rejoice,' for χαρyω, answering to s. hŕsh-yâ-mi; and μαίν-ε-ται, 'he rages,' for μαν-yε-ται, answering to s. mán-ya-té. Sometimes this y forms a diphthong with the root-vowel in Greek, where the Sanskrit drops the root-vowel, e. g. δαί-ω, 'I flame,' for δα-yω, s. d-yâ-mi. Again, we meet with this y in the form of ε, which, in some cases, must have very closely resembled it in pronunciation: for example, in πίστεως, 'of faith,' where εω is pronounced as one syllable. Thus we have ὠθ-έω, 'I push,' for ὠθ-yω.

Latin verbs of the third conjugation in -io belong to this class, e. g. l. cup-io, 'I desire;' s. kup-yâ-mi, 'I am angry;' l. cap-io, 'I take;' go. haf-ju, 'I lift.' Such forms as pi-yu-ṇ, 'I drink,' in Old Slavic, may belong to this class. But as the y occurs between two vowels, it may be only euphonic. Gothic verbs in -ja (=ya) are of this class, e. g. vahs-ja, 'I grow' (wax); bid-ja, 'I beg' (bid). When Sanskrit ô is changed to a in Gothic, y is also changed to i, and forms with a the diphthong ai, e. g. vai-a, 'I blow,' for va-ja; lai-a, 'I despise;' sai-a, 'I saw.'

Probably no roots originally ended in diphthongs. Those which now appear in that form resulted from contraction, and belong to this class, e. g. gá'yati, from gâ, not from gai; dháyati, from dhâ, not from dhai. So also dyáti is from dâ, as is clear from the Participle dâ-tus, 'cut off,' and the Substantive dâ-trum, 'a sickle.'

122. The *Tenth Class* gunaes the root-vowel like the first class, and, like the sixth class, it *accents the part inserted* between the root and the ending. This class, instead of *a* of the first and sixth, and *ya* of the fourth, inserts *aya* between the root and the ending, and

84   ROOTS

places the accent on the first vowel of this part. It is
thus identical in form with the Causative verbs, e. g.
chôr-áyâ-mi, 'I steal,' from chur.

From this form have arisen most Greek verbs in
-αζω, -αω, -εω, -οω, and Latin verbs of the 1st, 2nd, and
4th conjugations. Slavic verbs in -ayun belong to this
class, e. g. sl. rúd-ayu-n, 'I lament,' for a. ród-áyâ-mi,
'I cause to weep.' In Gothic we have ja, the first a
of aya being dropped (just as in the Latin form -io of
the fourth conj.). Sometimes the last a is dropped,
and y changed to i, as in hab-ai-s. This i also is
dropped before nasals, e.g. hab-a-m. When y is dropped,
a+a produces ô in Gothic, which corresponds to â in
the Latin first conjugation, e. g. go. laig-ô-s, 'thou
lickest,' for a. léh-áya-si; l. laud-â-s, 'thou praisest.'
The intermediate step is found in Pracrit, where
gan-aa-di, 'he wanders,' is for a. gan-áya-ti.

123. We now come to the SECOND CONJUGATION of
Sanskrit verbs, including the other six classes. They
all *affix the ending immediately to the root*, without
any connecting vowel. Four of the classes, however,
add an inorganic syllable or nasal letter as an enlargement of the *root*.

124. The *Second Class* accents the 'heavy' terminations, but before the 'light' terminations it gunaes
and accents the *root*-vowel, e. g. é'mi, 'I go;' imás,
'we go.' This difference of accentuation is not observed
in Greek, e. g. εἰμι, ἴμεν. Almost all the Greek *roots*
which belong to this class end in a vowel, i, φâ, βâ, δω,
πâ, θη. The only *root* ending in a consonant, which
immediately adds the terminations, is *as*, e. g. s. ás-ti,
gr. ἐσ-τί, l. es-t, go. is-t, 'is.' In Latin i, da, stâ, fâ,
flâ, qua (in-quam), as well as some forms of *fer*, and
vel, belong to this class.

125. The *Third Class* prefixes a syllable of *reduplication*, and places the accent on this syllable, e. g. *dádâ-ti*, 'he gives;' *dídhá-ti*, 'he puts.' The Greek language has many forms belonging to this class, e. g. δίδω-τι, τίθη-τι, βίβη-τι. In Latin the second *i* in *sisti-t*, *bibi-t*, is a shortened form for Sanskrit *â*; *seri-t* for *sisi-t*, with the common softening of *s* to *r* between vowels, and the usual change of *i* to *e* before *r*, is another instance of a *reduplicated* form of this class, as is indicated by the participle *sa-tus*.

126. The *Seventh Class* inserts in the *root* the syllable *na* before the 'light' endings, and this is reduced to *n* before 'heavy' endings, being changed, when necessary, to a nasal of the same organ with the final consonant of the *root*. In the last case words of this class coincide with those of the sixth, except in having no connecting vowel. Most of the corresponding words in Latin insert a connecting vowel, and agree with the *first*, instead of the *second*, Sanskrit conjugation. The accent in Sanskrit is placed upon *na* in the first case, and upon the endings in the second, e. g. *yunáj-mi*, 'I bind;' *yunj-más*, 'we bind;' *bhinád-mi*, 'I split;' *bhind-más*, 'we split;' *chhinád-mi*, 'I cut;' *chhind-más*, 'we cut.' In Latin the corresponding words have the syllable in both cases reduced to the mere nasal, and a connecting vowel inserted, e. g. *jung-o*, 'I join,' *jung-i-mus*; *find-o*, 'I cleave,' *find-i-mus*; *scind-o*, 'I cut,' *scind-i-mus*. In Greek some verbs exhibit the characteristics of two classes, a nasal inserted and another appended to the root, e. g. λαμβάνω, 'I take,' λιμπάνω, 'I leave,' μανθάνω, 'I learn,' from the roots λαβ, λιπ, μαθ, as in ἔ-λαβ-ον etc. In Gothic a nasal is inserted in the Present tense of *standa*, Pret. *stóth*; a. s. *stunde*, *stód*; e. *stand*, *stood*. In this word the final consonant *d* appears to be inorganic, as it does not exist in Sanskrit, Greek, or Latin. A similar phenomenon appears in *mita*, e. *mete*, compared with s. *mâ*, 'to measure.'

127. The *Fifth Class* adds *nu* to the root, and this syllable is both gunaed and accented before 'light' endings, but 'heavy' endings both prevent guna and themselves take the accent, e. g. *stṛ-nó'-mi*, 'I spread;' *stṛ-nu-más*, 'we spread;' gr. στόρ-ῐ ῠ́-μι (where the vowel is lengthened instead of being gunaed), στόρ-νῠ́-μες.

128. The *Eighth Class* probably ought to be incorporated with the fifth. It is said to add only *u* to the *root*; but as all the *roots*, except one, terminate in *n*, this may easily be supposed to have caused the omission of the second *n*. Guna and accent are the same as in the fifth class: *tan-ó'-mi*, 'I stretch,' *tan-u-más*, 'we stretch,' gr. τάν-υ-μαι; ἄν-υ-μι, 'I complete;' γάν-υ-μαι, 'I delight in;' ὄλ-λυ-μι, 'I perish,' from ὄλ-νυ-μι.

129. The *Ninth Class* adds *nâ* before 'light,' and *ní* before 'heavy' endings, and accentuates like the fifth class. The Greek has *νη* before 'light,' and *νᾰ* before heavy endings. This is irregularly shortened in such forms as δάκ-νο-μεν, 'we bite;' e. g. s. *yu-nấ'-mi*, 'I bind,' *yu-ní-más*, 'we bind;' gr. δάμ-νη-μι, 'I tame,' δάμ-νᾰ-μεν; s. *stṛ-nấ'-mi*, 'I strew,' *stṛ-ní-más*, 'we strew,' l. *ster-no*, *ster-ni-mus*.

130. The following is a brief list of *roots* which may serve further to illustrate the relation of these languages one to another. It will have become obvious how the modifications of the different classes of roots are almost entirely lost in English, thus illustrating the progress of phonetic decay.

Sanskrit.	Zend.	Greek.	Latin.	Gothic.	English.
gâ	—	βῆ-ναι	—	gagg-an	go
dhâ	dâ	θῆ-ναι	—	—	do-n, do-ff
jnâ	żnâ	γνῶ-ναι	gno-sco	—	know
wâ	—	—	—	vi-nds	wi-nd
sthâ	stâ	στῆ-ναι	sta-re	sta-nda	sta-nd
i	—	ἴ-τε	i-re	—	—
żwl	—	κύ-ειν	—	hau-hs	hi-gh
smi	—	μει-δ-άω	—	—	smi-le
pri	fri	φιλ-ειν	—	frij-on	frie-nd
żi	—	κεῖ-μαι	qui-eo	—	—
plu	fru	πλε-ειν	plu-o	—	floo-d
tru	zrâv	κλύ-ειν	clu-eo	—	—
lû	—	λύ-ειν	lu-o	liu-san	loo-se
bhû	—	φύ-ειν	fu-i	bau-an	be
ad	—	ἔδ-ω	ed-o	it-an	eat
dru	—	ἔ-δρα-μ-ον	—	—	—
bandh	band	ἔ-πιθ-ον	fid-o	bind-an	bind
stig	—	ἔ-στιχ-ον	—	stoig-an	sti-le
ruh	rudh	—	—	—	rood, rod
bhrâj	—	φλέγ-ειν	flag-rare	bairh-ts	brigh-t
râj	râz	—	—	reik-s	rich
sach	—	ἕπ-ομαι	sequ-or	—	seek
as	as	ἐσ-τί	es-t	is	is
iksh	—	ὄπ-ός	oc-ulus	aug-o	eye
jush	zausha	γεύ-ω	gus-tare	kius-an	choose
diż	diż	δείκ-νυμι	dic-o	teih-an	teach
jiv	jva	βιό-ω	viv-o	qiu-s	quick

V. STEMS.

131. We have seen that in some cases letters or syllables intervene between the root of a verb and the endings which denote person and number. Thus, in the Latin *regit*, 'he rules,' *t*, meaning 'he,' 'she,' or 'it,' is not added to the simple root *reg*, but to the compound form *regi*. So, in the Perfect tense *rexit*, 'he ruled,' *t* is added to another compound form consisting of *reg*+*s*+*i*. So also, in nouns, the endings which denote case and number are similarly added to a compound form; thus, in *regem* the sign of the Accusative Singular *m* is added, not to *reg*, but to *rege*. This compound form, in distinction from the root, is called a *stem*, in harmony with the same figure of speech. The complete word, conveying intelligence, is not the bare root, nor the root and the connecting medium, or the *stem*, but the entire tree with its branches and fruit.

132. *Nominal Stems* of this kind are used with case-endings to form primitive nouns, e. g. Gen. S. *regi-s*, 'of a king;' and without case-endings as the first member in compound nouns, e. g. *regi-fugium*, 'king's flight.'

Different *genders* are sometimes indicated by different *stems* of the same word: ἀγαθ-ό-ς, 'good,' ἀγαθ-ό-ν, Mas. and Neut., have the same *stem* ἀγαθο, but ἀγαθ-ή Fem. a different one. So in Latin *bon-u-s*, 'good,' Mas., *bon-u-m* Neut., have the same stem *bonu*; but *bon-a* Fem. a different one. This distinction is preserved somewhat incompletely in Gothic, confusedly in Anglo-Saxon, and in English the word, e. g. *good*, is reduced again to its root form, all indication of *stem*, case, and number being lost. The *Neuter* gender at first doubtless was employed in reference to things which had no natural distinction of sex. In course of time it has, in some languages, acquired a wider application, as in English; and in others has entirely gone out of use, as in French.

The *number* of nouns is usually denoted by a modification of the case-ending. In Sanskrit *bhyam* is sometimes the ending of the Dative Sing., *bhyâm* the Dat. Dual, and *bhyas* the Dat. Plural. The *Dual* number, which was very carefully employed in earlier times, gradually lost its power, and then entirely disappeared, so that it no longer exists in the principal living languages of the Indo-European family. The Sanskrit has it most perfectly, both in the noun and the verb. The Zend has it rarely in the noun, but frequently in the verb. The Greek preserves it extensively, the Latin only in *duo* and *ambo*. It is in the Gothic pronoun and verb, as well as the Anglo-Saxon pronoun, but apparently in no other Germanic language.

Terminations of Nominal Stems.

133. In Sanskrit all the three vowels *a, i, u,* occur at the end of Nominal Stems. They are usually of the Masculine gender. *a* is always either Masculine or Neuter. It is represented by *a* in Zend, and in a few cases in Gothic; by *o* in Greek and Latin. In later times the Latin *o* was in some cases changed to *u*, e. g. λόγ-ο-ς, 'word;' δῶρ-ο-ν, 'gift;' *domin-u-s*, 'lord,' *domin-o-rum*; *regn-u-m*, 'dominion,' *regn-o-rum*; s.

vṛk-a-s, 'wolf,' gr. λύκ-ο-ς, l. lup-u-s. i occurs in all three genders. It is ι or ς in Greek, πόλι-ς, πόλε-ως, and i or e in Latin, fucil-i-s, 'easy,' fucil-e-m; a. vá'ri, 'water;' l. mare, 'sea,' Nom. Pl. mari-a. u occurs in the three genders. The same letter is preserved in the other languages: a. sûn-ú-s, go. sun-u-s, 'son;' a. svâd-ú-s, 'sweet,' gr. ἡδ-ύ-ς. The fourth declension in Latin furnishes examples.

134. The *stems* ending in the long vowels *â*, *î*, *û*, in Sanskrit, are generally Feminine, seldom Masculine, and never Neuter. *â* is shortened to *a* in the other languages. But the Gothic has *ô* in some oblique cases, and in the Nominatives: só, 'that' (she), for s. sâ, and hvó, 'who,' for s. kâ. *î* is often employed in Sanskrit and Zend to form Feminine derivatives, e. g. mahat-î', 'great,' from mahât. A further addition is made to it where it is preserved in Greek and Latin; *a* or *δ* is added in Greek, and *c* in Latin. Thus, a. svâd-û-s M., svâd-û N., becomes svâd-î' in the Fem.; but in gr. ἡδ-ύ-ς M., ἡδ-ύ N., becomes ἡδ-εῖ-α in the Fem.; a. jani-trî, gr. γενέτειρα for γενετρια, l. genetrix (genetrî-c-s); λῃστρίς, Gen. λῃστρί-δ-ος, for s. -trî. The placing of ι a syllable further back, as in γενέτειρα, frequently occurs in the Greek language. We have noticed other instances above. But sometimes a much greater change occurs in the terminations which we are now consider- ing. The ι retains its place, but is ultimately changed to σ. Thus from δολο- is formed δολο-ϝντ- by an affix which appears in Sanskrit as -vant, and in weaker forms as -vat (e.g. dhâna-vati Fem.), for which the correspond- ing Greek form would be σι. Hence we obtain the Fem. δολο-ετ-ια, then δολο-ισ-ια, and finally the clas- sical form δολό-ισ-σα, 'cunning.' The change of *t* to a sibilant is illustrated by the English pronunciation of *t* before *i* in such words as *nation*. This word may also serve to illustrate another change in the Greek Feminine termination -ια; for as in 'nation' the *i*, after giving a sibilant sound to *t*, is omitted in pronunciation, so in such participles as φέρουσα, 'bearing' (for φεροντ-ια), the *ι* disappears after having produced its effect on the preceding consonant; the only difference being that in Greek the writing is adapted to the new sound, whilst in English the old spelling is preserved with the new pronunciation. In Gothic the long vowel, written *ei*, is followed by an inorganic *n* in the Present Participle, e. g. a. *bhárant-í*, go. *bairand-ei-n*, 'bearing.' Or *i* is changed to *j* (y), and followed by *ó*, e. g. *frijond-s* M., *frijond-jó* F., 'friend;' *thius-s* M., *thiu-jó* F., 'servant.' *ú* is rare in Sanskrit. But there occur *zwazrú*, l. *socrus*, 'mother-in-law;' *bhrú*, gr. ὀφρύ-ς, 'eyebrow.'

135. There are a few instances of *stems* with diphthongal terminations: *rái*, 'riches,' becomes *rá* before consonants, and answers to the Latin *ré*; *dyô* is from the root *div*, and forms some of its cases from *dyâu*. The Nom. Sing. *dyaus* corresponds to Greek Ζεύς, *d* being dropped, *y* changed to ζ, and *á* shortened to *s*. The Latin has added *i* to the *stem* in *Jov-i-s*. s. *gó*, 'ox,' is in Zend *gau*, gr. βοῦ, L. *bó* or *bov*; s. *nau*, 'ship,' gr. ναῦ-ς, L. *nav-i-s*. The *stem* is preserved, without the additional *i*, in *nau-fragus*, 'shipwrecked.'

136. In Sanskrit CONSONANT STEMS, i. e. *stems* ending in consonants, are confined to the letters *n*, *t*, *s*, *r*. Several other consonants occur at the end of *roots*, which are used in the formation of nouns. In Greek and Latin a consonant appears sometimes in addition to the vowel *stem* in Sanskrit, e. g. the patronymics in -ιδ, and L. *pecu-d-is* compared with s. *pazu*, go. *faihu*, 'flock' (e. *fee*). *s* frequently occurs in Sanskrit, and serves to explain some otherwise obscure forms in Greek and Latin. Thus it appears that the σ in μένος, 'mind,' γένος, 'race,' belongs to the stem, and therefore the genitives μένεος, γένεος are for μενεσος, γενεσος. So also the first σ in τεύχεσ-σι, ὄρεσ-σι, belongs to the stem, and the second only to the case-ending. The compounds σακίς-παλος, 'wielding the spear,' τελίς-φορος, 'completing,' preserve the original σ in the first member of the compound. In Latin this *s* coming between two vowels is softened to *r*, e. g. *genus*, 'race,' *generis*. An analogous modification of the preceding vowel also takes place in these two languages; the Nom. Sing. having *o* for *s* in Greek, and *u* for *e* in Latin, a change similar to that which occurs in the connecting vowel of verbs before nasal consonants.

137. In Sanskrit the *stem* sometimes assumes three different forms — the 'strong,' 'middle,' and 'weak.' The 'strong' forms are used with the lightest case-endings, the 'weak' with the heaviest, and the 'middle' with those of intermediate weight: e. g. *rud*, 'weep,' has a reduplicated preterite, the participle of which has Acc. Sing. M. rurud-wấ'ns-am, Loc. Plu. M. and N. rurud-wát-su, Gen. Sing. M. rurud-úsh-as, where the *stem* ends in the strong -*wáns*, the middle -*wat*, and the weak -*ush*. More generally the *stem* has but two forms, when the 'weak' includes the 'middle' and 'weak' in the previous classification. The 'weak,' in the division into three, only includes the Gen. M. and N. of the three numbers. The eight cases of Sanskrit (and Zend) are therefore divided into two classes — the 'strong,' those which have the *strong stem*; and the 'weak,' those which have the *weak stem*. The following example will show which they are: —

THEIR CONSTRUCTION 93

		Strong Cases.	Weak Cases.
Sing.—	Nom. Voc.	bhár-an(t), 'bearing'	
	Acc.	bhár-ant-am	
	Instr.		bhár-at-á
	Dat.		bhár-at-ê
	Abl.		bhár-at-as
	Gen.		bhár-at-as
	Loc.		bhár-at-i
Dual.—	Nom. Voc. Acc.	bhár-ant-âu	
	Instr. Dat. Abl.		bhár-ad-bhyâm
	Gen. Loc.		bhár-at-ôs
Plu. —	Nom. Voc.	bhár-ant-as	
	Acc.		bhár-at-as
	Instr.		bhár-ad-bhis
	Dat. Abl.		bhár-ad-bhyas
	Gen.		bhár-at-âm
	Loc.		bhár-at-su

This arrangement is not carried out so fully in Zend as in Sanskrit. The accentuation of words with monosyllabic *stems*, where this difference of strength in the *stems* cannot be made, sometimes coincides with this arrangement of cases. And, singularly enough, the Greek retains the same position of the accent: e. g. s. vâk and gr. ὄπ-ς are of the same origin, and are thus accentuated.

94 STEMS

		STRONG CASES.		WEAK CASES.	
Sing.—	Nom. Voc.	vâk ('voice')	ὄπ-ς		
	Acc.	vâ'ch-am	ὄπ-α		
	Instr.			vach-â'	
	Dat.			vach-ê'	
	Abl.			vach-âs	
	Gen.			vach-âs	ὀπ-ός
	Loc. (gr. Dat.)			vach-î'	ὀπ-ί
Dual—	Acc. Voc.	vâ'ch-âu	ὄπ-ε		
	Instr. Abl.			vâg-bhyâ'm	
	Dat.			vâg-bhyâ'm	ὀπ-οῖν
	Gen. Loc.			vâch-ó's	
Plu.—	Nom. Voc.	vâ'ch-as	ὄπ-ες		
	Acc.	vâ'ch-as	ὄπ-ες		
	Instr.			vâg-bhís	
	Dat. Abl.			vâg-bhyás	
	Gen.			vâch-â'm	ὀπ-ῶν
	Loc. (gr. Dat.)			vâk-shú	ὀπ-σί

The Acc. Plu. is here placed among the strong cases, because of the position of the accent. Again, in πατερ, μητερ, θυγατερ, the ε is dropped only in the weak cases. In Gothic also a is dropped before r and changed to i before n in the weak cases: e. g. brôthar becomes in the Dat. brôthr, Gen. brôthrs; ahan, Dat. ahin, Gen. ahins.

138. When a case-ending which begins with a vowel has to be added to a *stem* which ends in a vowel, a euphonic consonant is inserted between them, e. g. in the Instr. Sing. and Gen. Pl. in Sanskrit, n; in the Gen. Pl. of three declensions in Latin, r.

VI. FORMATION OF CASES.

139. In Sanskrit and Zend there are *eight cases*, of which the Greek preserves only *five*; the Latin, *six*; the Gothic, *five*; Anglo-Saxon, *five*; and English, none. Some isolated instances remain in different languages, of a case which no longer forms part of their grammar; as, for instance, single words referable to the Locative case in Greek and Latin.

THE NOMINATIVE SINGULAR.

140. The sign of the *Nominative Case Singular*, in the Masculine and Feminine, is *s*. It forms ô with a preceding *a*, sometimes in Sanskrit, always in Zend. It is omitted at the end of consonant stems, and if the stem ends in two consonants, the latter of these is also dropped, e. g. Nom. *bibhrat*, 'bearer,' for *bibhrats*; *tudán* Nom., 'striker,' for tudants. In Zend the *s* is preserved, e. g. Nom. *afs*, 'water.' Stems in *n* omit this letter as well as the Nominative sign, lengthening the preceding vowel as a compensation, e. g. Nom. *dhanî*, 'rich,' from dhanín; Nom. *râ'jâ*, from râ'jan. The same occurs in Zend, except that the vowel is lengthened only in monosyllables, e. g. Nom. *spâ*, 'dog,' from *span*; *ashava*, 'pure,' from ashavan. Stems in -*ar*, -*âs* omit both their final consonant and the Nom. sign, lengthening the preceding vowel when short, e. g. Nom *pitâ'*, 'father,' from pitar; *dâtâ'*, 'giver,' from dâtâr. The Zend omits the lengthening of the short vowel, e. g. Nom. *brâta, dâta*. Stems in -*as* omit the Nom. sign, and lengthen the preceding vowel, e. g. Nom. *dúrmanâs*, 'evil-minded,' from durmanas. Of vowel stems the Feminines in -*â* always, and those in -*î* generally, omit the Nominative sign, e. g. Nom. *živâ* from živa, Nom. *nadî* from nadî, but Nom. *bhís* from bhî.

The Greek and Latin languages preserve the Nom. sign in consonant stems, omitting the stem consonant if it be a Dental, e. g. χάρι-ς for χαριτ-ς, *virtu-s* for virtut-s. So also τιθει-ς, *aman-s*, for τιθεντ-ς, amant-s. But Gutturals and Labials in the stem are preserved, e. g. κόραξ-ς, λαῖλαπ-ς, lex (leg-s). Greek stems in -ν sometimes preserve this consonant, and sometimes the Nominative sign, but never both, and generally a preceding short vowel is lengthened, e. g. μίλᾱ-ς (μελαν-), τέρην (τερεν). In Latin there is the same diversity, and in many cases both consonants are omitted, e. g. *sanguis* (**sanguin**-), *flumen* (**flumin**-), *homo* (**homin**-). -ρ is generally preserved and the Nom. sign omitted: ἔαρ, 'spring' (ἐαρ-), but μάρτυ-ς, 'witness' (μαρτυρ-). The stem consonant *r* is likewise preserved in Latin, and the Nom. sign omitted, e. g. *marmor, ver*. Stems in *s* lengthen the preceding vowel, as in Sanskrit, to compensate for the omission of the stem consonant or of the Nom. sign, e. g. δυσμενής- from δυσμενεσ-, Gen. δυσμενέ(σ)-ος. The same remark holds good of the Latin words *môs, flôs*, etc., where the *s* may be regarded either as belonging to the stem and softened to *r* between two vowels in the oblique cases, or as being the Nom. sign before which the stem consonant is dropped.

In Gothic *a* and *i* are omitted before the Nom. sign where it is possible, that is, in all but monosyllabic words and such words as *harja*, 'an army.' The *a* is weakened, however, to *i* in the Gen. *harjis: ji* thus formed are often contracted to *ei* (=i), in other cases diminished to *i* or altogether dropped, e. g. *wulf-s*, 'a wolf;' *gast-s*, 'a guest;' *althei-s*, 'old;' *sûti-s*, 'sweet;' *gamein-s*, 'common.' After *r* the Nom. sign is sometimes omitted, e. g. *vair*, 'man;' *fingr-s*, 'finger.' *va* after a long vowel loses *a* in the Nom., and after a short vowel the *v* is also changed to *u*, e. g. *snaiv-s*, 'snow;' *qviu-s*, 'living.' *n* is dropped, but *nd* is fully preserved before the Nom. sign, e. g. Nom. *ahma*, 'mind,' from ahman; *bairand-s*, 'bearing.' The *n* in Feminines, preceded by *ô* or *ei*, is inorganic, e. g. *viduvôn*, a *vidhavâ*, l. *vidua*; *quivôn*, a *jivâ'*.

The Neuter has no special form for the Nominative case; the Accusative form is used in its stead.

141. The following list contains illustrations of the Nominative case Masculine and Feminine:

FORMATION OF CASES

	Sanskrit.	Zend.	Greek.	Latin.	Gothic.	Ang.-Sax.	English.
m.	ŭwa-s	açpa-s	ἵππο-ς	equus-s	vulf-s	wulf	wolf
f.	ǵivâ	hizvâ	χώρᾱ	equa	giba	gifu	gift
m.	páti-s	paiti-s	πόσι-ς	hosti-s	gast-s	gæst	guest
f.	prĭti-s	áfriti-s	ὄϊ-ς	ovi-s	avi	cowu	ewe
m.	sûnu-s	paçu-s	υἱεύ-ς	pecu-s	sunu-s	sunu	son
f.	hanu-s	tanu-s	γένυ-ς	socru-s	hanitu-s	hand	hand
f.	bhrû	—	ὀφρύ-ς	—	brav	brəw	brow
m.f.	gâu-s	gâu-s	βοῦ-ς	bô-s	—	cû	cow
f.	vâk	vâk-sh	ἔπ-ς	voc-s	—	—	—
m.	bhâran	barain-z	φέρων	feren-s	fijand-s	feónd	fiend
m.	ǵinâ	azmâ	δαίμων	sermo	ahma	—	—
m.	bhrâ'tâ	brâtâ	φράτηρ	frâter	brôthar	brother	brother
f.	duhitá'	dughdhâ	θυγάτηρ	mâtor	dauhtar	dóhtor	daughter
m.	dâtá'	dâtâ	δοτήρ	dator	—	—	—

THE ACCUSATIVE SINGULAR.

142. The sign of the *Accusative Singular* is *m* in Sanskrit, Zend, Latin, and perhaps in the English word *him*. In Greek the sign is *ν*. The Gothic and Anglo-Saxon preserve this ending only in the Masculine of pronouns of the third person, the former adding *a* and the latter *e*, and both having *n* instead of the original *m*. Thus go. *tha-na*, a.s. *tho-ne*, = s. *ta-m*, gr. τό-ν, l. *is-tu-m*. A vowel is inserted between the termination and consonant stems. Hence we have in s. *bhrâ'tar-am*, z. *brâtar-ĕm*, gr. φράτορ-α (for older *ν*), l. *fratr-em*. Monosyllables in *î*, *û*, *âu* develope a half-vowel in Sanskrit, and then insert the vowel between the stem and the Accusative ending, e. g. *bhíy-am*, *súv-am*, *nâ'v-am*, from *bhî*, 'fear;' *sû*, 'sow;' *nâu*, 'ship.' Similarly Greek Accusatives in *ε-α* have probably passed through an intermediate stage in *-εϝα*, from which the digamma was afterwards dropped, e. g. βασιλέ-α from βασιλεϝ-α. So also the Latin forms *su-em*, *gru-em* may have been formed from the stems suv-, gruv-, like *bov-em*. Otherwise *em* may have been irregularly added instead of *m* to make the words dissyllabic. Accusatives like *ignem* should be divided into *igne-m*, since the stem ends in *i* or *e*.

Stems in *-a* in Sanskrit, and the corresponding forms in other languages, take *m* as the Accusative sign in the *Neuter*, and the form thus obtained is employed for the Nominative, e. g. Nom. and Acc. Neut. s. *śáyana-m*, 'a bed,' z. *zayanĕ-m*, gr. δῶρο-ν, l. *dônu-m*. Other Neuter stems have no sign for either Nominative or Accusative, but employ the unaltered stem in their place. Final *ν* in Greek and *s* in Latin belong to the stem, e. g. γένος, genus. In the cases where this letter would come to stand between two vowels, it is dropped in Greek and softened to r in Latin, e. g. Gen. γένε-ος, gener-is. Some Greek adjectives and participles have final s in the neuter, probably only as a euphonic substitute for τ, which cannot stand at the end of a word, e. g. τετυφός, τέρας, for τετυφοτ-, τερατ-; like πρός for προτί when the ι was dropped. Or it may have been added, by a false analogy, to the Nom., and then to the Acc., just as in Latin we have felix Nom. and Acc. Neut. for felic. In Gothic the Neuter omits the Accusative sign even in the a stems, e. g. daur, 'door,' for a. dwā'ram. In Anglo-Saxon duru is placed by Rask in the third class of his third declension, which consists of Feminine substantives. It has there the same form for Nom. and Acc., and u may be regarded as a weakened form of a, as in gifu for go. giba. But it has also some of the forms of the Neuter substantives of the first declension, which have no case sign in the Accusative. Stems in ja drop a, changing the j to i in Gothic, and this again to e in Anglo-Saxon, e. g. go. reiki, a. s. rice, s. rā'jya-m. The Gothic has no Neuter stems in i, and only one in u, i. e. faihu, for which the Anglo-Saxon has feoh (e. fee), dropping the stem-vowel.

Pronominal Neuter Stems form the Accusative with t in Sanskrit, ḍ in Zend, τ in Greek, d (for t) in Latin, t (with the addition of a) in Gothic, t in Anglo-Saxon, which also remains in English: e. g. s. (i-t wanting) ta-t, ka-t; z. (i-ḍ wanting) ta-ḍ, ka-ḍ; gr. (ι-τ wanting) το-τ, ὅ-τ, as in ὅτ-τι; l. i-d, is-tu-d, quo-d; go. i-ta, tha-ta, hwa-ta; a. s. hi-t, thæ-t, hwæ-t; e. i-t, tha-t, wha-t. The Greek language generally drops τ when final. Hence we have τό, ὅ, for the above forms. For the sake of uniformity the Vedic kat is used above instead of the s. chit.

143. The following list illustrates the different forms of the Accusative case:

	Sanskrit	Zend	Greek	Latin	Gothic	Anglo-Sax.	English
m.	ṡiva-m	aṡpe-m	ἵππο-ν	equu-m	vulf	wulf	wolf
n.	dâ'na-m	dâta-em	δῶρο-ν	dônu-m	daur	duru	door
f.	tivê-m	hizva-ñm	χώρα-ν	equa-m	giba	gifu	gift
m.	páti-m	paiti-m	πόσι-ν	hoste-m	gast	gæst	guest
a.	vâ'ri	vairi	ἴδρι	mare	—	—	—
f.	prîti-m	áfriti-m	πόπρι-ν	turri-m	anst	—	—
m.	sûnú-m	paṡu-m	υἱύ-ν	pecu-m	sunu	sunu	son
n.	mádhu	madhu	μέθυ	pecū	faihu	feoh	(fee)
f.	hânu-m	tanû-m	γένυ-ν	socru-m	handu	hand	hand
m.f.	gâ-m	ga-ṃm	βοῦ-ν	bov-em	—	cū	cow
m.	bhárant-am	barent-em	φέροντ-α	ferent-em	fijand	feond	fiend
n.	nâ'ma	nãma	νάμαν	nômen	namô	(nama)	name
m.	bhrâ'tar-am	brâtar-em	φράτερ-α	frâtr-em	brôthar	brodher	brother
f.	duhitár-am	dughdhar-em	θυγατέρ-α	mâtr-em	dauhtar	dohtor	daughter
m.	dâtâ'r-am	dâtâr-em	δοτῆρ-α	datôr-em	—	—	—
n.	vâchas	vachô	ἴπος	genus	—	—	—

THE INSTRUMENTAL SINGULAR.

144. The *Instrumental* case remains in but few languages. The sign of this case is *â* in the Vedas, forming, with *a* stems, *â* for *a + â*, or connected with them by *y*, and thus forming *-ayâ*, e. g. *mahitwâ'*, from *mahitwá*, 'greatness;' *urúyâ*, from *urú*, 'great.' In later Sanskrit this case-ending is connected with *a* stems by *n*. It is then shortened, and the preceding *a* is changed to *é*, e. g. *áçwêna* from *áçwa*. But with other vowel-stems the *â* is preserved long, and the stem-vowel not changed, e. g. *agni-nâ*, *sûnú-nâ*. The pronouns of the first and second person have the same form as in the Vedas, e. g. *ma-yâ*, *twa-yâ*, from *ma*, *twa*. *Páti* and *sákhi* change *i* to *y* and do not insert *n*, e. g. *páty-â*, *sákhy-â*. Feminines do not insert *n*, but change *â* of the stem to *ay*, e. g. *áçway-â*, from *áçwâ*, 'mare.' The Greek and Latin languages have not this case. Some remains of it appear in the Germanic languages. In Gothic, *thé*, 'by that;' *hvé*, 'by what;' *své*, 'by such.' In Anglo-Saxon, *thâ*, *hû* (for *hwâ*, probably to distinguish it from the Nom. Sing. Masc. of the Interrogative pronoun), *swâ*, and in English *thus* (irregular for *thô*), *how* (derived from the a. s. *hû*, the same reason probably holding against the regular form *whô*), and *sô*. The meaning and form of these words justify their being referred to the Instrumental case. The way in which both forms *sva* and *své* in Gothic occur, induces Grimm (*Geschichte etc.*, 929) to think they are both ultimately derivable from the same source, and have distributed between them the words and meanings which, according to the analogy of *hvé*, would have belonged to *své* alone, if *sva* had not come into use. The above forms are the only instances of an Instrumental case traceable in Gothic. But Anglo-Saxon, as well as Old German, contains many examples both in substantives and adjectives, e. g. *fŷrené sweordé*, 'with a fiery sword' (Cædmon, 18, 17; 95, 8).

The following is a list of Sanskrit and Zend words in the Instrumental case:

	m.	n.	f.	m.	f.
Sans.	áźwe-n-â	mahitwâ´	áźway-â´	páty-â	prí'ty-â
Zend.	aźpa	dâta	hizvay-a	patay-a	áfriti

	m.	f.	m.f.	f.	m.
S.	sunú-n-â	kánw-â	gáv-â	vâ´ch-â	bhárat-â
Z.	poźv-â	tanv-a	gav-a	vâch-a	barent-a

	m.	n.	m.	f.	n.
S.	áźman-â	nâ´mn-â	bhrâ´tr-â	duhitr-â´	váchas-â
Z.	aźman-a	nâman-a	bráthr-a	dugbdhèr-a	vachaṇh-a

THE DATIVE SINGULAR.

145. The original *Dative* case has been more extensively preserved than the Instrumental. Its sign in Sanskrit is *ê*, and with Feminine stems in *â*, and polysyllables in *i*, *û*, it becomes *âi*, preceded by *ây* instead of *â*, e. g. *áźwây-âi* from *áźwâ*. Masculine stems in *i*, *u*, are gunaed, and Feminines, if the case-ending is *ê*. Neuter vowel stems insert *n*. The same sign is preserved in Zend, but *âi* is preceded by *ay* instead of *ây*. Masculine *a* stems make *âya* ($=a+ay+a=a+ê+a$) in Sanskrit, and *âi* ($=a+ai=a+ê$) in Zend. The use of guna is also only partial in the *i* and *u* stems. What is called the Dative in Greek and Latin corresponds in origin to the Sanskrit Locative, and will be considered in connection with that case.

In Latin the ending is *i*. If in Latin as in Greek this case was originally the Locative case, the long quantity of the final vowel must be referred to a general tendency in the Latin language which increases the quantity of this vowel at the end of a word without organic cause. To the general rule that final *i* is long there are but very few, and those isolated, exceptions. Although, therefore, the quantity of this vowel induces Bopp to regard this case in Latin as originally a Dative, yet the great probability that Greek and Latin both adopted the same course, and the existence of a sufficient reason in the genius of the Latin language to account for the subsequent change of quantity in the vowel, justify our regarding the Latin Dative as originally a Locative case.

In Gothic this Dative ending is entirely lost, unless the *i* in *gibai* (for giba-i) be regarded as a remains of it in the Feminine *á* stems. The gunaed forms of the stems in *i, í, u, ú,* are retained; but in the first of these cases the final *i* is dropped, e. g. *gasta* (for *gastai*), *anstai, sunau, kinnau,* from gasti-, ansti-, sunu-, kinnu-.

146. The *Pronouns* are in so far peculiar that in several cases, of which the Dative is the first that comes under our notice, they insert the syllable *sma* between the stem and the case-ending. This syllable is capable of many modifications by omission of one or other of the letters, and by euphonic changes. It appears consequently in many fragmentary forms in different languages; e. g. the Dat. Sing. of *ka* is *kásmái*, 'to whom?' ($= ka + sma + \acute{e}$). The syllable appears in Zend as *hma*, in Pracrit as *mha*. This inversion of letters resembles that in the English word *who* for the Anglo-Saxon *hwa*, and it renders less startling the connection between the Sanskrit *sma* and the Gothic *nsa*: the *s*, being a Dental, changes the preceding Labial *m* to the corresponding Dental *n*. It thus becomes easy to identify the English *us* and the Sanskrit *asmân*. For, as s. *asmân* is probably for *asmans*, the vowel being lengthened to compensate for the *s*, it is clearly the same as the go. *unsis* (for u-nsa-s), where *s* is preserved and *n* dropped. But this *unsis* has already become *us* in Anglo-Saxon as well as English, merely by that system of abbreviation which Horne Tooke so convincingly showed to be an inherent characteristic in the history of language. This particle, however, assumes no less than six different forms in Gothic, viz. *nsa, zva, gka, gqva, mma,* and *s*. The first, *nsa*, occurs in the Accus., Dat., and Gen. Plur. of the first personal pronoun, and the second, *zva*, in the same parts of the second personal pronoun, i. e. *u-ns-*, 'us,' *u-nsi-s*, 'to us,' *u-nsa-ra*, 'of us;' *i-zvi-s*, 'you,' *i-zvi-s*, 'to you,' *i-zva-ra*, 'of you.' In the corresponding cases of the Dual the first person has *gka*, and the second *gqva*, i. e. *u-gki-s*, 'us two,' *u-gki-s*, 'to us two,' (*u-gka-ra*); *i-gqvi-s*, 'you two,' *i-gqvi-s*, 'to you two' *i-gqvi-ra*, 'of you two.' The *g* here stands for *n* (*ng* before Gutturals). The fifth form, *mma*, occurs in such Datives as *i-mma*, 'to it,' *hi-mma*, 'to him,' *hva-mma*, 'to whom?' where *mm* is by assimilation for *sm*. The sixth form, *s*, appears in the Datives, *mi-s*, 'to me,' *thu-s*, 'to thee,' *si-s*, 'to one's self.' Bopp also ascribes the same origin to the *s* in the Nom. Plur. *vei-s*, 'we,' and *ju-s*, 'you.'

In the Feminine forms of the third personal pronouns in Sanskrit, the Dative, Genitive, and Locative Sing. end in *-sy-âi, -sy-âs, -sy-âm*, of which the first part *sy* may be for *smy*, and this for *smi*, an ordinary Feminine equivalent in Sanskrit for *sma*. A confirmation of this view is obtained from the Zend, which preserves forms like *yahmyu* for s. *ya-sy-âm*. For Zend *hmy* presupposes a Sanskrit *smî*. In Gothic, *ô* is a Feminine termination, which would give the form *smô* to this particle. If then *m* be dropped as in Sanskrit, the remainder *sô* serves to explain such words as Gen. Sing. thi-zô-s, the *s* being regularly softened to *z* between two vowels, as it is in Latin to *r*.

In Anglo-Saxon a further change has taken place. The Gothic *nsa* has perhaps entirely disappeared in the Acc. and Dat. *u-s*, Gen. *u-re*. The *ow* in the Acc. and Dat. *eow*, Gen. *eower*, may be an equivalent for the *v* (or *w*) in the Gothic *zvâ*. In the Dual of the first person (Acc. and Dat. *u-nc*, 'us two,' Gen. *u-nce-r*, 'of us two') and the Dual of the second person (Acc. and Dat. *i-nc*, 'you two,' *i-nce-r*, 'of you two'), the remains of this particle are almost as complete as in Gothic. Why has the Dual preserved fuller forms than the Plural? Probably because the Dual had, for a long time, been of rare use in common language, and the antique forms were therefore preserved, whilst the everyday use of the Plural caused it to be still further abbreviated. This conjecture is confirmed by the existence of *u-se-r* as an older poetical form for *u-re*. The fifth Gothic form, *mma*, is represented by *m* in Dat. *him*, *thâm*, *whâm*. The *s* of *mis*, *thus*, has disappeared in *me*, *the*. In the Feminine *hire*, *thære*, as compared with the Gothic *thi-zô-s*, the *s* appears weakened still further to *r*, and the vowel from *ô* to *e*. In English, as the Dual is lost, the third and fourth Gothic forms of course disappear. The rest is nearly in the same state as in Anglo-Saxon. First person plural, *us*, *our*; second person plural, *you*, *your*. The Anglo-Saxon *e* before vowels was pronounced *y*, and the *ow* probably *ó*, as in the vulgar pronunciation of *yô*, *yô-er*, for *you*, *your*, at the present day. *Him*, which was both singular and plural in Anglo-Saxon, is now restricted to the Singular, and the Plural 'them' borrowed from 'that,' which has no variation of cases. *Whom* answers to *hwâm*. The Feminine *r* is preserved in *her* for Anglo-Saxon *hire*.

In Greek ἡμεῖς or ἄμμες for *α-σμε-s*, and ὑμεῖς or ὕμμες for *υ-σμε-s*, exhibit the same particle, almost as complete as in Sanskrit; whilst in the Latin forms *no-s*, *vo-s*, it is much abbreviated.

147. The following instances of the Dative case in Pronouns illustrate the use of the particle *sma*:

	Sanskrit.	Greek.	Gothic.	
Nom. Plu.	asmê	{ ἡμεῖς / ἄμμες }	veis	'we'
Acc. Plu.	asmân	ἡμᾶς	unsis	'us'
Instr. Plu.	asmâbhis	——	——	'by us'
Gen. Plu.	asmâkam	ἡμῶν	unsara	'of us'
Nom. Sing.	kásmâi	——	hvamma	(to) whom?
Abl. Sing.	yásmât	——	——	'from whom'
Loc. Sing.	tásmin	——	——	'in that'

The following list illustrates the Dative case:

	Sanskrit.	Zend.	Gothic.	English.
m.	áśw-áya	ażp-ái	vulfa	wolf
f.	áżwáy-ái	hizvay-ái	gibai	'gift'
m.	pátay-ê	paithy-ai	gasta	guest
f.	pri'tay-ê	áfritay-ai	anstai	——
m.	súnáv-ê	paźv-ê	sunau	son
f.	hánav-ê	tanu-y-ê	kinnau	chin
m.f.	gáv-ê	gav-ê	——	cow
f.	vách-ê'	vách-ê	——	——
m.	bhárat-ê	barent-ê	fijand	fiend
m.	áżman-ê	ażmain-ê	ahmin	——
n.	ná'mn-ê	námain-ê	namin	name
m.	bhrá'tr-ê	brátlir-ê	bróthr	brother
f.	duhitr-é'	dughdher-ê	dauhtar	daughter
m.	dátr-ê	dátlir-ê	——	——
n.	váchas-ê	vachanh-ê	——	——

THE ABLATIVE SINGULAR.

148. Except in Sanskrit, Zend, and Latin, the *Ablative* has but few representatives. Its sign in the above languages is *t*, *d*, *d*, respectively.

In Sanskrit it is preserved only in the *a* stems. The vowel is lengthened to *á*, e. g. *vŗká-t*, 'from a wolf.'

In Zend *a* becomes lengthened, as in Sanskrit, before the ending, e. g. *vehrká-d*; *i* is gunaed, e. g. *áfrítôi-d*, 'benedictione;' *u* assumes the forms *au*, *eu*, *v*, *av*, e. g. *anhau-d*, 'mundo,' 'from the world;' *mainyeu-d*, 'animo,' 'from the mind;' *tanau-d*, *tanv-ad*, or *tanav-a-d*, 'corpore,' 'from the body.' Consonant stems insert a connecting vowel, e. g. *ap-a-d*, 'aquâ,' 'from water;' *áthr-a-d*, 'igne,' 'from fire.'

In old Latin inscriptions the vowel stems add *d*, and the consonant stems insert a connecting vowel *e*, e. g. *præda-d, alto-d, mari-d, senatu-d, dictator-e-d*. The vowel of the *a* stems is not lengthened. But the long quantity of the final vowel in the Ablative Sing. of the first and second declensions, is probably a compensation for the loss of the consonant, i. e. *animâ* for anima-d, and *animô* for animo-d. The termination *-met* which occurs in some pronouns probably originated from the particle *sma*, as Ablative Sing. *â-smâ-t* in Sanskrit; though *t*, in Latin, is irregular for *d*. *Med, ted*, though used as Accusatives, are probably original Ablatives, corresponding to Sanskrit *mat, twat*. The conjunction *se-d* is the Ablative of *se*, and is used pronominally in *S. C. de Bacch*.

In Greek there are few instances, and in them the final *t*, as usual, appears changed to *s*, or dropped. These words are mostly adverbs, and Latin Ablatives have a similar adverbial use. The vowel before *s* is always long, and is made long even with consonant stems, e. g. ὁμῶ-ς, 'altogether;' οὕτω-ς, 'thus;' ὡ-ς, 'as;' οὕτω, ὧδε, 'thus,' etc. = s. *samâ-t* etc. So also σωφρόν-ω-ς, 'wisely,' etc. An instance of the preservation of δ preceded by a short vowel, as in Latin, is furnished by ἀφρο-δ-ίτη, if the meaning 'sprung from foam' is correct.

Gothic adverbs in *ð* furnish examples of an Ablative case, for *ð* = s. *â*, and final *t* is uniformly dropped, so that the termination *-ð* corresponds to s. *ât* in such words as *thathr-ð*, 'from there,' *hvathr-ð*, 'from where,' from stems in *-thara*, containing the expression for the comparative degree. The two adverbs in Anglo-Saxon answering to the above in meaning are differently formed, viz. *hwanon, thanon*. From these we have the

English words *whence, thence,* containing an additional adverbial ending. But many Anglo-Saxon adverbs in *-e*, being equivalent in meaning to the Latin Ablative, appear to be of this case, e. g. the first word in *micl-e mâre* = l. *multo magis,* 'much more.'
The following are a few instances of Ablative terminations:

	Sanskrit.	Zend.	Greek.	Latin.	Gothic.	Anglo-Sax.
m.	áçwâ-t	aspâ-ḍ	ὅμω-ς	alto-d	hvathrô	micle
f.	prî′té-s	âfrîtôi-ḍ	——	navale-d	——	——

THE GENITIVE SINGULAR.

149. Unlike the Ablative, the *Genitive* case is very extensively represented in various languages. In Sanskrit it assumes four different forms, viz. *sya, âs, as, s.* The first, *sya,* is employed with *a* stems, and one other word, the personal pronoun *amu,* e. g. *vṛka-sya,* 'of a wolf;' *ta-sya,* 'of this;' *amu-shya,* 'of that.' The second, *âs,* is used with Feminine stems which end in a vowel; but if the vowel *i* or *u* be short, either the second or the fourth form may be used. The same is the case also with monosyllables in *í, ú,* e. g. *áçwây-âs,* 'of a mare;' *bhávanty-âs; vadhw-â′s.* But *prî′té-s* or *prî′ty-âs; hánô-s* or *hánw-âs.* The third form, *as,* is used with consonant stems, e. g. *pad-ás,* 'of a foot;' *vâch-ás,* 'of a voice.' The fourth form is used with masculine vowel stems, but *i* and *u* are gunaed, e. g. *prî′té-s,* from priti, 'favour;' *súnô′-s,* from *súnú,* 'son.' All these forms of the Genitive ending appear to be of the same origin, the variety being occasioned by the stems to which the form is applied.

The first form generally appears in Zend as *hé*, e.g. *vehrka-hé*; *túiryê-hé*, 'of the fourth.' The fuller form *hya* is also found, with the final vowel lengthened; *martiya-hyâ*, 'of man.' In Greek *y* becomes *ι*, and *s* is usually dropped between two vowels. The Epic form *οιο* answers therefore to the Sanskrit *a-sya*, as in λύκοιο, 'of a wolf,' τοῖο, 'of the;' and the subsequent omission of *ι* reduces the whole to *οο*, from which by contraction the Attic Genitive *ου* is formed, as in λύκου, τοῦ. Some dialectic forms have an additional *s*, as *ἐμοῦς* for *ἐμοῦ*, 'of me.' The same appears to be the case in the Genitive of the Latin pronouns *hu-jus*, 'of this,' *cu-jus*, 'of which,' where *jus* is supposed to be for *ju*, and this for *syu*. The Gothic and Anglo-Saxon have no remains of this fuller Genitive, but have reduced the ending of the *a* stems to the same form as the other masculine vowel stems, *s*: e. g. go. *vulfi-s*, *thi-s*; a. s. *wulfe-s*, *thæ-s*; e. '*wolf-'s*,' 'of the.'

The second form is in Zend *-âo*, e.g. *hizvay-âo*, *bavainty-âo*. The only indication of this form in Greek is where the vowel is long in the Genitive, though short in the Nom. and Acc., e. g. σφύρᾱς, 'of a hammer,' compared with σφῦρα, σφῦραν. So also in the old Latin forms *familiâ-s*, 'of a family,' *escâ-s*, 'of food,' *terrâ-s*, 'of the earth,' the vowel is long, though short in the Nominative. In Gothic the vowel is long in *gibô-s* from *giba*, and *gunaed* in *anstai-s* from *ansti*. In Anglo-Saxon *gife* the *s* is dropped, but the vowel lengthened from *gifû*. The same phenomena (i. e. the omission of *s* and the change of the vowel to *e*) appear in Gen. Sing. *thæ-re* compared with Gothic *thi-zô-s*.

The third form, *as*, appears in Greek as *os*, the regular form of the Genitive of the third declension; but it is also extended to the *i* and *u* stems, e. g. ποδ-ός, 'of a foot;' πόσι-ος, 'of a husband;' νέκυ-ος, 'of a corpse.' In Latin the later form is *is*, *ped-is*, 'of a foot;' but there is also an older form. *us*, e. g. *nomin-us*, 'of a name;' *Vener-us*, 'of Venus.' If the *i* stems adopted this form, as in Greek, the vowel was afterwards shortened; but the *u* stems of the fourth declension have the vowel long in the Genitive, which seems to have arisen from employing the third form of the Genitive ending. Hence Gen. *exercitûs*, 'of an army,' but Nom. *exercitus*. Indeed, *exercituus* is found on inscriptions, and *senatu-os* in the *S. C. de Bacch.* The Zend also has *ô* (for *as*) with *u* stems, e. g. *danhv-ô*, 'of a place,' and *danhav-ô*, from *danhu*. Even in Sanskrit *páty-us* and *sákhy-us* occur as Genitives of páti and sákhi.

The fourth form, *s*, is displaced by the third in Greek, and partly in Latin; though it is preserved perhaps in such forms as *hosti-s*, 'of an enemy.' We find it in Gothic *gasti-s* and Anglo-Saxon *gæste-s*, 'guest's.' It is also, as we have seen, extended in these two languages to the *a* stems.

150. The following list contains illustrations of the various forms of the Genitive ending:

THE GENITIVE SINGULAR

	Sanskrit.	Zend.	Greek.	Latin.	Gothic.	Ang.-Sax.	English.
m.	âiwa-sya	aspa-hê	ἱππο-ιο	—	vulfi-s	wulfe-s	wolf's
m.	kê-sya	ka-hê	—	cujus	hvi-s	hwæ-s	who-se
f.	âiwây-âo	hisvay-âo	χώρᾱ-ς	terræ	gibô-s	gife	'gift'
m.	pâtê-s	paiti-s	(πόσι-ος)	hosti-s	gasti-s	geste-s	guest's
f.	prîtê-s	âfritôi-s	(φόσι-ος)	turri-s	anstai-s	—	—
m.	sûnô-s	pazeu-s	(υἰευ-ος)	pecû-s	sunau-s	suna	son's
f.	bênô-s	taneu-s	(γίνυ-ος)	socrû-s	kinnau-s	—	—
m.f.	gô-s	geu-s	βο-ός	bov-is	—	—	—
f.	vâch-âs	vâch-ô	ὀπ-ός	vôc-is	—	—	—
n.	nâman-as	nâman-ô	τλαν-ος	nomin-is	namin-s	naman	name's
n.	vâchas-as	vachanh-ô	ἐπε(σ)ος	gener-is	—	—	—

THE LOCATIVE SINGULAR.

151. The *Locative* case is expressed in Sanskrit and Zend by *i* in the *a* stems and the consonant stems. In the first of these cases *a* and *i* are contracted into *ê* in Sanskrit, and to *é* or *ói* in Zend, e. g. s. *áśwé*, z. *aśpé*; s. *mádhyé*, z. *maidhyói*; s. *nấ'mn-i*, z. *nấmain-i*.

152. In Greek this form appears as a Dative case, and is indicated by the ι added to consonant stems, and by ι *subscriptum* with vowel stems, e. g. χώρᾳ, λόγῳ, ποδ-ί. The Locative meaning is preserved in many expressions which have come to be regarded as adverbial, e. g. Δωδώνι, Μαραθώνι, Σαλαμῖνι, 'at Dodona,' etc.; ἀγρῷ, 'afield,' 'in the field;' οἴκοι, 'at home;' χαμαί, 'on the ground.'

The Latin Dative has *î* with the consonant stems, where the length of the *i* is probably the result of a general tendency in the Latin language, in which this letter is almost always long when final. The *i* is preserved distinct in all the declensions in the older stages of the language, e. g. *familia-i, populo-i, ped-i, fluctu-i, re-i*. In later times the first declension reduced this ending to *e*, making a diphthong with the stem-vowel as in *familia-e* (æ), and the second incorporated it with the stem-vowel, which consequently became long, as in *populó* for populŏ-i. Some writers also have *fluctû* for fluctŭ-i etc. in the fourth declension. The stem is not subject to the same amount of modification as in Sanskrit.

In Latin the Locative form is said to be used for the Genitive case in the second declension, where *î* appears as a contraction of *o + i*. Both Bopp and Rosen adopt this view of the Locative origin of the Latin

Genitive in the second declension. Yet it seems to do some violence to the general spirit of language. The meanings of the two cases lie very far apart, and the form i may be for $o+i$ out of a a-sya. This would make the proximate forms of both Genitive (i) and Dative (δ) to be the same, $o+i$. The reason for the difference in the ultimate forms may be that in the Genitive the case-ending represented by i was 'heavier' than the stem-vowel o; and therefore the sound of the former predominated when the whole was reduced to one syllable, and i was the result. On the other hand, in the Dative, the case-ending i being 'lighter' than the stem-vowel o, the sound of the latter predominated, and the i had no other effect on it than that of lengthening it to δ.

In this view the Greek and Latin forms harmonise together. In the Genitive the consonant stems have -os in Greek and -is in Latin. The Masculine and Neuter a stems have ov for oo from $o(\sigma\iota)o$ in Greek, and i for oi from $o(s)i(o)$ in Latin. The Feminine $\hat{a}$ stems have -s preceded by $\bar{a}$ in Greek, and -s preceded by $\hat{u}$ in Latin (paterfamiliâs). In the Dative the consonant stems have ι in Greek, and i (for i) in Latin; the Masculine and Neuter a stems have ω from $o+\iota$ in Greek, and δ from $o+i$ in Latin; the Feminine a stems have *iota subscriptum* in Greek, and e (for i) in Latin.

153. One of the most unsatisfactory rules of Latin syntax is that which Zumpt (§ 398) expresses as follows: — 'In answer to the question *where?* the names of towns in the Singular, if of the first or second declension, are in the *Genitive*; if of the third, in the *Ablative* case.' The rule would be much simpler and more satisfactory if it could be thus expressed: — 'In answer to the question *where?* the names of towns in the Singular are in the *Dative* case.' At first sight there are two objections to this — one in regard to the meaning, and the other in regard to the form, of the words in question. The usual *meaning* of the Dative is not adapted to answer the question *where?* If, however, the Latin Dative, like the Greek Dative, is in reality the Locative case substituted in place of the Dative, the first objection disappears, because it is very likely that with the old form some remains of the original meaning should be preserved. The objection that the words in question are not in the *form* of the Dative does not apply at all to the first declension, for *Romæ* is as much a Dative as a Genitive in form. In the third declension the difference between *e* and *i* can hardly be looked upon as determining the case in the Singular, for these letters not unfrequently change; e. g. *hosti-s* and *hoste-m* have the stem-vowel as *i* in the one case, and as *e* in the other. Besides this, the words in question sometimes are found with the usual Dative form *i*, e. g. *Tibur-i, Carthagin-i*, meaning 'at Tibur,' 'at Carthage.' There remains the second declension. But in the Singular the Datives *Abydo, Corintho*, etc., not unfrequently occur. It is only, therefore, in some instances of the second declension that any real difficulty occurs as to the form, and these are doubtless the result of a false analogy which led Roman authors to write words belonging to a case (Locative) of which they had no consciousness like a case (Genitive) with which they were well acquainted.

All these names of towns, therefore, of whatever declension they appear, with a Locative meaning may be regarded as Latin Datives, that is, original Locative cases. A few other words are similar in meaning and admit of the same explanation, i. e. *domi*, 'at home;' *ruri* or *rure*, 'in the country;' *humi* or *humo*, 'on the ground,' etc. Corresponding words in the Greek language which are clearly Datives (originally Locatives) confirm this view of the Latin words: οἴκοι, 'at home,' χαμαί, 'on the ground,' compared with *domi, humi*. Comp. Sect. **152.**

It is easy to see how this confusion arose. When the Locative case was generally employed as a Dative, the meaning appeared inconsistent with the idea that the words in question belonged to that case. They were, however, manifestly case forms, and were assigned to such other cases as they resembled. For instance, in the passage, *Romæ Consules, Carthagine Sufêtes, sive judices, quotannis creabantur* ('At Rome Consuls, at Carthage Sufêtes, or judges, used to be appointed yearly'), as *Romæ* and *Carthagine* were supposed by their meaning not to be Datives, they were referred to the other cases which they resembled, i. e. Romæ to the Genitive, and Carthagine to the Ablative. The difficulty as to the meaning, however, was only altered, not removed, by this method; whilst referring these words to the Locative case fully justifies the sense in which they are employed.

154. There are three other forms of the Locative case in Sanskrit. The *first, âu*, is used with Masculine *i* and *u* stems, and sometimes with Feminines; but the stem-vowels *i* and *u* are dropped (except in *páty-âu, sákhy-âu*), e. g. *prí't-âu, sûn-âú*. This Bopp regards as really a Genitive ending, viz. *âu* for *âs*. The Zend has *ô*, which is also a Genitive form.

The *second* additional Locative form, *in*, is used only in the pronouns of the third person, e. g. *tásm-in,* 'in that;' *kasm-in,* 'in whom?' The third, *âm*, is used with Feminine stems ending in a long vowel, and sometimes with those ending in *i* or *u*, e. g. *bhiy-âm,* 'in fear.' Perhaps this form of the Locative is preserved in such Latin expressions as *ante diem quartum Nonas Januarias*, '*on* the fourth day before the Nones of January;' where the preposition *ante* governs *Nonas*, and *diem* means '*on* the day.' The employment of the Locative in regard to time is not without example in other languages, e. g. a. *divasé*, '*in* the day,' *niśi*, '*in* the night;' gr. τῇ αὐτῇ ἡμέρᾳ, '*on* the same day,' νυκτί, '*at* night.' The similar use of the Latin forms *die, nocte, interdiu, noctu*, 'by day,' 'by night,' makes it probable that they were originally Dative, that is, really Locative cases. The Dative and Ablative forms fluctuate, not only in the cases quoted above, but also in the employment of both *vespere* and *vesperi* for '*in* the evening;' *luce* and *luci* for '*during* the day,' etc. The Ablative gradually absorbed these and similar meanings to itself, and the Ablative *form* was substituted where no preposition occurred, whilst the use of a preposition in such expressions as *ante diem quartum Nonas*, etc., caused forms in *m* which look like an Accusative to be preserved.

155. The following is a list of instances of the Locative case:

	Sanskrit.	Zend.	Greek.	Latin.
m.	áśwê	aźpê	ἵππῳ	equo
f.	áśwây-âm	hizvay-a	χώρᾳ	equae
m.	páty-âu	——	πόσει	hosti (i + i)
f.	prít-âu	——	πέρυσι	——
n.	vári-ṇ-i	——	ἴδμει	fideli (i + i)
m.	sûn-âá	——	υἱεῖ-ι	pecû (u + i)
f.	hán-âu	——	γένυ-ι	socrû (u + i)
n.	mádhu-n-i	——	μέθυ-ι	pecû (u + i)
m.f.	gáv-i	——	βοϝ-ί	bov-i
f.	vách-í	——	ὀπ-ί	voc-i
m.	átman-i	aímain-i	δαίμον-ι	sermon-i

THE VOCATIVE SINGULAR.

	Sanskrit.	Zend.	Greek.	Latin.
n.	nā́mn-i	nâmain-i	ráλαν-ι	nomin-i
m.	bhrā́tar-i	brâthr-i	φράτορ-ι	frātr-i
f.	duhitár-i	dughdher-i	θυγατρ-ί	matr-i
n.	váchas-i	vachah-i	ἔπι(τ)-ί	gener-i

THE VOCATIVE SINGULAR.

156. The *Vocative* has no distinctive sign. A few instances occur of the Nominative form being employed for the Vocative, i. e. in Latin neuters and in such words as θεός, deus, where the familiarity implied in the short Vocative form is not allowable. In some instances the stem-vowel is lightened: e. g. gr. ε and l. e of the second declension for o or u. In Sanskrit the accent is drawn back to the first syllable, and in some Greek words it is placed as far back as possible.

157. The modifications of the Vocative will be easily understood from the following list:

	Sanskrit.	Zend.	Greek.	Latin.	Gothic.
m.	áçwa	açpa	ἵππε	eque	vulf
n.	dā́na	dâta	δῶρο-ν	dónu-m	daur
f.	áçwē	bizva	χώρά	equa	giba
m.	pátē	paiti	πόσι	hosti-s	gast
f.	prī́tē	âfriti	πόρτι	turri-s	anstai
n.	vā́ri	vairi	ἴδρι	mare	—
m.	sū́nō	paçu	νίεν	pecu-s	sunau
f.	hánō	tanu	γίνυ	socru-s	kinnau
n.	mádhu	madhu	μίθυ	pecû	—
m.f.	gâu-s	gâu-s	βοῦ	bô-s	—
f.	vâk	vâksh-a?	ὀπ-ς	voc-s	—
m.	átman	açman	δαῖμον	sermo	ahma?
n.	nā́man	nâman	ráλαν	nômen	namô?
m.	bhrā́tar	brâtare	φράτορ	fràter	bróthar
f.	dúhitar	dughdhare	θύγατιρ	mâter	dauhtar
n.	ráchas	vachō	ἔπος	genus	—

THE NOMINATIVE PLURAL.

158. The *Nominative Plural* in Sanskrit has the sign *as*, e. g. *átman-as, vṛk-ás, pátay-as*. The *a* and *á* stems, of course, make the Nom. Plur. end in *-ás*, and the *i* and *u* stems are gunaed.

In Zend the original ending is represented by *-aś* when the conjunction *cha* is added. In other cases *s* appears as *o*, and *as* as *ó*, e. g. *aśman-aśchu, aśman-ó*, 'stones;' *vehrk-áo*, 'wolves.' The gunaing of *i* and *u* stems is arbitrary. One word preserves the original *s* when final, viz. *geu-s*.

In Greek the ending is *-es*. The *i* and *u* stems are not gunaed. The *a* and *á* stems exhibit *ι*, making with the stem-vowels οι and αι, e. g. πατέρ-ες, 'fathers;' πόσι-ες, 'husbands;' ἵπποι, 'horses;' χῶραι, 'lands.'

In Latin consonant stems have *-ēs*, with the vowel long. The *i* and *u* stems are not gunaed, but form with the ending *-ēs* and *-ús*, for *i-es, u-es*. The *a* and *á* stems form *í* and *œ* (for ai), which resemble the Greek οι and αι, e. g. *patr-és*, 'fathers;' *host-ēs*, 'enemies;' *exercit-ús*, 'armies;' *animí* 'minds;' *familiæ*, 'families.'

In Gothic the ending is reduced to *s* in the consonant stems. The *i* and *u* stems form, with the endings, *is (eis)* and *jus (yus)*, where the stems may be regarded as gunaed, since the guna-vowel in Gothic is *i*; the ending would then be *s* only, as in the consonant stems. Or *í* and *ju* may be regarded as lengthened forms of the stem-vowel, like the Latin *é* and *ú*, caused by the vowel of the ending. The *a* and *á* stems have *-os*, which answers to the Sanskrit *-ás*, e. g. *ahman-s, gastei-s, sunju-s, vulfôs, gibos*.

In Anglo-Saxon -*as* is preserved in Rask's second class of the second declension, which includes all the Masculine nouns not ending in *a* or *u*. Elsewhere the Nominative Plur. ends in -*a*, including the stem-vowel, e. g. *dag-as*, 'days;' *suna*, 'sons.' In English *s* still appears as the sign of the Nominative Plural.

The ending of the Nom. Plur. *Neuter* presents some difficulty. It appears generally as -*a*, e. g. L. *gener-a*, etc. With *a* stems it would form -*â*, an equivalent for which appears in some pronouns, e. g. l. *quæ*, 'which,' *hæ-c*, 'these;' go. *hvô, thô;* a. s. *huâ, thâ*. In the Latin forms *quæ, hæ-c*, the original ending -*a* is reduced to *e*. In nouns, however, the long quantity thus obtained is reduced to *ă*. In Sanskrit this *a* appears already weakened to *i*, which is connected with vowel stems by *n*. If the stem-vowel be short, it is lengthened, e. g. *dâ'nâ-n-i, vâ'rî-n-i, mádhû-n-i*, from dâ'na, vâ'ri, mádhu.

This *a* Bopp regards as an abbreviation of the form -*as* which appears in the Masculine and Feminine. But the reason which is given for *s* never having been used in the Singular will apply also to the Plural Neuter. This *a* may therefore be regarded as the original ending of Neuter nouns in the Nominative Plural.

A peculiarity appears in the Nom. Plur. of the first and second declensions in Greek and Latin—viz. instead of -*as* we find *ι* and *i* (e) added to *a* and *â* stems. The same form appears in Sanskrit, Zend, and Gothic, restricted, however, to pronominal stems in -*a*, e. g. s. *té* (for ta-i), z. *té*, go. *thai*, e. *they*. Bopp regards this *i* as an inorganic enlargement of the stem, and thinks the case-ending to be entirely lost. But if we suppose *s* of the original -*as* to be dropped, which is frequently the case with final *s*, and *a* then weakened to *i*, as in the Sanskrit Neuter nouns, we reach the same result without supposing any step so arbitrary as enlarging the stem without apparent reason.

159. The following list contains illustrations of the Nominative Plural:

	Sanskrit.	Zend.	Greek.	Latin.	Gothic.	Ang-Sax.	English.
m.	áśvás	—	ἵπποι	equi	vulfôs	wulfas	wolves
f.	śivás	hizvåo	χῶραι	equæ	gibôs	gifa	gifts
n.	dânâ-n-i	dâta	δῶρα	dôna	daura	dura	doors
m.	pátay-as	patay-ô	πόσι-ες	hostes	gasteis	gæstas	guests
f.	prítay-as	áfritay-ô	πόλι-ες	turrës	anteis	—	—
n.	vấri-n-i	var-a?	ἴδρι-α	mari-a	thrij-a	—	—
m.	sûnáv-as	pazav-ô	υἱεύ-ες	pecûs	sunjus	suna	sons
f.	hánav-as	tanav-ô	γλυκέ-ες	socrûs	handjus	handa	hands
n.	mádhû-n-i	madhv-a	μέθυ-α	pecu-a	—	—	—
m.f.	gấv-as	geu-s	βοῦ-ες	—	—	cû	cows
m.	bhárant-as	barent-ô	φέροντ-ες	ferent-ës	fijand-s	fynd	fiends
m.	áximán-as	aiman-ô	δαίμον-ες	sermôn-ës	ahman-s	—	—
n.	nấmân-i	nâman-a	τάλαν-α	nômin-a	namn-a	naman	names
m.	bhrấtar-as	bratar-ô	ῥήτορ-ες	frâtr-ës	brôthrjus	brôthra	brothers
f.	duhitár-as	dugbdhar-ô	θυγατέρ-ες	matr-ës	dauhtrjus	dôhtru	daughters
n.	vấchâns-i	vachão	ἔπη(σ)α	gener-a	—	—	—

THE ACCUSATIVE PLURAL.

160. The ending of the *Accusative Plural* appears to have been *ns*, of which letters, however, only one is usually preserved. In Sanskrit, vowel stems have *n* in the Masculine and *s* in the Feminine, e. g. *áśwân*, 'horses;' *áśwâs*, 'mares.' If the stem-vowel be short, it is lengthened, to compensate for the lost consonant. The consonant stems have *as*, in which *a* is either a connecting vowel or a substitute for *n*, e. g. *bhárat-as*, 'bearing.'

In Zend *-ns* of the consonant stems is also extended to those in *i* and *u*, so that *n* occurs only with *a* stems without lengthening the vowel, e. g. *aźpa-ñ*, 'horses.' When *s* and *as* are final, they are replaced, as usual, by *o* and *ô*, except in *gâu-s*, 'cows,' and *-eus* after *-ar* stems, which is equivalent to Greek *-ovs*.

In Greek, again, *n* does not appear at all, but *s* universally. *as* is applied to the *i* and *u* stems as well as to those in consonants. The terminations are *-ás* in the first declension, with *á* stems; *-ovs* in the second declension, with *a* stems; and *-as* in the third declension, with consonant and *i* and *u* stems. *-ovs* corresponds to the same letters in *-ovσι* of the third person plural of verbs, where, e. g., τύπτουσι, 'they strike,' is for τυπτονσι, and this for τυπτοντι.

In Latin also *s* is universally preserved, and *n* not at all. The terminations are *-âs*, *-ês*, in the first and fifth declensions, with *â* stems; *-ôs* in the second, with *a* stems; *-ês* in the third, with consonant and *i* stems; and *ûs* in the fourth, with *u* stems. In the third declension *ês* probably includes the stem-vowel *i*, and the consonant stems have irregularly adopted the long vowel instead of the short, as in the Nom. Plur., thus presenting -*és* for Sanskrit -*as*.

In Gothic, which in this case presents an older form than even the Sanskrit, both consonants are preserved in the *a*, *i*, and *u* stems, but *s* only in the *â* and consonant stems. In the last case, however, *s* is not preceded by *a* as in the other languages, e. g. *fijand-s*, 'foes;' *gasti-ns*, 'guests.'

In Anglo-Saxon the Accusative has the same forms as the Nominative, and probably presents no evidence of the original form of the Accusative.

161. The following is a list of Accusatives:

THE ACCUSATIVE PLURAL

	Sanskrit.	Zend.	Greek.	Latin.	Gothic.	English.
m.	áçvā-n	açpa-ō	ἵππω-ς	equō-s	vulfa-ns	wolves
f.	áçvā-s	hizvā-ō	χώρā-ς	equā-s	gibō-s	gifts
m.	páti-n	paithy-ō	πόλι-ας	host-ēs	gasti-ns	guests
f.	prĭti-s	áfrithy-ō	τόρτι-ας	turr-ēs	anstí-ns	—
m.	sūnū'-n	paçv-ō	νέκυ-ας	pecū-s	sunu-ns	sons
f.	hánū-s	tanv-ō	γένυ-ας	socrū-s	handu-ns	hands
m.f.	gā-s	gāu-s	βό-ας	bov-ēs	—	cows
f.	vā'ch-as	vach-ō	ὄπ-ας	voc-ēs	—	voices
m.	bháranṭ-as	barent-ō	φέροντ-ας	ferent-ēs	fijand-s	fiends
m.	áçman-as	açman-ō	δαίμον-ας	sermon-ēs	ahman-s	—
m.	bhrā́tṛ̥-n	brāthr-eus	φράτορ-ας	frātr-ēs	brothar-s	brothers
f.	duhitṛ́-s	dughdher-eus	θυγατέρ-ας	matr-ēs	dauhtar-s	daughters

THE INSTRUMENTAL PLURAL.

162. The *Instrumental Plural* in Sanskrit ends in *-bhis*, e. g. *vâ'ribhis*, from vâri, 'water.' But with *a* stems the initial consonant is dropped, and the case-ending reduced to *-is*, e. g. *żivais* for żivâ-is, from żiva, 'fortunate,' where the stem-vowel is lengthened. In Zend *a* stems have *-is*, and others *-bis*. This case and its sign have disappeared from several later languages.

Sanskrit.	m. áżwá-is	f. áżwá-bhis	m. páti-bhis	f. pri'ti-bhis
Zend.	ażpā-is	hizvā-bis	paiti-bis	áfriti-bis
Sanskrit.	m. sûnú-bhis	f. gō'-bhis	m. átma-bhis	n. váchô-bhis
Zend.	pażu-bis	gau-bis	ażma-bis	vache-bis

THE DATIVE AND ABLATIVE PLURAL.

163. These two cases have one and the same form. It is in Sanskrit *-bhyas*, Zend *-byô*, Latin *-bus*, and Gothic *-m* (Dative only). The *a* stems in Sanskrit change *a* to *é*; in Zend they change *a* to *aii*; and in Latin have *-is*, including the stem-vowel. The consonant stems take a connecting vowel *i* in Latin. The stem-vowel *u* is also weakened to *i*. The first declension of *â* stems also reduces the case-ending to *s.* The Lithuanian has *mus*, and later *ms*. Through similar changes perhaps the Gothic has passed, and has ultimately retained only *m*. The Anglo-Saxon has *-m* in the Dative Plural of nouns, where *m* is always preceded by *u*, whatever may have been the original stem-vowel. In English there is a remains of this case probably in the pronouns *hi-m* (now restricted to the Singular), *who-m*, *the-m*; Anglo-Saxon, *him* (both Singular and Plural), *hwâ-m*, *thâ-m*.

For the Greek Dative, see the Locative case below.

164. The following list will serve for illustration:

	Sanskrit	Zend	Latin	Gothic	Ang.-Sax.
m.	áçwá-bhyas	açpaii-byô	equt-s	vulfa-m	wulfu-m
f.	áçwá-bhyas	hizvá-byô	equá-bus	gibô-m	gifu-m
m.	páti-bhyas	paiti-byô	hosti-bus	gasti-m	gæsta-m
f.	príti-bhyas	áfriti-byô	turri-bus	ansti-m	—
m.	sûnú-bhyas	paçu-byô	peca-bus	sunu-m	suna-m
f.	vág-bhyás	—	vôc-i-bus	—	—
m.	bhárad-bhyas	buren-byô	feront-i-bus	fijandu-m	fcôndu-m
m.	átma-bhyas	áçma-byô	sermôn-i-bus	ahma-m	—
m.	bhrátṛ-bhyas	brátar-e-byô	frátr-i-bus	brôthar-u-m	brôdhru-m
n.	váchô-bhyas	vache-byô	gener-i-bus	—	—

THE GENITIVE PLURAL.

168. The sign of the *Genitive Plural* is in Sanskrit -âm, in Zend -anm, in Greek -ων, in Latin -um (ûm), in Gothic -ê, and in Anglo-Saxon -a.

In Sanskrit n is inserted between vowel stems and the case-ending. Pronouns of the third person, however, have s in place of this n. Monosyllabic vowel stems develope a corresponding half-vowel instead of inserting a consonant. The vowel before the inserted n or s is always made long, e. g. *pad-â'm*, 'of feet;' *áśwâ-n-âm*, 'of horses;' *tâ'-s-âm*, 'of these;' *gáv-âm*, 'of oxen.'

In Zend the vowel is short, and the nasal appears as -nm. The same consonant is inserted as in Sanskrit, but a preceding short vowel is not lengthened. Polysyllabic u stems also change u to v instead of inserting a consonant, e. g. *atpa-n-anm*, 'of horses;' *aitai-sh-anm*, 'of these;' *gav-anm*, 'of oxen;' *patv-anm*, 'of cattle.'

In Greek no connecting letter is inserted, but the ending is affixed immediately to either consonant or vowel stems, and ā of the stem is incorporated with the termination, e. g. ποδ-ῶν, 'of feet;' ἱππ-ων, 'of horses;' τ-ῶν, 'of the;' βο-ῶν, 'of oxen.'

In Latin the third and fourth declensions, embracing the consonant and *i* and *u* stems, add the ending immediately to the stem, e. g. *ped-um*, 'of feet;' *hosti-um*, 'of enemies;' *exercitu-um*, 'of armies.' The first, fifth, and second declensions, embracing the ā and a stems, insert *r*, which is the Latin equivalent for Sanskrit *s*, between two vowels: *equâ-r-um*, 'of mares;' *ré-r-um*, 'of things;' *equó-r-um*, 'of horses.'

In Gothic *n* appears only with the ā stems, and *s* is

softened to *z*. The latter occurs only in pronouns and strong adjectives, e. g. (*gibô-n-ô*), 'of gifts;' *thi-z-ê* Masc., *thi-z-ô* Fem., 'of these;' *blindai-z-ê* Masc., *blindai-z-ô* Fem., 'of the blind.' The half-vowel *v* is developed in the *u* stems, which are gunaed, whilst the vowel of the *a* and *i* stems is dropped or incorporated with the termination, e. g. *suniv-ê*, 'of sons;' *vulf-ê*, 'of wolves.'

In Anglo-Saxon *-a* is connected with Feminine vowel stems by *n*; and the pronouns *thâ-r-a*, *this-s-a*, exhibit remains of the original *s* as it appears in Sanskrit.

166. The Greek and Latin forms of the Genitive Plural supply a strong reason for regarding *s* as the consonant originally inserted in all instances. The change from *s* to *n*, as in Sanskrit, will be more fully discussed on a subsequent occasion. The absence of this consonant in Greek is consistent with the general tendency of the language which causes *s* to disappear between vowels. In Latin also, as a rule, *s* becomes *r* in the same position. Hence the use of *r* in the Genitive Plural of the first, second, and fifth declensions. The remains in Gothic and Anglo-Saxon also are in harmony with the view of *s* being the original consonant.

167. The following list includes the above modifications of the Genitive Plural:

130 FORMATION OF CASES

	Sanskrit.	Zend.	Greek.	Latin.	Gothic.	Ang.-Sax.	English.
n.	ázwâ-n-âm	aśpan-anm	ἵππ-ων	equô-r-um	vulf-ê	wulf-a	wolves'
f.	ázwâ-n-âm	bizva-n-anm	χωρ-ῶν	equâ-r-um	(gibô-n-ô)	gife-n-a	gifts'
un.n. trî-ŋ-âm	thry-anm	τρι-ῶν	tri-um	thrij-ê	three-r-a	'of three'
m.	páti-n-âm	paiti-n-anm	ποσί-ων	hosti-um	gast-ê	gæst-a	guests'
f.	prîtî-n-âm	áfriti-n-anm	πορτί-ων	turri-um	anst-ê	—	—
f.	vári-n-âm	vairi-n-anm	ἰχθύ-ων	mari-um	—	—	—
m.	súnú-n-âm	paśv-anm	υἱύ-ων	pecu-um	suniv-ê	sun-a	sons'
f.	hánú-n-âm	tanu-n-anm	γενύ-ων	socru-um	handiv-ê	hand-a	hands'
n.	mádhú-n-âm	madhu-n-anm	μεθύ-ων	pecu-um	—	—	—
m.f.	gâv-âm	gav-anm	βο-ῶν	bo(v)-um	—	cu-a, cu-n-a	cows', of kine
f.	vâch-âm	vâch-anm	ὀπ-ῶν	vôc-um	—	—	—
m.n. bhárat-âm	barent-anm	φέροντ-ων	ferent(i)-um	fijand-ê	feónd-a	fiends'
m.	áźman-âm	aśman-anm	δαιμόν-ων	sermôn-um	ahman-ê	—	—
m.	bhrátṛ́-ṇ-âm	brâthr-anm	φρατέρ-ων	frâtr-um	brothr-ê	brothr-a	brothers'
f.	duhitṛ́-ṇ-âm	dughdher-anm	θυγατέρ-ων	mâtr-um	dauhtr-ê	dóhtr-a	daughters'
n.	váchas-âm	vachanh-anm	ἐπέ-ων	gener-um	—	—	—

THE LOCATIVE PLURAL.

168. The *Locative Plural* has disappeared from several languages. Its sign is in Sanskrit -*su*, in Zend -*hu*, and in Greek -σι.

In Sanskrit the laws of euphony change -*su* in certain cases to -*shu*. The same takes place in Zend, where we find -*shva* and -*hva*, which makes it probable that in Sanskrit also the original form was -*swa*. In Greek *i* is added to the *a* and *â* stems, as in Sanskrit it is to the *a* stems. A connecting vowel, *e*, is sometimes added to the *i*, *u*, and consonant stems in Greek; and the forms ending in -σσι perhaps contain the half-vowel which appears in Zend, assimilated to the preceding consonant. Therefore -σσι is for σfι, corresponding to Sanskrit -*swa*. In later times the final ι was dropped in the first and second, i. e. the *â* and *a* declensions. In -σιν of the third declension ν is inorganic.

169. The following is a list of Plural Locatives:

	Sanskrit.	Zend.	Greek.
m.	áçwê-shu	azpai-shva	ἵπποι-σι
f.	áçwâ-su	hizvâ-hva	χόραι-σι
n.	dâ'nê-shu	dâtai-shva ?	δώροι-σι
m.	páti-shu	paiti-shva ?	πάσι-σι
f.	prî'ti-shu	âfriti-shva	πόρτι-σι
n.	vâ'ri-shu	vairi-shva	ἴδρι-σι
m.	sûnú-shu	pazu-shva	νέκυ-σι
f.	hánu-shu	tanu-shva	γένυ-σι
n.	mádhu-shu	madhu-shva	μέθυ-σι
m.f.	gó'-shu	gau-shva	βου-σί
f.	vák-shú	vâkh-sva ?	ὀπ-σί
m.n.	bhárat-su	———	φέρου-σι

κ 2

	Sanskrit.	Zend.	Greek.
m.	kámā-su	azma-hva	δαίμο-σι
n.	nā'ma-su	nāma-hva	τάλα-σι
m.	bhrā'tṛ-shu	brātar-e-shva	φράτορ-σι
f.	dubitf-shu	dughdber-e-shva	θυγατρά-σι
n.	váchas-su	vachô-hva	ἔπεσ-σι

DUAL.

170. The *Dual* has but three forms for the eight cases, and appears only in the declension of the Sanskrit, Zend, and Greek.

THE NOMINATIVE, ACCUSATIVE, AND VOCATIVE DUAL.

These three cases have for their sign in Sanskrit *-âu*, in Zend *-âo*, and in Greek *-ε*.

From the Sanskrit and Zend it appears probable that *-âs* was the original form, and a confirmation of this is found in such Zend words as *huru-âoż-cha*, where the *s* (necessarily changed to *ż* before *ch*) is preserved. The Veda forms have only *-â*. This is further reduced to *-í* in the Sanskrit Neuter stems, as well as in the Feminine *â* stems, whilst the *i* and *u* stems merely have their vowel lengthened, except monosyllables, which develope a half-vowel and take *âu*.

In Zend *-a* appears as well as *-âo*. The Masc. and Fem. *i* and *u* stems have the stem-vowel lengthened without any further addition, and the Neuters, as well as the Feminines in *â*, have only *i* added.

In Greek the stem-vowel in the *â* and *a* stems is lengthened only. Elsewhere the case sign is *s*.

All these may be regarded as successive abbreviations of the original *-âs*.

171. The following list exhibits the different forms:

THE DUAL NUMBER 133

	Sanskrit.	Zend.	Greek.
m.	áçw-âu or â	aṡp-âo or a	ἵππω
f.	íçw-ê	hizv-ê	χώρᾱ
n.	dá'n-ê	dàt-ê	δώρω
m.	páti	paiti ?	πόσι-ε
f.	pri'ti	âfriti ?	πόρτι-ε
n.	vá'ri-ṇ-î	—	ἴδρι-ε
m.	sûnú'	paṡû	νίσυ-ε
f.	hánû	tanû	γένυ-ε
n.	mádhu-n-î	madhv-i	μέθυ-ε
m.f.	gâv-âu or â	gâv-âo or a	βό-ε
f.	vá'ch-âu or â	vâch-âo or a	ὄπ-ε
m.	bhárant-âu or â	barant-âo or a	φέρουτ-ε
m.	ázmân-âu or â	asman-âo or a	δαίμον-ε
n.	nâ'mn-î	namain-i	τάλαν-ε
m.	bhrâ'tar-âu or â	brâtar-âo or a	φράτορ-ε
f.	duhitár-âu or â	dughdhar-âo or a	θυγατέρ-ε
n.	váchas-î	—	ἔπι(σ)-ε

THE INSTRUMENTAL, DATIVE, AND ABLATIVE DUAL.

172. The ending for these cases is in Sanskrit *-bhyâm,* in Zend *-bya,* and in Greek *-ιν.*

The stem-vowel *-a* is lengthened in Sanskrit and becomes *-aii* or *ôi* in Zend. In Greek the older form was *-φιν,* which caused the connecting vowel in the *i, u,* and consonant stems to be *o* instead of *ε,* in accordance with the general law in Greek which requires the connecting vowel to be *o* before Labial consonants. The change of an original final *m* to *ν* in Greek is usual.

The fuller form, *-byanm,* is preserved only in one word in Zend, viz. *brvad-byanm,* 'with the two eyebrows.'

The following list is sufficient to illustrate these forms:

	Sanskrit	Zend	Greek
m.	áçwâ-bhyâm	azpaii-bya	ἵππο-ιν
m.	páti-bhyâm	paiti-bya	πόσι-ο-ιν
m.	bhárad-bhyâm	baran-bya	φέροντ-ο-ιν

THE GENITIVE AND LOCATIVE DUAL.

173. In Greek the *Genitive* has the form of the Dative. In Zend there are but few instances of the Genitive and Locative. The ending appears as $\bar{o}$, e. g. *aṇhv-ô*, 'in the two worlds;' *zaćtuy-ô*, 'of the (two) hands.'

In Sanskrit the form is *-ôs*, and is extensively represented, e. g. *áçway-ôs, páty-ôs, hánw-ôs, vách-ô's*. The $\bar{a}$ stems change this vowel to *ay*. The Masc. and Fem. *i* and *u* stems change their vowel to *y* and *w*. The Neuter *i* and *u* stems insert *n*, e. g. *vá'ri-n-ôs, mádhu-n-ôs*.

VII. ADJECTIVES.

174. The declension of adjectives is the same as that of substantives, but they are subject to other changes of a peculiar character. They differ from substantives, which are the names of things, in expressing the *qualities* by which things are distinguished. These qualities may exist in a greater or less, in the greatest or least degree. This difference is denoted by terminations peculiar to adjectives. The terminations which denote more or less are usually called *Comparative*, and those which denote most or least, *Superlative*.

In Sanskrit the comparative is generally indicated by -*tara*, and the superlative by -*tama*; sometimes by Comp. -*iyâns*, and Sup. -*ishṭha*. The first forms are affixed to the stem of the positive, e. g. *púnya*-**tara**, *púnya*-**tama**, from *púnya*, 'pure;' *mahát*-**tara**, *mahát*-**tama**, from *mahát*, 'great.' The second forms cause the omission of the formative syllable, and sometimes even more than that, in the positive to which they are affixed, e. g. *mát*-**iyas**, *mát*-**ishṭha**, from *matimát*, 'intelligent;' *bál*-**iyas**, *bál*-**ishṭha**, from *bálavat*, 'strong.'

The first forms in Zend are -*tara* and -*tĕma*, and are affixed to the Nominative case of the positive, not to the stem as in Sanskrit, e. g. *huskŏ*-**tara**, from *huska*, 'dry;' *spĕntŏ*-**tĕma**, from *spĕnta*, 'holy.' The second forms are -yaś, Fem. yéhí, and -iṣṭa, e. g. (maś-yô) maś-yêhí and maś-iṣṭa, from maś, 'great.'

175. In Greek the first forms are -τερο, -τατο, added to the stem of the positive, whose final short vowel, however, is lengthened, if preceded by a short syllable, e. g. δεινό-τερο-ς, δεινό-τατο-ς, from δεινο, 'terrible;' but σοφώ-τερο-ς, σοφώ-τατο-ς, from σοφο, 'wise.' The second forms are -ιον, -ιστο-ς. In ιον, ι represents the Sanskrit íy, and ον the Sanskrit án, the á of which becomes short also in Sanskrit in the weak cases. The special form for the Feminine of the comparative, which is in Sanskrit and Zend, disappears, e. g. Gen. M. F. ἡδ-ί ον-ος, ἡδ-ιστο-ς, from ἡδυ, 'sweet.' In the Superlative ισ corresponds to the Sanskrit ish, and is the contracted form of the comparative yâns, from which án disappears, and y is vocalised. With dental and guttural stems we find the comparative terminates in -σσων, including the stem consonant. The half-vowel probably at first produced some such change in the sound of the consonants as we see effected by e and i in the English pronunciation of Greek and Latin words, e. g. nation, contagion, where $ti = sh$ and $gi = j$. If the change were made at once to the dental sibilant, it would resemble the French modification of Greek and Latin words; for in the French pronunciation of nation $t = s$. Hence we have the comparatives κρείσ-σων, from κρατ-ύς, 'strong;' βάσ-σων, from βαθ-ύς, 'deep;' γλύσ-σων, from γλυκ-ύς, 'sweet;' βράσ-σων, from βραχ-ύς, 'short.' Both the stem consonant and the ς of the comparative are represented in the two sigmas. In (μείζων) Ionic μέζων, from μεγύς, 'great,' it is not, however, so easy to trace them. Probably the pronunciation of ζ was such as to represent the effect produced by the combination of γ and ι, the spelling being then adapted to the pronunciation, as would be the case if we were to write *contajon* instead of *contagion*.

176. In Latin the comparative is taken from the second forms, and the superlative from the first. The comparative is formed by *iōr*. At an earlier stage in the language it was *iōs*, of which a few remains are still preserved, e. g. *ma*-**jōs**-*ibus*, *mel*-**iōs**-*ibos*, in Festus. The Latin and Greek forms of this comparative supply each other's defects, the former dropping the nasal and preserving the sibilant (*iōs* for a. *yâ(n)s*), and the latter dropping the sibilant and preserving the nasal (*ιοb* for s. *yan(s)*). The Latin also preserves the long quantity of the vowel which has been shortened in Greek. The Neuter Nom. and Acc. Singular, having a short vowel and the preserved sibilant, very closely resemble the Sanskrit form, i. e. l. *mel*-**ius**, s. *māt-iyas*. The Latin superlative form is *tumu*, later *timu*, and is an exact representative of the Sanskrit *tama*. The *t*, however, changes to *s* after gutturals, e. g. *op*-**timu**-*s*, 'best;' *maximus* (*mag*-**simu**-*s*), 'greatest.' It is also assimilated to *l* and *r*, e. g. *facil*-**limu**-*s*, 'easiest;' *pulcher*-**rimu**-*s*, 'most beautiful.' Those superlatives which end in -*issimus* are probably formed from *is* and *simu*-*s*, the former of which corresponds to Sanskrit *ish*, the contracted form of the comparative *iyas*. We have thus the comparative of the second forms followed by the superlative of the first forms to make a compound superlative. The Greek superlatives in εσ-τατος and ισ-τατος are capable of the same explanation. The comparative of the first forms, though not used in the ordinary declension, occurs in several Latin prepositions, e. g. *in*-**ter**, 'within;' *præ*-**ter**, 'without;' *prop*-**ter**, 'on account of;' as well as in *sub*-**ter**, 'under;' *obi*-**ter**, 'in passing,' where the original *-tara* is reduced to *-ter*.

The second forms are employed almost exclusively in the Germanic languages.

177. In Gothic the comparative is *-iz* or *óz* when followed by a vowel, and *is* or *ós* when final, in which the original syllable is still further reduced than we find it in Greek or Latin. *is* is = Sanskrit *ish* for *îyas*, employed in forming the superlative, and *ós* resembles the Latin *iós*, but with the loss of the first vowel; *is* occurs in adverbs, e. g. *ma*-**is**, 'more;' *hauh*-**is**, 'higher.' In some cases *i* is dropped: *min*-**s**, 'less;' *vair*-**s**, 'worse,' from which *vair*-**siza** is formed like the English '*wor*-**ser**.' In Greek and Latin we saw the comparative and superlative united in one form, i. e. in *ισ-τατος* and *is-simus*; we have here the comparative used twice in the same form. *seith*-**s**, 'later,' 'since.' The addition of *-an* in the ordinary declension causes the *s* to become *z*, e. g. *ma*-**iz**-*an*, 'greater.' The Feminine has a special form, as in Sanskrit and Zend, e. g. *ma-iz-ei-n*, 'greater.' The following are instances of the less usual form, *óz*: *svinth*-**óz**-*an*, 'stronger;' *fród*-**óz**-*an*, 'more prudent;' *frum*-**óz**-*an*, 'earlier.' And of adverbs in *ós*: *sniumund*-**ós**, (σπουδαιοτέρως), 'more carefully;' *aljaleik*-**ós** (ἑτέρως), 'otherwise.'

The formative syllable of the positive is dropped as in Sanskrit, e. g. *sut-iza*, 'sweeter,' compared with s. *swâd*-**ú**-*s*; *hard-iza*, 'harder,' from *hard*-**u**; *reik-iza*, 'richer,' from *reik*-**ja**.

In English the original *s*, which in Gothic is reduced to *z* between vowels, is still further softened to *r*, whilst the stem is subject to the same curtailment as in Gothic. The above examples furnish an illustration of both points, i. e. *sweet*-**er**, *hard*-**er**, *rich*-**er**. In the last word the softening of the original guttural to *ch* was probably the effect of the half-vowel which belonged to the adjective stem, as seen in the Gothic *reik-ja*.

The Gothic superlative is formed by -*ista*, which corresponds to s. *ishṭha* and gr. ιστο of the second forms, e. g. *minn*-**ist**-s, 'least.' The usual form in English is -*est*, e. g. *great*-**est**.

178. The first forms are applied to a few pronouns which imply a comparison with one or more others. Even those languages, viz. Latin and Teutonic, which have not preserved the forms in adjectives, have preserved them in these pronouns. In Sanskrit *ka*-**tará**-*s* means 'which of two;' *ka*-**tamá**-*s*, 'which of several;' *éka*-**tará**-*s*, 'one of two;' *éka*-**tamá**-*s*, 'one of several.' In Greek, πό-τερο-*s*, 'which of two;' ἑκά-τερο-*s*, 'one of two;' ἕκα-στο-*s*, 'each;' differing in both termination and meaning from the Sanskrit. In Latin, *u*-**ter**, 'which of two;' *al*-**ter**, 'another;' *cœ*-**teru**-*s*, 'the other.' In Gothic, *hva*-**thar**, 'which of two;' *an*-**thar**, 'another.' In Anglo-Saxon, *hwæ*-**dher**, *ó*-**dher** (for an-dher), *â*-**dher**, 'one of two;' *æg*-**dher**, 'either' (*g* for *gh*). In English, *whe*-**ther**, 'which of two' (*whe* for *hwe* = s. *ka*); *o*-**ther** (*o* for *an*, same as *al* in Latin *al-ter*, and *an* in Sanskrit *an-yá*), *ei*-**ther**, 'one of two,' (*ei* for Sanskrit *éka*).

179. The ordinal numerals are formed in a similar way. The second has the comparative, and the rest the superlative ending, e. g. s. *dwit*-**í'ya**, gr. δεύ-τερο-*s*, l. *al*-**ter**. The word *secundus*, meaning 'following,' is of later use, from the verb *sequor*. The superlative ending appears as -*tama* in s. *viṅzati*-**tamá**-*s*, 'the twentieth;'

— as -*ta* in s. *chatur*-**tha**; gr. πρῶ-το-s, τέταρ-το-s, etc.; l. *quar*-**tu**-*s*, *quin*-**tu**-*s*, etc.; go. *fimf*-**ta**, etc.; a. s. *fif*-**ta**, etc.; e. *four*-**th**, *fif*-**th**, etc.;—as -*ma* in s. *pancha*-**ma**-*s*; gr. ἕβδο-μο-s; l. *pri*-**mu**-*s*, *septi*-**mu**-*s*; go. *fru*-**m**-*s*, 'first;' a. s. *for*-**ma**, e. *fore*-**mo**-*st*, with two superlatives united, as the comparative is repeated in *wor*-*s*-*er*, and as the superlative is followed by the comparative in *for*-*m*-*er*.

VIII. NUMERALS.

a) CARDINAL NUMERALS.

180. The formation of the Cardinal Numerals is still somewhat obscure. The forms which remain in the Indo-European languages were evidently of identical origin. But the nature of the changes which some have undergone, and the original elements themselves, still require explanation.

181. (1.) The word for *one* in Sanskrit is *é'-ka* = ai-ka; Zend *ai-va*; Greek (*oi-vo-s*) *ol-o-s* and *ἶν* (for *οἱ-ν-*); old Latin *oi-no-s*, later *ú-nu-s*; Gothic *ai-na*; Anglo-Saxon *ân*; English *one*. The half-vowel *w*, which is heard at the beginning of the English word, was probably also heard in Gothic and Anglo-Saxon, just as another half-vowel, *y*, is heard in the Scotch pronunciation of the same word; and we have in this an easier explanation of the *w* in the Lithuanian word *wé'-na-s*, than by supposing, as Bopp does, that it is for an original *m*, and making the word for 'one' to be *mé'-nas*, meaning 'little.' The origin of the gr. *μία*, *μόνος*, and the Armenian *mino*, is too obscure to be relied upon for the explanation of the Lithuanian *wé'nas*. The second part of the Sanskrit *é'-ka*, 'one,' Bopp thinks, is preserved in the following Gothic words as *ha*, viz. *haihs*, stem **ha**-*iha*, corresponding to the Latin *ca-icu-s*, *cœ-cu-s*, 'one-eyed,' 'blind;' **halts**, from *ha*-litha, 'one-legged,' 'lame,' '*halt*;' **hanfs**, from *ha*-nifa, 'one-handed' (*nifa* = Scotch *nieve*, 'hand'); **halbs**, from *ha*-liba, 'of one part,' '*half*.'

182. (2.) The word for *two* is in Sanskrit and Zend *dwa*; Greek δύω, δύο; Latin *duo*, declined wholly or in part as duals; Goth. *tvai*, and Anglo-Saxon *twá*, declined as plurals; English *two*. In composition this word is reduced in Sanskrit to *dwi*; Greek to δι; Latin and Zend to *bi*, the *d* being dropped, and *u* changed to *b*, as in *b*-ellum for *du*-ellum; Gothic *tvi*; Anglo-Saxon *twi*; English *twi*, e.g. **twi**-*light*. The adverbial forms are s. *dwis*, gr. δίς, l. *bis* (a. s. has twawa), e. *twice*. In English the final *e* only indicates that *c* stands for *s*.

183. (3.) The word for *three* is in Sanskrit *tri*; in Zend and Gothic *thri*. In Zend the aspirate *th* is occasioned by the letter *r*. The declension is regular. The *i* becomes *ij* in Gothic before vowel endings, and in Sanskrit the Genitive *trayá-n-á'm* is formed from *traya*. In both Sanskrit and Zend the Feminine is formed from the stem *tisar*. In Greek, M. F. τρεῖς, N. τρία; in Latin, M. F. *trés*, N. *tria*; both declined as plurals. In Gothic *thri*, and in Anglo-Saxon *threo*, as a plural. In English *three*.

184. (4.) *Four* is expressed in Sanskrit by *chatwá'r*, in weak cases *chatúr*, and Feminine *chatasar*; in Zend by *chathwár*, weak cases *chathru*; in Greek by τέτταρες, τέσσαρες, Æol. πίσυρες, Homeric πίσυρες; in Latin by *quattuor*, *quadru*- in composition; in Gothic by *fidvôr*, *fidur*- in composition; in Anglo-Saxon by *feôwer*, both separately and in composition; in English by *four*, sometimes *for*- in composition. The first three of these languages regularly decline this numeral; but the Sanskrit and Zend insert *n* in the Genitive, as with vocal stems. In Greek the initial π corresponds to Sans. *ch*, but τ is an unusual deviation. The double consonant results from assimilation, i. e. ττ for *tw*. In Latin the guttural initial stands for Sans. *ch*, and *w* is vocalised to *u*; whilst in the Ordinal **quar-***tus* the whole is abbreviated similarly to the English in **for**-ty. In Gothic the initial *f* is the regular representative of the gr. π.

185. (5.) For *five* we have in Sanskrit *pánchan*; Zend *panchan*; Greek πέμπε, πέντε; Latin *quinque*; Gothic *fimf*; Anglo-Saxon *fíf*; Engl. *five*. The final nasal of the first two is perhaps inorganic. In the Greek forms there are both π and τ for the Sanskrit *ch*, as in the number four. In Latin there is the guttural for *ch*, and also for the initial *p*. The Gothic follows the Greek in having labial consonants. This word is declined only in Sanskrit and Zend, and there not in Nom., Acc., and Voc.

186. (6.) The word for *six* is in Sanskrit *shash*; in Zend *khsvas*; Greek ἕξ; Latin *sex*; Gothic *saihs*; Anglo-Saxon *six*; Engl. *six* — all undeclined. As *sh* is a derived sound and begins no other word in Sanskrit, it may originally have been preceded by the guttural which is preserved in Zend; and Bopp thinks the other forms are transpositions for *xes*, etc. Hence s. *kshash*, Latin *ksex*, etc. The Greek aspiration is here, as in many other instances, for an original sibilant. Gothic *h* stands regularly for an older *k*, which in English has been reduced again to the earlier form, *siks*. A similar inversion to that here supposed occurs in a. s. *acs-ian* and *asc-ian*, e. *ax* and *ask*.

187. (7.) For *seven* Sanskrit has *sápta*; Zend *hapta*; Greek ἑπτα; Latin *septem*; Gothic *sibun*; Anglo-Saxon *seófon*; Engl. *seven*. The declension of the Sanskrit and Zend shows that the stem is *saptan*. The Greek *a* also, as in the Accus. Sing. of the third declension, stands for a nasal preceded by a short vowel. In Latin *m* instead of *n* is an apparent deviation. In Gothic *b* probably stands, like the *d* in *fidvór*, for the vocal aspirate *bh*, since the regular law of consonant changes requires in Gothic *dh* for Sanskrit *t*, and *bh* for Sanskrit *p*. The English *v*, which represents *bh*, confirms this view. Possibly the Gothic *b* was in this case pronounced like *v*.

188. (8.) The word for *eight* is in Sanskrit *áshṭa*, and the dual form *ashṭâu*; in Zend *asta*; Greek ὀκτώ; Latin *octo*; Gothic *ahtau*; Anglo-Saxon *eahta*; Engl. *eight*. *sh* and *s* are derived from the original guttural. In Gothic and Anglo-Saxon *h* stands for the guttural aspirate, whilst in Engl. the aspirate is fully written *gh*, though not pronounced.

189. (9.) For *nine* we have in Sanskrit *náva*; Zend *nava*; Greek ἐννέα; Latin *novem*; Gothic *niun*; Anglo-Saxon *nigon*; English *nine*. The original stem appears to have been *navan*. In Greek the *a* indicates the final nasal, whilst the prefixing of a vowel and the doubling of the consonant at the beginning are not unusual. In Latin, again, *m* is in place of *n*, and in Gothic *va* is reduced to *u*, which in English is represented only by the long quantity of the *i*. The *g* in Angl.-S. is irregular: perhaps it was pronounced *y*, and was developed out of *i*.

190. (10.) For *ten* we have in Sanskrit *dáża*; Zend *daża*; Greek δέκα; Latin *decem*; Gothic *taihun*; Anglo-Saxon *týn*; English *ten*. *ż* is for an original guttural, which in Gothic is represented by *h*, and altogether dropped in Angl.-S. and English. In Greek *a* includes a final nasal, and in Latin *m* is instead of *n*.

191. The following is a list of the above numerals:

CARDINAL NUMERALS

Sanskrit.	Zend.	Greek.	Latin.	Gothic.	Ang.-Sax.	English.
ê-ka (=ai-ka)	ai-va	(ai-v-) ἷν	oi-no-s / ū-nu-s	ai-na	â-n	one
dwa	dwa	δύω, δύο	duo	tva	twâ	two
tri	thri	τρεῖς (τρα-ες)	trēs (tre-es)	thri	threo	three
chatwâr-as	chathwâr	τέτταρ-ες / τέσυρ-ες	quattuor	fidvôr	feower	four
pánchan	panchan	πέντε / πέμπε	quinque	fimf	fíf	five
shash	khsvas	ἕξ	sex	saihs	six	six
sáptn	hapta	ἑπτά	septem	sibun	seofon	seven
áshṭa	asta	ὀκτώ	octo	ahtau	eahta	eight
návn	nava	ἐννέα	novem	niun	nigon	nine
dáśa	daśa	δέκα	decem	taihun	týn	ten

L

192. The numerals from *eleven* to *nineteen* are as follows:

Sanskrit.	Zend.	Greek.	Latin.	Gothic.	Anglo-Saxon.	English.
ékadaśan	aivandaśan	ἕνδεκα	undecim	ainlif	endlufon	eleven
dwádaśan	dvadaśan	δώδεκα	duodecim	tvalif	twelf	twelve
trayódaśan	thridaśan	τρεισκαίδεκα	tredecim	thritaihun	threotyne	thirteen
chaturdaśan	chathrudaśan	τεσσαρεσκαίδεκα	quattuordecim	fidvôrtaihun	feowertyne	fourteen
pánchadaśan	—	πεντεκαίδεκα	quindecim	fimftaihun	fiftyne	fifteen
shôḍaśan	—	ἑκκαίδεκα	sedecim	saihstaihun	sixtyne	sixteen
sáptadaśan	—	ἑπτακαίδεκα	septendecim	sibuntaihun	seofontyne	seventeen
śahṭádaśan	—	ὀκτωκαίδεκα	duodeviginti	ahtautaihun	eahtatyne	eighteen
návadaśan	—	ἐννεακαίδεκα	undeviginti	niuntaihun	nigontyne	nineteen

193. In the above list the *units* are prefixed to the word for *ten*, and generally without anything to connect them together, e. g. s. *êkâdaźan* = 'one-ten;' go. *fimf-taihun* = 'five-ten;' e. *seventeen*. In Greek the numbers after twelve are connected by καί, 'and,' which is a later modification. In Sanskrit, Greek, etc., the word for ten is preserved unchanged, except the slight change of *e* to *i* in Latin, e. g. *undecim* for *undecem*. In Gothic the first two of the above numbers have the word ten changed in a very peculiar manner; viz. *-lif*, stem *libi*, is used, where *b* is for *v*, as in *sibun*, 'seven.' It seems, however, to be the same word originally as that used in the following numbers, *taihun* = s. *daźan*; for there are several examples of the change of an original *d* to *l* instead of to *t*, and that this change was made in the present case appears from the Lithuanian equivalent *lika*, which is extended to the numbers beyond twelve, e. g. *dwy-lika*, 'twelve;' *try-lika*, 'thirteen.' In Prâcrit the word for ten, in these compounds, is changed to *raha*, and in Hindustanee to *rah*, in one case *lah*, i. e. *só-lah*, 'sixteen.' The Gothic equivalent for the second consonant *k* would be the aspirate *gh*, for which we usually find the aspirate only, as in *tai*h*un*: but the substitution of *f* or *v* for this aspirate frequently takes place in the Germanic languages, and in English where *gh* is written *f* is pronounced in such words as rou**gh**, *t*ou**gh**. So that the Gothic *lif*, stem *libi* (probably pronounced *livi*), appears to be only a somewhat unusual modification of the original word for ten, s. *daźan*, go. *taihun*. Nor is the change so great as one which even modern history has witnessed, i. e. of the Latin *decim* to French *ze* in *on-ze*, *dou-ze*, for *un-*decim, *duo-*decim. In Anglo-Saxon the same change of consonants has taken place as in Gothic, in *end-*

lufon and *twelf*, but in the former the second syllable of the word for 'ten' is preserved in the form of -*on*, whilst in the latter even the *i* in *lif* is dropped, so that both vowels of the original word are lost. The *f* in both languages may have been pronounced *v*. The word *tyne* is as much abbreviated as the English equivalent *teen*. In English there is also a loss of the intervening vowel of the first syllable in one word, *twe-lv-e*, though it is retained in the other, *e-lev-en*; the second syllable is preserved as *en*. The word for 'one' loses its final vowel in Greek, Latin, Gothic; and in English the *n* also is dropped, as is usually the case with the article (*an*) before consonants.

The comparison of the Gothic words *sibun* and -*lif*, stem -*libi*, with the English words *seven* and *eleven*, leads to the conclusion either that the sound *bh* was changed in Gothic to *b*, or that the Gothic *b*, in some instances, was pronounced *bh* or *v*.

194. The following are the numbers from twenty to a hundred:

CARDINAL NUMERALS

	Sanskrit	Zend	Greek	Latin	Gothic	Ang.-Sax.	English
20	vin-zátí	vi-zaiti	εἴ-κοσι	vi-gintī	tvantigus	twentig	twenty
30	trin-zát	thri-inta	τριά-κοντα	trī-ginta	thrinatigus	thrītig	thirty
40	chatwārin-zát	chathwaro-sata	τεσσαρά-κοντα	quadrā-ginta	fidvōrtigus	feowertig	forty
50	panchā-zát	panchā-zata	πεντή-κοντα	quinquā-ginta	fimftigus	fīftig	fifty
60	shash-tí	khsvas-ti	ἑξή-κοντα	sexā-ginta	(saihstigus)?	sixtig	sixty
70	sapta-tí	haptāi-ti	ἑβδομή-κοντα	septuā-ginta	sibun-tēhund	hund-seofontig	seventy
80	aśī-tí	—	ὀγδοή-κοντα	octō-ginta	ahtau-tēhund	hund-eahtatig	eighty
90	nava-tí	navāi-ti	ἐννενή-κοντα	nōnā-ginta	niun-tēhund	hund-nigontig	ninety
100	śatá-m	śatō-m	ἑ-κατό-ν	centu-m	hunda	hund-teontig	hund-red

149

195. The small numbers are placed first, as in the previous series, and a derivative from the word for ten is employed to express 'ten times,' viz. s. *dażata*, differently abbreviated in various words to *dażat, żati, żat, ti*; z. *żaiti, żata, ti*. In the Greek and Latin κοντα and *ginta*, a nasal is inserted, and *k* changed to *g* in Latin; both have the form of Neuter Plurals. In Gothic, *tigu-s*, in 20—60, has *g* in place of *gh*, as in the previous list the same word retains only *h* for *gh*. The fuller form, with addition of *d* and *ê* for *ai*, is used in 70—90. Both are declined. In this respect also *g* for *gh* resembles *b* in *libi* for *bh*, and admits of a similar explanation, viz. that *gh* was in Gothic reduced to the sound *g*, or that in some cases *g* represents the *gh* sound. If we add the case of *fidvor*, where *d* is for dh (=*th* in *then*), we have the same phenomenon in regard to all the soft or vocal aspirates; i. e. *gh, dh, bh* are all reduced to the corresponding vocals, *g, d, b*, or these latter were all pronounced in some cases in Gothic as aspirates, viz. *gh, dh, bh*. Of these the first is a sound not preserved in the English language, the second is represented by *th* in *then*, and the third by *v*. In Anglo-Saxon, *tig* admits the same explanation as in Gothic. *Hund-* for go. -*téhund* is prefixed, and the usual *tig* superadded, in 70—90; *hund* is used alone for 100, as *hunda* in Gothic, but *hundred* also is found as in English. In the English -*ty* only the first syllable of the word is preserved. The *y*, however, may be regarded as the representative of the second consonant, which, in English, would be *gh* as in Gothic, so that e. *ty*=a. s. *tig*. In many English words this sound, being lost in the living language, is represented by *y*, e. g. *day* for *da*g**h**, compared with the German *ta*g; *lay* for *la*g**h**, compared with the German *la*g. The same word in Latin, with the termination of the Neuter Singular, *m*, serves to express a hundred, *centum*; in Greek, with *ἑ* prefixed, and *a* for *ov*, *ἑκατόν* (perhaps for *ἑν-κατον*) = 'one hundred.' The Gothic *hund* in *hund-a*, where *d* is for *dh*, is the exact counterpart of the Latin *cent* in cent-um.

b) ORDINAL NUMERALS.

196. The Ordinal Numerals are adjectives formed from the Cardinals, generally by the superlative ending *-tama*, which, in some cases, is reduced to *-ta*, and in others to *-ma*, as will be seen in the following list:

	Sanskrit.	Zend.	Greek.	Latin.	Gothic.	Ang-Sax.	English.
1	pratha-má-s	frathê-mô	πρω̂-το-ς	pri-mu-s	frum-s	for-ma	fir-st
2	dwi-tî'ya-s	bi-tyô	δεύ-τερο-ς	al-ter	an-thar-s	ô-ther	second
3	tṛ-tî'ya-s	thri-tyô	τρί-το-ς	ter-tiu-s	thri-dja	thry-dde	thir-d
4	chatur-thá-s	tuir-ya	τέταρ-το-ς	quar-tu-s	(fidvôr-dja)	feor-tha	four-th
5	pancha-má-s	pukh-dhô	πέμπ-το-ς	quin-tu-s	fimf-ta	fíf-ta	fíf-th
6	shash-thá-s	khs-tvô	ἕκ-το-ς	sex-tu-s	saihs-ta	six-ta	six-th
7	sapta-má-s	hapta-thô	ἕβδο-μο-ς	septi-mu-s	sibun-da	seofo-tha	seven-th
8	ashta-má-s	astê-mô	ὄγδο-ος	octa-vu-s	ahtu-da	eahta-tha	eigh-th
9	nava-má-s	nâu-mô	ἔννα-το-ς	non-u-s	niun-da	nigo-tha	nin-th
10	daça-má-s	daça-mô	δέκα-το-ς	deci-mu-s	taihun-da	teô-tha	ten-th
11	êkâdaça-s	aivandaçô	ἑνδέκα-το-ς	undeci-mu-s	(ainlif-ta)	endlyf-ta	eleven-th
20	vinçati-tamô-s	vîsaiti-tê-mô	εἰκο-στό-ς	vicê-simu-s	——	——	twenti-eth

197. The word for *first* is an exception to the rule, inasmuch as it is not formed like the rest from the corresponding cardinal numeral. In all the above languages the word, however, is of one and the same origin. The first syllable appears in the various forms of *pra, fra, πρω, pri, fru, for, fir*, which present no modification but what has been abundantly illustrated in other cases. A peculiar ending appears in the word for 'third' in all except the Greek τρί-το-s, which is regular. This ending appears to have been *ta-ya* instead of *tama*, contracted to *tya*, and then enlarged to *tīya* in Sanskrit. In Gothic, Anglo-Saxon, and English, *d* is in place of the aspirate *dh*. In English *ir* is, by a transposition of letters, for *ri*. In the word for 'second' the comparative ending is employed, except in z. *bi-tyô*, which perhaps has been altered under the influence of *thri-tyô*, and in s. *dvi-tī'ya-s*, which may have originally ended only in *tya-s*, one of the comparative forms, and, as in Zend, have adopted *t* in imitation of *tr-tī'ya-s*. In English 'other' has been appropriated to another use, and *second*, from the Latin *secundus*, substituted among the Ordinals. Secundus is also employed in Latin as a Numeral in place of *alter*. In the z. *tuīr-ya* the ending is reduced to *ya*, as in the s. *tŭr-ya*, which also occurs. In Old Slavic this *ta-ya* or *ya* occurs in all the words.

There is a difficulty in deciding to which part of the word a letter belongs in some of the above forms. For instance, if the Latin word be divided into *septim-u-s*, *m* of the cardinal *septem* is preserved, and that of the ending *mu* is dropped; but if it be divided into *septi-mu-s*, the former *m* is dropped and the latter preserved. In ὄγδο-ο-s the *m* is dropped, and in *octa-vu-s v* is substituted for it. In *ékúdazá-s* either *a-m* or *ma* has been dropped from *ékúdaza-má-s*.

In Gothic the ending *ta* has preserved the original *t* in some cases, from the influence of the preceding consonant; in other cases *d* may have been pronounced as an aspirate, i. e. *dh*. In Anglo-Saxon *-ma* occurs in 1st, as in all the other languages except Greek and English. In 2nd the comparative form is used, and in the other numbers, except 3rd, *-ta* occurs in the regular equivalent form of *-tha*, or as *-ta* or *-te*, where the preceding consonant prevents the *t* from being aspirated. In 3rd *-dde*, by assimilation from *dya*, is equal to go. *-dja*, and this is a regular equivalent for the s. *tya* (tiya), the *d* being pronounced as *dh*. In English the aspirate occurs in all except *thir-d*, where, since no vowel follows as in Anglo-S., the difficulty of pronunciation explains the change. It is evident that the Ordinal Numerals have been considerably modified since the separation of these languages, for the formative endings are not alike in any two of them, except the more modern Go., Anglo-S., and Engl.; and yet the original analogies have not been lost sight of, for no absolutely new ending occurs in any of them.

c) NUMERAL ADVERBS.

198. In the formation of Numeral Adverbs *s* is frequently employed, as in—

Sanskrit.	Zend.	Greek.	Latin.	Anglo-Saxon.	English.
dwi-s	bi-s	δί-ς	bi-s	(tu-wa)	twi-ce
tri-s	thri-s	τρί-ς	ter(s)	(thry-wa)	thri-ce
chatúr(s)	chathru-s	——	quater(s)	——	'four times

It is singular that this s (ce) appears in English though lost in Anglo-Saxon.

The omission of s after r in *ter, quater, chatur,* is regular. *źas* (from *kas*) is also used in Sanskrit, and κις in Greek, e. g. *bahú-źas*, πολλά-κις, 'many times.' In Sanskrit *vat (vant)* or *kṛt-vas*, and Latin *ien-s, iê-s,* for *uent-s, uet-s,* are used to denote 'possessed of' or 'times,' e. g. *daźa-*kṛ́tvas, 'ten times;' *quotiês, quo-*tiens, 'how many times.' 'Distribution into' is expressed by a. *dhâ,* gr. χα, e. g. *dwi-*dhâ' = δί-χα, 'by twos.'

IX. PRONOUNS.

199. The original elements of which the Pronouns are formed are very obscure, and the words have undergone such great changes that many of the forms admit only of conjectural explanations.

a) PRONOUNS OF THE FIRST AND SECOND PERSON.

The Pronouns of the First and Second Persons are similarly inflected, and may conveniently be considered together. They have the following forms:

Pronouns of the First and Second Person Singular.

	Sanskrit.	Zend.	Greek.	Latin.	Gothic.	Anglo-Saxon.	English.
Nom.	ah-ám tw-am	az-ĕm tû-m	ἐγών σύ	eg-o tu	ik thu	ic thû	I (k) thou
Acc.	má-m twá-m	me-ñm twa-ñm	μέ σέ	mê tê	mi-k thu-k	me (meh, mec) the (thch, thec)	me thee
Inst.	má-yá twá-yá	— —	— —	— —	— —	— —	'by me' 'by thee'
Dat.	má-hyam tú-bhyam	mai-byâ thw-ôi	μοί σοί	mi-hi ti-bi	mi-s thu-s	me the	me thee
Abl.	ma-t twa-t	ma-d thwa-d	— —	me-d te-d	— —	me the	'from me' 'from thee'
Gen.	má-ma táva	ma-na thwa-byâ	μοῦ σοῦ	me-i tu-i	mei-na thei-na	mi-n thi-n	my, mi-ne thy, thi-ne
Loc.	má-yi twá-yi	— thwa-hmi	— —	— —	— —	— —	'in me' 'in thee'

200. There are two stems in the above forms of the first person, one for the Nominative alone, and the other for the remaining cases. The Nom. has for the first person in Sanskrit *ah*, and for the second *twa*. The Latin and Greek seem to have preserved the original consonant in the first person; for the Germanic languages have *k* and *kh* (germ. *ch*), which presuppose *g* in the earlier languages. The Sanskrit *h* and Zend *z*, therefore, are corruptions of the original sound. Modern English, *I*, has lost the consonant as compared with the old English *ik*, like the Italian *io* as compared with the Latin *ego*.

The ending of the Nominative is s. *-am*, z. *-ěm*, gr. *-ον* in the archaic forms *ἐγ-ών*, *τούν*, l. *o*. It is lost in the other languages, and is a form which appears originally to have been confined to a few pronouns, i.e. *ah-ám*, *tw-am*, *ay-ám*, *sway-ám*, etc.

The stem in the oblique cases of the first person is *ma*, that of the second person *twa* (or *tu*, changed to *tw* in some cases). The Accusative, Instrumental, Ablative, and Locative coincide with the declension of nouns. The Dative and Genitive differ. The former cases have in several languages lost the case-ending. Even Sanskrit and Zend have Acc. *má* and Gen. *mé* as well as the fuller forms. The *k* in Gothic and sometimes in Anglo-S. Acc. appears to be the remains of a demonstrative particle, as in Latin *hi-c*, *hun-c*, *tun-c*, etc.

The ending of the Dative is *-bhyam*, which occurs with modified forms in the dual *-bhyám* and plural *-bhyas* of nouns. It is reduced in the Sanskrit first person to *-hyam*, in Zend to *-byĭ* and *-ŏi*, in Greek to *-ι* (unless the Greek forms are really Locatives), in Latin to *-hi* and *-bi*. It is quite lost in the Germanic languages.

The Genitive appears to be a reduplication of the stem, *má-ma*, *tá-va* for ta-twa, and this for twa-twa. The Greek and Latin are greatly abbreviated, and the Gothic as well as the Anglo-Saxon and English words have an adjective form, which is doubtless of later origin, and occasioned by the reduced reduplication being no longer understood as a Genitive sign. In English this adjective ending is again dropped before consonants, e. g. 'mine own,' but 'my house.'

In Greek the stem consonant σ in the second person is the regular substitute for an older *t*, and many archaic forms preserve τ, e. g. τοί, τοῖο, etc.

201. The Plural forms of the First and Second Persons are:

FIRST AND SECOND PERSON PLURAL

	Sanskrit.	Zend.	Greek (Æolic.)	Latin.	Gothic.	Anglo-Saxon.	English
Nom.	{vay-ám / a-smé} / {yu-shmé / yuy-ám}	va-ēm / yū-shēm	á-μμε-ς / ύ-μμε-ς	nō-s / vō-s	vei-s / jū-s	wē / gē	we / you
Acc.	a-smā́-n / yu-shmā́-n	nō / vō	á-μμε / ύ-μμε	nō-s / vō-s	u-nsi-s / i-zvi-s	ús (úsih, úsic) / eów (eówih, eówic)	us / you
Instr.	a-smā́-bhis / yu-shmā́-bhis	— / —	— / —	— / —	— / —	— / —	— / —
Dat.	a-smá-bhyam / yu-shmá-bhyam	mai-byō / yu-shmaii-byō	á-μμι-(ν) / ύ-μμι-(ν)	nō-bis / vō-bis	u-nsi-s / i-zvi-s	ús / eów	us / you
Abl.	a-smá-t / yu-shmá-t	yū-mna-ḍ	—	—	—	ús / eów	—
Gen.	a-smā́-kam / yu-shmā́-kam	a-hmá-kēm / yu-smá-kēm	á-μμέ-ων / ύ-μμέ-ων	nostri / vestri	u-nsa-ra / i-zva-ra	ú-re / eów-er	our / your
Loc.	a-smā́-su / yu-shmā́-su	—	á-μμί-σι	—	—	—	—

159

The stem of the first person is *a-sma*, and of the second *yu-shma* (for yu-sma). The full forms occur throughout in Sanskrit, together with some abbreviated forms. The abbreviations in Zend are similar to what have been already illustrated. The Accusatives correspond to *nas, vas*, which are used in Sanskrit. In Greek (Æolic) *sma* assumes the form μμε, in which *s* is assimilated to the following letter. In the Attic forms the rough breathing is used for *s*, as in many other cases, e. g. ἲξ for *sex*, etc. But the stem-vowel of the first person is lengthened to η, and the rough breathing prefixed. Hence we have ἡμῖς, ὑμεῖς, for ἡμσ-ες, ὑμσ-ες, and these for ἠ-σμε-ες, ὐ-σμε-ες. The older forms have been placed in the table in order to show more clearly the correspondence of the Greek with other languages. The forms ἡμῖν, ὑμῖν, for ἡμσ-ιν, ὑμσ-ιν, exhibit ιν for *y-m* of the Sanskrit ending *-bhyam*, the rest being dropped. The Genitives agree with the declension of nouns, to which they have perhaps been assimilated in later times. As there is a proper Dative to these pronouns in the Plural, the Locative has disappeared in the classical language, though a reminiscence of it is preserved in the Æolic ἀ-μμέ-σι. In Latin we find *nô, vô*, with the addition of *s* in the Nominative and Accusative, and of *bis* in the Dative. In Sanskrit, also, *na-s, va-s* are used in the Accusative, Dative, and Genitive. Corresponding forms occur in Zend. The fact that *s* appears in three cases besides the Nominative makes it unlikely that it should be the sign of that case. Bopp thinks it is a remains of *sma*, whilst *nô, vô, na, va* are modifications of *ma, twa*, which appear in the singular, *a* in the plural of the first person being also a corruption of *ma*. This explanation of the stem needs further confirmation, and the entire absence of all trace of *sma* from *nó-bis*, *vó-bis*, is an evidence against its existence in the Latin plurals. In *ego-met*, *tu-met*, *nos-met*, the assumption of the existence of *sma* is not without difficulty, for *met* appears to be affixed to the Nominative case, which suggests that these are late formations. The Genitives *nostri*, *vestri*, etc., may be readily admitted to be adjectives.

In Gothic the Nominatives *vei-s*, *ju-s*, have stems corresponding to those Sanskrit ones which have not *sma* affixed (i. e. *vay-âm*, *yuy-âm*), but *s* occasions the same difficulty as in Latin; perhaps in both cases the simpler hypothesis would be that it was adopted in later times in imitation of nouns. In the oblique cases *u* (before a nasal) and *i* represent the Sanskrit *a* and *yu*. The changes of the latter *yu* to *y* and then to *i* contain nothing unusual. There is no difficulty either in supposing *sma* to have become *msa*, as in Zend *mha*, and then *s* to have caused the change from *m* to *n*. So that Gothic *nsa*, *nsi* correspond to Sanskrit *sma*. In *zva*, *zvi*, the softening of the *s* is due to the preceding weak vowel *i*, and the change from *m* to *v* is one which extensively occurs. The final *s* in the Accusative, as in Latin, is probably for *ns*, as in the Accusative plural of nouns. In Sanskrit the other consonant, *n*, is preserved. In the Dative also a final *s* occurs. Perhaps we ought to divide the Latin words into *no-bi-s*, *vo-bi-s*, leaving only *bi* of the original ending *-bhyam*, as in the singular *mi-hi*, *ti-bi*. In Latin the *s* is probably an imitation of the nominal declension, where the original form *bhyas* ends in *s*; or it is the Instrumental used as a Dative. In Gothic its origin remains obscure. It is not likely to be a remains of *sma*, which would make *u-nsi-s* for *u-nsi-nsi*. Probably the Gothic Dative is really the Accusative used for the Dative. The Genitives, except

in Greek, appear to be all possessive adjectives, i. e.
'our,' 'your,' for 'of us,' 'of you.' In Anglo-Saxon the
reduction had already proceeded almost as far as in modern English. In *ge* and *eów*, *g* and *e* were pronounced
y. In *ûs* the length of the *û* shows some remains of
the syllable *sma*, whilst *s* appears to correspond to the
final *s* in Gothic, since in the Genitive *û* is for u + sma,
and the final *ra* preserved as *re*. In *eów*, on the contrary,
the final *s* is lost. The older forms *û-si-h*, *û-si-c*,
eów-i-h, *eów-i-c*, also occur.

202. The forms of the Dual for the First and
Second Persons are:

	Sanskrit.	Greek.	Gothic.	Ang.-Sax.	English.
Nom.	â-vâ'-m	νώ-ι	vi-t	wi-t	'we two'
	yu-vâ'-m	σφώ-ι	———	gi-t	'ye two'
Acc.	â-vâ'-m	νώ-ι	u-nki-s	u-nc	'us two'
	yu-vâ'-m	σφώ-ι	i-nqvi-s	i-nc	'you two'
Instr.	â-vâ'-bhyâm	———	———	———	'by us two'
	yu-vâ'-bhyâm	———	———	———	'by you two'
Dat.	â-vâ'-bhyâm	νώ-ιν	u-nki-s	u-nc	'to us two'
	yu-vâ'-bhyâm	σφώ-ιν	i-nqvi-s	i-nc	'to you two'
Abl.	â-vâ'-bhyâm	———	———	u-nc	'from us two'
	yu-vâ'-bhyâm	———	———	i-nc	'from you two'
Gen.	â-vŕ-yôs	νώ-ιν	u-nka-ra	u-ncs-r	'of us two'
	yu-vá-yôs	σφώ-ιν	i-nqva-ra	i-ncs-r	'of you two'
Loc.	â-vá-yôs	———	———	———	'in us two'
	yu-vá-yôs	———	———	———	'in you two'

In the dual *va* occupies the place of *sma* in the
singular and plural, *s* being dropped and *m* changed to

v, as in the Gothic forms of the second person both dual and plural. In Sanskrit the Nom. and Acc. end alike in *m*. In the Nom. it is most likely of the same origin as in the Singular and Plural *aham*, *vayam*, etc. In the Acc. it is the original case sign, preserved in the singular, preceded by a long vowel in the dual, and changed to *u* in some nominal forms: hence -*âu* for *â-m*. It is changed to *n* in the plural in consequence of being followed by *s*, which was afterwards dropped. The Accusatives *nâu*, *vâm*, appear to be abbreviations of the older forms, the stem syllables *a* and *yu* being dropped; *nâ* would then be an irregular form for *sma*. Bopp suggests the original to have been *nâ-smâu*. In Greek νω and σφω may also be regarded as strangely altered forms of *sma*, having the vowel lengthened as in the Sanskrit *vâ*. The Dative ending *ω* corresponds to the Sanskrit *bhyâm*. It is used irregularly for the Genitive. ι in the Nom. and Acc. may be for Sanskrit *i*, which occurs in some nouns. In Gothic the stems are the same as in the plural; the syllable *sma* in the oblique cases assumes the forms *nki*, *nka*, *nqvi*, *ṅqva*, *qv* being equal to *k*, and *k* standing in place of Sanskrit *s*. The final *s* in the Acc. and Dat. is the same as in the Plur., the nasal, which is preserved in Sanskrit, being here dropped. The final *t* in the Nom. of the first person, Bopp says, 'clearly belongs to the designation of the number two (stem *twa*).' The Anglo-Saxon preserves much older and fuller forms in the Dual than in the Plural. The reason probably is that the former were less used, and therefore less worn and wasted, than the latter. We have the Nominative of both persons, and both alike add *t* to the Plural. In the other cases *nc* clearly corresponds to the go. *nk*, *nq*, as representative of *sma*. The personal endings are lost in the Accusative and Dative. *U-nci-t, i-nci-t,* also occur for *unc, inc.* An Ablative is given, but identical in form with the Dative as in the Sing. and Plur. An Ablative might perhaps with equal propriety be assigned to the Gothic.

b) PRONOUNS OF THE THIRD PERSON.

203. There is a great variety of Pronouns of the Third Person. Their forms in different languages mutually help to explain each other, and the comparison of them serves to elucidate many isolated words, which otherwise would be inexplicable.

The Reflexive Pronoun is —

	Zend.	Greek.	Latin.	Gothic.
Acc.	——	σφί, ἕ	sē	si-k
Instr.	——	——	——	svê
Dat.	hă, hôi	οἷ	sibi	si-s
Gen.	hê, hôi	εἷο, οὗ	sui	sei-na

The Sanskrit, Anglo-Saxon, and English have lost the use of this pronoun in a separate form, but the Sanskrit has *swa* and *sway-am* in some compounds, e. g. *swa-bhu, swayam-bhu,* 'to be self-originated;' *swayam-prabha,* 'to be self-glorified;' *swa-tas* is also used in the sense of 'self.' As a possessive pronoun, fully declined, *swa* is also used of all persons and numbers, in the sense of 'my,' 'thy,' 'his,' 'our,' etc. In this usage it corresponds to the Greek σφό-ς.

In the Reflexive Pronoun the original *w* appears only in Greek Acc. as φ, and Latin Gen. as *u*. The *s* has become *h* in Zend, and *spiritus asper* in Greek.

In Zend this pronoun occurs in the form of *qha* in

compounds (e.g. *qha-dhâta,* 'self-produced'), and of *hwa*
as a possessive. In Latin *i-pse* is explained as being
by inversion for *i-spe,* and *sp* for Sanskrit *sw,* as in
sponte. A similar inversion occurs in the Doric ψίν
for σφίν. The change of Sanskrit *w* to Latin *p* is
illustrated in l. *por-ta* = s. *dwấra,* 'door.'

The Reflexive Pronoun is not preserved in Anglo-
Saxon and English, unless it be in the word *self,* as in
the German *selbst,* in which *lf* as in *loaf,* and *lb* as in
laib, are an expression for 'body' or 'person;' *se-lf* =
'one's own person.'

Demonstrative Pronouns. TA.

204. The Demonstrative stem **ta**, Fem. *tâ,* is extensively employed. Its forms are the following:

Singular.	Sanskrit.		Zend	Greek.	Latin.	Gothic.	Ang.-Sax.
Nom. m.	sa-s	hō		ὁ	is-te	sa	se
Nom. n.	ta-t	ta-ḍ		τό	is-tu-d	tha-ta	that
Acc. m.	ta-m	tḕ-m		τόν	is-tu-m	tha-na	thone
Acc. n.	ta-t	ta-ḍ		τό	is-tu-d	tha-ta	that
Instr.	tḗ-na	(tā)		—	—	thē	—
Dat.	tá-smâ-i	(ta-hmâ-i)		—	—	tha-mma	thám
Abl.	tá-smâ-t	—		—	—	—	thy
Gen.	tá-sya	(ta-hē)		τοῖο	is-tius (is-to-ius)	this	thæs
Loc.	tá-sm-in	(ta-hmi)		τῷ	is-tî (is-to-i)	—	—

DEMONSTRATIVE PRONOUNS 167

		Sanscrit.	Zend.	Greek.	Latin.	Gothic.	Ang.-Sax.
Plur.							
Nom.	m.	tê	tê	τοί, οἱ	is-ti	tha-i	—
	n.	tấ-ni	tâ	τά	is-ta	thô	thá
Acc.	m.	tấ-n	(ta-n)	τό·νς, το·ὑς	is-tô-s	tha-ns	thá
	n.	tấ-ni	tâ	τά	is-ta	thô	thá
Instr.		tấ-is	(tâ-is)	—	—	—	—
D. Abl.		tế-bhyas	taii-byô	—	is-ti-s	tha-im	thám
Gen.		tế-shâm	(tai-shañm)	τῶν	is-tô-rum	thi-zê	tha-ra
Loc.		tế-shu	(tai-shwa)	τοί-σι	—	—	—
Dual.							
N. Acc.		tâu, tâ	tâo, tâ	τώ	—	—	—
I. D. Abl.		tấ-bhyâm	(taii-bya)	τοῖν	—	—	—
G. L.		tấ-yôs	(tê-yo)	τοῖν	—	—	—

Fem. Sing.	Sanskrit.	Zend.	Greek.	Latin.	Gothic.	Ang.-Sax.
Nom.	sâ	hâ	ἁ, ἡ	is-ta	sô	seó
Acc.	tâ-m	(tā-ṁm)	τἀ-ν, τἠ-ν	is-ta-m	thô	thâ
Instr.	tâ-yâ	(tā-hmya)	—	—	—	—
Dat.	tâ-syâi	ta-ṅhâi	—	—	—	—
Abl.	tâ-syâs	ta-ṅhâḍ	—	is-ta(d)	thi-za	thæ-re
Gen.	tâ-syâs	ta-ṅhâo	τᾶ-ς, τῆ-ς	is-tius-s	thi-zos	thy
Loc.	tâ-syâm	ta-hmya	τῇ	is-ti	—	thæ-re
Plur.						
Nom.	tâ-s	(tâ-o)	ταί, αἱ	is-tæ	thô-s	thâ
Acc.	tâ-s	(tâ-o)	τἀ-ς	is-tâs	thô-s	thâ
Instr.	tâ'-bhis	(tâ-bis)	—	—	—	—
D. Abl.	tâ'-bhyas	(tâ-byô)	—	is-tis	thæ-im	thǽm
Gen.	tâ'-sâm	ta-oṅhanhm	τά-ων, τῶν	is-tâ-rum	thi-zo	thâ-ra
Loc.	tâ'-su	tâ-hwa	ταῖ-ση	—	—	—
Dual						
N. Acc.	tê	tê	τἀ	—	—	—
I. D. Abl	tâ'-bhyâm	tâ-bya	τα-ῖν	—	—	—
G. L.	tâ-yôs	—	τα-ῖν	—	—	—

The Nominative singular, Masc. and Fem., has a stem, *sa*, *sâ*, different from the rest of the pronoun. The Loc. **sá**-*smin* in the Védas, the Latin archaic forms **sum**, **sam**, **sôs**, for *eum*, *eam*, *eôs*, and **sa**psa for *ea-ipsa*, as well as the Greek σή-μερον, σή-τες, render it probable that this stem (*sa*) was at first completely declined, and that in the above forms we have parts of two separate pronouns, just as several languages form the substantive verb from two or more roots, which were each originally fully conjugated. Possibly also the Greek plurals *οἱ*, *αἱ*, are further remains of this once complete pronoun, whilst τοι, ται belong to the other.

The *stem* in the rest of the pronoun undergoes but slight changes. In Sanskrit the Masc. and Neut. is sometimes *tâ* or *tê* in accordance with general usage, whilst in the Fem. the vowel is in some cases shortened. In Zend the instances adduced are mostly conjectural. In Greek the stem is preserved with great regularity in all genders. In Latin the stem does not appear separately as a pronoun, but it is preserved in several adverbs and conjunctions, i. e. **tu**-*m*, **tu**-*nc*, **ta**-*m*, **ta**-*ndem*, **ta**-*men*, **ta**-*lis*, **ta**-*ntus*, **to**-*t*, **to**-*tidem*, **to**-*ties*. As a pronoun it is compounded with *is* in *is*-**te**, of which the *s* may be the Nom. sign, as in *is*, *ea*, *id*. In this compound form it is probably of late origin, and for this reason it has the same stem in the Nom. Singular as elsewhere. In Gothic the stem assumes the regular forms **tha, thi, thô**, and in Anglo-Saxon **thæ, thŷ, thâ.**

The *endings* in Sanskrit are the same as in the *a* stems of nouns, with the insertion of -*sma* in the Dat., Abl., and Loc. Sing., and the addition of *n* in this last case. The Nom. Masc. also omits the case sign generally in the singular, and has *ê* = *a-i* for *âs* in the Nom. plural.

The Gen. plural has *-s-âm*. In Greek the declension agrees with that of nouns, omitting the case sign in the Nom. Sing. Masc. In Latin the greatest deviation from the nominal declension is in the Gen. singular *-íus* for a. *-a-sya*, *s* being dropped, *a+y* becoming *í*, and *a* becoming *u*. The final *s* causes some difficulty, but we see the tendency to introduce that letter in the first syllable *is-* of this pronoun, and in the Neut. *felix*, 'happy.' It may here also be an inorganic addition, which does not admit and does not require any further explanation. The Nom. Sing. Masc. has no case sign, *te* being a weakened form of the stem. In Gothic and Anglo-Saxon the endings require no special remark.

The same stem occurs in the Latin words *i-dem*, 'the same;' *qui-dem*, 'indeed;' *quí-dam*, 'some one,' as well as in **dum**, 'whilst;' **dêmum**, 'at length;' **dônec**, 'until;' **dudum**, 'before;' **dênique**, 'then.' *d* for *t* appears in a. *i-dam*; z. **dêm**, **dim**, for *têm*; gr. δέ, 'and.' In ὅδε, 'this' (Hom. Dat. plural τοίσδεσσι, τοίσδεσι), the two forms of the same stem appear combined, just as in the Latin *tandem*, 'at length.' Αὐ-τό-ς, 'he,' is a similar compound to the L. *is-te* and a. *ê-tá*; and οὗ-το-ς, 'this,' for ὁ-αυ-τος, consists of three pronominal stems. Bopp considers *ja, jav*, in *-aû-ja, -aû-jav*, etc., to be of the same origin. That the forms with *t* and *d* were originally identical is rendered probable by such words as l. *dêmum* compared with gr. τῆμος, 'then,' and s. *tâ'vat*; L. *dônec*, with gr. τηνίκα, 'at that time of day.'

The stem *ta* also forms a compound with *ya*, the stem-vowel of the first part being dropped. It thus forms Nom. Singular M. *sya*, F. *syâ*, N. *tya-t*, and is declined like *ta*.

I.

205. The pronominal stem *i* appears in several languages. In Sanskrit it forms part of the pronoun, M. **ay**-*ám*, N. **i**-*dám*, F. **iy**-*ám*. It is also used in several indeclinable words in Sanskrit and Zend, e. g. s. **i**-*tás*, 'from here;' **i**-*há* (for *i-dha*), z. **i**-*dha*, **i**-*thra*, 'here;' s. **i**-*ti*, z. **i**-*tha*, l. **i**-*ta*, 'so;' s. **i**-*dâ'nîm*, 'now;' **i**-*tthám*, 'so;' *chêt* (=*cha-it*), 'if;' *nêt* (=*na-it*), 'if not;' z. *nô-id*, 'not;' s. **i**-*tara-s*, 'the other;' **i**-*dŕśa*, 'such;' **iy**-*át*, 'so much.' In Greek, there is no pronoun of this stem, nor any trace of one, except perhaps the Acc. ἴ-ν. But the demonstrative *ι* added to many words, as ὀυτοσ-ί, 'this one,' etc., preserves the stem. In Latin, *i-s*, *e-a*, *i-d*, 'this,' is fully declined, the stem fluctuating, as is frequently the case in this language, between *i* and *e*, and some of the forms, as *e-u-m*, etc., having also been adapted, by the addition of *u*, to the second declension of nouns. An older form *i-m*, however, remains. The same stem appears also in **i**-*terum*, 'again;' **i**-*mmo*, 'nay,' for=*i*-smo-d = s. *i-smâ-t*. In Gothic the stem undergoes but slight modifications, and the endings are regular, e. g. :

		Nom.	Acc.	Dat.	Gen.
Sing.	m.	i-s	i-na	i-mma	i-s
	n.	i-t			
Plur.	m.	ei-s	i-ns	i-m	i-zê
	n.	ij-a			

A.

Another pronominal root of extensive application is *a*, which furnishes some of the cases of *i-dám* in Sanskrit,

e. g. Dat. a-*smá'i*, Abl. a-*smá't*, Loc. a-*smín*, etc. It is used in the adverbial forms á-*tra*, 'here;' a-*tás*, 'hence;' a-*dyá*, 'this day.' The usual Feminine form í has become *iy*, as in the Nom. singular **iy**-*ám*. Some cases combine *a* with *na*, e. g. Instr. singular a-*né'-na* (a-na-i-na). There is the same compound in Latin e-**nl**-*m*, 'for,' and the second part of it in **na**-*m*, 'for,' **nu**-*nc*, 'now,' **ne**-*mpe*, 'surely,' **nu**-*m*, **ne**. The Greek words νί-ν, 'him,' etc., νύ, 'well,' νῦ-ν, 'now,' as well as the Sanskrit **nu**, appear to contain the same root *na*. This root also furnishes the negative particles, s. **na**, gr. νη-, l. **ne**-, **nl**-, go. **ni**, a. s. **ne**, Old Engl. **ne**. The compound form *ana* appears in the conditional particle, gr. ἄν, l. **an**, go. **an** (not in a. s.), old e. **an**, 'if.' The following are instances of triple compounds with *a*, viz. a-*na-ya*, a-*na-tara*, which become a-*nyá-s*, a-*ntará-s*, 'other;' gr. ἄ-λλος, with change of *n* to *l* and assimilation of *y*; l. a-*lius* (with *y* changed to *i*), a-*ller*; go. a-*lja*, a-*nthara*; e. e-*l-se*, as an adverb, 'otherwise;' e. o-*ther* and a. s. ó-*dher*, with the *l* or *n* dropped after changing the vowel to *ó*.

AVA.

In Sanskrit *ava* has ceased to be used as a pronoun, but appears as a preposition, e. g. **ava**-*tar*, 'to come down.' In Zend it retains its pronominal character. In Greek it is compounded with *ta*, forming αὐ-τό-ς, in which and many similar forms the second *a* is omitted; αὐ-θι, 'in this place,' as a Locative, and αὐ-θεν as an Ablative, belong to the simple pronoun. αὐ has probably lost a case-ending. In αὐ-τάρ it is combined with the comparative suffix. In the l. **au**-*tem*, 'but,' the last syllable may be the superlative termination; in **au***t*

perhaps for *au-ti,* the ending is the same as in *u-ti,*
i-ti-dem, and s. *i-ti,* 'so.' *ov* is a more usual representative of a. *av* than *av*: hence we have *oû-v,*
'then,' *oủ,* 'not.' In go. **au-**k (a. s. **â-**c, ' but '), e. **ê-**ke,
the same pronoun appears, with a demonstrative particle, as in *mi-k,* etc.

Relative Pronouns. YA.

The Relative pronoun *ya* is declined in Sanskrit like
ta. In the Greek ὅς, ἥ, ὅ, the *spiritus asper,* as in
many other cases, is for Sanskrit *y*. In Zend this
pronoun has a demonstrative meaning. It is preserved
in go. **ei** and **ja-***bai* for *ja-ba,* 'if;' a. s. **gi-***f,* pronounced
yif, e. **l-***f.* The ending is the same as in the Interrogative *i-bai, i-ba.* Bopp supposes this *ba* (where *b* was
probably pronounced *v*) to be for s. *va,* which brings it
still nearer to the English *if,* where both syllables are
greatly abbreviated, viz. *i* standing for *ya,* and *f* for *va.*
Further, go. **ja-***u,* ' whether,' for *ja-v,* and that for *ja-va,*
preserves the same elements; go. **ju**, 'now,' 'already,'
l. **ja-***m,* are of the same origin. The Latin *m* for *v*
corresponds to l. *mare* for s. *vari.* Gothic **ja-***i,* **ja** (e.
yea), and **ja-***h,* 'also,' with an ending like the Latin *que*
in *quo-que,* 'also,' belong to the same root. Engl. **ye-***t*
is combined with the same particle as *na* is in s. *nêt*
for *na-it.*

Interrogative Pronouns. KA.

206. The root of the Interrogative has three forms
in Sanskrit, *ka, ku, ki,* all probably modifications of the
same original. The first is the more extensively applied,
and was doubtless originally complete in Sanskrit as in
Zend, Greek, and Latin; for the Nom. and Acc. singular

174 PRONOUNS

Neut. *kat*, instead of which *kim* is used, appears in *kách-chit* for *kat-chit*, and in *kád-adhwan*, 'a bad street,' lit. 'what a street.' The ordinary Greek form would be κο, which is also preserved in the Ionic dialect, e. g. κό-τε, 'once,' κῶ-ς, 'how?' κό-τερον, 'whether?' κό-σος, 'how great?' κο-ῖος, 'of what kind;' but in Attic Greek the consonant is changed to π, e. g. πό-τε, πῶ-ς, πό-τερον, πό-σος, πο-ῖος. The Latin **qui** also, in some cases, belongs to the *o* and *a* declensions, which answer to the Sanskrit *a* and *á*. It has the Latin characteristic *u* after the guttural. In the Nom. singular Fem. the *e* in **qua**-*e*, as well as in *ha-e-c*, is obscure. The forms of the go. **hva** belong to the same root, as well as the Anglo-Saxon **hwâ**, and English *who* (with an inversion in the order of the consonants) for *hwo*. The *h* in these languages regularly answers to Sanskrit *k*, and the *w* is developed similarly to the Latin *u*.

The second form of the Interrogative, *ku*, appears in some adverbs, e. g. **kû**-*tra*, 'where;' **kû**-*tas*, 'whence,' etc. The Latin forms which seem to belong to this stem, viz. **cu**-*jus*, 'of whom,' **cu**-*i*, 'to whom,' etc., are more probably abbreviations of *quo-jus*, *quo-i*, etc., where there is a similar curtailment of the first syllable as in the pronunciation of the English *who* for *hwo*, in which *o* is omitted and *w* sounded as *oo*. *ku* is used like *kat* in depreciatory compounds, **ku**-*tanu*, 'ugly-bodied,' lit. 'of what a body.' l. **u**-*ter* has lost the guttural which is preserved in go. **hva**-*thar*, a. s. **whæ**-*dher*, e. **whe**-*ther*. It is also wanting in L **u**-*bi*, **u**-*n-de* (but *ali-cu-bi*, *ali-cun-de*), **u**-*nquam*, **u**-*squam*, **u**-*spiam*, **u**-*sque*.

The third stem, *ki*, is used in Sanskrit to form the

Nom. and Acc. Singular Neut. **ki**-*m*, with the ending
of Neuter nouns. That *ki-t* was earlier in use seems
probable from l. **qui**-*d*. A Masc. **ki**-*s* is also employed
in the Vêda compounds *na*-**kís**-*s*, 'no one;' *má*-**kís**-*s*,
'let no one.' This stem is used in **kí**-*díža*, 'like what;'
kíy-*at*, 'how much;' **hi**, 'for.' Here *h* is for *k*, as in
hṛd compared with l. *cord*-, 'heart.' A similar change
appears in s. **hy**-*as* for *hi-as*, and this for *ki-divas*, gr.
χϑὲs with 9 inserted, l. **he**-*ri* (*hesternus*), go. **gi**-*s-tra*,
a. s. **gy**-*sternlic dæg*, e. **ye**-*s-ter-day*. Some confirmation of this etymology of *hyas* is derived from s.
žwas, perhaps for *ku-as*, 'to-morrow.' The abbreviation of words causes less difficulty in these cases than
the application of the interrogative pronoun in such a
sense. The familiar designations of time, however, generally involve the strangest modifications of language,
e. g. s. *parut*, 'in last year,' from *pára vatsá*. **qui**-*s*
and **hi**-*c* are Latin pronouns formed from this stem.
The latter has *h* instead of the original guttural. The *u* is
preserved in Gen. and Dat. **hu**-*jus*, **hu**-*ic*, and the original vowel lost as in *cu-jus*, *cu-i*. **qui**-*a* is the regular
Neuter plural, and **qu**-*és* the old Masc. Plural. Plautus
has Gen. plural **qui**-*um*. The stem appears in **ci**-*s*,
ci-*tra*, 'on this side,' retaining the guttural, but omitting the usual *u*. In **hi**-*c*, 'this,' the affixing of the
guttural at the end may have been a reason for changing the initial to *h*.

This final particle appears in different forms, as *c, ce,
que, quam, pe, piam*. It is from the same interrogative
stem, and is often affixed to interrogative pronouns.
The doubling of interrogatives destroys the interro-
gation, just as doubling a negative destroys the negation,
e. g. *quis*, 'who?' compared with *quisque*, 'whoever;'
quid, 'what,' compared with *quippe* (for quid-pe), 'what-

ever.' In Gothic *uh* is the representative of this particle, e.g. *hvas* = quis, and *hvaz-uh* = quis-que; *hvó* = quæ, and *hvo-h* = quæ-que. Does not the English *whoso* preserve a remains of this compound? In that case *s* would be the Nom. sign, and the particle reduced to a vowel. As in the other examples quoted, *who* is interrogative and *whos-o* indefinite. Of this compound form,

e. *whos*   =   go. *hvaz*   =   l. *quis*.
e. *ó*   =   go. *uh*   =   l. *qus*.
e. *whosó*   =   go. *hvazuh*   =   l. *quisque*.

The Gothic Dat. **hi**-*mma*, Acc. **hi**-*na*, Neut. Acc. **hi**-*ta*, are from this same stem, with the usual *h* for an older *k*. The adverb **hi**-*dré*, a. s. **hi**-*dher* and **hi**-*der*, as well as the English **hi**-*ther*, has the comparative ending. go. **hê**-*r*, in compounds *hir* (e.g. **hi**-*r-i*, **hi**-*r-ja-ts*, **hi**-*r-ji-th*, second person Sing., Dual, Plur. = 'come here'), and e. **he**-*re*, have the same ending, *r*, as *hvar*, 'where;' *thar*, 'there;' and exhibit the stem under consideration as *hi*, *he*. In Anglo-Saxon, **hê**-*r*, *thæ*-*r*, *hwæ*-*r* have the same ending. In Greek τί-s, τί-νο-s, 'who?' τί-ν, τι-νό-ς, 'some one,' originally identical, have τ for κ, like τέσσαρες, πέντε, so that the guttural of this pronoun is in Greek represented by all three classes of consonants, e.g. κῶς, πῶς, τίς. So also κα-ί, 'and,' for καιτ, corresponds to s. *chét* for **cha**-*it*, the first part of which, *cha* for *ka*, is used as a conjunction, and is the pronominal stem in its first form.

c) DERIVATIVE ADJECTIVE PRONOUNS.

207. This class of derivatives is formed by the terminations *ka*, *ĭya*, *vant*, *ti*, *dṛẑ*.

DERIVATIVE ADJECTIVE PRONOUNS 177

kā forms *máma*-**ká**, 'my,' *táva*-**ká**, 'thy,' from *mama, táva*; and in the Vêdas *asmá'*-**ka**, 'our,' *yushmá'*-**ka**, 'your,' from *asmát, yushmát*.

ï'ya forms *mad*-**i'ya**, 'my;' *twad*-**i'ya**, 'thy;' *as-mad*-**i'ya**, 'our;' *yushmad*-**i'ya**, 'your;' *tad*-**i'ya**, 'belonging to that one;' *sarv*-**i'ya**, 'belonging to all.' The words derived from the personal pronouns are formed from the Ablative case, whose *t* is softened to *d* between vowels. In Greek the ending -ιο-ς preserves this formative: ἴδ-ιο-ς, 'one's own,' from ιδ-= l. *id*, or for ἴδ, and that for σFιδ=s. *swat*, from the possessive pronoun *swa-s*; πο-ῖο-ς, 'of what kind;' το-ῖο-ς, 'of that kind;' ὁ-ῖο-ς, 'of which kind.' Bopp thinks this formative *ï'ya* is represented in Gothic by *a*, and the Ablative *d* (for *t*) by *r*, in the words *unsa-r-a*, *unka-r-a*, 'our;' *izva-r-a*, *inqva-r-a*, 'your.' If so, the *r* in the English words *our, your*, is a representative of the Ablative sign *d* (for *t*).

vant in certain cases is regularly weakened to *vat* or *vân*. It forms *tá'*-**vant**, 'so much;' *yá'*-**vant**, 'how much;' *kiy*-**ant** (dropping *v*), *iy*-**ant**. The Zend has Acc. *ch*-**want**-*ĕm*, Nom. *ch*-**wanz**, dropping the stem-vowel and preserving *v* (w) of the formative. In τῆ-μο-ς, 'then,' ἦ-μο-ς, 'when,' *v* is changed to *m*, and *μο* stands for s. *vat*. In Latin *qu*-**ant**-*us*, 'how much,' *t*-**ant**-*us*, 'so much,' both the stem-vowel and *v* are dropped; whilst *v* is changed to *l*, and *a* to *e*, in *opu-lent*-*us*, 'wealthy,' *viru*-**lent**-*us*, 'poisonous,' etc. In Gothic this formative appears as -*laud*- in *hvê*-**laud**-*s* = quantus, and in *sva*-**laud**-*s*.

ti forms *ká*-**ti**, *yá*-**ti**, 'how much;' *tá*-**ti**, 'so much.' In Latin *quo*-**t**, 'how many;' *to*-**t**, 'so many,' where the final vowel is dropped.

dṛś (also *dṛśa, dṛksha*), from *dṛś*, 'to look,' forms

N

many derivatives denoting 'resemblance to,' 'looking like,' e. g. *kí*-**dŕž**, 'like what;' *tá*-**dŕž**, 'like that,' etc. This *d* appears as *l* in several other languages; and *ž*, originally a guttural, appears as *k*. In Greek we find πη-λίκ-ος, 'how great;' τη-λίκ-ος, 'so great,' etc. In Latin *quá*-ll-*s*, 'like what;' *tá*-ll-*s*, 'such;' *æquá*-ll-*s*, 'equal,' where *k* is dropped, etc. In Gothic *hvé*-**leik**-*s*, *sva*-**leik**-*s*, etc. In Anglo-Saxon *hwy*-**lc**, *swy*-**lc**. In English *whi*-**ch**, *su*-**ch**, etc., the formative is preserved only in *ch* for the final guttural, whilst the meaning has been retained in *such*, but lost in *which*. The full form, however, is preserved in the adjective *like*. The *l* is preserved also in the corresponding German words *welch*-, *solch*-, and in the Scotch *quhilc*. The same formative also appears in the general ending, a. s. *-lic*, e. *-ly*; e. g. *leóf*-**lic**, *love*-**ly**.

Some possessive adjectives have only the pronominal stem, without any formative element, e. g. a. *swa*-*s*, *suá*, *swa*-*m*; gr. ἐμό-*s*, σό-*s*, ὅ-*s*, σφό-*r*; L *meu*-*s*, *tuu*-*s*, *suu*-*s*.

d) PRONOMINAL ADVERBS.

208. Pronominal Adverbs are formed by *tra*, *dha*, *tas*, *dú*, *tham*, *thá*, *ti*.

tra forms adverbs of *place*, e. g. s. *á*-**tra**, 'here;' *tá*-**tra**, 'there;' *amú*-**tra**, 'there;' *kú*-**tra**, 'where?' *yá*-**tra**, 'where.' z. *i*-**thra**, 'here;' *ava*-**thra**, 'there;' *ya*-**thra**, 'where.' L *ci*-**tra**, 'on this side;' *ul*-**tra**, 'on that side.' go. *hva*-**thrô**, 'whither;' *tha*-**thrô**, 'thither.' a. s. *hwœ*-**der**, *thi*-**der** (*d* probably pronounced as *dh*). e. *whi*-**ther**, *thi*-**ther**.

dha also forms adverbs of *place*. In Sanskrit it assumes the form *ha*, e. g. *i*-**há**, 'here;' in the Vēdas, *kú*-**ha**, 'where?' The preposition *sa*-**há**, 'with,' is similarly formed. z. ka-**dha,** 'here.' gr. ἐν-θα, ἐνταῦ-θα, 'here,' etc. l. perhaps in-**de,** 'from there,' etc. go. hva-**th,** or hva-**d,** 'where;' alja-**th,** 'elsewhere;' jain-**d** (a. s. geon-**d,** c. yon-**der**), 'there;' i-**th,** 'but.'

tas forms adverbs expressing 'origin' or 'source,' e. g. s. kú-**tas,** 'whence?' tá-**tas,** 'thence;' yá-**tas,** 'whence.' gr. πό-θεν, 'whence;' τό-θεν, 'thence;' ὅ-θεν, 'whence.' l. perhaps (c)un-**de,** 'whence;' **de,** in-**de,** 'thence.' The full form appears in swarga-**tás**; l. cœli-**tus,** 'from heaven;' gr. ἐν-τός, l. in-**tus,** 'within.'

dâ forms adverbs of time, e. g. ka-**dấ**, 'when?' ta-**dấ**, 'then;' ya-**dấ**, 'when;' éka-**dấ**, 'once;' sa-**dấ**, 'always;' ta-**dấ**-nim, 'then;' i-**dấ**-nim, 'now.' In the Vêdas, i-**dấ**. gr. perhaps πό-τε, 'once;' τό-τε, 'then;' ὅ-τε, 'when;' perhaps also ἤ-δη, 'already,' for ἤ-δη = ya-dá, with a long vowel, like ἤ-παρ for ya-kṛt.

tham, thâ, ti, form adverbs of manner, e. g. a. ka-**thám,** 'how?' it-**thám,** 'so;' anyú-**thà,** 'otherwise;' tá-**thâ,** 'so;' yá-**thâ,** 'as;' sarvá-**thâ,** 'every way;' i-**ti,** 'so;' ú-**ti** (prep.), 'over,' 'beyond;' u-**t** (prep.), 'upwards.' z. ui-**ti,** 'so.' l. i-**tem,** 'likewise;' au-**tem,** 'but;' i-**ta,** 'so;' aliu-**ta,** i-**ti,** i-ti-dem, u-ti, u-ti-nam, u-ti-que. Sanskrit áti appears in l. a-t-avus, 'primitive ancestor.'

X. VERBS.

a) THE CONSTRUCTION OF VERBS.

209. The verb is the most important part of speech. It sometimes forms a complete sentence by itself, and no opinion or determination or wish can be expressed without it. It undergoes a greater variety of changes than any other word. In some American languages it is said that a single verb may appear in six thousand different forms. So great a variety does not exist in any Indo-European language; yet in Sanskrit about a thousand possible forms, without including participles, may be assigned to one verb. In Greek, and still more in Latin, the number is very much reduced. In modern languages, the analytical method has brought the verb to an almost Chinese simplicity. An English verb, for instance, does not assume more than half a dozen different forms; and when we remember that the same word at one time had all the varieties which are found in the Sanskrit verb, we gain some idea of the great change which has been gradually made in the language of man. The method pursued has been the analytical, not the synthetical. The progress has been from the complex to the simple. History does not present to us a language growing out of a rude state, developing new forms, and in process of time acquiring expansion and symmetry. On the contrary, we see that it is most perfect in its earlier history. We see its ornamental leaves gradually fall off, its pliant branches broken, and ultimately but little remaining besides the gnarled trunk.

What is thus illustrated in language as a whole, is specially illustrated by the changes which the verb has undergone. Our examples, therefore, will necessarily be drawn chiefly from the older languages, and be comparatively few from those now spoken.

A verb may consist of several distinct elements. The Latin verb *amâbantur*, for example, may be thus divided: am-â-ba-nt-u-r. Of these parts, *am* is the root which appears in all the forms; *amâ* is the stem of several tenses, etc.; *ba* is the sign of the Imperfect Tense; *nt* is the sign of the Third Person Plural; and *r* is the sign of the Passive Voice, whilst *u* is merely a connecting vowel inserted between the consonants *nt* and *r*, without affecting the sense of the word at all. Again, in *amârentur*, *re*, like *ba*, represents the Imperfect Tense, but differs from *ba* in denoting also the Conjunctive Mood.

In verbs, therefore, besides the root or stem, there may be expressions for Voice, Mood, Tense, and Person.

b) THE THREE VOICES.

210. There are three *Voices*, so far as the *meaning* of verbs is concerned. The Sanskrit has separate forms for all three; in other languages there are only two forms, and in some only one.

The three forms are the Active, Middle, and Passive. In Sanskrit the Active is called *parasmaipadam*, 'affecting another,' from *parasmai*, Dative Singular of *para*, 'another,' and *padam*, from the root *pad*, 'fall,' 'fall upon.' It is so called because the action expressed by the verb is not aimed at the acting person, but at some one else, e. g. 'I strike,' i. e. not myself, but some one else. The Middle is called in Sanskrit *âtmanêpadam*, 'self-affecting,' from âtmanê, Dative Singular of *âtman*, 'self,' and *padam*. In this case the person acting is also the object acted upon, which, as there is no such verbal form in English, has to be expressed by the addition of a pronoun, e. g. 'I strike *myself*.'

The terms Active and Middle are clearly inappropriate, for the Middle is as active as the so-called Active; and the word Middle, in itself, conveys no notion of the thing intended, but merely that, as in Greek, where this term is chiefly applied, since it is in some things like the Active, and in some things like the Passive, it may be conveniently supposed to be half-way between them. But these terms are so widely used and so generally understood, that we shall adhere to them.

211. In Sanskrit the Middle is distinguished from the Active by the endings affixed to the stem; e. g. the Third Person Singular has -*ti* in the Active and -*tê* (for ta + i) in the Middle. The Passive has the same ending as the Middle, but *ya* is inserted between it and the root. Hence for Mid. -*tê* we have Pass. -*ya-tê*, e. g. from the root **dwish**, 'hate,' 3 Sing. Act. *dwésh-ti*, 'he hates' (some one else); Mid. *dwêsh-tê*, 'he hates himself;' Pass. *dwêsh-yá-tê*, 'he is hated' (by some one else).

In Greek the Middle form is also used to express the Passive voice, e. g. 3 Sing. Act. τύπτ-ει (for τυπτ-ε-τι), 'he strikes' (some one else); Mid. and Pass. τύπτ-ε-ται, 'he strikes himself' and 'he is struck' (by some one else). There are, however, a few special Passive forms.

In Latin likewise one form serves for both Middle

and Passive verbs. It consists in affixing the reflexive pronoun *se* to the Active. We thus from the 3 Sing. Act. *amat* obtain *amat-u-se*, the *u* being introduced as a connecting vowel between the consonants, or *tu* may be a modified form of the pronoun used to express the Third Person Singular, which in Sanskrit is *ti*, in Greek σι. These latter instances make it probable that in Latin also, at an earlier period, a vowel followed such forms as *amat*. Which of the above explanations of *u* is adopted will depend on the period in the development of the language at which it is supposed the Middle and Passive were formed, whether before or after the loss of the vowel in the personal endings. It is, further, one of the euphonic laws of the Latin language, that *s* between two vowels is softened to *r*, and hence from amatuse we obtain amature, and from this again, by the very common loss of the final vowel, *amâtur*. Such forms ending in *r* occur both as Deponent verbs, which exhibit instances of Middle verbs (i. e. verbs with both Active and Reflexive meaning), and as Passive verbs.

212. The above will perhaps throw some light upon the formation of the Middle verbs in Greek. For whilst in Latin *s* between two vowels is usually softened to *r*, in Greek, when occurring in the same position, it is entirely dropped. Indeed, the reflexive pronoun itself, in Greek, is already changed from σε or σι to ἱ; it is therefore easy to suppose that -τασι would become -ται. This view gains confirmation from the fact that it brings the Greek and Latin languages into agreement where they have been supposed to be utterly at variance; for they thus appear to agree, not only in each having one form for both voices, but in both having the same form.

Bopp regards the Middle forms in Sanskrit and Greek as resulting from the repetition of the personal pronouns, i. e. a. *-mê, -sê, -tê*, etc., for *mami, sasi, tati*, etc.; gr. *-μαι, -σαι, -ται*, etc., for *μαμι, σασι, τατι*, etc. But this supposes not only the dropping of *s* and *t*, which may perhaps be referred to general laws, but also of *m*, which cannot be so justified. Besides, whilst this method *cannot* have originated the Latin forms, the employment of the reflexive pronoun *may* have originated both the Sanskrit and Greek, as it certainly has the Latin, forms.

The following are the endings of the singular in the present tense:

	Sanskrit.	Greek.	Latin.		
1. Act.	mi	μι	m		
Mid.	ê	μαι	r	from	masi
2. Act.	si	σι	s		
Mid.	sê	σαι	ris	„	sasi
3. Act.	ti	τι	t		
Mid.	tê	ται	tur	„	tasi

In Sanskrit the First Person drops both *m* and *s*, and then contracts a + i, as is usually done, to *ê*; the Second and Third Persons merely drop *s*, and make the same contraction of the vowels. In Greek all three persons are perfectly regular, there being in each only the omission of σ, which always takes place when it would be between two vowels. The preservation of *a*, though in the Active it is weakened to *ι*, is owing to the fact that it was followed by a consonant. The same phenomenon appears in Sanskrit, *tê* being for ta + i, whilst the

Active ends in *ti*. In Latin the First Person is more mutilated than in Sanskrit. The personal pronoun is altogether lost, and only the consonant (r) of the reflexive pronoun preserved. In the Second Person the personal pronoun appears as *ri* for *si*, the *s* being changed to *r* between two vowels. This has caused the reflexive pronoun to retain its original consonant (*s*). The usual change to *r* is prevented by the fact that the previous syllable (*rise*) begins with *r*. In the Third Person the final vowel is dropped. The personal pronoun appears as *tu*, the reflexive as *r*.

In the examination of these few forms we find a striking illustration of the uses of Comparative Grammar. What one language has lost the others have preserved. Thus the original forms may be constructed out of the fragments which are scattered abroad in various places, and what has become obscure in each language may be explained by the help of the rest. In the above instances, the *m* which has disappeared from the Sanskrit (*é*) and the Latin (*r*) is preserved in the Greek (μαι), the final vowel which is lost in Latin remains in Sanskrit and Greek, and the *s* which they have lost the Latin has retained.

The forms in the plural are the following:

		Sanskrit.	Greek.	Latin.		
1.	Act.	mas	μεν	mus		
	Mid.	mahê	μεθο	mur		from mahasi
2.	Act.	tha	τε	—		
	Mid.	dhwê	σθε	—	,,	dhwasi
3.	Act.	nti	ντι	nt		
	Mid.	ntê	νται	ntur	,,	ntasi

In Sanskrit all three persons have dropped *s*, as in the singular, and contracted the vowels *a*, *i*, in a regular way, to *ê*. In Greek the reflexive pronoun is entirely lost, except that the Third Person preserves *i* like the Sanskrit. The *a* of the First Person also shows that it was previously followed by the reflexive pronoun. From the Latin language alone it is not easy to say how the First Person (*mur*) was formed. If the vowel was originally short, *mur* may be merely the termination of the Active, with the necessary change of *s* to *r*, and the following part dropped; *mur* being, therefore, for mur-uri. But the tendency in the language, which caused the final syllable of all words ending in one consonant to be considered in later times as short, leaves us at liberty to suppose that the vowel, in this case, may have been originally long, and have arisen from the contraction of two vowels. A similar change of *û* to *u* appears in the ending of the Genitive Plural of nouns. (See Sect. **165**, p. 128.) The ending *mûr* would thus be for *muur*, where the first *s* of musus*i* is dropped, and the second preserved as *r*, the final vowel being omitted as usual. This point, which the other two languages above referred to leave in doubt, may be cleared up by a reference to the Lithuanian, which retains several forms elsewhere lost. In that language the corresponding syllable is long, which Schleicher (*Compendium*, p. 122) regards as exceptional, and as resulting from the affixing of a consonant to the short vowel of the Active. It is evidently the result of contracting two vowels together. Lith. *vėżame* = l. *vehimus*, the final consonant being lost. Lith. *vėżamės* = l. *vehimur*. The reflexive pronoun is here preserved as *s*, the rule in Latin which changes it to *r*, or that in Greek by which it is dropped, not applying in this case in Lithuanian. The vowel is long because originally the active *me* was not only followed by a consonant (*s*), but also by another vowel, as is manifest from the Active plural in the Vêdas, -*masi*. These two vowels contracted together form *ê*, and by affixing the reflexive pronoun we obtain *més* = 1. *mûr*.

This view is confirmed by the second person singular in Lithuanian, e. g. *vežês* = 1. *veheris*, in which *ê* does not arise from the preservation of an originally long vowel (Schleicher, *Comp*. p. 122), but from the contraction of two originally short ones; for both the vowels in the corresponding Latin word, and in similar forms in Sanskrit, are short. The pronominal sign, which is *s* in Sanskrit and *r* (between vowels) in Latin, is dropped in Lithuanian as it is in Greek, τύπτ-ῃ being for τυπτ-εσαι, and that for τυπτ-εσασι. We have here again an illustration of the way in which languages supply each other's defects. The Greek preserves the vowel of the reflexive pronoun as *ι* subscriptum, and loses the consonant (*ϱ*), whilst the Lithuanian preserves the consonant and loses the vowel (*ês*). There is the same mutual relation between Greek and Latin in the Third Person Plural, i. e. νται from νπασι, and *ntur* from *nturi*.

The Second Person presents the greatest anomalies; but, whatever view be adopted as to the origin of the Middle forms, these anomalies still remain in Sanskrit and Greek, whilst the Latin language avoids them by satisfying itself with participial forms ending in -*mini* = gr. -μενοι, s. -*manâs*.

The dual forms are:

	Sanskrit.			Greek.		
	1	2	3	1	2	3
Act.	vas	thas	tas	(μεν)	τον	τον
Mid.	vahê	thê	ê	μεθον	σθον	σθον

In Sanskrit, as far as regards the reflexive pronoun, the dual exactly coincides with the plural. In Greek the s of the pronoun, instead of being dropped, as in the plural, appears to have changed to ν, as it did in the First Person Plural Active, μεν for μες.

The secondary forms exhibit a still greater abbreviation than the primary in the Middle as well as the Active.

In the singular we have:

	Sanskrit.	Greek.	Latin.		
1. Act.	m	ν	m		
Mid.	ê, i	μην	r		from masi
2. Act.	s	s	s		
Mid.	thâs	σο	ris	„	sasi
3. Act.	t	—	t		
Mid.	ta	το	tur	„	tasi

In Sanskrit the First Person has ê, as in the primary forms for the first conjugation, but reduced to i for the second. The Second Person has th for the personal pronoun, which is t in the pronoun, though s in the verbal forms. The consonant of the reflexive pronoun is preserved, but the vowel lost as in Latin. In the Third Person a shows the pronoun formerly was added, for when nothing followed, ta was reduced to ti or t.

In Greek, again, the First Person preserves μ of the personal pronoun, whilst s of the reflexive pronoun is changed to ν, just as in the Active First Person Plural, -μεν for μες. In this case, therefore, μην is for μης from μασι. The ο of the Second and Third Persons indicates the previous presence of the reflexive pronoun in the form of ν.

In Latin the secondary do not differ from the primary forms.

In the plural we have:

	Sanskrit.	Greek.	Latin.	
1. Act.	ma	μεν	mus	
Mid.	mahi	μεθα	mur	from mahasi
2. Act.	ta	τε	—	
Mid.	dhwam	σθε	—	,, dhwasi
3. Act.	n, s	ν	nt	
Mid.	nta	ντο	ntur	,, ntasi

In Sanskrit the First and Third Persons have merely reduced $a+i$ of the primary forms to i and a. The Second Person preserves the consonant, and drops the vowel of the reflexive pronoun, as in the singular. The s, however, is reduced to a nasal (m), as in Greek.

In Greek the Third Person only differs from the primary forms; and here the ο, as in the singular, indicates the previous presence of ν for σ of the reflexive pronoun.

In the dual we have:

	Sanskrit.			Greek.		
Act.	va	tam	tâm	(μεν)	τον	την
Mid.	vahi	thâm	tâm	μεθον	σθον	σθην

The nasal in both these languages appears to be from the reflexive pronoun.

c) PERSONS.

213. The terminations which denote the First, Second, and Third Persons, are amongst the most interesting and instructive phenomena of language. They are most of them easily analysed, and illustrate the progressive transformation of grammar. They consist of the personal pronouns affixed to the verbal stems. The personal endings appear sometimes in a fuller, sometimes in a more mutilated form, and may accordingly be distinguished as *heavier* or primary, and *lighter* or secondary, endings. The former are affixed to the principal tenses (in Greek), viz. the Present, Future, and Perfect; the latter to the secondary tenses, viz. the Augmented Preterites (Imperfects and Aorists), as well as the Non-Indicative Moods, except the Lêṭ and the Greek Conjunctive. In Latin the First Person Singular preserves *m* of the lighter forms, e. g. *amabam*, 'I was loving;' *amem*, 'I may love:' but has lost *mi* of the heavier forms, e. g. *amo*, 'I love;' *amabo*, 'I shall love;' *amavi*, 'I loved.' The other parts have dropped the additional vowel (i) of the heavier forms, and thus the two classes in Latin are alike. In Gothic the heavier forms have preserved *t* and *nt* (as *th* and *nd*) of *ti* and *nti*, whilst the lighter have dropped the *t* which had no vowel after it. Compare *bair-i-*th, 'he beareth,' with s. bhár-a-ti; *bair-a-*nd, 'they bear,' with s. bhár-anti; but *bair-ai* with s. bhár-ê-t, 'he can bear.' As in Latin, in the First Person Singular, *mi* has disappeared, but *m* has been preserved (as *u*). Compare *bair-a*, 'I bear,' with s. bhár-â-mi, but *bair-a-***u**, 'I can bear,' with s. bhár-êy-am.

The First Person Singular.

214. The first personal pronoun has two stems, one for the Nominative case and the other for the oblique cases. The latter is *ma*, and in the weakened form -*mi* is employed in the primary, and still further reduced to -*m* in the secondary forms, as an affix, to denote the First Person Singular of verbs. The following instances are taken from the ten classes of Sanskrit verbs:

Primary Forms.

1st Conjugation, Present.

Class 1. 1. bô′dh-â-mi, 'I know'
 ,, 6. tud-â′-mi, 'I strike'
 ,, 4. zuch-yâ-mi, 'I am pure'
 ,, 10. chôr-âyâ-mi, 'I steal'

2nd Conjugation.

Class 2. 2. dwḗsh-mi, 'I hate'
 ,, 3. bibhar-mi, 'I bear'
 ,, 7. yunáj-mi, 'I join'
 ,, 5. chi-nó′-mi, 'I gather'
 ,, 8. tan-av′-mi, 'I stretch'
 ,, 9. yu-nâ′-mi, 'I bind'

Secondary Forms.

Imperfect (Single-formed Augmented Preterite).

á-bôdh-a-m, 'I was knowing'
á-tud-a-m, 'I was striking'
á-zuch-ya-m, 'I was pure'
á-chôr-aya-m, 'I was stealing'

á-dwḗsh-a-m, 'I was hating'
á-bibhar-a-m, 'I was bearing'
á-yunáj-a-m, 'I was joining'
á-chi-nav-a-m, 'I was gathering'
á-tan-av-a-m, 'I was stretching'
áyu-na-m, 'I was binding'

The primary forms always lengthen the characteristic vowel of the first conjugation to *â*, whilst the secondary forms leave the vowel short. The reason seems to be, that the heavier ending *mi* requires a stronger vowel to support it than the lighter ending *m*. The ending is made lighter in the secondary forms probably in consequence of the word being lengthened, here by the augment, and in the moods by the mood vowel.

Though the connecting vowel of the first conjugation is not lengthened in the secondary as it is in the primary forms, yet, on the other hand, a connecting vowel is introduced in the second conjugation, where *m* would otherwise follow a consonant or half-vowel.

In Greek the primary forms have -μι in the verbs corresponding to the Sanskrit second conjugation, and ω in the verbs corresponding to the Sanskrit first conjugation, where the connecting vowel may be supposed to be lengthened, according to the analogy of the Sanskrit, and -μι dropped. Thus we have ἵστη-μι, 'I stand,' and φέρ-ω, 'I bear.' In the secondary forms -ν occurs as the usual Greek equivalent for the Sanskrit *m* when final, e. g. in the Imperfect ἵστη-ν, 'I was standing,' and ἔ-φερ-ο-ν, 'I was bearing.'

In Latin this ending is almost universally lost, and -*o* left, like the ω in Greek verbs, in the primary forms, e. g. Present *st-o*, 'I stand;' *fer-o*, 'I bear.' There are a few exceptions, such as *su-m* and *inqua-m*, and even there only *m*, not *mi*, is preserved. In the secondary forms *m* is preserved as in Sanskrit and Greek (ν), e. g. Imperfect *staba-m*, 'I was standing,' and *fereba-m*, 'I was bearing.'

In Gothic the primary forms present only one instance of the preservation of -*m* for *mi* in the substantive verb *i-m*, 'I am;' and thus the work of destruction has gone further than even in Latin. In the other instances, e. g. *bair-a*, 'I bear,' etc., *a* is weaker than ω and ô in Greek and Latin. The secondary forms, however, preserve *u* for m, and in this vocalising of the consonant the language has again proved weaker than the Latin. Compare *bair-a-u*, 'I may bear,' with l. fer-a-m.

In Anglo-Saxon *eo-m*, and in English *a-m*, we have likewise the consonant of the original ending in a single word only. Elsewhere there is no trace of it.

The following list illustrates the formation of the First Person Singular:

THE FIRST PERSON

Sanskrit	Zend	Greek	Latin	Gothic	English
ás-mi	ah-mi	εἰ-μί	su-m	i-m	a-m
bhár-â-mi	bar-â-mi	φέρ-ω	fer-o	baír-a	'I bear'
váh-â-mi	vaz-â-mi	ἔχ-ω	veh-o	vig-a	{'I carry' 'wag-gon'}
(a)syâ-m	hyn-îm	ἔ(σ)ίη-ν	sie-m	sija-u	'I may be'
bháreya-m	—	φέροι-(μι)	fera-m	baíra-u	'I may bear'
ávaha-m	avuzê-m	εἶχο-ν	veheba-m	—	'I was carrying'

o 2

The First Person Plural.

216. The nominative plural of the pronoun in the Vêdas is *asmê*, probably for *masmê*, from ma-sma-i, including the pronominal particle *sma*. If this be the origin of the verbal affix, it has in most cases been greatly curtailed, which would not be surprising; for the addition of it as a whole would render the verbs very cumbersome, and we have seen that language resorts to many devices to prevent this. The Vêdas have the ending -*masi*, and the Zend -*mahi*, e. g. v. *dadmási* and z. *dadĕmahi*, 'we give.' They are the nearest approach to the supposed original *masmê*. In Sanskrit the primary forms have -*mas*, sometimes -*ma*, and the secondary forms regularly -*ma*. The connecting vowel of the first conjugation is lengthened as in the singular, e. g. *bhár-â-*mas and *bhár-â-*ma, 'we bear;' *sárp-â-*mas and *sárp-â-*ma, 'we creep;' *â-bhar-â-ma*, 'we were bearing.' The Greek has -μες in older and dialectic words, but elsewhere -μεν in both primary and secondary forms. The change of *s* to *v* is unusual, but not without example in other parts of the language, e. g. ἕρπ-ο-μες, 'we creep;' φέρ·ο-μες, 'we bear;' ἐ-φέρ-ο-μες, 'we were bearing.' The Latin likewise has but one form of this affix, i. e. -*mus*, e. g. *serp-i-*mus, *fer-i-*mus, *fer-e-ba-*mus. In Gothic the primary forms, as in the singular, have suffered greater loss than the secondary. For the Sanskrit -*mas* of the former we find only *m*, whilst the Sanskrit -*ma* of the latter is preserved entire, e. g. *bair-a-*m, 'we bear,' and *bair-ai-*ma, 'we may bear.' We see here the same relation between the endings and the previous syllable as in the Sanskrit forms *bó'dh-â-mi* and *á-bódh-a-m*; i. e. the

THE FIRST PERSON 197

stronger vowel *ai* sustains the heavier ending -*ma*, and the weaker vowel *a* the lighter ending -*m*. In Anglo-Saxon there is *n* in some forms, which may, however, be the third person used for the first. The English has entirely lost this affix.

The following list illustrates the First Person Plural:

Sanskrit.	Zend.	Greek.	Latin.	Gothic.	English.
s-mas	—	ἐσ-μέν	su-mus	siju-m	'we are'
bhárá-mas	bará-mahi	φέρο-μεν	feri-mus	baíra-m	'we bear'
váha-mas	—	ἔχο-μεν	vehi-mus	vigâ-m	'we carry'
syâ'-ma	—	εἴη-μεν	sî-mus	sijai-ma	'we may be'
bhárê-ma	barai-ma	φέροι-μεν	ferâ-mus	baíraí-ma	'we may bear'
ávahâ-ma	avazâ-ma?	εἴχο-μεν	veheba-mus	—	'we were carrying'

The First Person Dual.

216. The Sanskrit has *-vas* for the primary and *-va* for the secondary forms, differing from the plural affix in substituting *v* for *m*, a change which takes place in other parts of speech as well. Indeed, the plural of the first personal pronoun itself presents an instance of it in the nominative: **vayam** may be supposed to be for **mayam**, of which *am* is an affix as in *yúy-am*. We have, then, *may* or *ma+i*, which would be written *mé*, and differs from *masmé* (ma-sma+i, the supposed original of the Véda form *asmé'*) only in the absence of the particle *sma*, which is uniformly absent from the nominative in Sanskrit. *mé* would then correspond to *té*, Nom. Plur. of the third personal pronoun. If, then, *v* has resulted from an earlier *m*, the dual may be regarded as sprung from the plural. The first conjugation lengthens the connecting vowel to *á*, as in the singular and plural, e. g. *bhár-á-***vas**, 'we two bear;' *bhár-é-***va**, 'we two may bear.' In Gothic the Conjunctive has *-va* like the Sanskrit, e. g. *baír-ai-***va**, 'we two may bear;' the Present Ind. *-ôs* from *a-as*, and this from *a-vas*, e. g. *baír-ôs*, 'we two bear,' of which, however, properly only *-as* belongs to the affix; the Preterite has *-ú* for *uu*, and this for *u-v*, and again for *u-va*, e. g. *mag-ú*, 'we both could.' Here, again, only one *u* belongs to the affix. These cases also furnish instances of the stronger syllable supporting the heavier ending, and vice versâ. In Anglo-Saxon the verbs have no dual forms. In Greek the place of the First Person Dual is supplied by the forms of the First Person Plural. In Latin there is no dual.

The following list illustrates the First Person Dual:

Sanskrit.	Gothic.	English.
s-vas	sij-u	'we two are'
bhárâ-vas	bair-ôs	'we two bear'
váhâ-vas	vig-ôs	'we two carry'
syâ'-va	sijai-va	'we two may be'
bhárê-va	bairai-va	'we two may bear'
ávahâ-va	vag-û	'we two were carrying'

The Second Person Singular.

217. The second personal pronoun is in Sanskrit *twa* (probably from *tu*), a weakened form of which, -*si*, is employed as the verbal affix. The change of the consonant to -*s* is shown in the Greek pronoun, which is σύ. The secondary forms further reduce this affix to *s*, and euphonic laws in some cases change *si* to *shi*. The corresponding forms in Zend are -*hi* (for *si*) and -*s*, which is sometimes represented by -*o* as in the nominative of nouns, e. g. s. *bhávasi*, z. *bavahi*, 'thou art;' v. *kṛṇō'-shi*, z. *kěrěnůishi*, 'thou makest;' s. *ábrús* (ábravis), z. *mraus*, 'thou spakest;' s. *prú'zrâvayas*, z. *frazrávayō* (ō for *as*), 'thou didst cause to hear.' In Greek the full form -σι is found in old and dialectic forms, e. g. Doric ἐσ-σί, 'thou art;' but usually the ι is drawn back into the previous syllable, which is frequently the case in the Greek language when the consonant between it and a preceding vowel is not dropped, e. g. χαίρω for χαρίω. Thus both the primary and secondary forms in Greek end in *s*, e. g. τύπτε-ις (for τυπτ-ε-σι), 'thou strikest,' and ἔτυπτε-ς, 'thou wast striking.' In Latin likewise we have only -*s* in both primary and secondary forms, e. g. *amâs*, 'thou lovest;' *amâbas*, 'thou wast loving.' The vowel, however, in the primary forms may be supposed, as in Greek, to be incorporated in the preceding long syllable of the vowel stems, but preserved as a connecting vowel after the consonant stems, as in *leg-is*, 'thou readest,' etc. The Gothic also has the two forms -*is* and -*s*: gr. ἔχε-ις compared with go. *viga-is*, 'thou carriest,' and gr. εἴη-ς with go. *sijai-s*, 'thou mayest be.'

The original consonant of this affix was *t* (*twa*), and by a euphonic law in the Germanic languages this letter causes *t* of the root to become *s*; hence the Gothic verbs whose roots end in a dental terminate in -*st* in the Second Person Singular, e. g. *vaist*, 'thou knowest,' from the root *vid*; *baist*, from the root *bhid*. The same compound *st* was afterwards added to other verbs, and regarded as the normal ending of the Second Person Singular. This fact explains the -*st* of the corresponding English and German forms, e. g. *bringst*, *broughtest*, *praisest*, *praisedst*. In *art* the *s* has been softened to *r*. The *st* in the Latin Perfects is owing perhaps to a similar cause. In the Greek forms ἦσθα, 'thou wast,' and οἶσθα, 'thou knowest,' the dental affix of the latter has changed δ of οἶδα to σ, and in both cases σ has changed the following τ to θ. In several words, such as ἔφησθα, 'thou saidst,' for ἔφης, σθα has been used in imitation of οἶσθα, just as in Gothic *st* has been used for *t*.

The Imperative of the second conjugation in Sanskrit, and of the μι conjugation in Greek, has an aspirated affix, i. e. -*dhi* (sometimes weakened to -*hi*) in Sanskrit, -*dhi* (sometimes weakened to -*di*) in Zend, and -θι in Greek. This affix clearly contains the original dental of the pronoun, as does also the Latin Future Imperative amâ-to, 'love thou,' etc. But whence comes the aspiration in the former languages? In Greek the aspiration often serves as a substitute for σ. It may be so in this case: could it in the other languages, and, if so, from whence came the *s*?

The reduplicated Preterites have -*tha*, in which the aspiration may have resulted from the euphonic influence of some consonant in a particular case, and afterwards have been generalised by a process similar to that which gave rise to *st* in the Germanic languages. Bopp traces the aspiration to the *w* of the original pronoun.

The Second Person Singular is illustrated in the following list:

Sanskrit	Zend	Greek	Latin	Gothic	English	
á-si	a-hi	ἐσ-σί	e-s	i-s	a-rt	
bhára-si	bara-hi	φέρε-ις	fer-s	bair-is	bear-est	
váha-si	vaza-hi	ἔχ-ις	veh-is	vig-is		
syâ-s	hyâ-o	εἴη-ς	siê-s	sijai-s		'thou carriest'
bhárê-s	barôi-s	φέροι-ς	ferâ-s	bairai-s		'thou mayst be'
ávaha-s	avaz-ô	εἶχε-ς	vehebâ-s	—		'thou mayst bear'
						'thou wast carrying'

The Second Person Plural.

218. The Sanskrit and Zend both have -*tha* in the primary and -*ta* in the secondary forms; the Greek has -τε, the Latin -*tis*, and the Gothic -*th*, in both primary and secondary forms. The Latin has -*te* in the Imperative. There are no remains of it in English.

This ending seems to be formed from the singular of the personal pronoun, for the stem of the plural is *yu*. The aspiration in the Sanskrit and Zend may have originated in some euphonic peculiarity of these languages. It appears as a vocal aspirate in the Middle forms *dhwé* and *dhwam*. We have thus both aspirates in the plural, as we have noticed them in the singular. The Gothic *th* is the regular representative in that language of an older *t*. The Anglo-Saxon has likewise *th* (dh), *weorthadh*, 'ye become.' In many cases this form is lost, and the Third Person is used in its stead. The *s* in the Latin forms is difficult to account for. Bopp suggests that it may be a remains of the particle *sma* in a plural form, twasmé', similar to the asmé' (masmê) of the First Person Plural.

The following list contains examples of the Second Person Plural:

Sanskrit	Zend	Greek	Latin	Gothic	English
s-tha	——	ἐσ-τέ	es-tis	siju-th	'ye are'
bhára-tha	bara-tha	φέρε-τε	fer-tis	bairi-th	'ye bear'
váha-tha	vaza-tha	ἔχε-τε	vehi-tis	vigi-th	'ye carry'
syá'-ta	——	εἴη-τε	sié-tis	sijai-th	'ye may be'
bháré-ta	barai-ta	φέροι-τε	ferâ-tis	bairai-th	'ye may bear'
ávaha-ta	avaza-ta	εἴχε-τε	vehebá-tis	——	'ye were carrying'

The Second Person Dual.

219. The Sanskrit has -*thas* in the primary and -*tam* in the secondary forms; the Zend has -*thô* = s. *thas* in the primary forms; the Greek has -τον, and the Gothic -*ts*, in both. Sanskrit *m* and Greek ν, as a lighter substitute for *s*, occur also in other instances. These forms are therefore consistent with one another, with the re-appearance of the aspirate in Sanskrit and Zend. As the dual and plural are of the same origin, the *s* in these cases is supposed to furnish an additional confirmation of the view suggested above in regard to the plural, that the affix was originally supplied by a form containing the particle *sma*.

The following list exhibits the endings of the Second Person Dual:

Sanskrit	Zend	Greek	Gothic	English
s-thas	——	ἐσ-τόν	siju-ts	'ye two are'
bhára-thas	bara-thô?	φέρε-τον	baira-ts	'ye two bear'
váha-thas	vaza-thô?	ἔχε-τον	viga-ts	'ye two carry'
syá´-tam	——	εἴη-τον	sijai-ts	'ye two may be'
bháré-tam	——	φέροι-τον	bairai-ts	'ye two may bear'
ávaha-tam	——	εἴχε-τον	——	'ye two were carrying'

The Third Person Singular.

220. The third personal pronoun is *ta*. This, in Sanskrit, becomes *-ti* in the third person singular of the primary forms (*-tu* in the Imperative), and *-t* in the secondary forms, e. g. *dádâti*, 'he gives;' *dadyâ't*, 'he may give.' In Zend the ending is *-ti* and *ḍ*, e. g. *dadháiti* and *daidhyâḍ*. In Greek the primary forms have for the verbs in *-μι σι*, and for the verbs in *-ω ι*, the *τ* being dropped in accordance with a general euphonic law. The forms in which *τ* is changed to *σ*, and so preserved, are older than those in which the *τ* is lost. Both the first person and the third (*-ω* and *ι*), when compared with the earlier forms *-μι* and (*-τι* or) *-σι*, show the destructive effect of time. The original *-τι* is preserved in the substantive verb ἐστί, owing probably to its being preceded by a hard consonant. The ending has altogether disappeared from the secondary forms. According to the analogy of the other languages, and of the other personal endings in Greek, the secondary forms would end in *-τ*, but this letter, when final, is almost universally dropped, e. g. δίδωσι, 'he gives;' τύπτει, 'he strikes' (for τυπτε-τι); ἔτυπτη, 'he was striking' (for ετυπτε-τ). In Latin both forms have *-t*, the primary forms having dropped the final vowel, e. g. *dat* (comp. s. dádâti) and *det* (comp. s. dadyâ't). The Gothic has *-th* in the primary forms, and nothing in the secondary. *th* is the regular Gothic representative of an older *t*. It thus agrees with the Latin in the primary forms, but has suffered greater loss in the secondary forms, e. g. *itith*, 'eateth,' and *sijai*, compared with L *siet*, 'he may be.' In Anglo-Saxon the primary forms have likewise *th*, which is lost in the secondary. The older English agrees with the Gothic and Anglo-Saxon, e. g. *eateth* in the Present and *ate* in the Past tense. The *th* has in later times become reduced to *s*. This change of sound has become generalised in the German language, where *s* usually stands in place of *th*, which would be the proper equivalent for an English *t* and for an older *d*, e. g. L. *quod*, e. *what*, ger. *was*.

The following is a list of verbs in the Third Person Singular:

Sanskrit	Zend	Greek	Latin	Gothic	English
ás-ti	aí-ti	ἐσ-τί	es-t	is-t	'he is'
bhára-ti	barai-ti	φέρε-ι	fer-t	bairi-th	beare-th
váha-ti	vazai-ti	ἔχε-ι	vehi-t	vigi-th	'he carries'
syá-t	——	εἴη	sie-t	sijai	'he may be'
bháré-t	barói-ṭ	φέροι	fera-t	bairai	'he may bear'
ávaha-t	avaza-ṭ	εἶχε	veheba-t	——	'he was carrying'

The Third Person Plural.

221. The Sanskrit has in the primary forms for the Third Person Plural -*nti* (-*ntu* in the Imperative); *n* is dropped in the reduplicated verbs of the third class, probably to lighten the word at one end, as the reduplication makes it heavier at the other. The secondary forms have -*n* only in some cases and -*s* in others. Where the stem ends in a consonant the connecting vowel *a* (*u* before *s*) is inserted, e. g. *tishṭhanti*, 'they stand;' *dádati*, 'they give;' *ábharan*, 'they were bearing;' *tishṭhéyus*, 'they may stand.' The Zend has -*nti* and -*n* in the two forms, with a connecting *ĕ* where necessary, e. g. *histĕnti*, 'they stand,' and *histayĕn*, 'they may stand.' 'n Greek the primary forms have -ντι in earlier examples, with a connecting *o* after consonant stems. In later examples τι is changed to σι, whilst ν is vocalised, so that by it the preceding vowel is lengthened or changed to a diphthong. Hence the forms -ουσι, -ᾱσι, e. g. Doric διδόντι, Attic διδοῦσι, 'they give;' Doric ἱστάντι, Attic ἱστᾶσι, 'they stand.' In the Epic ἐντί and the Attic εἰσί, *ε* alone represents the verbal root -*es*, whilst, in εἰσί, ν of the ending is represented by ι. In the Doric *ἐοντι* the connecting vowel *o* indicates the presence originally of the full verbal root, making ἐοντι. The secondary forms have -ν, e. g. ἔφερον, 'they were bearing.' The Latin has preserved -*nt* in both forms, e. g. *stant*, 'they stand;' *stent*, 'they may stand.' The Gothic has -*nd* in the primary forms, in which *d* may have been pronounced *dh* (the Gothic representative of an older *t*), as we have seen to be probable in other cases; or, as Bopp suggests, the change may be referred to a preference for the combination *nd*. The Gothic Preterite has -*u-n*,

analogous to the Sanskrit -*u-s* in the Reduplicated
Preterite, e. g. *haihaitun*, 'they were called,' compared with s. *â'sus*, 'they were.' It is important to
notice the relation of the nasal and sibilant (*n* and *s*)
in these cases. We have had other instances in the
Greek forms for the First Person Plural (-μεν and -μες).
We shall find another illustration of it in the Third Person Dual. The secondary forms have -*na*, in which they
agree as usual with the Greek, but are inferior to the
Latin in the loss of the *t*. No very satisfactory reason
appears for the final *a*. e. g. *sind*, 'they are;' *bai-
raina*, 'they may bear.' In Anglo-Saxon *nd* is only
partially preserved, and in modern English not at all.

The following is a list of verbs in the Third Person
Plural:

Sanskrit	Zend	Greek	Latin	Gothic	English
as-nti	hě-nti	ἐ-ισί	su-nt	si-nd	'they are'
bhára-nti	barě-nti	φέρο-υσι	feru-nt	baira-nd	'they bear'
váha-nti	vaze-nti	ἔχο-υσι	vehu-nt	viga-nd	'they carry'
syu-s	——	εἶε-ν	sie-nt	sijai-na	'they may be'
bháreyu-s	baraye-n	φέροιε-ν	feru-nt	barai-na	'they may bear'
ávaha-n	avaze-n ?	εἶχο-ν	veheba-nt	——	'they were carrying'

The Third Person Dual.

222. The Third Person has -*tas* for the dual in the primary and -*tâm* in the secondary forms of Sanskrit verbs, e. g. *bháratas*, 'they two bear,' and *ábharatâm*, 'they two were bearing.' *m* and *s* seem here to be interchangeable, as we found *n* and *s* in the Second Person Plural. The long vowel in -tâm may be owing to a similar cause to that which produces it in the First Person Singular and Plural Present, i. e. -â-mi and -â-mas, though it seems as if there must at some time have been an addition to -*m* in the dual to give it this power; for in the secondary forms of the first person -*m* has not this power, but leaves the connecting vowel short, as in *ábharam*. In Zend the primary forms have -tô, e. g. *vakhsayatô*, 'they two (i. e. the cloud and the rain) cause to grow.' There are no instances of the secondary forms. In Greek we find -τον in the primary and -την or -των in the secondary forms, e. g. φέρετον, 'they two bear;' ἐφερίτην, 'they two were bearing;' φερίτων, 'let the two bear.' The nasal ν (the usual representative of the Sanskrit final *m*) occurs in all these instances. In Gothic there is no Third Person Dual.

The following list contains instances of the Third Person Dual:

VERBS

Sanskrit	Zend	Greek	English
s-tas	t-tô	ἐσ-τόν	'they two are'
bhára-tas	bara-tô?	φέρε-τον	'they two bear'
váha-tas	vaza-tô?	ἔχε-τον	'they two carry'
syá'-tâm	—	εἴη-την	'they two may be'
bháré-tâm	—	φέροί-την	'they two may bear'
ávaha-tâm	—	εἴχέ-την	'they two were carrying'

d) THE WEIGHT OF THE PERSONAL ENDINGS.

223. An important source of change in words lies in the difference in the weight of affixes which Bopp discovered while endeavouring to account for the change of vowels in the Germanic languages. He supposes the influence of this principle to have been recognised, but only to a small extent, before the separation of languages. The loss of the root-vowel of the substantive verb before the heavy affixes in Sanskrit, at the same time as it is retained in the Greek and some other languages, shows that no such influence was allowed to the heavy affixes as long as these languages formed one, e. g.:

Sanskrit.	Greek.
Singular.	
ás-mi, 'I am'	ἐμ-μί (from ἐσ-μί)
á-si	ἐσ-σί
ás-ti	ἐσ-τί
Plural.	
s-mas	ἐσ-μές
s-tha	ἐσ-τέ
s-ánti	(σ)-εντί
Dual.	
s-was	—
s-thas	ἐσ-τόν
s-tas	ἐσ-τόν

After the separation of languages each seems to have followed the general tendency, but with some peculiar modifications. The stem usually retains its original form, or is strengthened or enlarged, when the ending is light; but when the ending is heavy, the stem is commonly abbreviated.

The following list shows this variety of operation:

Sanskrit.	Zend.	Greek.	Latin.	English.
Singular.				
dádâ-mi	dadhâ-mi	δίδω-μι	do	'I give'
dádâ-si	dadhâ-hi	δίδω-ς	da-s	'thou givest'
dádâ-ti	dadhâi-ti	δίδω-σι	da-t	'he gives'
Plural.				
dad-más	dad-mahi	δίδο-μες	da-mus	'we give'
dat-thá	daz-ta?	δίδο-τε	da-tis	'you give'
dád-a-ti	dad-ê-nti	διδο-ῦσι	da-nt	'they give'
Dual.				
dad-wás	—	—	—	'we two give'
dat-thás?	daz-tô?	δίδο-τον	—	'you two give'
dat-tás	daz-tô?	δίδο-τον	—	'they two give'

The root-vowel is preserved, though in a shortened form (ο), in the Greek plural and dual, whilst in Sanskrit the corresponding forms have entirely lost the root-vowel. This is accounted for by the fact that in Greek the endings are lighter upon the whole than in Sanskrit.

A similar difference appears in the Imperfect. In the Aorist, however, in cases where the reduplication is not employed, the Sanskrit preserved the root-vowel long, the Greek short, as follows:

	Imperfect		*Aorist*	
	Sanskrit	Greek	Sanskrit	Greek
Singular.				
	ádadâ-m	ἐδίδω-ν	ádâ-m	(ἔδω-ν)
	ádadâ-s	ἐδίδω-ς	ádâ-s	(ἔδω-ς)
	ádadâ-t	ἐδίδω(τ)	ádâ-t	(ἔδω-(τ))
Plural.				
	ádad-ma	ἐδίδο-μεν	ádâ-ma	ἔδο-μεν
	ádat-ta	ἐδίδο-τε	ádâ-ta	ἔδο-τε
	ádad-us	ἔδο-ν Epic for ἐδίδοσαν	ád-us	ἔδο-ν Epic for ἔδοσαν
Dual.				
	ádad-va	—	ádâ-va	—
	ádat-tam	ἐδίδο-τον	ádâ-tam	ἔδο-τον
	ádat-tâm	ἐδιδό-την	ádâ-tâm	ἐδό-την

In the above list the Sanskrit seems to have suffered no diminution of the Aorist stem (except in the 3rd Plur.), probably because the words, not having a reduplication, were not felt to need any such relief. In the Greek a different principle seems to have been followed, and the same reduction of the stem has been made in the plural and dual as in the Imperfect. A similar difference appears between the Sanskrit *bhá'mi*, 'I shine,' and the Greek φημί, 'I say,' both being from the same root, and conjugated in the Present and Imperfect Indicative as follows :

THE WEIGHT OF THE PERSONAL ENDINGS 219

Sanskrit.	Greek.	Sanskrit.	Greek.
Present.		*Imperfect.*	
Singular.			
bhá-mi, 'I shine'	φη-μί, 'I say'	ábha-m	ἔφη-ν
bhá-si	φή-s for φη-σι	ábha-s	ἔφη-σ(θα)
bhá-ti	φη-σί Doric φα-τί	ábha-t	ἔφη-(τ)
Plural.			
bhá-mas	φα-μέν	ábha-ma	ἔφα-μεν
bhá-thá	φα-τέ	ábha-ta	ἔφα-τε
bhá'-nti	φα-σί Doric φα-ντί	ábha-n	ἔφα-ν Poet. for ἔφα-σαν
Dual.			
bhá-vas	—	ábha-va	—
bhá-thás	φα-τόν	ábha-tam	ἔφα-τον
bhá-tás	φα-τόν	ábha-tām	ἐφά-την

The omission of guna before heavy endings is another illustration of their influence, as in the following examples from the root *i*:

Sanskrit.	Greek.
Singular.	
é'-mi, 'I go'	εἶ-μι
é'-shi	εἶ-ς
é'-ti	εἶ-σι (-τι)
Plural.	
i-más	ἴ-μεν
i-thá	ἴ-τε
y-ánti	ἴ-ασι
Dual.	
i-vás	—
i-thás	ἴ-τον
i-tás	ἴ-τον

In Gothic the influence of the weight of the endings is manifest in such Preterites as *bait*, 'he bit,' where, though the ending is entirely gone, the guna is preserved as in the Sanskrit reduplicated form *bibhé'da*; whilst it is omitted in the plural *bit-um*, 'we bit,' as in the Sanskrit *bibhid-imá*. The difference in Anglo-Saxon is similar, i. e. *bát* and *bit-on*. For the same reason the 2 Sing. *ban-st*, 'thou didst bind,' has the stronger vowel *a* with the lighter ending, originally only *t*; whilst *bund-um*, 'we bound,' has the weaker *u* with the heavier ending. In Anglo-Saxon the 2 Sing. and the 1 Plur. both have *u*, *bund-e* and *bund-um*. The same cause admits or prevents guna in Gothic, just as we saw to be the case in Sanskrit and Greek, e. g. from the root *vid*:

Sanskrit.	Greek.	Gothic.	Ang.-Sax.
Sing.			
vê'd-a, 'I know'	οἶδ-α	vait	wât
vê'ṯ-tha	οἶσ-θα	vais-t	wâs-t
vê'd-a	οἶδ-ε	vait	wât
Plur.			
vid-má	ἴδ-μεν	vit-u-m	wit-o-n
vid-á-(tha)	ἴσ-τε	vit-u-th	wit-e
vid-ús	ἴσ-α-σι	vit-u-n	wit-a-n
Dual.			
vid-vá	——	vit-û	——
vid-á-thus	ἴσ-τον	vit-u-ts	——
vid-á-tus	ἴσ-τον	——	——

The o in the Greek οι corresponds to Sanskrit *a*, as well as the more usual ε does, and therefore οι is a proper equivalent for s. έ (for a+i).

In some cases, especially in Sanskrit, endings which were originally heavy appear as light ones, because some of their letters have been lost or weakened, but their original influence on the root remains; e. g. *ábi-*bhr-*i* has a lighter ending now than *ábi*bhar-*am*, yet the latter has guna and the former not —the reason being that the guna was prevented in ábibhri by the Middle ending, of which *i* is only a slight remains. So also τε in ἴσ-τε represents an originally heavier ending than θα in οἰσ-θα; the former therefore prevents, but the latter permits guna.

The following is a list of the two classes of endings in Sanskrit and Greek:

Light:	mi	si	ti	m	s	t
	μι	σ(ι)	τι	ν	ς	(τ)
Heavy:	vas	thas	tas	wa	tam	tâm
	—	τον	τον	—	τον	την
	—	tha	nti	ma	ta	n(t)
	μεν	τε	ντι	μεν	τε	ν(τ)
	ê	sê	tê	a, i	thâs	ta
	μαι	σαι	ται	μην	σο	το
	vahê	âthê	âtê	vahi	âthâm	âtâm
	μεθον	σθον	σθον	μεθον	σθαν	σθην
	mahê	dhwê	ntê	mahi	dhwam	nta
	μεθα	σθε	νται	μεθα	σθε	ντο

The law which thus reduces or enlarges the body of a word to counterbalance the greater or less weight which has to be added to the end appears to have been almost as powerful in Gothic as in Greek and Sanskrit, whilst in Latin it has been comparatively inactive. This adds another instance to several already noticed in which the Gothic resembles the Greek language more than it does the Latin.

e) CONJUGATIONS.

224. The Conjugation refers to the manner in which the stem and ending of verbs are united together. Every variety of this kind, however, does not form a distinct conjugation. Those methods which nearly resemble one another are classified together, and thus but few separate conjugations appear in each language. The conjugations of two different languages rarely coincide. The forms which are classed together in one language are distributed amongst two or three conjugations in another language; and those which in one are separated are united in the other.

The Sanskrit verbs, as we have already seen, are subdivided into ten classes. These classes, again, are arranged in two divisions forming two conjugations. The ground of this distinction is, that the verbs in one division insert some letter or letters between the root and the ending, whilst those in the other division add the ending immediately to the root.

The first conjugation, in which *a connecting letter or letters are inserted between the root and the ending*, includes four of the ten classes. These four classes are 1, 6, 4, and 10. The *first* inserts a and gunaes and accents the root-vowel, e. g. *bó'dh-a-ti*, 'he knows,' from the root *budh*; the *sixth* inserts an accented *a* likewise, but omits guna, e.g. *tud-á-ti*, 'he thumps' (Engl. *thud*), from *tud*; the *fourth* accents the root without guna, and inserts *ya*, e. g. *zúch-ya-ti*, 'he is clean,' from *zuch*; and the *tenth* inserts *aya* with guna, and accents the first syllable of *aya*, e. g. *chór-áya-ti*, 'he steals,' from *chur*.

The second conjugation, which *affixes the ending immediately to the root*, or to the root enlarged by the syllable *na* (nu), includes the other six classes, i. e. 2, 3, 5, 7, 8, 9. The place of the accent is modified by the weight of the affixes. In this conjugation the *second* class gunaes the root, e. g. *dwé'sh-ti*, 'he hates,' from *dwish*; the *third* reduplicates and gunaes the root, e.g. *bibhar-ti*, 'he bears,' from *bhṛ*; the *seventh* inserts *na* in the root, e.g. *yunák-ti*, 'he joins,' from *yuj*, *j* being changed to *k* by the influence of the hard consonant *t*; the *fifth* and *eighth*, which may be considered as belonging to one and the same class, affix *nŏ*, the gunaed form of *nu*, to the root, e.g. *chinŏ'-ti*, 'he gathers,' from *chi*, and *tanŏ'-ti*, 'he stretches,' from *tan*; and the *ninth* adds *nâ* and (before 'heavy' endings) *nî* to the root, e.g. *yunâ'-ti*, 'he binds,' and *yunî'-mas*, 'we bind,' from *yu*.

Strictly speaking, there are only three classes, viz. 2, 3, and 7, which add the ending *immediately* to the root, and none to the mere unaltered root. The 5, 8, and 9 might very appropriately be put with the first conjugation, as inserting a connecting syllable; for *nâ* of the ninth is as much a connecting syllable as *ya* of the fourth class, neither of them affecting the sense of the word. Indeed, we find that these forms are united under one conjugation in the Greek language.

225. The -ω conjugation in Greek answers to the first in Sanskrit, but it includes also several other forms. Those which have ε as a connecting vowel (o before nasals), without guna, like λεγ (e.g. λέγ-ε-τε, 'ye say;' λέγ-ο-μεν, 'we say'), answer to the s. sixth class; those which also guna the root-vowel, like φυγ (e.g. φεύγ-ε-τε, 'ye flee;' φεύγ-ο-μεν, 'we flee'), answer to the s. first class. Such verbs as τάσσω belong to the s. fourth class; for τάσ-σε-τε, 'ye order,' τάσ-σο-μεν, 'we order,' are for ταγ-ιε-τε, ταγ-ιο-μεν, in which ιε and ιο are equivalent to s. *ya*. The pure verbs, i.e. those in -ἰω, -όω, -άω, belong to the s. tenth class, *y* being lost, unless perhaps *a* represents *ay*; e.g. φιλ-έε-τε, 'ye love,' δηλ-όε-τε, 'ye show,' and τιμ-άε-τε, 'ye honour,' are for φιλ-α(y)a-τε, δηλ-a(y)a-τε, and τιμ-aya-τε. But the -ω conjugation also includes such words as δάκνω, 'I bite,' which belongs to the ninth class, with the vowel, however, short, e. g. δάκ-νε-τε. In τύπ-τε-τε we have the addition of *ta* to the root, which is found in none of the Sanskrit classes, as well as several other forms which are peculiar to the Greek, showing that in the arrangement of their conjugations each language has acted independently. The general character of the -ω conjugation is that ε (ο before nasals) connects the ending to the stem, as its equivalent α does in Sanskrit.

The -μι conjugation omits this connecting vowel, and adds the ending either (1) immediately to the root, without or with guna, e. g. ἐσ-τί, 'he is,' from ἐσ, εἶ-σι, 'he goes,' from ἰ; or (2) to the root enlarged by νυ (υ), as in the Sanskrit fifth and eighth classes, but without guna, unless the long quantity be considered an equivalent for guna, e. g. δείκ-νυ-σι, 'he shows;' or (3) to the root enlarged by νη (νᾰ), answering to the ninth class in Sanskrit, e. g. δάμ-νη-σι, 'he tames.'

It thus appears that although the arrangement of the conjugations is based in these languages upon the same general principles, yet that the details were not settled till after they had become separate and independent of one another. This is singularly illustrated in the treatment of the root *yuj*, the Greek equivalent for which is ζυγ. The s. form *yŭ-na-k-ti* has no guna, and inserts *na* in the middle of the root *yu-j*, whilst the gr. form ζεύγ-νῡ-σι, 'he yokes,' has guna *in* the root, and adds *νῡ after* the root. These forms do not appear to be the representatives of the same common original, nor to be derived one from the other, but to be independently constructed out of similar materials and upon the same general principles.

226. The Latin language has four conjugations.

Of these, however, three, i. e. the 1, 2, and 4, are only modifications of the tenth class in Sanskrit. They thus severally resemble the Greek verbs in -άω, -έω, and -όω, and, like them, should be classed in one conjugation. The s. *aya* becomes $a+a$ or $â$ in the first, $a+i$ or $ê$ in the second, and $o+i$ or $î$ in the fourth conjugation. The third conjugation in Latin includes a great variety of verbs taken indiscriminately from almost all the ten classes in Sanskrit. The fourth class is recognisable in the 1 Sing. of such verbs as *capio*, though the other forms are reduced to a resemblance with those verbs which belong to the sixth class; e. g. in *cap-i-mus*, only *i* intervenes between the root and ending, as in *leg-i-mus*.

227. The Gothic language has preserved *ya* of the fourth class more completely than is done in Latin, in the forms *ja* and *ji*, pronounced ya and yi.

The resemblance between Sanskrit and Gothic, and their difference from the Latin, are seen in the following instances:

CONJUGATIONS

	Sanskrit	Gothic	Latin
Sing.	lúbh-yâ-mi, 'I desire'	haf-ja, 'I lift' (heave)	cap-i-o, 'I take'
	lúbh-ya-si	haf-ji-s	cap-i-s
	lúbh-ya-ti	haf-ji-th	cap-i-t
Plur.	lúbh-yâ-mas	haf-ja-m	cap-i-mus
	lúbh-ya-tha	haf-ji-th	cap-i-tis
	lúbh-ya-nti	haf-ja-nd	cap-i-unt
Dual.	lúbh-yâ-vas	haf-jô-s	—
	lúbh-ya-thas	haf-ja-ts	—
	lúbh-ya-tas	—	—

f) FORMATION OF TENSES.

228. In the original construction of language it is evident that there was the intention of marking the difference of time by a corresponding variety in the forms of expression. In the Indo-European languages slight modifications in the forms of the same word were at first made to answer this purpose. What was the primitive meaning of the letters or syllables added to form tenses it is not easy in all cases to determine; but it is possible to classify the forms actually in use, and by comparing them one with another to throw some light upon this difficult question.

Whatever the primitive signs of tense were, they have in progress of time been gradually mutilated and destroyed, so that they are almost as entirely obliterated from the leading languages of Western Europe as the original inhabitants are from its soil. The analytical method has completely established its power in this respect over a large part of the English language; but its operation has been so symmetrical as well as complete, that the English language has a considerable advantage over most others with regard to the precision with which the *time* of an action can be expressed. We mention the subject somewhat in detail here for the purpose of reference when examining each particular tense.

229. The three main divisions of time, viz. Past, Present, and Future, are presented in at least four different modifications, expressed by distinct forms of speech. For, in regard to each of these tenses, an action is represented as incomplete or complete at that time. Each of these incomplete or complete actions is either narrated or described. Thus there are furnished four varieties for each tense. We will take the word 'go' as an example:

Present Tense, Incomplete.	*Complete.*
Narrative: 'I go'	'I have gone'
Descriptive: 'I am going'	'I have been going'

Past Tense, Incomplete.	*Complete.*
Narrative: 'I went'	'I had gone'
Descriptive: 'I was going'	'I had been going'

Future Tense, Incomplete.	*Complete.*
Narrative: 'I shall go'	'I shall have gone'
Descriptive: 'I shall be going'	'I shall have been going'

The difference in regard to time between the primary divisions is very obvious: 'went' cannot be used of to-morrow, nor 'shall go' of yesterday. The distinctions expressed by the secondary divisions are not so great, but still they are considerable. For instance, the Narrative forms may express a single action, and the Descriptive a succession of actions; the former may denote what is done at once, the latter may express the continuance of an action through a long space of time. Again, the idea expressed by the Incomplete is very different from that expressed by the Complete forms. 'I gain an advantage' denotes that I am at present receiving the advantage, but may not have yet acquired its full amount. On the other hand, 'I have gained an advantage' denotes that I have no more of that advantage to acquire, but that at the present time the gain is complete.

There are many ways in which the difference between these four modifications of the same tense might be illustrated, but the above will sufficiently answer the purpose of showing how methodically and completely the analytical method expresses the relations of time. We have no less than twelve different forms for as many varieties of tense. The end is gained in modern languages by means of auxiliary verbs, which is characteristic of the analytical method; but in most of the languages under our present consideration the synthetical method is employed for the same purpose, and seems to have been employed exclusively in their original structure. It consists in making various inflexions of one verb answer the end which we have seen accomplished by means of auxiliaries.

The same primary distinctions of time, viz. Past, Present, and Future, belong to both systems. We begin with the Present, as containing the simpler forms.

The Present Tense.

230. The incomplete and the complete are distinguished as Present and Perfect, but no distinction of form is made in the older languages between the narrative and descriptive of the Present.

The first of the above twelve forms has no auxiliary, therefore properly no indication of time. It is doubtful whether it is the same in the synthetical system. Some suppose the strengthened forms of the Present tense were intended to denote the present time; others suppose that they contain no such meaning, but that the present is sufficiently indicated by the absence of all reference to

THE PRESENT TENSE

any other time. We will first take an example of the Present Tense Indicative from the first Sanskrit conjugation, in order to illustrate this difference of opinion:

Sanskrit	Zend	Greek	Latin	Gothic	English
Singular.					
váh-â-mi	vaz-â-mi	ἔχ-ω	veh-o	vig-a	'I carry'
váh-a-si	vaz-a-hi	ἔχ-ε-ις	veh-i-s	vig-i-s	'thou carriest'
váh-a-ti	vaz-ai-ti	ἔχ-ε-ι	veh-i-t	vig-i-th	'he carries'
Plural.					
váh-â-mas	vaz-â-mahi	ἔχ-ο-μεν	veh-i-mus	vig-a-m	'we carry'
váh-a-tha	vaz-a-tha	ἔχ-ε-τε	veh-i-tis	vig-i-th	'ye carry'
váh-a-nti	vaz-ê-nti	ἔχ-ο-νσι	veh-u-nt	vig-a-nd	'they carry'
Dual.					
váh-â-vas	—	—	—	vig-ô-s	'we two carry'
váh-a-thas	vaz-a-thô?	ἔχ-ε-τον	—	vig-a-ts	'ye two carry'
váh-a-tas	vaz-a-tô	ἔχ-ε-τον	—	—	'they two carry'

The Anglo-Saxon *wæg-an* or *weg-an* has little trace of the connecting vowel. In examining these forms, we see that between the root of the verb and the personal terminations different vowels are inserted, which, however, have probably all originated from the same. In Sanskrit they are *a* and (before Labials) *â*; in Zend *a*, (before Labials) *â*, and *ǝ*; in Greek *ε* and (before Nasals) *o*; in Latin *i* and (before *n*) *u*; and in Gothic *i* and *a*. The origin of them all is the *a* which appears in Sanskrit. Is this merely a 'connecting' vowel, or is it intended to express the Present tense? It can hardly be the latter, because it is used also in the Past, i. e. the Imperfect tense. Again, in other verbs, syllables containing also a consonant are similarly inserted, and with a greater variety in Greek than in Sanskrit. Are we, with Pott, to regard these as the grammatical expressions of the present time? If so, why are they also used in Past tenses (e. g. the Imperfect), and why is such a variety of forms adopted to express one idea? On the other hand, if they are not intended to express the relations of time, for what purpose are they inserted?

In regard to guna, Bopp thus expresses himself in the second edition of his *Vergl. Grammatik*, vol. ii. p. 378:

'I cannot ascribe a grammatical meaning to the guna in the conjugation of Sanskrit and its sister languages, but explain it as resulting merely from a desire for fulness of form which causes the lighter vowels *i* and *u* to be strengthened—to be propped up as it were—by prefixing *a*, whilst *a* itself, being the heaviest vowel, needs no foreign help. If, as is done by Pott (*Et. Forsch.* i. 60), guna be regarded in the Present and Imperfect as an expression of the continuance of an action, a difficulty will be felt, which he also found, in the fact that guna is not confined to these tenses, but, in verbs with the lighter stem vowels *i* and *u*, accompanies the root through almost all tenses and moods, not only in Sanskrit but also in its sister languages in Europe, wherever this mode of forming diphthongs is preserved at all. As, for example, in Greek, λείπω and φεύγω cannot free themselves again from the ι inserted in the roots λιπ, φυγ, except so far that ι is changed to ο in λέλοιπα, and the Aorist ἔλιπον, ἔφυγον has the pure root, which I cannot ascribe to the meaning of this Aorist, but to the circumstance that the Second Aorist generally inclines to preserve the original form of the root, and hence sometimes has a lighter but sometimes also a heavier vowel than the other tenses, as in ἔτραπον as compared with ἔτρεψα and ἔτριπον. In meaning, too, the Second Aorist agrees with the First, and yet the latter retains the guna if it belongs to the verb at all. Considering this inclination of the Second Aorist to preserve the root unchanged, the distinction between such forms as ἔλιπον, ἔφυγον, ἔτυχον, and the Imperfect, cannot be found in the circumstance that the action of the Aorist is not represented as a lasting one, whilst, on the contrary, in the Imperfect and Present continuance is symbolically indicated by guna.'

If, then, as seems the more likely, these letters and syllables inserted between the root and the personal ending were not intended as expressions of time, the Present tense contains no indication of time. A statement is supposed to refer to the present time when it does not expressly refer to any other. The fact that a distinct indication of time is given with the Past and the Future naturally suggests the idea that there may be something analogous in the Present. And yet it is not difficult to conceive that a necessity for it might be felt in the one case and not in the other. We feel no need for any expression to show that 'I go' refers to the present; but if it is to refer to the future, we feel the need of adding a word to state this: 'I *shall* go.' There is, therefore, a close analogy in this between the old and modern languages — between the synthetical and analytical systems. There is, moreover, a striking similarity between this indication of tenses in verbs and the expression of number in nouns; for whilst the number is specially indicated in the Plural and Dual, there is nothing to denote number in the Singular. We thus see in the original representation of tense and number the operation of the same mental laws.

The Imperfect Tense.

231. The Imperfect Tense generally coincides in meaning with the first and second forms of the Past in the table on page 229, viz. 'I went' and 'I was going.' The Imperfect includes the Single-formed Augmented Preterite in Sanskrit, and the Imperfect in Greek and Latin.

The following examples are from the first conjugation:

Sanskrit	Greek	Latin	English
Singular.			
á-bhar-a-m	ἔ-φερ-ο-ν	fer-e-ba-m	'I was carrying'
á-bhar-a-s	ἔ-φερ-ε-ς	fer-e-ba-s	'thou wast carrying'
á-bhar-a-t	ἔ-φερ-ε	fer-e-ba-t	'he was carrying'
Plural.			
á-bhar-â-ma	ἐ-φέρ-ο-μεν	fer-e-bā-mus	'we were carrying'
á-bhar-a-ta	ἐ-φέρ-ε-τε	fer-e-bā-tis	'ye were carrying'
á-bhar-a-n	ἔ-φερ-ο-ν	fer-e-ba-nt	'they were carrying'
Dual.			
á-bhar-â-va	—	—	'we two were carrying'
á-bhar-a-tam	ἐ-φέρ-ε-τον	—	'ye two were carrying'
á-bhar-a-tâm	ἐ-φερ-έ-την	—	'they two were carrying'

The root and the connecting vowel, i. e. *bhar*, *a*, are the same as in the Present. The personal endings differ only in being the light instead of the heavy forms, which is probably intended to compensate for the additional vowel which is prefixed to the word, viz. *a-* in Sanskrit and *ì-* in Greek. This prefix, which is called the *Augment*, constitutes the only essential difference of the Imperfect from the Present in form; and as it is universally preserved, it is evidently for the purpose of denoting the difference in meaning, which is also uniform. The difference is that of *past* instead of *present* time; therefore the Augment is the sign of the Past tense.

When the secondary endings were fully identified with the Past tense in the Indicative, they were felt to be a sufficient distinction from the Present, and hence we find the Augment in many cases omitted. In Zend the Augment is usually wanting, e. g. in the first conjugation, z. *frâdaizaêm*, 'I showed' = s. *sprâdêzayam*, 'I caused to show;' in the second conjugation, z. *dadañm* = s. *ádadham*, 'I put.' In Latin, whilst the Augment is omitted, a syllable is inserted between the connecting vowel and the personal endings. This syllable *ba* is probably a part of the substantive verb as it appears in the Perfect *fui*, or an older form *fua*. From this *ba* would come by changing *u* to *b*, and dropping the preceding consonant, as is done in **b**-*ellum* for *d***u**-*ellum*. The omission of the Augment, and the insertion at the same time of a weakened form of the substantive verb, are not confined to the Latin language. The same is done in the Armenian, Lithuanian, and Slavonian. In this, however, all these languages rather resemble in form the Greek Weak (First) Aorist and Sanskrit Multiform Augmented Preterite than the

Imperfect; for those also, as we shall see, insert the substantive verb, though they preserve the Augment at the same time. In the Latin third conjugation the connecting vowel is lengthened, merely in imitation of the long vowel in the other conjugations.

In the cases already noticed the Augment, preceding a consonant, forms an additional syllable, and it is therefore called the *Syllabic Augment*. When prefixed to words beginning with a vowel, it is usually contracted into one syllable with the initial vowel of the word. It then does not form an additional syllable, but increases the *time* of that already existing, and is hence called the *Temporal Augment*. This latter will be illustrated in the Imperfect tense of the substantive verb, whose root is *as-*:

	Sanskrit.	Greek.	Latin.
Sing.	â's-a-m, 'I was'	ἦ(σ)-ν	er-a-m
	â's-î-s	ἦ(σ)-s(θα)	er-â-s
	â's-i-t	ἦ-ν	er-a-t
		for ηs-ν(ησ-s-ν)	
Plur.	â's-ma	ἦ(σ)-μεν	er-â-mus
	â's-ta	ἦ(σ)-τε	er-â-tis
	â's-n-n	ἦσ-α-ν	er-a-nt
Dual.	â's-va	——	——
	â's-tam	ἦ(σ)-τον	——
	â's-tâm	ἤ(σ)-την	——

In Sanskrit the connecting vowel *i* has been changed

from *a*, probably in imitation of the Aorist. In Latin *a* and *â* resemble the usual Imperfect forms in *ba* and *bâ*. *s* becomes *r*, as usual in Latin; hence er-a-m, etc., are for es-a-m, etc. In Greek the *s* is dropped in a similar position, and two syllables are then contracted into one, e. g. ἦ-ν for ἤ-ο-ν, and that for ἦσ-ο-ν; ἦ-ς for ἤ-ε-ς, and that for ἤσ-ε-ς, etc. In the first syllable a. ἆς is for *a-as*; gr. ἦσ for ἔ-ἐσ; l. *er* is short, from the Augment not being used, but *a* and *â* represent ba and bâ in other Imperfects.

232. The most satisfactory explanation of the Augment appears to be that which represents it as the negative particle, applied to denote that an action *is not now* going on, and thus suggesting that it *was* going on *before*. If we say 'he shot a bird,' it is evidently implied that he is *not now* shooting it. So, in the celebrated phrase 'fuit Troja,' the assertion of the past is made to imply a denial of the present. There 'was a Troy,' or there 'has been a Troy,' is used to denote 'there is a Troy no longer.' But if we say 'he is not shooting,' it does not suggest that he once was; and yet perhaps it is merely habit which makes the implied idea more natural in the one case than in the other. It may be objected that the negative particle appears as *an* before a vowel and *a* before consonants, whilst the Augment is *a* in both cases; but the appropriation of the particle to a special purpose may easily be supposed to have been connected with a modification of form.

We have seen that in several languages where the Augment is omitted a part of the substantive verb is inserted as a characteristic of the Imperfect tense. We can easily see how that verb may denote the futurity of an action, for the difference between 'he leaves' and 'he *is* to leave' shows it at once. The former expression, if nothing be added to it, is supposed to apply to a present action or to a habit which includes the present; whilst the latter evidently excludes the present, and leads us almost instinctively to supply an expression of some future time, as 'to-morrow.' Again, it is probably only habit which makes it seem more natural to us that prefixing the substantive verb to the Infinitive should form a Future Tense than a Past Tense. In Latin we shall see that it is inserted in the verb to form both.

We thus find two means of indicating past time in the Imperfect Tense, viz. the negative particle in the Augment, and the substantive verb in the Latin *ba*.

In the Sanskrit word *anuttamás*, 'supreme,' used of the Divine Being, the negative particle *an* is prefixed to *uttamás*, the superlative of *ut*, and meaning 'highest;' but *uttamás* means the 'highest in comparison with the rest,' whilst *anuttamás* means 'not the highest in comparison with the rest,' because too high to be compared with any, and hence 'supreme.' So also *anḗka*, 'many,' is formed by the negative particle being prefixed to *ḗka*, 'one,' so that 'not one' means 'many.' Indeed, the same thing is illustrated in the phrase 'not one, but many.' Such an undoubted use of the negative particle removes part of the objection to supposing the Augment to be of the same origin.

The Aorist Tense.

233. The Aorist agrees generally in meaning with the first, in distinction from the second, of the four forms of the Past in the table on page 229, 'I went,' in distinction from 'I was going.' In this tense, however, we shall find both a great variety of forms and a considerable diversity of meanings. The term Aorist, or 'Indefinite,' is most appropriate in the Greek language, to which it was originally applied, and from which the name is derived. It is used to narrate, as the Imperfect is to describe, the events of the past. In Sanskrit the Aorist comprises the meanings of the Greek Imperfect and Aorist; and the Latin Perfect expresses the meanings of the Greek Aorist and Perfect.

In Sanskrit there are seven forms of the Aorist, hence called the Multiform Augmented Preterite. They are divided into two classes, the first of which, corresponding to the 'Weak' (or First) Aorist in Greek, includes four forms; the second class, corresponding to the 'Strong' (or Second) Aorist in Greek, includes three forms. The Augment is prefixed in both classes.

234. The four forms of the first class all agree in this, that they insert the substantive verb *as* between the root and the personal endings. The *first* form adds the substantive verb *immediately* to the root, but the root is subject to guna or vriddhi, e. g. *á-nái-**sh**-í-t*, 'he led,' from *ní*; the *second* adds the subst. verb to the unaltered root, e. g. *á-dik-**sh**-a-t*, 'he showed,' from *diś*; the *third* unites the subst. verb to the root by means of the vowel *i*, but the root is subject to guna or vriddhi as in the first form, e. g. *á-sáv-i-**sh**-a-m*, 'I bore,' from *su*; and the *fourth* adds a reduplicated form of the subst. verb immediately to the unaltered root, e. g. *á-yá-**sish**-a-m*, 'I went,' from *yá*.

This increase in the body of the word subjects the personal endings to great changes, so that in many cases they are recognised with difficulty.

The following list contains an example from each of the four forms in the first class of Sanskrit Aorists:

THE AORIST TENSE

	1 'I led'	2 'I showed'	3 'I knew'	4 'I went'
Sing.	ánâi-sh-am	ádik-sh-am	ábôdh-ish-am	áyā-sish-am
	ánâi-sh-is	ádik-sh-as	abôdh-î-s	áyā-sî-s
	ánâi-sh-ît	ádik-sh-at	abôdh-î-t	áyā-sî-t
Plur.				
	ánâi-sh-ma	ádik-sh-âma	ábôdh-ish-ma	áyū-sish-ma
	ánâi-sh-ta	ádik-sh-ata	ábôdh-ish-ṭa	áyā-sish-ṭa
	ánâi-sh-us	ádik-sh-an	ábôdh-ish-us	áyū-sish-us
Dual.				
	ánâi-sh-wa	ádik-sh-âva	ábôdh-ish-wa	áyū-sish-wa
	ánâi-sh-ṭam	ádik-sh-atam	ábôdh-ish-ṭam	áyā-sish-ṭam
	ánâi-sh-ṭâm	ádik-sh-atâm	ábôdh-ish-ṭâm	áyū-sish-ṭâm

The Zend is but scantily supplied with examples of the Aorist tense. The following, however, are instances in the first class: *manżta*, 'he spoke,' like the a. Mid. *ámansta*, 'he thought,' from the root *man*; *rusta*, 'he rose,' from *rudh.*

In Greek the 'Weak' or First Aorist furnishes numerous examples formed upon the same principles as those in Sanskrit, but apparently by an independent action; e. g. ἔδειξα, 'I showed' (ἰδεικ-σ-α), agrees with ádik-sh-a-m in adding the subst. verb immediately to the root, but differs from it in the root being subject to guna, i. e. δεικ for δικ.

In Latin this class of Aorists is represented by those Perfect tenses which are formed by adding s to the stem, e. g. *dixi* (dic-si), the Augment being lost, as in all cases in Latin, and the personal ending dropped, as it is also in Greek in the 1st person sing. *Dicsi*, therefore, is the exact counterpart in Latin of (*a*)-*dik-sh-a-*(*m*) in Sanskrit.

In the following list these Greek and Latin words, which represent large classes, are compared with the Sanskrit second form:

	Sanskrit.	Greek.	Latin.
Sing.			
	ádik-sh-am, 'I showed'	ἰδεικ-σ-α	dic-s-i (dixi)
	ádik-sh-as	ἰδεικ-σ-ας	dic-s-isti
	ádik-sh-at	ἰδεικ-σ-ε	dic-s-it
Plur.			
	ádik-sh-âma	ἰδείκ-σ-αμεν	dic-s-imus
	ádik-sh-ata	ἰδείκ-σ-ατε	dic-s-istis
	ádik-sh-an	ἰδεικ-σ-αν	dic-s-êrunt

	Sanskrit.	Greek.	Latin.
Dual.	ádik-sh-âva	—	—
	ádik-sh-atam	ἐδείκ-σ-ατον	—
	ádik-sh-atâm	ἐδεικ-σ-άτην	—

The irregular personal endings of the second person sing. and plur. in Latin may be supposed to have sprung from some false analogy, or from some particular case of euphonic influence, as other irregularities have arisen (see **217**), rather than, as Bopp supposes, that they are the representatives of the Middle endings which in Sanskrit are -*thas* and -*thwam*.

235. The second class of Sanskrit Aorists includes the 5, 6, and 7 forms. They are distinguished from the first class by not inserting the substantive verb, and from the Imperfect by not using the stem of the present tense, but the pure or verbal root. The *fifth* form affixes the personal endings to the root, e.g. *á-dâ-m*, 'I gave,' from *dá*; the *sixth* inserts *a* between the root and the personal ending, e. g. *á-bhar-a-m*, 'I bore,' from *bhar* or *bhṛ*; the *seventh* reduplicates the root and inserts *a*, e. g. *á-papt-a-m*, 'I fell,' from *pat*.

In Greek the fifth is represented by such forms as ἔ-δω-ν, the sixth by such as ἔ-λιπ-ο-ν, and the seventh by such as ἐ-πεφν-ο-ν.

The last form is doubly represented in Latin by such Perfects as *cucurri*, *tutudi*, and *cecini*, and by such as have a long vowel in the first syllable, which may be explained from reduplication, e. g. *cêpi, frêgi, fêci, lêgi, fôdi, scâbi, vîdi, fûgi*, for ce+ipi, etc., from cecipi, etc.

In Zend we have an instance of the seventh form in *urârudhusha,* 'thou didst grow,' from *rudh*, where the initial *u-* is for the augment. The instances of the other forms are hardly to be distinguished from the imperfect.

The following are instances of the fifth and sixth forms:

	Fifth Form			Sixth Form		
	Sanskrit	Greek		Sanskrit	Zend	Greek
Sing.	ádhâ-m, 'I put'	ἔθη-ν		ábhar-a-m, 'I bore'	bar-ĕ-m	ἔφερ-ο-ν
	ádhâ-s	ἔθη-s		ábhar-a-s	bar-ô	ἔφερ-ε-s
	ádhâ-t	ἔθη-		ábhar-a-t	bar-a-ḍ	ἔφερ-ε
Plur.	ádhâ-ma	ἔθε-μεν		ábhar-â-ma	bar-â-ma	ἐφέρ-ο-μεν
	ádhâ-ta	ἔθε-τε		ábhar-a-ta	bar-a-ta	ἐφέρ-ε-τε
	ádhu-s	ἔθε-ν Ep. and Dor. for ἔθεσαν		ábhar-a-n	bar-ĕ-n	ἔφερ-ο-ν
Dual.	ádhâ-va	—		ábhar-â-va	—	—
	ádhâ-tam	ἔθε-τον		ábhar-a-tam	—	ἐφέρ-ε-τον
	ádhâ-tâm	ἔθε-την		ábhar-a-tâm	—	ἐφερ-έ-την

The Perfect Tense.

236. The Sanskrit and Greek both have reduplicated forms which differ from the seventh form of Aorists in having no augment, e. g.:

a. Aor. á-paptam, from pat ; Perf. bubó'dha, from budh
gr. ,, ἐ-κεκλόμην, ,, κελ ; ,, κέκληκα, ,, καλ

The Sanskrit reduplicated forms generally correspond in meaning to the Greek Aorists. In Latin the reduplicated forms of the Perfect are mixed up with those of the Aorist under the general name of Perfect Tense; for, as the Latin language has no augment, these two tenses do not differ in form. They are also identical in meaning, and both equally include the Aorist and Perfect significations.

The meaning of the Greek Perfect is that of the third form of the Present, or the Completed Present, in the table on p. 229, ' I have gone.' This meaning is included in the Latin Perfect, but not in the Sanskrit. The latter language employs compound forms, such as gató' smi for gatas asmi, 'gone am I '=I have gone; uktávân asmi, 'possessed of speaking am I '= I have spoken. This employment of auxiliaries bears a striking resemblance to the general usage in modern languages. Indeed, the employment of a possessive adjective and of the verb *have*, which also denotes possession, indicates nearly the same mental process in both forms. In many instances the Sanskrit language resorts to a circumlocution, in which the passive participle and the instrumental case of the personal pronoun are used, e. g. gatám (asti) asmâ'i, 'done by me,' similar to such English forms as 'it has been done by me,' for ' I have done it.'

237. The mode of reduplication was perhaps uniform at first, but it has become subject to great modifications in course of time. The reduplication now appears more or less defective and obscured. In some languages it can scarcely be recognised.

In Sanskrit, when the root begins with a single consonant, the reduplication consists of that consonant and the vowel following it, e. g. **ba**-*bándha*, 'I bound,' from *bandh*. If, however, the consonant be an aspirate or a guttural, the aspiration is omitted and the guttural changed to a palatal, e. g. **bu***bhaúja*, 'I bent,' from *bhuj*; **cha***ká'ra*, 'I made,' from *kṛ*. When the root begins with two consonants, only the first is taken; or if the first be a sibilant and the second a mute, the second is taken, e. g. **cha**-*kránda*, 'I wept,' from *krand*; **pa**-*spárza*, 'I touched,' from *spṛz*. When the vowel is long, it becomes short in the reduplication, and of two vowels only the second is taken, e. g. **pi**-*práya*, 'I loved,' from *prí*; **bu**-*bó'dha*, 'I knew,' pres. *bó'-dâmi* for *baudâmi*. Thus the general principle of taking the *first consonant and the vowel following it* for the syllable of reduplication is subject only to such modifications as render the syllable lighter, and so make its subordinate character perceptible to the ear.

The Zend, on the whole, resembles the Sanskrit, but with considerable irregularity in the vowel of the reduplicated syllable.

In Greek the same general principle and modifications hold good, with the exception that when a verb begins with a sibilant followed by a mute, the sibilant, in the form of the *spiritus asper*, is reduplicated, e. g. ἕ-στηκα, 'I placed.' So in ἀφίσταλκα for ἀπ-ἐσταλκα, 'I sent away,' the aspiration is for the σ of reduplication. In many cases the reduplicated consonant is dropped, as in ἤψαλκα, 'I sang;' ἔφθορα, 'I spoilt.' The vowel is made light in ἔ-αγα, 'I broke;' ἔ-ούρηκα, 'minxi.' The general employment of this vowel *a* in reduplication, instead of the various vowels in Sanskrit, shows a decay of vitality.

In Latin the reduplicated forms are fewer. They follow the above rules with some exceptions. Two initial consonants are preserved in reduplication, but lightened in the root, e. g. **spo**-*pondi*, 'I engaged,' from *spondeo*. The root vowel is retained in reduplication, e. g. **tu**-*tudi*, 'I struck,' from *tundo*, except when it is *a*, which, being the heaviest vowel, had more need of being made lighter than the others: hence **ce**-*cini*, 'I sang,' from *cano*; **ce**-*cidi*, 'I fell,' from *cado*.

In Gothic the reduplication is preserved, but the compound tense is also used for the Perfect. The first of two consonants is reduplicated; but when a sibilant is followed by a mute, they are both repeated, e. g. **skai**-*skaith*, 'I separated.' The vowel always becomes *ai*. The root vowel *ê* becomes *ô*, e. g. **gai**-*grôt*, 'I wept,' except in **sai**-*zlêp*, 'I slept.' In *vôhs*, *stôth*, from *vahsja*, *standu*, reduplication is omitted. The general tendency to contract reduplication and root into one syllable has produced in many the appearance of unreduplicated verbs. Even in Sanskrit there is the commencement of this reduction of two syllables to one, e. g. **tên**-*ivá* for *tatan-iva*; **sêd**-*imá*, 'we sat,' for *sasad-ima*; go. **sêt**-*um* for *saisat-um*.

In Anglo-Saxon *sæt* as compared with *sit*, and in English *sat* as compared with *sit*, have a heavier vowel, and only in this preserve an indication of the double syllable.

238. The *personal endings* in Sanskrit are those of the secondary forms, but still further weakened in consequence of the word being burdened with a prefixed syllable. They are: S. *a-*, *i-tha*, *a-*; Pl. *i-ma*, *a-*, *u-s*; D. *i-va*, *a-thus*, *a-tus*. In Sanskrit the first and third persons singular and the second person plural end in *a*, entirely losing the personal signs *m*, *t*, and *ta*. The second and third persons dual, *thus*, *tus*, approach nearer to the primary forms. The third plural has *u-s*, preserving *s* in place of the usual *n* of the secondary forms. *tha* in the second singular appears in some Greek forms as 9α (οἶσ-9α), and in Gothic as *th*.

babándha, 'I bound.'

Sing.	Plur.	Dual.
babándh-a	babandh-i-má	babandh-i-vá
babándh-i-tha	babandh-á	babandh-á-thus
babándh-a	babandh-ús	babandh-á-tus

In Greek the personal endings are: S. *a*, *a-s*, *ε*; Pl. *a-μεν*, *a-τε*, *ά-σι*; D. —, *a-τον*, *a-τον*. The singular shows a similar abbreviation to the Sanskrit, but has the usual *s* in the second person. The vowel *o* in the dual corresponds to *u* in Sanskrit. The plural has the primary endings, except that the third person has *ά* for *αν* instead of *ον* for *ον*.

τέτυπα, 'I have struck.'

Sing.	Plur.	Dual.
τέτυπ-α	τετύπ-α-μεν	—
τέτυπ-α-s	τετύπ-α-τε	τετύπ-α-τον
τέτυπ-ε	τετύπ-ά-σι	τετύπ-α-τον

In the First Perfect κ, or ' in its stead, is inserted between the stem and the ending, e. g. πεφίλη-κ-α, τετυφ-α (for τετυπ-'-α).

The Gothic has: S. —, t, —; Pl. u-m, u-th, u-n; D. ú, u-ts, —. In the singular the connecting vowel is lost, which was preserved in Sanskrit and weakened in Greek. t of the second person agrees with the Sanskrit and differs from the Greek. The connecting vowel appears in the dual and plural as u. In the first person dual ú is for uu, out of s. a-va. The second person plural preserves the consonant (th) as in Greek, which is lost in Sanskrit. The final vowel of the personal endings is in all cases lost. a of the root is changed to u in the plural, because of its being followed by heavier endings. When i in the root is for an original a of the present, the past tense has é, and this from the contraction of two syllables into one, as in Sanskrit tén-imá for tatan-ima. So go. sét-um for saisat-um.

In the following examples, as compared with the s. babándha, the reduplicated syllable is lost:

band, 'I bound.'

Sing.	Plur.	Dual.
band	bund-u-m	bund-ú
bans-t	bund-u-th	bund-u-ts
band	bund-u-n	

In Anglo-Saxon the endings are reduced almost as much as in English, e. g.:

Sing. band, 'I bound'
bund-e, 'thou boundest'
band, 'he bound'
Plur. bund-o-n, 'bound,' for all persons.

The root vowels *i* and *u* have guna or vriddhi both in Sanskrit and Gothic, but only in the singular (that is, before the light endings), e. g. s. *bibháida,* 'I bit,' from *bhid;* *bubhañja,* 'I bent' (bow), from *bhuj;* go. *bait,* from *bit;* *baug,* from *bug.* Anglo-Saxon *bát,* from *bit;* *beah,* from *bug.* In the s. *bhuj, j* is for *k*; in the go. *bug, g* is for *gh*, as we have seen in several other cases, and this is represented by *w* in the e. *bow.* The Greek carries guna through all numbers, e. g. πεποί-θαμεν, πεφεύγαμεν, etc.

239. Verbs of the tenth class (i. e. those which insert *aya*), as well as causative and derivative verbs generally, do not admit of the reduplication of their roots, but form a verbal noun in -*â*, to which in the accusative case is affixed the Reduplicated Preterite of the substantive verb *as* or *bhu,* 'be,' or of *kr*, 'put,' 'make,' e. g. *chórayâ'mása* or *chôrayâ'nchakûra,* 'he was stealing;' 'he made' or 'did stealing,' for 'he stole,' from *chur, choraya.*

Other verbs of a similar meaning to *kr* were used in this way. One of them is *dhâ,* 'put' or 'do,' which appears in the formation of the past tenses of the Germanic languages. The Gothic *sôkidédum,* 'we sought,' has in the ending -*déd-um* the reduplicated form of this verb, whilst the singular *sóki-da,* 'I sought,' has only one syllable. The Anglo-Saxon *sóh-te* has *te. d* is changed to *t* by the influence of the preceding consonant *h*, which here has taken the place of *k.* Though this consonant is not now pronounced in the word *sought,* yet the change which it once produced of *d* to *t* is still preserved. In English the whole of this is reduced to the letter *d*, which is the regular, or 'weak,' form of the past tense, e. g. *praise-d, boun-d,* etc.

The verb thus abbreviated in the formation of a

particular tense is used separately in English to make emphatic tenses, both present and past, of other verbs, e. g. 'he *does* praise,' 'he *did* praise.' In *sók-i-da, i* represents Sanskrit *aya*, but there are verbs in Gothic which affix the auxiliary immediately to the root, as in Sanskrit some verbs not belonging to the tenth class affix a similar auxiliary, especially such as begin with a vowel (except *â*) long by nature or position, e. g. *ízá'n-chakâra*, 'I ruled,' from *íz*. So in Gothic *brah-ta*, 'I brough-t;' *skul-da*, 'I shoul-d;' *vis-sa* for *vis-ta*, 'I knew,' 'I wist.' The changes in the *d* are caused by the preceding consonant. Four 'weak' verbs drop the *i* (for *aya*): *thah-ta*, 'though-t;' *bauh-ta*, 'bough-t;' *vaurh-ta*, 'wrough-t;' *suh-ta*, 'sough-t;' a. s. *thûh-te*, *bôh-te*, *worh-te*, and *sôh-te*. The exact correspondence of the English with the Gothic and Anglo-Saxon forms is one of the most interesting phenomena of language, showing the preservation of a peculiar form through many centuries, whilst the language has been undergoing great changes in almost every department. These fossil-like remains, imbedded in modern speech, perpetuate the evidence of a former organism and vitality which no longer exist.

The same auxiliary, but not reduplicated, appears in the Greek First Aorist, and consequently also the First Future, Passive, as $\vartheta\eta$, e. g. τύφ-θη-ν, 'I was struck;' τυφ-θή-σομαι, 'I shall be struck.'

The following examples show the reduction of the reduplication and root to one syllable in the plural and dual:

Sanskrit	Gothic
Sing.	
sasâ'd-a, 'I sat'	(sai)sat
sasát-tha	(sai)sas-t
sasâ'd-a	sai-sat
Plur.	
sêd-i-má	sêt-u-m
sêd-á	sêt-u-th
sêd-ûs	sêt-u-n
Dual.	
sêd-i-vá	sêt-û ?
sêd-á-thus	sêt-u-ts
sêd-á-tus	——

The following examples show the guna or vriddhi in the singular (in Greek throughout the tense), with the loss of the reduplication syllable in Gothic:

Sanskrit.	Gothic.	Greek.
Sing.		
bibhaíd-a, 'I bit'	bait	πέποιθ-α, 'I trusted'
bibhaíd-i-tha	bais-t	πέποιθ-α-ς
bibhaíd-a	bait	πέποιθ-ε
Plur.		
bibhid-i-má	bit-u-m	πεποίθ-α-μεν
bibhid-á	bit-u-th	πεποίθ-α-τε
bibhid-ús	bit-u-n	πεποίθ-ᾱσι
Dual.		
bibhid-i-vá	bit-û	——
bibhid-á-thus	bit-u-ts	πεποίθ-α-τον
bibhid-á-tus	——	πεποίθ-α-τον

The Pluperfect Tense.

240. The Pluperfect corresponds in meaning to the third form of the Past in the table on p. 229, i. e. 'I had gone.'

The Sanskrit has no special form for this tense, as it has none for the Perfect, from which the Pluperfect would be formed; and to express the meaning it employs a gerund or the Locative Absolute.

In Greek the Pluperfect is formed from the perfect by prefixing the augment, just as the imperfect is formed from the present. The endings cause some difficulty. -ειν, -εις, -ει, etc., may be for the imperfect tense of the substantive verb ἦν, ἦς, ἦ, etc. This would involve a repetition of the augment which appears in the initial ε, but would make the Greek strikingly resemble the Latin forms *amav-eram*, 'I had loved,' etc. Or ει may be for *as*, in the same way as in εἰ-μί = s. ás-mi; and Latin *er* in *amav-er-am* may be regarded also as equivalent to *as* in the Sanskrit verb. This view is confirmed by the third person plural, ἐτετύφ-εσ-αν, 'they had struck,' where the root of the substantive verb is preserved as in ἐσ-μέν. It is true that the σ in the same part of the imperfect and second aorist of verbs in μι (e.g. ἐδίδο-σ-αν, 'they were giving;' ἔδο-σ-αν, 'they gave'), and in the Latin perfect (e. g. *fuerunt*, 'they were' = fu-es-unt), at first sight suggests a doubt whether the σ in the third person plural of the Pluperfect implies its previous existence in the rest of the tense; yet the Latin Pluperfect again removes the doubt, for it has *er* in all parts of the tense. The absence of the substantive verb in the middle and passive may have been occasioned by the greater weight of the endings.

In Latin the uniform correspondence of the latter

part of the Pluperfect with the imperfect of the substantive verb *eram*, etc., at once suggests that *er* is for Sanskrit *as* in *ásmi*. The general practice of dropping a preceding in favour of a succeeding vowel supports the division amav-er-am, in preference to amave-r-am, whilst in the Conjunctive amav-is-sem *is* may be as exact a representative of s. *as*, as *er* in the Indicative, for s. *a* often appears both as *i* and as *e* in Latin; so that the difference between *es-sem* and the latter part of amav-*is-sem* would be unessential.

Examples.

	('I had struck') Greek.	('I had loved') Latin.
Sing.	ἐτετύφ-ει-ν	amav-er-am
	ἐτετύφ-ει-ς	amav-er-as
	ἐτετύφ-ει	amav-er-at
Plur.	ἐτετύφ-ει-μεν	amav-er-amus
	ἐτετύφ-ει-τε	amav-er-atis
	ἐτετύφ-εσ-αν	amav-er-ant

The connecting vowel *a* is needed in all the forms in Latin because the consonant of *er* is everywhere preserved, but it is needed only in the 3 Plur. in Greek because σ of *εσ* is preserved only there.

The Future Tense.

240 *a.* The Future is one of the principal modifications of time expressed by verbal forms. In Sanskrit there are two modes by which it is expressed.

1. The first consists in affixing the present tense of the substantive verb to the abbreviated form of the

Nom. Sing. Masc. of the participle in -tár, e. g. dátá'si (dátá-asi), 'thou wilt give.' In the third person the substantive verb is generally omitted, but the participle retains its full form in the dual and plural, e. g.:

Sing. datá'-smi   Plur. datá'-smas   Dual. datá'-swas
      datá'-si   datá'-stha   datá'-sthas
      datá'   datá'ras   datá'ráu

This participle is rarely used separately in a Future sense.

2. The second method of expressing the Future is by affixing *sya*, a form of the substantive verb, which does not exist independently in Sanskrit as a Future tense, but is found in the s. Potential *syâm, syâs, syát*, etc., and in the Latin *siém, siés, siét*, etc. (later *sim*, etc.), and as a Future tense in *ero, eris*, etc., for *eso, esis*, etc. The latter forms also preserve the root vowel of the substantive verb, *er* = s. *as*. The change of *s* to *r* between two vowels is a common occurrence in Latin, and appears in the imperfect tense of this same verb, *eram*, etc. In *ero, erunt*, the *i* is dropped, probably through an imitation of the present tense, e. g. *rego*, 'I rule;' *regunt*, 'they rule.'

In Greek this omission of *i* or *ι* for *y* has become general; yet there are sufficient remains of it to make it probable that it was once universally employed, and that the Greek, in this respect, started from the same point as the Sanskrit. The Futures in σι-ω and σι-ομαι, and those with σσ, which is for σι, clearly point to the Sanskrit *sy*. The Doric Futures in σῶ are for σέω, and that for σίω. Illustrations of the modifications of this old form are πραξίομεν, 'we shall do;' ἔσσομαι, 'I shall be;' στελῶ, 'I shall send.'

In Latin the first and second conjugations have another form for the Future, derived from the verb which is in Sanskrit *bhu*, meaning 'to come into being;' l. *fu*. It is not used in Latin in the present tense, but forms the perfect *fu-i*, etc., of the substantive verb. It appears as *b-o*, *b-is*, *b-it*, etc., for u-o, u-is, u-it, etc., and these for fu-o, fu-is, fu-it, by similar changes to those which made *b-ellum* out of du-ellum. The participle in *tûr-us*, *tûr-a*, *tûr-um*, is also used in Latin, like *târ-* in Sanskrit, in a future sense, with or without the auxiliary verb, and in that sense it distinguishes the genders, which is not done by the Sanskrit participle.

Future formed by *b-*	Future formed by *tûr-*	
('I shall love')	('I am going to love')	
S. amâ-b-o	amâ-tûr-us (-a, -um)	sum
amâ-b-is	amû-tûr-us (-a, -um)	es
amâ-b-it	amâ-tûr-us (-a, -um)	est
PL. amâ-b-imus	amâ-tûr-i (-æ, -a)	sumus
amâ-b-itis	amû-tûr-i (-æ, -a)	estis
amâ-b-unt	amâ-tûr-i (-æ, -a)	sunt

To return to the form *sya*, used so extensively in the Future Tense, we observe that it has the appearance of being compounded of *as-* and *ya*, the former being the root of the substantive verb, and the latter from a root *yâ*, denoting 'go.' The root *i*, 'go,' and (by Bopp) *î*, 'wish,' are also supposed to be employed in forming this Future. Some objection lies in the fact that either of these roots must be supposed to be enlarged in the Future *s-ya*, instead of being reduced as is generally the case, e. g. *b* compared with the root *bhu*. As to meaning, the one would serve as well as the other.

Indeed, *i* and *í* were probably identical, one form serving to express both meanings. The English word *go* has evidently also expressed the idea of 'to wish.' The evidence of it, like many other original meanings, is preserved in provincial or vulgar forms of expression, e. g. 'I did n't *go* to do it,' for 'I did n't *intend* to do it.' That this meaning may easily be adapted to express futurity is evident from such English phrases as 'he is *going* to do,' etc., in the sense of 'he will do,' etc. We have here the substantive verb, 'is,' and the participle of the word 'go,' used to denote the same as the Sanskrit *s-ya* in the Future tense.

A similar use of *ya* appears in the formation of verbal participles corresponding to the Latin forms in *-dus*, and denoting necessity or duty, which differs little from futurity. In the Greek verbal adjectives in -τέος, denoting the same as the Latin forms in *-dus*, this very *ya* was perhaps originally contained (like the Doric Futures in -έω for -ίω, and that for -s-yâ-mi), i. e. τέος for τ-ιο-ς, and this for τ-ya-ς. These two meanings of *ya*, 'duty' and 'futurity,' meet together in the English word *shall*, which in the present tense is used to express the Future, 'I shall go;' and in the past, to denote duty, 'I should go.'

The Old Slavic, which preserves a few remains of the older forms, already resorts in general to the analytical method of employing auxiliary verbs, separately from the principal verb, to express the Future tense. Verbs denoting 'have,' 'begin,' 'will,' are commonly employed for this purpose. In Greek some traces of this method appear in the use of μέλλω, ἐθέλω, etc. μέλλω — sometimes with the Future Infinitive, e. g. θήσειν γὰρ ἔτ' ἔμελλεν ἐπ' ἄλγεα Τρώεσιν, 'for he *was going* to inflict further woes upon the Trojans' (*Il.* ii. 39); also with the Present Infinitive, e. g. μέλλοντι δ' αὐτῷ πολυθύτους τεύχειν σφαγὰς κῆρυξ ἀπ' οἴκων ἵκετο, 'but there came to him from home, as he *was going to* prepare multifarious sacrifices, a herald.' ἐθέλω—e. g. εἰ δὲ θελήσει, τούτου τελευτήσαντος, ἐς τὴν θυγατέρα ταύτην ἀναβῆναι ἡ τυραννίς, 'but if, when he dies, the royal power *shall* come to this daughter' (*Her.* i. 109).

In the following examples of the synthetical Future, an archaic Latin word is given (faxo). In both Greek and Latin, *s* and *i* must be supposed to be the remains of *yā*; or they are the ordinary connecting vowel, and *yā* is entirely lost, leaving only σ, *s*, as the sign of the Future.

THE FUTURE TENSE

	Sanskrit	Zend	Greek	Latin	
Sing.	bhav-i-shyá́-mi	bû-shyê-mi	φύ-σ-ω	fac-s-o	da-b-o
	bhav-i-shyá-si	bû-shyê-hi	φύ-σε-ις	fac-si-s	da-bi-s
	bhav-i-shyá-ti	bû-shyê-iti	φύ-σε-ι	fac-si-t	da-bi-t
Plur.	bhav-i-shyá́-mas	bû-shyâ-mahi	φύ-σο-μεν	fac-si-mus	da-bi-mus
	bhav-i-shyá-tha	bû-shya-tha	φύ-σε-τε	fac-si-tis	da-bi-tis
	bhav-i-shyá-nti	bû-shya-nti	φύ-σο-νσι	fac-su-nt	da-bu-nt
Dual.	bhav-i-shyá́-vas	—	—	—	—
	bhav-i-shyá́-thas	bû-shyo-thô	φύ-σε-τον	—	—
	bhav-i-shya-tas	bû-shya-tô	φύ-σε-τον	—	—

In Gothic ULFILAS translates Greek Futures by the Conjunctive mood, just as in Latin the third and fourth conjugations have Conjunctive forms for the Future tense. But the auxiliary 'have' is also employed in Gothic for the Future, e. g. taujan *haba* ('I have to do' = I shall do) for ποιήσω, 2 Cor. xi. 12; visan *habaith* ('he has to be' = he will be) for ἔσται, John xii. 26. *Vairtha* = a. s. *weordhe*, 'become,' is sometimes used for the Future of the substantive verb, but otherwise 'will' and 'shall' are employed.

The Anglo-Saxon has no special form for the Future. In English, as in the Germanic languages generally, the synthetical Future is altogether lost; even go. *vairtha*, a. s. *weordhe*, has disappeared, whilst 'shall' and 'will' are the usual auxiliaries. There are also many phrases employed to express futurity, e. g. 'I am going to do,' 'I have to do,' 'I am to do,' 'I am about to do,' etc.

We see, therefore, that, even at a very early period in the development of languages, there existed a great variety in the methods of expressing the relations of time. The idea of time is one of the most abstract that the human mind conceives, and it is not surprising that it was found very difficult to fix so subtle a thing in verbal forms. The difficulty is manifest from the multitude of methods resorted to. The relation of a noun to possession, place, instrumentality, etc., is much more easily appreciated than the relation of a verb to the time when an action takes place; and it is possible that the former was determined much earlier than the latter. The original forms of the various cases of nouns were evidently the same in the great mass of Indo-European languages, which is a strong evidence in favour of the conclusion that the cases were fixed when all those languages were one and the same. But the modes of indicating the

THE POTENTIAL, OPTATIVE, CONJUNCTIVE

tenses, especially the Future tenses of verbs, whilst they are so analogous as to show that they are the result of the same mental laws, are nevertheless so different in verbal expression as to suggest the idea that it was after the different tribes had separated from one another that they began to define those relations more exactly in their language. So long as the children of the family remained under the parental roof, the Present alone possessed importance; but when the brothers and sisters separated and wandered into the wide world, the memories of the Past and the aspirations of the Future filled a larger space in their mental existence, and demanded a more definite expression.

g) MOODS.

a. *Potential,* gr. *Optative,* l. *Conjunctive.*

241. Among the almost infinite variety of circumstances which may accompany the expression of thought, such as its being in the form of a command, a desire, a supposition, etc., a few are distinguished by the special forms of the verb. These special forms are called Moods, or modes of expression. Even when formed by the same elements, they differ considerably in name and meaning in different languages.

The same original element, *yâ,* is employed in forming the Potential of the second conjugation in Sanskrit, the Optative of Greek verbs in μι, and the Present Conjunctive in Latin, e.g. a. *dad*-**yâ**′-*m,* gr. διδο-ίη-ν, L. *d-ê-m,* 'I may give.' An older form exists of a few Latin words, which brings that language sufficiently near to the others; e.g. *du-i-m* preserves *î,* and *s-iê-m* preserves *iê,* for the original *yâ.* All take part, more or less, in the gradual abbreviation of this Mood-sign. In Sanskrit it becomes *yu* for *yâ* in the third person plural, and *i* in the first conjugation, forming *é* with the class vowel *a*. In Zend it is *ya* in several places. In Greek it becomes *ie* in the third person plural (διδο-ῖε-ν, 'they might give'), and *ι* in the ω conjugation (τύπτο-ι-μι, 'I might strike'). In Latin it is reduced generally to *í* (*s-i-mus*, 'we may be'), and in the third person singular to *i* (*s-i-t*). In Sanskrit Atmanêpadam (Middle) it is uniformly *í*; in the Greek Middle and Passive, *ι* (διδο-ί-μην, τυπτο-ί-μην). In the past tense of the Gothic Conjunctive this syllable assumes three forms, in which it appears successively abbreviated from *yâ* to *ya*, *í* (*ei*), and *i*, according to the general laws of the language:—1. êt-ja-u, for êt-ja-m, 'I might eat.' 2. et-ei-s, 'thou mightest eat.' 3. ét-i, 'he might eat.' In Anglo-Saxon it remains only in the singular as *e*, e.g. ic êt-e, 'I might eat.'

Besides these three different Moods, the same element *-yâ* is used to form the Imperative in Old Slavic and Lithuanian, which adds further evidence that these verbal forms, if at all existing, were but imperfectly determined before the entire separation of languages.

The following list will serve to illustrate these Moods, viz. the Sanskrit and Zend Potential, the Greek Optative, and the Latin and Gothic Conjunctive.

THE POTENTIAL, OPTATIVE, CONJUNCTIVE

First Conjugation.

	Sanskrit. 'I can give'	Zend	Greek. 'I would give'	Latin. 'I may give'	Gothic. 'I may eat'
Sing.	dad-yâ′-m	daidh-yã-ñm	διδο-ίη-ν	du-i-m	ét-ja-u
	dad-yâ′-s	daidh-yâ-o	διδο-ίη-s	du-i-s	ét-ei-s
	dad-yâ′-t	daidh-yâ-ḍ	διδο-ίη	du-i-t	ét-i
Plur.	dad-yâ′-ma	daidh-yâ-ma	διδο-ίη-μεν	du-i-mus	ét-ei-ma
	dad-yâ′-ta	daidh-ya-ta	διδο-ίη-τε	du-i-tis	ét-ei-th
	dad-yû-s	daidh-ya-n	διδο-ῖε-ν	du-i-nt	ét-ei-na
Dual.	dad-yâ′-va	—	—	—	ét-ei-va
	dad-yâ′-tam	—	διδο-ίη-τον	—	ét-ei-ts
	dad-yâ′-tâm	—	διδο-ιή-την	—	—

Second Conjugation.

Sanskrit.	Zend.	Greek.	Latin.	Gothic.
'I can bear'		'I would bear'	'I may bear'	
bhár-ê-yam	bar-ôi	φέρ-οι-(μι)	fer-a-m	bair-a-u
bhár-ê-s	bar-ôi-s	φέρ-οι-s	fer-â-s	bair-ai-s
bhár-ê-t	bar-ôi-ḍ	φέρ-οι	fer-a-t	bair-ai
bhár-ê-ma	bar-ai-ma	φέρ-οι-μεν	fer-â-mus	bair-ai-ma
bhár-ê-ta	bar-ai-ta	φέρ-οι-τε	fer-â-tis	bair-ai-th
bhár-ê-yus	bar-ay-ən	φέρ-οι-εν	fer-a-nt	bair-ai-na
bhár-ê-va				bair-ai-va
bhár-ê-tam		φέρ-οι-τον		bair-ai-ts
bhár-ê-tâm		φερ-οί-την		

242. The tenth class in Sanskrit forms *ayê* from *aya-i* (*kâm-ayê-s*). In corresponding Greek verbs the *ι* appears separately, e. g. τιμάο-ι-ς, φιλέο-ι-ς, δηλόο-ι-ς, and in Latin its effect is seen, e. g., in *amês* for *amá-i-s*. In some old Latin forms, as *verber-i-t*, the *yâ* is reduced to *i*, unless the vowel is long, and so *î* stands for *ê*. In the second and fourth Latin conjugations the mood-vowel is indicated only by the long quantity of the *â*, *mon-eâ-s*, *aud-iâ-s*. The future of the third and fourth conjugations contains the same element, and a more regular indication of the half-vowel in *ê* for *ai* than is in *â*. In the Gothic strong conjugations the Conjunctive has *ai*, except in the first person singular, where *a* only occurs, just as in the Latin futures, e. g. 1. *fer-a-m*, *fer-ê-s*; go. *bair-a-u*, *bair-ai-s*. In the weak conjugations the mood-vowel disappears in *ô*, from *a+a*, and that from *aya*. The Conjunctive and Indicative thus coincide, except in the omission of the personal ending in the third singular Conjunctive.

The Imperative Mood.

243. The Imperative Mood, in its oldest forms, differs but little from the indicative. The personal endings are generally of the secondary class. In course of time they have become much abbreviated, and in some cases entirely dropped. In Sanskrit they are: S. -*â-ni*, *a-*, *a-tu*; Pl. *â-ma*, *a-ta*, *a-ntu*; Du. *â-va*, *a-tam*, *a-tâm*. Of these *ni*, *tu*, *ntu* belong to the primary class, and are but modifications of *ma*, *ta*, *nta*, which appear as *mi*, *ti*, *nti* in the indicative mood. The second person singular has lost the personal ending in the first conjugation, but in the second conjugation it has -*dhi*. Verbs of the tenth class in Sanskrit terminate in the second person singular in *aya*, which in the corresponding forms in Greek becomes *as* (*á*), *es* (*ıs*), *os* (*ου*), e. g. τίμ-ά, φίλ-ει, δήλ-ου; in Latin, *â, ê, î*, e. g. *am-â, hab-ê, aud-i*; go. *t (ei), ô, ai*, e. g. *tam-ei*, 'tame;' *laig-ô*, 'lick;' *hab-ai*, 'have.' The second person plural in Latin perhaps preserves the secondary form in not having the final *s* which appears in the indicative. The forms with *tô*, both in Greek (-τω) and Latin (-*to*), to which the Vêda -*tât* has some resemblance, may have been suggested and occasioned by the mood which appears as Lêt in the Vêdas and as conjunctive in Greek. The long vowel, which is characteristic of this mood, appears also in the three first persons of the second Sanskrit conjugation.

The following are examples of the Imperative:

	Sanskrit.	Zend.	Greek.	Latin.	Gothic.
Sing.					
2.	bhár-a	bar-a	φέρ-ε	fer	bair
3.	bhár-a-tu	bar-a-tu	—	—	—
Plur.					
2.	bhár-a-ta	bar-a-ta	φέρ-ε-τε	fer-te	bair-i-th
3.	bhár-a-ntu	bar-a-ntu?	—	—	—
Dual					
2.	bhár-a-tam	—	φέρ-ε-τον	—	bair-a-ts
3.	bhár-a-tâm	—	φερ-έ-των	—	—
Lêt.					
3. S.	váh-a-tât	—	ἐχ-έ-τω	veh-i-to	—

The Conditional Mood.

244. There is a Conditional in Sanskrit, though it is rarely used. It appears to be formed from the auxiliary Future in -*syâm*, etc., by prefixing the augment and substituting the secondary for the primary personal endings, *a-syam*, etc., e. g. Future *dâsyâ'mi*, 'I shall give;' Conditional **adâsyam**, 'I would give.' The Latin language seems to have resorted to a similar method in forming the Imperfect, Perfect, and Pluperfect Conjunctive, for the endings -*rem*, *rim*, and *es-sem* have the same relation to the Future in -*ro* that the Sanskrit *a-syam* has to -*syâmi*, e. g.:

Future	Perf. Conj.	Imperf. Conj.	Plup. Conj.
amâve-ro	amâve-ri-m	amâ-re-m	amâvi-sse-m
amâve-ri-s	amâve-ri-s	amâ-rê-s	amâvi-ssê-s
amâve-ri-t	amâve-ri-t	amâ-re-t	amâvi-sse-t
amâve-ri-mus	amâve-ri-mus	amâ-rê-mus	amâvi-ssê-mus
amâve-ri-tis	amâve-ri-tis	amâ-rê-tis	amâvi-ssê-tis
amâve-ri-nt	amâve-ri-nt	amâ-re-nt	amâvi-sse-nt

The original *s* is preserved in the Pluperfect; in the other instances it is regularly changed to *r* in consequence of being between two vowels. The difference in the quantity and character of the vowel after *s* or *r* is the result of the different treatment of the original *yâ*.

245. There is a striking analogy to these Latin forms in the resemblance between the Future and Conditional in those modern languages which have a close relation to the Latin. It is the more interesting, as exhibiting the operation of the synthetical principle in comparatively recent times, and in languages which, upon the whole, follow the analytical method:

	Future.	Imperf. Opt.
Italian.	ame-rò	ame-rei
	ame-rai	ame-resti
	ame-rà	ame-rebbe
	ame-remo	ame-remmo
	ame-rete	ame-reste
	ame-ranno	ame-rebbono

	Future.	Conditional.
French.	aime-rai	aime-rais
	aime-ras	aime-rais
	aime-ra	aime-rait
	aime-rons	aime-rions
	aime-rez	aime-riez
	aime-ront	aime-raient

	Future.	Imperf. Conj.
Spanish.	ama-ré	ama-ría
	ama-rás	ama-rías
	ama-rá	ama-ría
	ama-rémos	ama-ríemos
	ama-réis	ama-ríais
	ama-rán	ama-rían

The Passive Voice.

246. The Passive forms in Sanskrit, in the special tenses and perhaps originally also in the general tenses, have the accented syllable *yá* between the root and the personal endings which are of the secondary kind. The Passive, therefore, resembles the Middle of the fourth class, except in the place of the accent, e. g. Pass. *bhar-yá-tê*, 'he is borne;' Mid. bhár-a-tê, 'he bears for himself.' As in this example the connecting vowel *a* is omitted, so in general the insertion of the syllable *ya* causes the root to lose those increments which it admits in the special tenses of the Active and Middle, and sometimes also subjects the root to a further abbreviation, e. g.:

3 Sing. Pres. Pass.	Middle.	Active.		
Class 1.				
budh-yá-tê	bó'dh-a-tê	bó'dh-a-ti from	*budh*,	'know'
Class 3.				
bhri-yá-tê	bíbhr-tê'	bibhár-ti	,, *bhr* or *bhar*,	'bear'
Class 7.				
yuj-yá-tê	yunk-té'	yúnak-ti	,, *yuj*,	'join'
Class 5.				
star-yá-tê	str-nu-tê'	str-nó'-ti	,, *str* or *star*,	'strew'

In the above instances the guna, reduplication, insertion of *na* and addition of *nu*, which are modifications of the root admitted in the Active and Middle, are absent from the Passive. In the following instances the root itself is also diminished: **uch**-*yá-tê*, 'is spoken,' from *vach*, 'speak;' **prch**-*yá-tê*, 'is asked,' from *prach*, 'ask;' **di**-*yá-tê*, 'is given,' from *dâ*, 'give;' *ni-***dho**-*yêi-nté*, 'are laid down,' from a. *ni-dhâ*, 'lay down.'

This form of the Passive, which is probably from the root *yâ* = 'go,' is general in Sanskrit and extensively used in Zend, but is rarely met with in the other languages. The Latin verbs *morior* and *fio* present remains of it in the *i*. In *fio* we have the root (*fu*) also in a diminished form, as in the instances noticed above. In Gothic, *us-ki-ja-na* (of which *us* is a preposition), 'enatum,' presupposes a Pres. Ind. *ki-ja*, abbreviated from kin-ja, like s. *ji'-yê* for *jan-yê*. That the root *yâ* = 'go' was the origin of this Passive formative, is rendered the more probable from the fact that in Bengalee and Hindostanee the Passive is expressed by the auxiliary verb 'go,' just as in English it is expressed by the verb 'be,' e. g. *kŏrû yâi*, 'I go made' = 'I am made.' The same verb is also used as an auxiliary in such Latin Passive forms as *amatum iri*, etc.

Causal Verbs.

247. The most common form of Causal Verbs is that in which *aya* is found inserted between the root and the personal endings. It corresponds exactly with the tenth class, e. g. *kâr-áyâ-mi*, 'I cause to make,' from the root *kṛ* or *kar*. This formative may have sprung from the root *î*, 'wish;' for the expression 'I wish (you) to make' may easily have come to mean 'I cause (you) to make.' The verb 'have' in English has been similarly appropriated to a special meaning, for 'I have (or 'have had') a house built' is the same as 'I cause (or 'have caused') a house to be built;' and even 'I have built a house' has come to mean 'I have had a house built.'

This formative appears as -*ja* in the first class of Gothic weak verbs, e. g. a. *sâd-áyâ-mi*, go. *sat-ja*, 'I set,' from a sad, go. sat, e. sit. So lag-ja, 'I lay,' from lig-a, 'I lie;' nas-ja, 'I make well,' from nas, 'to get well;' sanqv-ja, 'I cause to sink,' from sinqv-a, 'I sink' (of myself); drank-ja, 'I cause to drink,' e. drench, from drink-a, 'I drink.' In the English word drench, although no part of the original aya is preserved, yet the influence of y is apparent in the change of k to ch. The difference of formation between the causative and non-causative verbs is indicated in English in a few cases by the former having the heavier, the latter the lighter vowel, e. g. set, sit; lay, lie; drench, drink.

In Greek, καλέω, 'I call' 'I cause to hear,' seems to be a Causative of κλύ-ω, 'I hear;' the root κλυ has become καλ, and ε represents the aya in Sanskrit, as it generally represents aya of the tenth class in verbs in έω.

In Latin the long vowels â, ê, î of the first, second, and fourth conjugations represent the p. aya of the tenth class, and amongst them are some Causatives, e. g. nec-â-re, 'cause to die;' sed-â-re, 'set,' 'cause to sit;' plor-â-re, 'weep,' 'cause to flow;' mon-ê-re, 'cause to think;' sop-î-re, 'cause to sleep.'

The following instances will show the agreement between the Sanskrit and the Latin:

272 VERBS

	Pres. Ind. Sanskrit	Latin	Pot. Sanskrit	Conj. Latin
Sing.	swâp-áyâ-mi ('I cause to sleep')	sôp-i-o	swâp-áyê-yam	sôp-iâ-m
	swâp-áya-si	sôp-i-s	swâp-áyê-s	sôp-iâ-s
	swâp-áya-ti	sôp-i-t	swâp-áyê-t	sôp-iâ-t
Plur.	swâp-áyâ-mas	sôp-i-mus	swâp-áyê-ma	sôp-iâ-mus
	swâp-áya-tha	sôp-i-tis	swâp-áyê-ta	sôp-iâ-tis
	swâp-áya-nti	sôp-iu-nt	swâp-áyê-yus	sôp-ia-nt

After roots in -â, p is inserted in Sanskrit and k (c) in Latin; e. g. yâp-áyâ-mi, 'I cause to go,' from yâ, is the same as l. jac-i-o. The i is reduced in quantity, and the whole assimilated to the third conjugation, as in capio. So also a bhav-áyâ-mi, 'I cause to be,' is the same as the l. fac-i-o, where c is for v, as in vixi (vic-si) from vivo; jnâp-áyâ-mi, 'I cause to know' (from *jnâ*); L. *doc-e-o*. In *râp-áyâ-mi*, 'I cause to go,' 'move' (from *rû*) = 1. *rap-i-o*, the Latin preserves *p*.

In some cases *l* is inserted in Sanskrit Causatives, and corresponding forms are found in Greek, e. g. a. *pál-áyâ-mi*, from *pâ*, 'to rule.' So in Greek, βάλλω for βαλ-γ-ω, 'I cause to go,' from βâ (in ἔ-βη-ν, etc.); στέλλω, 'I cause to stand,' for στελ-γ-ω, from στâ (in ἔ-στη-ν, etc.); ἰάλλω, 'I cause to go,' for ἰαλ-γ-ω, from γâ (2 Aor. of ἵημι has ἰ-, where the *spiritus asper* is for *y*), like the Latin *jac-i-o*.

Desideratives.

248. Desideratives are formed by inserting between the reduplicated form of the root and the personal endings *sa* in Sanskrit, σκε in Greek, and *sci* in Latin, of which the following are illustrations:

Pres. Sanskrit	Greek	Latin	Imperf. Sanskrit	Greek
Sing.				
jijnâ-sâ-mi	γιγνώ-σκω	no-sco	ájijnâ-sa-m	ἐγίγνω-σκο-ν
jijnâ-sa-si	γιγνώ-σκε-ις	no-sci-s	ájijnâ-sa-s	ἐγίγνω-σκε-ς
jijnâ-sa-ti	γιγνώ-σκε-ι	no-sci-t	ájijnâ-sa-t	ἐγίγνω-σκε
Plur.				
jijnâ-sâ-mas	γιγνώ-σκο-μεν	no-sci-mus	ájijnâ-sâ-ma	ἐγιγνώ-σκο-μεν
jijnâ-sa-tha	γιγνώ-σκε-τε	no-sci-tis	ájijnâ-sa-ta	ἐγιγνώ-σκε-τε
jijnâ-sa-nti	γιγνώ-σκο-νσι	no-scu-nt	ájijnâ-sa-n	ἐγίγνω-σκο-ν
Dual.				
jijnâ-sâ-vas	—	—	ájijnâ-sâ-va	—
jijnâ-sa-thas	γιγνώ-σκε-τον	—	ájijnâ-sa-tam	ἐγιγνώ-σκε-τον
jijnâ-sa-tas	γιγνώ-σκε-τον	—	ájijnâ-sa-tâm	ἐγιγνώ-σκέ-την

The Sanskrit changes the original guttural *g* to the palatal *j* in *jíjnâ-sâmi*, 'I desire to know.' The Latin loses the reduplication and (except in some compounds, e. g. *ignosco*) the first consonant of the root. In many of the words which have this form, the Desiderative meaning has not been preserved. In Latin the root *vid* has produced the Desiderative *ví-si* by adding *si* = s. *sa*, and not *sci* as in the former instances. The English form *know* confirms the view that the original consonant was *g*, and the *w*, which appears also in the a. s. *cnaw-an*, is probably the remains of the Desiderative form. The formative *sa* is reduced in Sanskrit for the general tenses to *s*, and is altogether absent from those tenses in Greek and Latin.

Intensives.

249. In the Intensives the personal endings are sometimes connected with the reduplicated root by *í*. The vowel in the syllable of reduplication also, contrary to the usual practice, is made as heavy as that in the root syllable, or even heavier, e. g. *vévéz-mi*, from *viz*, 'to enter;' *ló'lôp-mi*, from *lup*, 'cut off,' 'lop.' Instances in Greek are τωθάζ-ω, παιπάλ-λω, ποιπνύ-ω, etc. If the root begins with a vowel, the whole syllable is repeated in the reduplication; but if the vowel is short, it is lengthened in the root syllable, e. g. *atát*, from *at*, 'go;' *azáz*, from *az*, 'eat.' To these correspond some nominal forms in Greek, e. g. ἀγωγ-ός, 'guide;' ἀγωγ-εύς, 'remover.' But the vowel is shortened in the root of ὀνίν-ημι, ὀπιπτ-εύω, ἀτιτ-άλλω, and not lengthened in ἀλαλ-άζω, ἰλελ-ίζω. Those which begin with a consonant, if they end in a nasal, do not lengthen the root vowel, e.g. s. *jaṅgam*, from *gam*, 'go;' gr. παμφαίνω,

'I shine brightly;' go. *ganga*, 'I go;' n. a. *gange*. If the root ends in a liquid, this is either changed to a nasal or displaced by a nasal, e.g. *chañchal*, from *chal*, 'move;' *pamphal*, from *phal*, 'burst;' *chañchar*, from *char*, 'go.' In Greek, πίμπλημι, 'I fill;' πίμπρημι, 'I set on fire,' etc. Sometimes, however, the liquid remains unchanged in Greek, e.g. μαρμαίρω, 'I glimmer;' βορβορύζω, 'I rumble,' &c. A few Intensive forms have been discovered in Zend and in Latin, as *gingrire*, 'to gaggle.'

h) DENOMINATIVES.

250. Denominatives, i.e. verbs formed from nouns (*de nominibus*), have, in Sanskrit, *ya*, *aya*, *sya*, or *asya* inserted between the nominal stem and the personal ending. If, however, the nominal stem ends in a vowel, it is dropped, e.g. a. *kumâr-áya-si*, 'thou playest,' from *kumárá*, 'boy;' *sukh-áya-si*, 'thou delightest,' from *sukha*, 'delight;' *yóktr-áya-si*, 'thou embracest,' from *yó'ktra*, 'band;' *ksham-áya-si*, 'thou endurest,' from *kshamá'*, 'endurance.'

The examples in Latin are numerous in the first, second, and fourth conjugations, where *â*, *é*, *í* represent Sanskrit *aya*, e.g. *laud-â-s*, 'thou praisest,'from lauda, 'praise;' *can-ê-s*, 'thou art grey,' from canu-s, 'grey;' *sit-í-s*, 'thou thirstest,' from siti-s, 'thirst.' In nouns of the fourth declension, *u* shows more tenacity in keeping its place in the Denominatives, e.g. *fluctu-â-s*, 'thou wavest,' from fluctu-s, 'wave.'

In Greek also many of those verbs which resemble the 10th class in Sanskrit are Denominatives, i.e. such as end in -άω, -έω, -όω, -άζω, -ίζω. In these cases the a. *aya* is represented by different letters. Examples are τιμᾷς (for τιμα-ε-ις), 'thou honourest,' from τιμή; πολεμεῖς (for πολεμε-ε-ις), 'thou warrest,' from πόλεμο-ς; δηλοῖς (for δηλο-ε-ις), 'thou makest manifest,' from δῆλο-ς, 'manifest;' ἀγοράζεις (for ἀγορα-ζε-ις), 'thou attendest market,' from ἀγορά, 'market;' δειπνίζεις (for δειπνι-ζε-ις), 'thou feastest,' from δεῖπνο-ν, 'feast.' Denominatives in σσ, λλ, correspond to Sanskrit forms in ya, having assimilated y to the preceding consonant, e. g. ἀγγέλλω for ἀγγελ-yω, from ἄγγελο-ς; μαλάσσω for μαλακ-yω, from μαλακό-ς. This y, instead of being assimilated after ν or ρ, is transferred to the preceding syllable in the form of ι, e. g. μελαίνω for μελαν-yω, from μέλαν; καθαίρω for καθαρ-yω, from καθαρό-ς. The Denominatives in -ευ-ω perhaps arose from an interchange of half-vowels, i. e. w (v) for y, e. g. δουλεύει, 'he is a slave,' from δοῦλος.

In Gothic j (y) represents the formative element, e. g. audag-j-a, 'I call happy,' from audaga, 'happy;' gaur-j-a, 'I make sad,' from gaura, 'sad;' skaft-j-a, 'I create,' from skafti, 'creation.' The stem-vowel of the noun is dropped, except sometimes u, as in Latin and Greek, e. g. thaurs-j-a, 'I thirst,' from thaursu, 'dry;' and ufar-skadv-j-a, 'I overshadow,' from skadu, 'shadow.' In some cases the Gothic has ô for aya, like the Latin â, e. g. fisk-ô-s, 'thou fishest,' from fiska, 'fish.' In a few cases n is inserted before the ô, and the stem-vowel preserved in a weakened form, e. g. hôrin-ô-s, from hôra, e. whore = gr. κόρη, Dor. κώρα, 'girl,' 'wench.'

Some Passive Denominatives in Gothic are formed by -n, which seems to be connected with the Sansk. Passive Participle in -na, continued in the Germanic strong verbs, e. g. e. broke-n, etc. Go. Passive Denom. (which may be compared with such Passives as and-bund-n-a,

'I am unbound') are *full*-n-*a*, 'I am filled,' Act. *full*-j-*a*, 'I fill,' from *fulla*, 'full.' Perhaps such forms are the source of the double meanings in such English verbs as 'I fill,' both intransitive and transitive = 'I become full' and 'I make full.'

Some Denominatives in Sanskrit, like some Causatives, prefix *p* to *aya*, lengthening the stem-vowel, e. g. *arthâ-páyâ-mi*, from ártha, 'thing;' *satyâ-páyâ-mi*, from satyá, 'truth.'

Some Sanskrit Denominatives correspond in meaning to the Desideratives, e. g. *patî-yâ'mi*, from páti, 'a husband;' *putrî-yâ'mi*, from putrá, 'child.' So in Greek θανατ-ιάω, from θάνατο-ς, 'death,' etc. Such Latin forms as coenaturio, ending in -*turio*, are verbal derivatives, but equio (equ-i-o) is a Denominative with a Desiderative meaning, from equu-s, 'horse.'

Denominatives with a Desiderative meaning are formed in Sanskrit also by *sya* (*asya*), e. g. *vrsha-syâ'-mi*, from *vrshá*, 'bull;' *aśwa*-syâ'-*mi*, from aźwá, 'stallion;' *madhw*-asyâ'-*mi*, from madhú, 'honey.' Latin forms in -*sso*, denoting *imitation*, correspond to these Sanskrit forms in *sya*, the *y* being assimilated to *s*, e. g. *attici*-sso, from atticu-s; *graci*-sso, from graecu-s. Latin Inchoatives in -*asco*, -*esco*, also resemble the Sanskrit forms with -*asya*, e. g. *flamm*-esco, 'I begin to flame,' from flamma, 'flame.'

XI. DERIVATION AND COMPOSITION.

a) DERIVATIVES.

NT or NTA.

251. *The Present Participle Active* is formed by inserting *nt* or *nta* between the verbal stem and the personal ending. The weak forms, however, generally drop the *n* in Sanskrit, while in the Greek and Latin the *n* is preserved throughout. The Gothic has *nda*, where *d* was pronounced probably as an aspirate, for the older mute generally becomes an aspirate in the Gothic language. Examples are s. Gen. *bhára*-**ta**-*s*, but Acc. *bhára*-**nta**-*m*; gr. Gen. φέρο-ντ-ος, l. *fere*-**nti**-*s*, go. *baira*-**ndi**-*ns*. In Greek the *i* is lost, as is seen from the plural M. φέρο-ντ-ες, N. φέρο-ντ-α. The parallel forms in Latin show that the *i* is preserved in that language, e. g. *fere*-nté-*s*, *fere*-nti-*a*. The feminine is formed in Sanskrit by *nt*+*i* in the first conjugation, and by *t*+*i* in the second, e. g. *vása*-**ntî** F., 'inhabiting,' from *vas*; *dáhu*-**ntî** F., 'burning,' from *dah*; *sa*-**tî**' F., 'being,' from *as*. In Greek ντιδ for a. *ntî*, like τριδ for a. *trî*, occurs in 9ερaπó-ντις, Gen. 9ερaπó-ντιδ-ος. In these Participles the Masc. form is used also for the Fem. in Latin. In Gothic the feminine has *ndi* for *ndhi*, with the addition of an inorganic *n*, e. g. *visa*-**ndei** F., 'remaining,' stem *visa*-**ndein**.

The Participle of the substantive verb has lost the

entire root in both Greek and Latin: Gen. ὄντ-ος, L. enti-s, contain only the formative ὀντ, enti, and the case-ending os, s. The Epic and Ionic form ἐοντ indicates the previous existence of ἐσ-οντ; and the compounds præ-sens, ab-sens, Gen. præ-s-enti-s, ab-s-enti-s, contain the root consonant s. The feminine of this Participle in Greek is somewhat obscured from the fact that ν has become υ, as usual in such a position, and τ become σ through the influence of ι, whilst the ι itself then disappears. οὖσα is therefore for ο-ντι-α.

The same element appears in the s. *Auxiliary Future*, e. g. Acc. S. dâ-syá-**nta**-m, 'about to give;' in the gr. *First Future*, δώ-σο-ντ-α, and *First and Second Aorist*, e. g. λύσα-ντ-α, 'having loosed,' λιπό-ντ-α, 'having left.' These letters therefore indicate the Participial character of the word in which they are inserted, and have no reference to any peculiarity of tense, for they are applied to Past, Present, and Future alike.

WANS.

251 a. The reduplicated preterite in Sanskrit forms an *Active Participle* by inserting *wâns* (vâns), *wat* (vat), or *ush*, according to the different weight of the case, between the stem and the personal ending, e. g. Acc. S. rurud-**wâ'ns**-am, Loc. Pl. rurud-**wât**-su, Acc. Pl. rurud-**ûsh**-as, from rud, 'weep.' -ush-î forms the feminine, e. g. rurud-**ûshî**. In the Greek perfect, which is also a reduplicated tense, this formative is employed in M. and N. -οτ, probably for an earlier ϝοτ = s. wat, but applied alike to both heavy and light cases, e. g. Acc. S. τετυφ-ότ-α, 'having struck.' The feminine is νι-α for υσι-α = s. ushî, σ in Greek being usually dropped between two vowels, e. g. τετυφ-υῖ-α. In Latin the word *securis*, 'axe,' for *sec-ns̆i-s*, means 'cutting;' and in Gothic, Nom. Pl. M. *bêr-us̆j-os* means 'those who have borne,' i. e. 'parents.' The Latin adjectives in -*ŏs-us* may also have been formed by *wâṅs*, to which *ŏs* corresponds very much as *ǒr* (*ŏs*) does to *âṅs* in the comparative forms, e. g. meli-ôr-; so *fam-ŏs-us* from fama, though the *s* is not softened in the latter as it is in the former case.

MANA.

252. *The Participle for the Present, Perfect, and Future Middle* ends in *mâna* in the first conjugation, and *âna* in the second. The latter seems to be only a weakened form of *mâna*, just as the plural of the first personal pronoun has *a* for *ma* of the singular, and for the same reason. Hence also, in those parts of the first conjugation which need a lighter ending than the others, viz. the tenth class and the reduplicated preterite, the form *âna* is used. The accent is on the last syllable of the ending, where, in the indicative, it would be on the personal ending; otherwise it is on that part of the stem where the indicative has it. In Greek the perfect has the accent on the last syllable but one of the ending; elsewhere the accent follows the general rule. The following are examples:

	SANSKRIT.	
Present.	Perfect.	Future.
dâd-ána-s	*tutup-ánâ-s*	*dâ-syá-mána-s*
	GREEK.	
διδό-μενο-ς	τετυμ-μένο-ς	δω-σό-μενο-ς

Again we see that the participial *mâna*, μενο, has nothing to do originally with the expression of tense, for, like the form previously noticed, viz. s. *nta*, gr. *ντ*, l. *nti*, it is used for present, past, and future alike.

In Sanskrit, the *Passive Participle* differs from the middle in the same way as the passive voice generally does from the middle voice; i.e. *yá* is inserted in place of the class characteristic, e.g. Mid. *dád-ána-s* (for dada-mâna-s), Pass. *di-yá-mána-s*. In Zend and Greek the same form serves for the passive as is used for the middle, e.g. *burè*-**manè**-*m* = gr. $\phi\epsilon\rho\acute{o}$-$\mu\epsilon\nu o$-$\nu$, *vazè*-**mne**-*m* = gr. $\dot{\iota}\chi\acute{o}$-$\mu\epsilon\nu o$-ν. In the first of these instances the vowel *â* is reduced in Zend as in Greek; in the second it is dropped, as we shall find to be the case in Latin. In using this form for both voices, the Zend already anticipates the practice in Greek, whilst the Latin almost exclusively appropriates it to the passive voice, i.e. in the second person plural.

The Latin forms for the second person plural passive, *amâ*-**mini**, 'being loved,' for *amâ-mini estis*, 'ye are (being) loved,' etc., are clearly instances of this participial form in the nominative plural masculine, and were probably at first used with the substantive verb as another participle is used in the perfect passive, i.e. *amâ-mini estis* like *amâ-ti estis*. *Alu*-**mnu**-*s* is also a passive participle of *alere*, whereas a middle or active meaning is more suited to *Vertu*-**mnu**-*s* and *Vollu*-**mna**. In the last three instances the vowel *â* is dropped, as was found to be the case in Zend.

The element thus appropriated to the formation of the middle participles also appears in *Substantives* and *Adjectives*. In Sanskrit *mân* in strong and *man* in weak cases forms *substantives* with an active or passive meaning, e.g. *túsh*-**man** M., 'fire' (the drier); *vē̆*-**man** M., 'weaving loom' (weaver). l. *fē̆*-**mln**-*a* and e. *wo*-**man** may be similarly formed from this root (s. *vé* or *wé*), denoting 'weaver'—'spinster' is still employed of the unmarried females of the family. (See Sec. **256**.) *hár-i-***mán** M., 'time' (that takes away, *hurries*); *dhar-i-***mán** M., 'form' (what is borne), as 1. *for-***ma** from *fer-*re, and e. bear-*ing* from bear. The neuters are more numerous than the masculines: *dhá'-***man** N., 'house' (what is put or made, so e. build-*ing* = what is built); *kár-***man** N., 'deed' (as 1. fac-**tum** from facere, and e. deed from do); *tó'-***man** N., 'hair' (what grows). *Adjectives* in *-man* are rare: *éár-***man**, 'happy.'

In Greek there are *Abstract Substantives* in -μονη, e.g. φλεγ-μονή, 'inflammation;' χαρ-μονή, 'pleasure.' *Masculine Substantives* in -μον (lengthened in the Nom. S. to μων) are πνεύ-μων, 'lungs' (breather); δαί-μων, 'god' (shining one). These have the accent on the stem; but others, with a connecting vowel, have the accent on the last syllable, both as in Sanskrit, e.g. ἡγ-ε-μών, 'leader.' The same formative also occurs as μεν (Nom. μην), e.g. ποι-μήν, 'shepherd' (feeder). The long quantity of *á* in mâna is preserved in some instances, as in κευθ-μών, Gen. κευθ-μῶν-ος. The same is the case with μίν in such words as κά-μιν-ος, 'oven' (καίω, κάω); ὑσ-μίνη, 'contest' (a contending), connected with s. *yudh,* 'contend.' *Neuter Substantives* have assumed the form -ματ (reduced to μα in the Nom. S.), e.g. Gen. S. ποιή-ματ-ος, πράγ-ματ-ος, ὀ-νό-ματ-ος. The original ν of this last word appears in νώνυ-μνο-ς, 'nameless.'

In Latin, *Masculine Substantives* preserve the long vowel in *món* (reduced to *mó* in the Nom. S.) = gr. μων, s. mân-a, e.g. Gen. S. ser-**món**-*is*, 'of speaking.' A further development of this form appears in those words which end in -mônia, -mônium, e.g. *ali*-**mônia**, *ali*-**mônium**, 'support,' from the same root as alumnu-s. The *Neuter Substantives* have *min* (enlarged to *men* in Nom. S.), e. g. sê-men, 'seed,' Gen. S. *sê*-**min**-*is*; nô-men, 'name,' Gen. S. *nó*-**min**-*is*. It is not clear whether this formative is in homo, Gen. S. *ho*-**min**-*is*, e. *goom* (with *r* inserted in bridegroom, which in Anglo-Saxon is *bryd-guma*), ger. Braüti-*gam*.

In Gothic, *Masculine Substantives* with *man* are *ah*-**man**, 'spirit' (that thinks, from *ah-ja*); *hliu*-**man**, 'ear' (that hears: comp. gr. κλυ); *blô*-**man**, 'flower' (that blows). The formative is curtailed in the a. s. *blô*-**ma**, and still more in the e. *bloo*-**m**. *mâna* is probably compounded of *ma* and *na*, each of which is employed separately in a similar way. We have also seen that *ta* and *ma* of the comparative suffix *tama* are employed separately. *ma* appears in s. *ruk*-**má**-*m*, 'gold' (the shiner); *yug*-**má**-*m*, 'a pair' (e. *yoke* of oxen, etc.); *dhú*-**má**-*s*, 'smoke' (set in motion); *ish*-**má**-*s*, 'love' (wishing). In Greek the suffix is accented like the Sanskrit, e. g. στολ-μό-*s*, 'equipment;' παλ-μό-*s*, 'wielding.' Ϛ is inserted in κλαυ-ϑ-μό-*s*, 'weeping;' μυκη-ϑ-μό-*s*, 'bellowing.' In Latin there are a few examples, such as *an-i*-**mu**-*s*, 'breath' (that blows); *fû*-**mu**-*s*, 'smoke' = s. dhû-má-s; *pó*-**mu**-*m*, 'apple;' *for*-**mu**-*s*, 'warming' = gr. ϑερ-μό-*s*, 'warm,' s. *ghar*-**má**-*s*; *fir*-**mu**-*s*, 'strong' ('bearing,' from *fer*-re); *al*-**mu**-*s* (for al-i-mu-s), 'nourishing.' In the Germanic languages the instances are few and obscure: go. stem *bag*-**ma**, 'tree,' e. *bea*-**m**; go. st. *ar*-**ma** (ard-ma), 'poor;' *bar*-**mi**, 'womb' (bar = 'bear'); e. *di*-**m** = s. dhu-ma, 'smoke;' e. *drea*-**m**, from the root *drâ*, 'sleep' (as in Latin *somnium* and *somnus* are connected together); e. *sea*-**m** from scw.

This formative also appears as *mi*, gr. μι, in s. *dal-***mi**-*s*, 'thunderbolt' (splitter); δύνα-μι-*s*, 'power;' φῆ-μι-*s*, 'speech;' δί-μι-*s*, 'justice.' μη is its feminine form, as in γνώ-μη, 'opinion;' μνή-μη, 'remembrance.' l. *ma*, as in *flam*-**ma**, 'flame' (flag-ma); *fâ*-**ma**, 'fame,' from the root *bhâ*, 'speak.' Latin nouns in -*mulu*-*s* (stem *mulo*-) are perhaps for *munu*-*s* = a. *mâna*, e.g. *fa*-**mulu**-*s* (fac-mulu-s, doer, worker), 'servant;' *sti-mulu*-*s* (stig-), 'stimulant' (pricker).

NDO.

253. In Latin, the *Future Passive Participle in* -*ndus* (stem -*ndo*) Bopp supposes to be of the same origin with -*nti* of the present active. The interchange of *d* and *t* is not without example. We have also seen instances of the same formative being used for different tenses and even for different moods. Though it is undoubtedly rare for all these differences to meet in one and the same instance, yet this does not perhaps form an insuperable difficulty. 1. The formative which appears as *tôr* in Latin is either *târ* or *dâr* in Persian: p. *dâ*-**dâr** = l. *dâ*-**tôr**. 2. The Persian *fer*-*e*-**ndo**-*h* is both active and present in sense, agreeing with l. (*fer*-*e*-**nti**) *ferens*, 'bearing;' but in form agreeing with l. *fer*-*e*-**ndu**-*s*. In the Latin language itself, moreover, there is an instance in which the form -*ndo* agrees in meaning with -*nti*; for *secu*-**ndu**-*s*, 'second,' means 'the following,' from the same root as *sequ-or*. Besides this, the Latin gerunds in -*ndo* have both a present and an active meaning: *reg*-*e*-**ndo**, 'by ruling.'

It thus becomes not improbable that in the adjectives ending in -*bundus*, also, the same formative is employed in a present and active and even a transitive sense, e. g.

vitâ-bu-ndus castra (Liv. 25, 13), 'carefully avoiding the camp;' *mirâ-bu-ndu-s* vanam speciem (Liv. 3, 38, 8), 'greatly admiring an empty show.'

TAR.

254. *The Participle of the Future Active* is formed in Sanskrit by *tú'r* (sometimes reduced to *tṛ*). But it is also used to form *Nomina agentis*, e. g. s. *dá-tấ'r*, Nom. S. *dátấ'*, 'going to give' and 'giver.' In the 1st and 2nd persons of all genders it is joined with the substantive verb to form the *Future Tense*, but in the 3rd person it is the future tense without the substantive verb. In Greek there is no participle in this form, but there are *Nomina agentis* in τήρ, τη, and τορ, e. g. δο-τήρ, 'giver;' μαχη-τή-s, 'fighter.' In Latin *tŭr-o* forms a *Future Participle*, and *tôr* forms *Nomina agentis*, e. g. *dâ-tŭr-u-s*, 'going to give;' *dá-tôr*, 'giver.'

The Feminine forms are s. *trí*, gr. τριδ and τρια, l. *tric*. The abbreviation from *tŭr* to *tr* is caused by the additional weight at the end, and the addition of δ in Greek and *c* in Latin is what we have seen take place in other instances. Examples of these feminines are s. *dá-tri'*, 'the giver;' gr. λησ-τρίs (Gen. λησ-τρίδ-os), 'robber;' ποιή-τρια, 'poetess.' Both ἱκέ-τη-s M. and ἱκέ-τι-s F. (Gen. ἱκέ-τιδ-os), 'applicant,' show a loss of ρ.

255. *The names of family relations in tar, tr,* appear to be *Nomina agentis*, so that each was named from what he was occupied in. s. *pi-tár*, gr. πα-τήρ (τηρ enlarged in the Nom. from τερ), l. *pa-ter*, go. *fa-der* (*d* pronounced as *dh*), a. a. *fœ-der* (*d* pronounced as *dh*), e. *fa-ther* (*th* pronounced as *dh*), from *pâ*, 'nourish' or 'rule;' s. *má-tár*, gr. μη-τήρ (τηρ enlarged from τιρ in Nom.), l. *mâ*-ter, go. *mô*-der, a. s. *mo*-der and *mo*-dor, e. *mo*-ther (*d* and *th* pronounced *dh*), from *mâ*, which itself means 'measure,' but in compounds has the meaning of 'produce,' 'bring forth;' and Bopp has found in the first book of the Rig-Véda, Hymn 61, 7, the Genitive *mâ-túr* as a masculine, meaning *creatoris*, and in the Old Persian the Acc. Sing. *fra-mâ*-târ-*am* = '*imperatorem*.'

256. May not *fê-mina* in Latin be a participial form of the same root? The change of *m* to *f* is certainly unusual; but they are both labials, and the interchange would not do much violence to the genius of language. Besides, we have an instance of a Latin *f* for Greek *μ* in *formīca* compared with μύρμηξ. *m* and *w* are more frequently interchanged: indeed, we have an instance probably in German **mit** and English **with**. In Bohemian, **mlh** corresponds in meaning, and probably also in origin, to the ger. **wolke**, e. **welk**-in. Is it not therefore possible that **wo**-*man* may be from the same root as **mo**-*ther*, and similarly formed with the Latin *fê-mina*? If so, two words for which hitherto very unsatisfactory etymologies have been given would be traced to their origin, and shown to have a very appropriate meaning. (See Sec. **252.**) s. *bhrâ'*-**tar** (gr. φρά-τωρ, member of a brotherhood), l. *frä*-**ter**, go. *brû*-**der**, a. s. *brô*-**dher** and *bro*-**dher**, e. *bro*-**ther**, is referred by Bopp to the root *bhar*, 'bear,' denoting the 'bearer' or 'supporter' of the family. s. *swás*-**âr** (*t* lost, but the vowel lengthened as in Latin) (gr. ἀδελφή), l. *sor*-**ór** (*t* lost and *o* lengthened as in Sans., and *s* between vowels changed to *r*), go. *svis*-**tar**, a. s. *swus*-**ter** and *sus*-**ter**, e. *sis*-**ter**, is referred by Pott and Bopp to the root *su*, *sû*, 'bear,' 'bring forth.' s. *duh-i*-**târ**, gr. θυγ-ά-τηρ (γ for χ) (L. filia), go.

288   DERIVATION AND COMPOSITION

dauh-**ter**, n. s. *dóh*-**ter**, e. *daugh*-**ter**, seems connected with the root *duh*, and to mean 'milker,' i. e. of cows. Bopp gives 'suckling' as the meaning, which is objectionable because it is quite as appropriate to son as daughter, whereas this word is used to distinguish one from the other.

257. From the same element (*tar*) arise the neuter -*tra* and the feminine -*trâ*, the former occurring in many words, the latter in few. They have an instrumental meaning; e. g. *né'*-**tra**-*m*, 'eye' (means of guiding, from *ní*); *zró'*-**tra**-*m*, 'ear' (means of hearing, from *zru*); *gâ'*-**trâ**-*m*, 'limb' (means of going, from *gâ*); *dánż*-**trâ**, 'tooth' (means of biting, from *danż*). In Greek the forms of the suffix are -τρο, -τρα, -θρο, -θρα. The change from a mute to an aspirate frequently occurs in Greek without any apparent cause: ἄρο-τρο-ν, 'plough,' from ἀρόω; καλυπ-τρα, 'covering,' from καλύπ-τω; ἄρ-θρο-ν, 'limb,' from ἀραρ-ίσκω; βά-θρα, 'step,' from βα-ίνω. In Latin *arâ*-**tru**-*m*, 'plough,' from arâ-re; *fulgé*-**trâ**, 'lightning,' from fulge-sco. The aspirate, which is only occasional in Zend and Greek, is regular in Gothic, Anglo-Saxon, and English: go. *maur*-**thr** (stem maur-*thra*), e. *mur*-**ther**, from the root *mar*, l. *mor*-ior. go. *blós*-**tra**, 'sacrifice,' which may be inferred from *blos-treis*, is from blôt-an, 'to sacrifice.' Without the formative the Anglo-Saxon *blot* means 'a sacrifice.' In e. *laugh*-**ter**, from laugh, the preceding consonant prevents *t* from being aspirated; and the same cause perhaps operated in *slaugh*-**ter**, the *gh* being pronounced at first. The consonant (*ch*) is pronounced still in both the corresponding words in German, i. e. lachen, schlachten. e. *wea*-**ther** is connected with the s. root *wâ*, 'blow.' go. *hulis*-**tr** (stem hulis-*tra*, the *t* not being aspirated in consequence of the preceding *s*); go. *fō*-**dr**, 'sheath,' s. s. *fó*-**dher** (stem fō-dra, d = dh), connected with the s. root *pâ*, 'to contain,' and so equal to s. *pâ'*-**tra**-*m*, 'container,' 'vessel.' c. *ru*-**dder**, ger. *ru*-**der**, is perhaps connected with gr. ῥεῖ-θρο-ν, 'stream,' from ῥέω, though with a meaning resembling the l. *ré*-mus, 'oar.' The *dd* is for the aspirate *dh*. go. *hlei*-**thra**, 'tent,' a. s. *hla*-**dre**, e. *la*-**dder** (*d* and *dd* for the aspirate).

With the change of *r* to *l*, which is of frequent occurrence, this formative becomes in Greek τλο, τλη, θλο, θλη, e. g. ὄχε-τλο-ν, 'carriage;' ἐχέ-τλη, 'handle;' θύσ-θλο-ν, instruments used in the worship of Bacchus; γενέ-θλη, 'birth.' In Gothic the corresponding form is *thla*, e. g. *né*-**thla**, a. s. *næ*-**dl**, e. *nee*-**dle** (*d* instead of the aspirate).

TA.

258. *The Participle of the Perfect Passive* is formed by *-ta*, F. *tá*. It takes the accent, e. g. *tyak*-**tá**-*m*, Acc. S., 'left.' In Greek *Verbal Adjectives* (but not participles) are similarly formed, e. g. πο-τό-ς, πο-τή, πο-τό-ν, 'drunk,' with a passive meaning, and the formative accented as in Sanskrit; but also πό-το-ς, 'the act of drinking.' In Latin the suffix is employed in forming the *Participle* as in Sanskrit, e. g. *du*-**tu**-*s*, *da*-**ta**, *da*-**tu**-*m*, from da-re. In the above instances *ta* is affixed immediately to the root. Sometimes *i* is inserted: s. *prath*-**i**-**tá**-*s*, 'stretched out,' from *prath*; gr. σκελ-ε-τό-ς, 'dried,' from σκέλ-λω; l. *mol*-**i**-**tu**-*s*, 'ground,' from mol-o. The characteristic of the tenth class (aya) is usually preserved in an abbreviated form, e. g. s. *púl*-**i**-**tá**-*s*, 'oppressed;' gr. φιλ-η-τό-ς, 'beloved,' l. *am*-**â**-**tu**-*s*.

U

Adjectives are also formed from substantives by *i-ta*, e. g. a. *phal-i-tá-s*, 'possessed of fruit;' gr. ἁμαξ-ι-τό-ς, 'possessed of waggons;' l. *patr-i-tu-s*, 'fatherly.' The Latin neuters in *-é-tu-m* are probably formed from denominatives of the second conjugation, e. g. *arbor-ê-tu-m*, from arbor-e-sco, Perf. -è-vi.

Abstract Nouns are formed from adjectives by the feminine *tá*, e. g. a. *çuklá-tâ*, 'whiteness.' go. *thô*, Nom. *tha*: *niuji*-**tha**, 'newness.' a. s. *dhe, dh* (also written *d*): *hal*-**dh**, *leng*-**dhe**; *gebyr*-**d**, 'birth.' e. *heal*-**th**, *weal*-**th**, *leng*-**th**, *dep*-**th**, *bread*-**th**, *heigh*-**th** (the last has in recent times dropped the *h* and become *heigh*-t). The Latin *juven*-**ta** belongs to this class of derivatives. The Sanskrit stem *yuvan* is in some cases contracted to *yun*. The same contraction takes place in the Latin comparative *jun*-ior. In Gothic the abstract *jun*-**da** is formed from this abbreviated stem, having *d*, as in so many instances, for *dh*; whilst the English *you*-**th** preserves the aspirate, but loses the final vowel and reduces the stem to *you* for *yu*.

Abstracts in *tát-i* occur in the Vêdas, with which may be compared the Greek τητ, the Latin *tât, tût*, and the Gothic *duth*, where the *d* is again for an aspirate, e. g. v. *arishṭá*-**tât**-*is*, 'invulnerability,' from *árishṭa*; gr. ἠλιθιό-τητ-ς, Gen. ἠλιθιό-τητ-ος, 'folly,' from ἠλίθιος; l. juven-tu-s, Gen. *juven*-**tât**-*is*, 'youthfulness,' from juvenis; sterilitas, Gen. *sterili*-**tât**-*is*, 'barrenness,' from sterilis; go. *ajuk*-**duth**-*s*, 'eternity;' *manag*-**duth**-*i*, 'abundance' (2 Cor. viii. 2); *mikil*-**duth**-*i*, 'greatness.' Similar words in Latin have *tûd-in*, perhaps from *tût* by changing *t* to *d* and adding *in*: Gen. S. *magni*-**tûdin**-*is*, 'greatness.'

Abstracts are formed from adjectives and substantives by *twá* added immediately to the stem, e.g. a. *amṛta*-

twá-m, 'immortality,' from amṛta. In Gothic the word *thiva*-dva, 'serfdom,' occurs (with d for the aspirate), from thiva, 'serf.' In English, -dom resembles the Latin forms in tû-din, from tût, in having added a nasal and changed t to d. In words which are not abstracts, the Gothic preserves the formative as *thva*, e. g. *fri-a*-thva, 'love;' *sal-i*-thva, 'an inn;' but also in *fi-a*-thva, 'enmity.'

NA.

259. *A Perfect Passive Participle* of a small number of verbs is formed in Sanskrit by the syllable *ná*, e. g. bhug-ná-s, 'bent,' from *bhuj*; bhag-ná-s, 'broken,' from *bhanj*; bhin-ná-s, 'split,' from *bhid*. A few Greek *Nouns* (but not participles) are similarly formed by νό, νή: σεμ-νό-s (for σεβνοs), 'venerated;' σκη-νή, 'tent' ('covered in'). The meaning shows that these forms are of participial origin. τέκ-νο-ν, 'child' (lit. 'brought forth'), has the accent irregularly thrown back. In Latin there are *plé*-nu-s, 'full' (lit. 'filled'); *reg*-nu-m, 'dominion' (lit. 'ruled over'). Here again the participial meaning is very obvious, although the form does not appear among the participles in any Latin conjugation. Many words have deviated more or less from the original meaning, e. g. *mag*-nu-s, 'great' (lit. 'grown'); *dig*-nu-s, 'worthy' (lit. 'talked of,' or 'pointed to'). A similar deviation appears in corresponding Greek forms, such as σεμνός, 'venerable' as well as 'venerated.' The formative, which thus appears to have only a fragmentary character in the older languages, extends in Gothic and Anglo-Saxon throughout the strong conjugations, answering to the strong or 'irregular' verbs in English. The syllable *na*, Nom. *n*, however, is joined to the root by means of a connecting vowel *a* or *e*, whereas in the languages which we have already noticed it is added immediately to the root, e.g. go. *bug-*a-n-s, n. s. *graf-*e-n, e. *grav-*e-n; s. *bhug-*nā́-s, 'bent.' In some Gothic *Participles* used as nouns, however, the syllable is added immediately to the root, e.g. the adjective *us-luk-*na-s, 'open' (lit. 'unlocked'), and the N. substantive go. *bar-*n (stem bar-na), a. s. *bear-*n, 'child' (lit. 'born;' so the Scotch *bair-*n).

260. *na* is used like *ta* to form *Possessive Adjectives* from substantives. In this application it also takes the connecting vowel *i*, e.g. a. *phal-*i-ná-s, 'possessed of fruit,' from phal-a; *mal-*i-ná-s, 'covered with dirt,' from mal-a. There are also feminine forms in *ní*, denoting 'wife of,' preceded by *á*, e.g. *Indr-*á-ní (*r* changes *n* to *ṇ*), 'wife of Indra.' gr. πεδ-ι-νό-ς, 'flat,' from πεδ-ίον; σκοτε-ι-νό-ς (for σκοτεσ-ι-νο-ς), 'dark,' from σκότος, st. σκοτες. Some adjectives, like ξύλινος, λίθινος, have the accent thrown back. An instance of this occurs in the Sanskrit word *çŕ̇ñg-*i-na-s, 'horned,' from *çŕ̇ñg-*a. Feminine forms in *νη*, preceded by *ω*, resemble the Sanskrit feminines in *á-ní*, e.g. 'Ακρισι-ώ-νη, 'daughter of' 'Ακρίσι-ος. Those in -αινα are for -α-νια, e.g. Θίαινα, λύκαινα. In Latin many words have *i* before -*nu* for the connecting vowel, as in Gothic, e.g. *stagn-*i-nu-s, from stagn-u-m, 'pool;' *bov-*i-nu-s, from stem bov (bos, 'ox'). After *r* the vowel is omitted, as in English, e.g. *ebur-*nu-s, from ebur, 'ivory;' *ver-*nu-s, from ver, 'spring.' Even in Sanskrit *í* occurs, e.g. *sam-*í'-na-s, 'yearly,' from samā́', 'year.' In Latin also a different vowel, viz. *á*, occurs, but it is perhaps of the same origin, e.g. *oppid-*á-nu-s, from oppid-u-m, 'town;' *Rom-*á-nu-s, from Rom-a. There are also feminines in -*na* and -*nia* preceded by *ó*, e.g. *Bell-*ó-na, *mátr-*ó-na, *Vall-*ó-nia. In Gothic *na*,

Nom. *n*, is preceded by *ei* (=*i*), e.g. *silubr*-ei-n-*s*, 'of silver;' *fill*-ei-n-*s*, '*pelliceus*;' *liuhad*-ei-n-*s*, 'light;' *sunj*-ei-n-*s*, 'true.' In English the connecting vowel has become *e*, and after *r* is lost, e.g. *wood*-e-n, *gold*e-n, *leather*-n. The later practice has been to use the substantive, without any formative addition, as an adjective, as in 'a *silver* knife,' 'a *gold* watch.' A trace of the feminine formative is found in the Anglo-Saxon *gyden* (gyd-e-n), *gyd*-e-ne, 'goddess.'

A few *Abstracts* are formed by *na*, F. *nâ*, e.g. s. *yaj*-nâ-*s*, 'honour;' *tṛsh*-nâ', 'thirst;' *swáp*-na-*s*, 'sleep;' gr. ὕπ-νο-*s*, τέχ-νη; l. *som*-nu-*s*, *rap*-i-na.

TI, NI.

261. *Feminine Abstracts* are formed by *ti* and *ni*, which are probably from ta and na, e.g. s. *yúk*-ti-*s*, 'union;' *úk*-ti-*s*, 'speech.' Some have *a* before *ti*, which is a connecting or class vowel. In these words the root is sometimes accented, e. g. *ár*-a-ti-*s*, 'fear;' *ram*-a-ti-*s*, 'the god of love;' *vah*-a-ti-*s*, 'wind.' gr. χῆ-τι-*s*, μῆ-τι-*s*, φά-τι-*s*, ἄμπω-τι-*s*. Elsewhere τ becomes σ, except when preceded by σ, which itself has come from a dental, e. g. πίσ-τι-*s* from πιϑ, ζεῦξις for ζευκ-σι-*s*. -σια has been formed from σι, as -τρια from a tri. It is seldom added to monosyllabic stems, e. g. ϑυ-σία, δοκιμα-σία, ἱππα-σία. These latter resemble in appearance such words as ἀϑανασ-ία from ἀϑάνατ-ος, which are not participial but nominal formations. Some in Greek, as in Sanskrit, have a connecting vowel before σι, and the same accentuation, e. g. νέμ-ε-σι-*s*, εὕρ-ε-σι-*s*. In Latin this enlarged form appears in *puer*-i-tia, *can*-i-tiê-*s*, *serv*-i-tiu-*m*, etc. A still greater increase of the formative appears in

-*ti-ón*, -*si-ón*, Nom. -ti-o, -si-o; e. g. *coc*-**tio** = s. *pák*-**ti-***s*, *junc*-**tio** = s. *yúk*-**ti-***s*. Adverbs in -*ti-m*, -*si-m*, retain the older and shorter form *ti*, e. g. *trac*-**ti**-*m*, *cur*-**si**-*m*. The same formative appears also in *mes*-**si-***s*, 'mowing;' *tus*-**si-***s*, 'coughing.' *mors*, *mens*, stem mort, ment, probably for *mor*-**ti**, *men*-**ti**, = s. *mṛ́*-**ti-***s*, *má*-**ti-***s*.

In Gothic this syllable assumes the forms *ti*, *di*, *thi*, Nom. *t*, *d*, *th*. The last is the regular form. The second was perhaps pronounced as *dhi*. The first has *t* from the influence of the preceding consonant. Examples are, *ga-baur*-**th-***s*, 'birth;' *ga-mun*-**d-***s*, 'memory;' *ga-skaf*-**t-***s*, 'creation;' *fra-lus*-**t-***s*, 'loss' (stem gabaurthi, etc.). Many English words retain this consonant, e. g. *bir*-**th**, *dea*-**th**, *soo*-**th**, *migh*-**t**, *sigh*-**t**, *frigh*-**t**. In some probably *gh* has been introduced from imitation of others, as in *fri*-**gh-t** from *fear*.

ni is not so extensively used as *ti*. It occurs in those words whose perfect passive participle has *na* for *ta*: s. *lū́*-**ni-***s*, 'loosening;' *glấ*-**ni-***s*, 'exhaustion;' *jī́'r*-**ni-***s*, 'age' (*n* changed to *ṇ* by *r*); gr. σπά-νι-*s*, 'rarity,' compared with σπα-νό-*s*. In Gothic *ana-bus*-**ni** (ana-biuda), 'command;' *taik*-**ni**, 'sign,' 'showing' (e. *tok*-**e-n**); *siu*-**ni**, 'seeing.' In these forms *i* is dropped before *s* of the Nom. The weak conjugations, which do not form the participle in *n*, have Abstracts in *ni*, Nom. *n*, preceded by *ei* in the first, *ó* in the second, and *ai* in the third conjugation, e. g. *gól*-**ei-n-***s*, 'salutation;' *lath*-**ó-n-***s*, 'invitation;' *bau*-**ai-n-***s*, 'edification.'

Masculine Substantives applied to agents are formed by *ti* in Sanskrit, e. g. s. *yá*-**ti-***s*, 'tanner;' *sáp*-**ti-***s*, 'horse' (lit. 'runner'); *pá*-**ti-***s*, 'lord' (lit. 'nourisher'); gr. πό-σι-*s*, 1. *po*-**ti-***s*. Is not the English word *foo*-**d** ('feeder') formed from the same root and in the same way, the regular *th* for *t* having become *d*? gr. μάντι-s, 'prophet;' L. vec-ti-s, 'lever' (lit. 'carrier'); go. ga-drauh-t-s, 'soldier;' gas-t-s, 'guest' (lit. 'eater'). In these Gothic words and the English gues-t, the t instead of th is from the influence of the preceding consonant.

ni also as well as ti is employed to form *Masculine Appellatives*, e. g. s. vṛsh-**ni**-s, 'ram,' and, applied to a different animal, perhaps l. ver-**re**-s for ver-**ni**-s, 'boar' (from the same root, s. vṛsh-á, 'bull'); s. ag-**ní**-s, 'fire' (lit. 'burner'); l. ig-**ni**-s. In Latin also pá-**ni**-s, 'bread' (lit. 'feeder'); fú-**ni**-s, 'rope' (lit. 'binder'), etc.

TU, NU.

262. As the interrogative pronoun appears in three forms, viz. *ka, ki, ku*, so the formatives which we are now considering appear as *ta, na; ti, ni*; and *tu, nu*. The Sanskrit *Infinitive* ends in *-tum*, of which *m* is the sign of the accusative case, e. g. dấ'-**tu-m**, 'to give;' sthấ'-**tu-m**, 'to stand;' át-**tu-m**, 'to eat,' from *ad*. In compounds *m* is dropped, e.g. *tyak*-**tu**-*kâmas*, 'desirous to leave.'

The Sanskrit -*tuấ* is an instrumental case of *tu*, formed by adding *â*, and is employed like Latin gerunds, e. g. *taṅ dṛsh*-**twâ'**, 'after seeing him' (lit. 'with seeing him'); *ity-uk*-**twâ'**, 'after so speaking' (lit. 'with so speaking').

The Dative case of abstract nouns is sometimes used in the sense of the usual *Infinitive* or accusative case, e. g. *gám*-**anâya**, 'to go;' *dárẑ*-**anâya**, 'to show.' The abstracts in *ana*, which appears in the above examples, are also employed in the Locative Singular in the same sense as the dative, instead of the infinitive, e. g. *anwésh*-**anê**, 'to seek.' The same form of infinitive becomes general in the Germanic languages: go. *an*, *gib*-**an**, 'to give;' a. s. *gif*-**an**, old e. *giv*-**en**, modern German *geb*-**en**. A similar formation appears in Greek. The oldest form of the *Present Infinitive* is -μεναι or ε-μεναι, which is a Dative (that is, a Locative) form of an abstract in -μενα or ε-μενα. Another form is -μεν or ε-μεν, which results from dropping αι of μεναι or ε-μεναι. Again, there are forms of the infinitive in -ναι, where the first syllable of μεναι is dropped, unless -ναι be the Dative (Locative) of να, as μεναι is of μενα, and thus be of distinct origin. This appears the more probable, because forms in -ναι occur as early as those in μεναι. The common classical form is -ειν for εν, and this from ε-μ-εν, e. g. εἰπ-έ-μεναι, εἰπ-έ-μεν, εἰπ-εῖν, βῆ-ναι.

263. An Aorist form in the Vêdas with the meaning of the *Infinitive* ends in *sê* (=sai), e. g. *mê′*-**shê** (*s* changed to *sh* by the preceding vowel), 'to throw.' This strikingly resembles the Greek First Aorist Infinitive in -σαι, e. g. λῦ-σαι, 'to loose;' τύψαι (τυπ-σαι), 'to strike;' δεῖξαι (δεικ-σαι), 'to show.' Both seem identical with the Latin -*se* after consonants, *re* after vowels, e. g. es-**se**, 'to be;' dic-*e*-**re**, 'to say.' *s* assimilates a preceding *t* in *pos*-**se**, from *pot*-*se*, and is itself assimilated to a preceding *l* and *r* in *vel*-**le** and *fer*-**re**, unless these are for vel-*e*-re (gr. βούλ-ο-μαι) and fer-*e*-re (φέρ-ο-μαι), in which case the only assimilation is that of *r* to *l* in *velle*. The *Perfect Infinitive* in Latin in archaic forms is also -*se*, e. g. *consum*-*se*, *admis*-*se* (for *admit*-*se*, from *admit*-*to*). As the Latin perfect generally corresponds in origin to the Greek aorist, these forms agree exactly with the aorists φῆν-αι (for φην-σαι, the σ being dropped after nasals) and τύψαι (for τυπ-σαι). The more common Latin forms in -*sse* are of later origin.

The *Passive Infinitive* in Latin was probably at first -*sese*, changed by the laws of euphony to -*rere*, and afterwards to -*ri-re* and -*ri-er*. Hence we meet with the older forms *amâ-rier*, *monê-rier*, *dici-er*, *mollí-rier*. The last syllable -*er* is wanting in the ordinary forms used in the classical works, and in conjugating the Latin verb; therefore *amâ-ri*, *monê-ri*, *dici*, *mollí-ri* are regarded as Passive Infinitives, though in fact they exactly agree in form with the Active Inf. *amâ-re*, etc., with the exception that the final -*e* was changed to -*i*, for euphonic reasons, when followed by *re* (*er*). There is also the further difference in the third conjugation, that -*re* of the Active *dice-re* is dropped. The so-called Passive Infinitives, therefore, are not Passive in *form*. The older termination *er* for *re*, and that for *se*, is the same reflexive pronoun as is employed in the form of *r* in the rest of the passive conjugation.

This *Véda Infinitive* in -*sê* occurs in sentences where its usage is exactly parallel with that of the *Dative of Abstract Substantives* in -*â*, and thus illustrates the meaning and force of the Infinitive, e. g. *vê'mi twâ púshann ṛnj-ásê*, *vê'mi stó't-avé*, 'I come to glorify thee, Pushann; I come for praising (thee).' ṛnj-ásê Inf., and stó't-avé Dat. S.

There is also a *Véda Infinitive* in the form of the accusative singular following the verb *żak*, 'to be able.' The English Infinitive without 'to,' after 'can,' resembles this construction, though the Infinitive has not the form of a case, e. g. *apalupan* (for apalupam, Acc. of apalupa) *nâ żaknuvan*, 'they could not (to) destroy.'

This verb *żak* is even used in the Passive form itself, *yadi żak-ya-té*, 'if it can,' lit. 'if it (is) can(ned).' A double Passive occurs even in Latin, e. g. *ut comprimi nequitur*, 'how incapable he is of being restrained' (Plaut. *Rud.* iv. 4, 20); *forma in tenebris nosci non quita est*, 'the form could not be distinguished in the dark' (Ter. *Hec.* iv. 1, 58). The Future Infinitive Passive in Latin has likewise the auxiliary in the passive form: *amatum iri*.

264. In later languages the expression of the *Passive* seems to have been felt to be difficult. The methods resorted to by Ulfilas, in his Gothic translation of the Scriptures, are various and singular; but in none of them is there a really passive form of the finite verb. The Passive Perfect Participle in *th* (originally *-ta*) is employed, but not as a past tense. The relations of time are expressed in the substantive verb connected with the participle, e. g. Mark xiv. 5, *maht vési ... frabugjan*, 'was able to be sold.' The word able, however, must be supposed to be Passive, as if *mayed* could be formed from *may* like *made* from *make*, and thus the *maht vési* might not only express the past tense of ἠδύνατο, but also the passive voice of πραθῆναι; for the Gothic word by which this latter is rendered is active, *frabugjan*, 'to sell,' instead of 'to be sold.' *skulds* (th-s) is also used in a similar way to express the passive of the accompanying infinitive: e. g. Luke ix. 44, μέλλει παραδίδοσθαι, 'is going to be given up,' is rendered *skulds ist abgiban*, 'is necessitated (Pass.) to give up' (Act.) for 'to be given up.' The Active Infinitive is also used for the passive when no passive form accompanies it, and the only method of indicating the voice is in the agent being expressed in the dative or instrumental case; e. g. πρὸς τὸ θεαθῆναι αὐτοῖς, 'in order to be seen by them,' is in Gothic 'in order to see by them,' *du saihvan im*. This use of the active for the passive infinitive, without the least indication of the difference, occurs extensively in the modern German language, e. g. *es ist zu sehen*, for 'it is to be seen.' In English it is rare, e. g. 'it is yet to do' for 'it is yet to be done.'

The preposition *to*, which is generally put before the infinitive in the Germanic languages, properly governs the dative case. The Gothic, however, from the habit of dropping the final vowel, has lost the case-sign. The old Saxon and Anglo-Saxon have *e* (for *ai*) as a reduced form of the dative ending *âya*. The *n* is also doubled without any apparent reason. Possibly it was intended to regulate the pronunciation of the preceding vowel, as in English the consonant is doubled after a short vowel when a suffix is added beginning with a vowel, e. g. *hitt-ing* for *hit-ing*, merely to prevent the first *i* from being pronounced long in the participle. A similar reason may have caused the forms o. s. and a. s. *farann-e* for *faran-e*.

As the Dative case, among other things, also expresses the goal at which an action aims, so the Germanic Infinitive, consisting of the preposition *to* with a Dative case, was at first confined to this meaning, and afterwards extended by analogy to others. Thus, in Gothic, 'a sower went out *to sow*' (*du saian*), i. e. for the purpose of sowing; 'he that hath ears *to hear*' (*du hausjan*), i. e. for the purpose of hearing. The following may serve as an illustration of the further use of this form: 2 Cor. ix. 1, *ufjô mis ist du mêljan izvis*, 'superfluous for me it is to write to you' (τὸ γράφειν, *du* mêljan, 'to write,' i. e. writing).

This mere action without any reference to aim or purpose is often expressed by the *Infinitive* which depends upon another verb, e. g. 'he began to go,' i. e. he began the act of going. So, in Lu. iv. 10, 'will enjoin upon his angels (the act) *of taking care of thee*;' go. *du gafastan thik*, τοῦ διαφυλάξαι σε.

In Gothic this *Infinitive* is also used without the preposition, sometimes in rendering a Greek infinitive, e. g. *galeithan*, ἀπελθεῖν, 'to go out;' and sometimes in rendering a Greek noun, e. g. Luke iv. 36, varth *afslauthnan* allans, ἐγένετο θάμβος ἐπὶ πάντας, 'there came *amazement* upon all.'

Verbs denoting an act of sensation often take two objects, the first expressed by an objective case, and the second by an infinitive without the preposition. The infinitive in this case denotes only the act, as in the dependent infinitive noticed above, e. g. 'I saw him go,' i. e. going, where *him* and (the act of) *going* are two objects seen and combined in one idea. The Greek has the participial form where the Gothic has this infinitive: John vi. 62, ἐὰν οὖν θεωρῆτε τὸν υἱὸν τοῦ ἀνθρώπου ἀναβαίνοντα, *jabai nu gasaihvith sunu mans ussteigan* (ἀναβαίνοντα, *ussteigan*, 'ascend up'). Where the governing verb does not denote an act of sensation, the nature of the governed infinitive is sometimes not quite so obvious. Yet in such cases as Matt. viii. 18, *haihait galeithan siponjons*, 'he commanded go the disciples,' i. e. the disciples to go, it is clear that both the act of going and the disciples were objects of command. So also Lu. xix. 14, *ni vileim thana thiudanon*, 'we refuse him to rule,' *him* and *ruling* are alike the objects of refusal.

265. In Greek we meet with the forms ε-μεναι, -ε-μεν, (ε-εν) -ειν (Ion. ην), -ε-ν (Dor.), and ναι. It is not difficult to trace all the others to the first, -ε-μεναι, which appears in the oldest documents; for -ε-μεν merely drops the final diphthong, (ε-εν) -ειν further drops μ, and regularly contracts the two vowels to ει, the Ionic shows another and less usual contraction to η, the Doric drops ι from ι-εν. Again, the original form after vowels is -μεναι, which, by dropping μι, becomes ναι. There is nothing in these changes very different from the usual course of abbreviation to which language is subject. The loss of αι all at once from μεναι is the least likely; but in Homer, where the full form occurs, very often the diphthong is elided in ἔμμεν for ἔμμεναι, and the elision of it, however rarely it occurs, indicates the possibility of its being dispensed with altogether. The derivation of -μεν from μεναι is also less improbable than that there should have been different sources of the infinitive present of εἰμί in the existing forms of ἔμμεναι, ἔμμεν.

If μεναι be referred to the Sanskrit -manê, dative singular of -man, it would make the Greek form αι fuller than the Sanskrit, which is very unlikely to be the case; but if it be referred to -mânâya, dative singular of -mâna, it would make the Greek a + ι for â + y, with the loss of the final a, a more regular representative of the Sanskrit form. The first part μεν answers to a. mân, as the participles in -μενο-ς to the s. part. mâna-s. Like other participial terminations, it was probably employed to form abstract nouns, and hence the Greek infinitive is a case of an abstract noun like other infinitives.

Bopp refers to the Middle forms, s. mê, sê, and gr. μαι, σαι, as showing that the s. ê may be represented in Greek by αι; but in this case there was a consonant between the vowels, which will account for the otherwise unusual preservation of the original vowels a ι in Greek. (Sec. **212**, p. 183.)

266. The *Passive Infinitive* has the form σθαι, which Bopp explains as consisting of the reflexive pronoun σ (for σέ, I) and the dative singular of an abstract noun formed from the same root as the auxiliary verb, signifying 'do' or 'put,' and appearing as $\vartheta\eta$ in the weak (or first) aorist and future passive $\vartheta\eta\text{-}\nu$, $\vartheta\eta\text{-}\sigma o\mu a\iota$. That σ represents the reflexive pronoun as expressive of the passive voice seems probable from the analogy of the Latin language, where the same pronoun serves the same purpose. There is this difference, however, that in Greek it is inserted between the root and the sign of the infinitive, whilst in Latin it is affixed to the infinitive, as it is to the finite forms, of the active, e. g. *amât-ur, amâri-er* (for *amare-er*). That $\vartheta a\iota$ is the dative singular of an abstract in *tha*, as the weak aorist active $\sigma a\iota$ is of an abstract in *sa* from the subst. verb, needs perhaps some further confirmation.

YA.

267. A considerable number of words are formed by *-ya*, and the secondary suffixes *tav-ya* and *an-i-ya*. *ya* is of the same form as the relative pronoun; in *tav-ya* the first part appears to be a gunaed form of *tu*, which is employed for the Sanskrit infinitive; the first part of *an-i-ya* is used as a suffix in forming abstracts, and *i* may be only a vocalised and lengthened form of *y* phonetically developed from the syllable *ya*.

ya occurs in *Gerunds*, and is probably an instrumental case, like *-twâ*, with which it corresponds in meaning. The Védas have an instrumental in *yâ* for *ya + â*, and the Sanskrit gerund *-ya*, being later, is also perhaps a shortened form for the same. The accent is upon the root, e. g. *ni-viż-*ya, 'having entered.' This suffix being used with compound verbs may account for the quantity of the vowel being shortened, whilst *-twâ* preserves its long vowel because it is used with simple verbs. If the root ends in a short vowel, *t* is inserted between it and this suffix, probably from a similar phonetic cause to that which doubles the consonant after a short vowel in English when a suffix beginning with a vowel is added, e. g. from *cut, cutt-ing*. Hence, in Sanskrit, *anu-śrú-*tya, 'having heard,' from *śru*.

In Greek the equivalent is ιω, in Latin *iu*. They are not used in forming gerunds, but *Abstract Nouns*, e. g. ἐρείπ-ιο-ν, *gaud-*iu-*m*. The instances in Greek are few; the Latin ones, like the Sanskrit, are usually compounds, e. g. *di-luv-*iu-*m, dis-sid-*iu-*m*.

Neuter Abstracts are formed in Sanskrit from nominal stems. The stem-vowel, except *u*, is dropped, e. g. *má'dhur-*ya-*m*, 'sweetness,' from *madhurá-s*, 'sweet.' Similar forms occur in Gothic, e. g. *unvit-*ja, 'ignorance,' from *unvit(a)-s*, 'ignorant;' *diub-*ja, 'theft,' from *diubs* (for *diuba-s*), 'thief.' So also in Latin *mendac-*iu-*m*, 'falsehood,' from *mendax* (mendac-s), 'false;' *jêjún-*iu-*m*, 'fast,' from *jêjúnu-s*, 'fasting.' There are a few in Greek, e. g. μονομάχ-ιο-ν, 'single fight,' from μονομάχο-ς, 'fighting singly;' also such words as κουρεῖον (κουρέϝ-ιο-ν), 'shearling,' from κουρεύ-ς, 'shearer.'

The feminine *-yá'*, with the accent, forms *Primary Abstracts*, e. g. *vid-*yá', 'knowledge.' In Greek *ía*, e. g. πεν-ία, 'poverty,' from πενέ-ω; ἀριστε-ία (ἀριστεϝ-ια), 'a noble act,' from ἀριστεύ-ω (ἀριστεϝ-ω), 'I am a noble.' In Latin *ia*, *iê*: *ined-*ia, 'hunger,' from *in + ed-ere*, 'not to eat;' *diluv-*iê-*s*, 'deluge,' from *dilu-ere* (diluv-ere). In Gothic *jô* (Nom. *ja, i*), e. g. *vrak-*ja, 'persecution,' Gen. *vrak-*jô-*s*, from a. *vraj*; *band-*i, 'bond,' from *bind-an*.

Both Latin and Gothic in some cases add *n*, e. g. 1. *con-tag-iô*, Gen. *con-tag-*iôn-*is*, 'touch,' from *con-tangere*; go. *vaih-jô*, Gen. *vaih-jôn-s*, 'contest,' from *vaiha*.

Both Greek and Latin form *Denominative Abstracts* in a similar way, e. g. σοφ-ία, 'wisdom;' l. *præsent-ia*, 'presence,' from *præsens* (*præsent-s*); *barbar-iê-s*, 'barbarity,' from *barbaru-s*; *un-iô*, Gen. *un-iôn-is*, 'union,' from *vnu-s*.

In Sanskrit *Future Participles Passive* are formed by *ya*, and *Substantives* resembling them in meaning, e. g. Part. *gúh-ya-s*, 'to be concealed;' Subst. *gúh-ya-m*, 'secret' (a thing to be concealed); Part. *bhój-yà-s*, 'to be eaten;' Subst. *bhój-yà-m*, 'food' (a thing to be eaten). Gothic *Adjectives* in *-ja* correspond to these participles in form and meaning, e. g. *anda-ném-ja*, 'agreeable' (to be received); *unqvéth-ja*, 'inexpressible' (not to be uttered). Similar *Adjectives* occur in Greek, with δ inserted after a short vowel, e. g. φθί-δ-ιο-s, 'perishable;' ἀμφά-δ-ιο-s, 'public' (to be seen); λατά-δ-ιο-s, 'broad' (to be spread out). Consonant stems also occur, e. g. πάλλα (for παλ-ια=s. *yâ* Fem.), 'ball' (to be hurled). In Latin *exim-iu-s*, 'eminent' (to be selected).

Denominative Adjectives are also formed by *ya*, e. g. s. *div-ya-s*, 'heavenly,' from *div*; *hṛd-ya-s*, 'hearty,' 'affectionate,' from *hṛd*; z. *yáir-ya*, 'yearly,' from *yárĕ*; gr. πάτρ-ιο-s, 'paternal,' from πατήρ; τέλs-ιο-s, 'perfect' (for τελεσ-ι'-s), from τέλος; οὐραν-ιο-s, 'heavenly,' from οὐρανός. In Latin they are less numerous than in the above languages. But there are *Appellatives* as well as adjectives, e. g. *patr-iu-s*, 'paternal,' from *pater*; *Mar-iu-s* from *Mar-s*, *Non-ia* Fem. from *nonu-s*.

It seems more natural to refer the *names of coun-*

tries to adjectives of this kind than to substantives, e. g. *Gallia, Germania,* to *Gall-iu-s, German-iu-s,* from *Gallu-s, Germanu-s,* i. e. *Gallia* (*terra*), etc., 'the land of the Gauls,' etc. Thus in more recent times we have Eng-land, Deutsch-land, named from the people as a whole, and not from an individual.

The corresponding *Adjectives* and *Appellatives* in the Gothic language end in Masc. -*ja*, Fem. -*jô*, whilst some add *n* and form -*jan*, e. g. *alth*-**ja**, 'old,' from *althi*; *leik*-**ja**, 'physician' (leech), from *leik*; *fisk*-**jan**, 'fisher,' from *fisks* (stem *fiska*).

268. *tav-ya* forms *Future Passive Participles*. It takes the accent, and is preceded by guṇa, e. g. s. *yók*-**távya**-*s*, 'to be joined,' from *yuj*; *dâ*-**távya**-*s*, 'to be given,' from *dâ*. gr. -τέο-ς, e. g. δο-τέο-ς, 'to be given,' for δο-τεfο-ς from δο-τεfιο-ς; L -*tivu-s*, e. g. *da*-**tivu**-*s*, where *tivu* is for *tiviu*. The meaning is somewhat altered, and even in *cap*-**tivu**-*s*, though the passive is expressed, it is referred to the present, not the future, time, i. e. 'taken,' not 'to be taken.'

269. *ani-ya* also forms *Future Passive Participles*: a. *yój*-**ani'ya**-*s*, 'to be joined,' from *yuj*. z. -*nya* (the í in Sanskrit being perhaps a later development), e. g. *ynt*-**nya**, 'to be adored.' The Gothic has the same form -*nja*, e. g. *ana-siu*-**nja**, 'visible' (to be seen).

270. s. *éya* seems to be from *é + ya*, of which the first part probably is only introduced for euphonic reasons. It generally retains the accent on the one or the other syllable. It is used similarly with the simple form *ya*, e. g. a. *dâs*-**èyá**-*s*, 'a slave's son,' from *dâsá*, 'slave;' *gáir*-**èyá**-*m*, 'mountain produce,' from *girí*, 'mountain.' gr. -ειο, and abbreviated to -ιο : λεόντ-ειο-ς and λεόντ-εο-ς, 'of a lion.' l. éju, and abbreviated to eu: Pomp-éju-s; ciner-eu-s, 'ashy.'

271. The stems of some *Nouns*, though not many, consist of the *root only*. In Sanskrit there are feminine *Abstracts* of this sort, e. g. a. bhí, 'fear;' mud, 'joy.' In Greek there are *Appellatives* so formed, e. g. ὄπ (ὄψ), 'eye;' φλογ (φλόξ), 'flame;' but στυγ (στύξ), 'hatred,' and διϛ (αἴξ), 'impetuous motion,' 'spring' (tide), are *Abstracts*. Latin *Appellatives*, e. g. duo (dux), 'leader.'

Bare roots are also used at the end of *Compounds*, and generally in the sense of the present participle governing the preceding noun, e. g. a. dharma-víd, 'knowing duty;' du:kha-hán, 'destroying pain;' gr. ψευσι-στυγ (ψευσίστυξ), 'hating lies;' κορυθ-αιϛ (κορυθ-αίξ), 'shaking the helm;' l. jū-dic (jūdex), 'uttering law;' au-cup (auceps), 'catching birds.'

The vowel a is sometimes lengthened, e. g. a. vách, 'speech' (r. vach); pari-vrâ'j, 'wandering about,' 'beggar' (r. vraj); gr. ὠπ (ὤψ), 'eye' (r. ὀπ); l. rég (rex), 'king' (r. reg).

After a short root vowel t is added, as in some other cases, e. g. a. pari-zrú-t, 'flowing round;' l. com-i-t (comes), 'attendant' (r. i).

A.

272. The suffix -a, which is the same, in form at least, as the demonstrative pronoun, is employed both as a primary and as a secondary suffix to form *Masculine Abstracts*. In Gothic these abstracts have acquired the neuter gender, as is seen from their not having s in the Nom. Sing., e. g. anda-beit (stem anda-beita), 'blame;' af-lét, 'forgiveness' (letting off). One neuter occurs in Sanskrit, i. e. *bhay-á-m*, 'fear,' from *bhî*, but M. *jay-á-s*, 'victory,' from *ji*.

The same suffix, with the accent, *-á*, also forms *Adjectives* resembling the present participle in meaning, as well as *Appellatives* which generally were at first *Nomina agentis*, e. g. *tras-á-s*, 'trembling;' *músh-á-s*, 'mouse' (lit. 'stealer'). In Greek *-ó*, e. g. φάν-ό-*s*, 'shining;' τροχ-ό-*s*, 'runner.' The meaning is sometimes passive, and the accent sometimes on the root both in Sanskrit and Greek. In the latter language δ is sometimes added, as we have seen *t* to be in many cases after a short vowel, e. g. δορκ-ά-*s* (stem δορκ-ά-δ-), 'gazelle'('gazer'); τυπ-ά-*s* (st. τυπ-ά-δ-), 'hammer' ('striker').

These forms occur especially at the end of compounds, e. g. s. *arin-dam-á-s* ('taming'), 'tamer of foes;' gr. ἱππό-δαμ-ο-*s*, 'tamer of horses;' l. *nau-frag-u-s*, 'shipwreck.' The e. *wreck* as well as *break* is of the same root as the Latin *frag* in *frang-ere*, 'break.'

Some words of this kind in Latin have the feminine form *-a = s. â* applied to both masculine and feminine genders, as in *parri-cid-*a, 'parricide,' from *cæd-*ere, and sometimes restricted to the Masc. as in *cæli-col-*a, 'dwelling in heaven,' from *col-*ere. Even *scrib-*a, 'writer,' 'secretary,' though not a compound, has the feminine form for the masculine. Some other *Masculine Appellatives* ending in *-a* are really Greek words which have dropped the final *s* of the Nom. Sing., like *poe-ta*, gr. ποιη-τή-*s*.

On the other hand, these compounds in Greek have the masculine form for both masculine and feminine.

The Gothic has a few instances of all these formations. Masculine, both compound and simple, e. g. *daura-vard-*a, 'door-keeper' (e. *ward*); *thiv-*a (Nom. *thiu-s*), 'lad,'meaning the 'strong,' 'muscular,' from *thu*, e. *thew*,

s. *tu*, 'grow,' 'become strong;' but *thiva* is in English degraded to 'thief.' Neut. *ga-thrask*-a, 'threshing-floor.' Fem. *daura-vard-ó* (Nom. *-vard-a*), 'porteress.' Adjectives, *laus*-a, 'loose;' *af-lét*-a, 'let off.'

A passive meaning belongs to these forms when compounded with the prefixes *su*, 'easy,' and *dus*, 'hard,' in Sanskrit, and with the corresponding ones εὐ, δυσ in Greek, e.g. s. *su-kár*-a-s, 'easy to be done;' *dush-kár*-a-s, 'hard to be done.' This explanation of these forms, which I have given in deference to Bopp's authority, seems to me somewhat arbitrary and unnecessary. The meaning is perhaps no more passive than in such Germanic forms as ger. *leicht zu thun*, e. *easy to do*, which some grammarians also represent as active forms used in a passive sense, whereas the true explanation is, by an ellipsis, *easy* (for any one) *to do*; so also *hard* (for any one) *to do*. The above Sanskrit and Greek forms may also be taken in an active sense. As these derivatives have originally the sense of the present participle active, e. g. s. *bhay-á-m*, 'fear' (lit. 'fearing'), so, when compounded with *su* or *dus*, they retain a similar meaning, e. g. *dush-kár*-a-s = 'hard doing,' not 'hard being done;' gr. εὐ-φορ-o-s = 'easy bearing,' not 'easy being borne.' The ease or difficulty in each case refers to the agent, not to the thing done or borne.

As a secondary suffix, *a* generally retains the accent, and is preceded by 'vriddhi.' It has a feminine in *-í*, and forms masculine substantives denoting *descent*, as well as neuters denoting *fruit*, etc., e. g. *mânav-á-s*, 'man' (descendant of Manú); *ászwatth-á-m*, 'fruit of the aświattha tree;' *sâmudr-á-m*, 'sea salt' ('sea produce'), from *samudrá*. In Greek the feminine patronymics in *-ι* have the usual δ affixed, e. g. Ἰναχ-ί-ς, Gen. Ἰναχ-ίδ-ος, 'daughter of Inachus;' μῆλ-ο-ν, 'apple,' from μηλι-δ-; ὀ(F)-ό-ν, 'egg.' In Latin pŏm-u-m, 'apple,' from pomu-s; ὄν-u-m, 'egg' ('bird's produce'), from avi-s.

Neuter Abstracts are also thus formed, s. yáuvan-á-m, 'youth,' from yúvan; and *Neuter Collectives*, s. kâpót-á-m, 'a flock of pigeons,' from kapô'ta.

Adjectives and *Appellatives* occur, e. g. s. áyas-á M. N., á'yas-î F., 'of iron,' from áyas; l. decŏr-u-s, 'proper,' from decus.

The feminine â' with the accent is also used to form *Abstracts*: s. bhid-â', 'a splitting;' gr. -η, φυγ-ή, 'flight;' l. -a, fug-a, idem; go. -ó, bid-ô, 'begging.'

I.

273. The suffix *i* is like the demonstrative pronoun *i*, but it may be only a weakened form of the suffix *a* noticed above, just as, in the Latin words *imbelli-s*, *multi-formi-s*, the *i* is for *u* (older *o*) in *bellu-m*, *multu-s*, which answers to the Sanskrit *a*.

This *i*, with the accent on the root, forms *Feminine Abstracts*, e. g. s. sách-i-s, 'friendship' (lit. 'following,' l. sequ-or); z. dâh-i-s, 'creation;' gr. μῆν-ι-s, 'wrath;' δ or τ is sometimes added, as in other cases: ἔλπ-ι-s (ἐλπ-ιδ-), 'hope;' χάρ-ι-s (χαρ-ιτ-), 'grace;' l. perhaps such as cæd-es (cæd-i-), 'cutting;' go. vunn-i, 'suffering' (wound).

It is also used, with the accent placed variously, in forming *Masculine Nomina agentis* and *Appellatives*, e. g. chhid-i-s, 'splitter;' áh-i-s, 'serpent' (mover, creeper); z. az-i-s, 'serpent;' gr. τρόχ-ι-s, 'runner;' ἴχ-ι-s, 'serpent;' sometimes δ again is added: κοπ-ί-s (κοπ-ιδ-), 'knife;' l. angu-i-s, 'serpent;' go. junga-laud-i, 'young man' (e. lud).

U.

274. The suffix *u*, without the accent, is employed to form *Adjectives* resembling in meaning the present participle of desiderative verbs, and governing the accusative case. With the accent it forms *Adjectives* without the desiderative meaning, e.g. s. *didṛkṣh-u*: *pitárâu*, 'desirous of seeing parents;' *tan-ú*, 'thin' (outstretched); *swâd-ú*, gr. ἡδ-ύ, l. *suâ-v-is*, 'sweet;' go. *thaurs-u-s*, 'dry.' In l. *i* is added to the suffix, and *suavis* is for suad-u-i-s.

Appellatives are also formed with an accented or unaccented *u*: *bhid-ú*, 'thunderbolt' (splitter); gr. νέκ-υ, 'corpse' (perishing); l. *curr-u-s*, 'carriage' (runner); go. *fôt-u*, 'foot' (goer).

AN.

275. *Appellatives* are formed by *an* (án) without accent, e.g. s. *snêh-an*, 'friend' (lover); *râ'j-an*, 'king' (ruler). In Greek this affix assumes several forms, αν, εν, ον, ην, ων, e.g. τάλ-αν, 'patient;' ἄρρ-εν, 'male;' σταγ-όν, 'drop;' πευθ-ήν, 'enquirer;' 'σκῆπ-ων, 'staff.' l. *ón, in*, e.g. *edó* (Gen. *ed-ón-is*), 'eater;' *pecten* (Gen. *pect-in-is*), 'comb.' go. *han-an*, 'cock' (crower, l. *can-ere*). A few *neuters* occur in this form: go. *ga-deil-an*, 'sharer.'

This suffix, weakened to *in* and accented, is employed at the end of compounds; with the root strengthened in s., e.g. *ṛta-vâd-in*, also in the simple *kâm-in*, 'lover;' l. *pect-in*; go. *stau-in-s*, Gen. of stau-a, 'judge.' It is also employed as a secondary suffix, e.g. *dhan-in*, 'rich,' from dhaná.

In Greek *ων* is applied to *place* and *time*, e.g.

ἱππ-ών, 'stable' (place for horses); ἀνδρ-ών, 'men's room;' ἐλαφηβολι-ών, 'month of El.' (stag-hunting time).

ANA.

276. Masculine and neuter *Appellatives*, with the root accented, are formed by a. *ana*, gr. *avo*, go. *ana*, e.g. s. *náy-ana-m*, 'eye' (leader); Fem. *yách-aná'*, 'begging;' gr. δρέπ-ανο-ν, 'sickle' (cutter); go. *thiudans* (st. *thiud-ana-*), 'king;' Fem. *ga-mait-anó-n*, 'cutting,' 'reaping.' In English we have *wagg-on*, with *g* doubled perhaps only in consequence of the shortened pronunciation of the first vowel. The same suffix accented also forms *Adjectives* in Sanskrit and Greek, e.g. s. *śóbh-aná*, 'beautiful' (shining); gr. σκεπ-ανό-ς, 'covering.'

AS.

277. The suffix *-as*, with the root vowel gunaed and accented, forms *Neuter Abstracts*, e.g. *máh-as*, 'greatness;' *táv-as*, 'strength,' from *tu*. gr. both primary, -ας (Nom. -ος), φλέγ-ος, 'flame' (burning), and secondary, γλεῦκ-ος, 'sweet wine' (sweetness, from γλυκύς). L. *-us*, Gen. *-er-is*; *-us*, Gen. *-or-is*; *-ur*, Gen. *-or-is*; *-ur*, Gen. *-ur-is*: *rób-ur*, 'strength' (s. root *rudh*); *fœd-us*, 'treaty' (for *foid-us* from *fid*). This suffix has in many cases become *-ōr*, and of the masculine gender: *sap-ōr*, 'taste' (Gen. *sap-ōr-is*). The long syllable is also employed in Latin to form secondary derivatives, e.g. *amar-ōr*, 'bitterness,' from *amaru-s*. go. *is-a* (Nom. *is*): *hat-is*, 'hatred;' *ag-is*, 'fright.' In English the *s* is softened to *r*: *hat-re-d*, *óg-re* (*re* for go. *sa*). Both primary and secondary forms are used with *l* added,

e. g. *svum*-s-l, 'pool' (swimming place); *svart*-is-l, 'blackness.' This suffix also occurs with the addition of *su*, perhaps for *tu*, e. g. *fraujin*-as-su-s, 'dominion;' *thiudin*-as-su-s, 'government.' The weak verbal stem from which these abstracts are formed ends in *n*, which has come to be regarded as part of the formative suffix. Hence the English -*ness* and German -*niss*, e. g. old ger. *drí*-nissa, a. s. *dhre*-ness, 'trinity' (three-ness), e. *mild*-ness, etc.

The same suffix also forms *Neuter Appellatives*, active or passive, e. g. s. *žráv*-as, 'ear' (hearer, from *tru*); *mán*-as, 'mind' (thinker); *páy*-as, 'water' (what is drunk); gr. μέν-ος, 'mind' (what thinks); τέκ-ος, 'child' (what is brought forth); l. *ol*-us (Gen. *ol*-er-*is*), 'vegetable.' *t* is sometimes inserted, e. g. s. *sró'*-t-as, 'stream;' gr. σκῦ-τ-ος, 'skin' (covering). In other cases *n* is similarly inserted, e. g. s. *ár*-n-as, 'water' (mover, from *r*); gr. δά-ν-ος, 'gift,' 'loan;' l. *pig*-n-us, 'pledge.'

A few *Adjectives* are thus formed with the meaning of a present participle and governing an accusative case, e. g. s. *nr-man*-as, 'thinking of men.' The same form occurs at the end of Greek compounds, e. g. ὀξυ-δερκ-ές, 'seeing quickly,' 'keen-sighted.'

LA, RA.

278. These two forms, *la*, *ra*, appear to be of identical origin. The final vowel sometimes changes to *i* or *u*, and in some instances *a*, *i*, *u*, *o*, or *e* is inserted between the stem and the suffix. These modifications, whilst they give great variety to the later forms of language, do not affect the meaning of the derivatives. e. g. s. -*la*, -*ra* : *zúk*-la, 'white' (glittering); *dip*-rá, 'shining.' gr. -λο, -ρο: βη-λό-s, 'threshold;' νεκ-ρό-s, 'corpse' (perishing). 1. Fem. -la, sel-la (sed-la), 'seat;' -ru (older ro), ca-ru-s, 'dear' (s. kam, 'love'). go. -lu, -ra: sit-la (Nom. sitls), 'nest' (sitting-place); lig-ra (Nom. ligrs), 'lair' (place to lie in). The formatives *l* and *r* remain in the English words. sett-le, denoting a place to 'sit' or 'set' upon; lai-r and lay-er; sadd-le, padd-le, an instrument for the foot, formed from the old root l. pés, ped-is.

-ri appears in s. ángh-ri-s, 'foot' (goer); gr. ἴδ-ρι-s, 'acquainted with' (knowing); l. cele-r (Gen. cele-ri-s), 'quick' (hurrying).

A few occur in -lu, -ru: s. bhí-lú, 'fearful;' áz-ru (dát-ru), 'tear;' gr. δάκ-ρυ, 'tear;' go. og-lu-s, 'heavy.'

Instances with the inserted vowel are: s. chap-alá, 'trembling;' mud-irá, 'a wanton;' an-ilá, 'wind' (blowing); vid-urá, 'knowing;' harsh-ulá, 'gazelle;' gr. τροχ-αλό-s, 'quick;' στιβ-αρό-s, 'strong;' τραπ-ελό-s, 'easy to turn;' φαν-ερό-s, 'visible;' φλεγ-υρό-s, 'burning;' καμπ-ύλο-s, 'bent;' l. ten-er (st. ten-ero), 'tender;' ag-ili-s, 'active;' teg-ulu-m, 'roof' (covering).

Some secondary derivatives are in these forms, e. g. s. azm-ará, 'stony;' śrí-lá, 'fortunate;' médh-ira and médh-ilá, 'intelligent;' gr. φθονε-ρό-s, 'envious;' χαμη-λό-s, 'on the ground;' l. carnú-li-s, 'fleshly.'

WA (VA).

279. The suffix -wa (va), Fem. wá (vá), generally without the accent, forms *Appellatives*, e.g. s. áz-wa-s, 'horse' (runner); z. az-pa, where *w* has become *p*; gr. ἵπ-πο-s = ἵκ-κο-s for ἰκ-Ϝο-s; l. eq-uu-s; s. s.

eóh, in which the formative is again dropped. Adjectives are also formed in the same way, e. g. a. *rish-wa*, 'offending;' gr. perhaps such forms as δρομ-εύ-s, 'runner;' L. *tor-vu-s*, 'stern' (piercing); go. *lus-ivs* (st. *las-iva-*), 'weak;' e. *laz-y*, the formative being represented only by *y*.

WAN (VAN).

280. The suffix *wân* or *wan* (*ván* or *van*), without the accent, forms: 1. *Adjectives* with a participial meaning, e.g. a. *vâja-dâ'-vân*, 'giving food.' 2. *Nomina agentis*, e.g. a. *yáj-wân*, 'sacrificer.' 3. *Appellatives*, e.g. a. *rúh-wân*, 'tree' (grower); z. *zar-wan*, 'time' (destroyer).

This suffix appears also with an additional *t* in *vant*, *mant* (*vat*, *mat* in weak cases). In Latin there is a change of *v* or *m* to *l*, and a further addition of *o* in *-lento*. In Greek the corresponding form would be ϝηντ or ϝεν, of which, however, the digamma is generally lost, and ντ, εν remain. The digamma is preserved in some instances in an inscription found in the island of Corfu in 1845, and published in 1846 by Professor Franz. (See *Zeitschrift für Vergleichende Sprachforschung*, i. 118, 119.) Among the instances where the digamma is preserved is one word containing the formative in question, i. e. στονόϝεσσαν for στονο-ϝεντ-ιαν. Other instances of this formative are: a. *átwa-vant*, 'having horses;' *marút-vant*, 'having Maruts' (Indra); gr. ὑλη-εντ- (ὑλήεις), 'having wood,' 'woody;' πυρό-εντ- (πυρόεις), 'having fire;' l. *pûru-lent-us*, 'having matter' (*pus*); *opu-lent-* (*opulens*), 'having wealth.'

NU.

281. *Adjectives* and *Substantives* are formed by -*nu* with the accent, e. g. s. *tras*-**nú**-*s*, 'trembling;' *bha*-**nú**-*s*, 'sun' (shiner); z. *taf*-**nú**-*s*, 'burning;' *jañf*-**nu**-*s*, 'mouth' (speaker); gr. λιγ-νύ-ς, 'smoke' (s. *dah*, 'burn'); l. *lig*-**nu**-*m* (fire) 'wood.'

MI.

282. This is perhaps only a weakened form of *ma*, Fem. *má*. It rarely occurs, but is found in a few *Appellatives* with the accent, e. g. s. *bhû*-**mí**-*s*, 'ground;' L *hu*-**mu**-*s*, go. *hai*-**m**-*s* (st. hai-*mi*-), 'village,' e. *ho*-**me**. The two last denote resting or sleeping place, from the root s. *śî*, gr. κει.

KA.

The suffix *ka* with the accent is rarely used in immediate connection with the root, e. g. s. *śush*-**ká**-*s* (for sus-ka-s), 'dry;' z. *hush*-**ka**; L *sic*-**cu**-*s* (for sus-cu-s). A vowel is usually interposed between the root and *ka*, which then has not the accent, e. g. s. *nárt*-**aka**-*s*, 'dancer;' *jálp*-**áka**, 'talkative;' *mû'sh*-**ika**-*s*, 'mouse' (stealer); *kâ'm*-**uka**, 'wanton;' *vávad*-**û'ka**, 'talkative;' gr. φύλ-ακο-ς, 'guard;' φεν-ακ-ς (φέν-αξ), 'deceiver;' κηρ-ὑκ- (κῆρ-υξ), 'herald;' γυν-αικ- for γυν-ακ-ι- (γυν-ή, 'woman'); l. *med*-**icu**-*s*, 'physician;' *am*-**icu**-*s*, 'friend;' *ed*-**âo**- (*edax*, 'devouring'); *vel-ôc*- (*velox*, 'swift,' *ô* = original *â*); *cad*-**ûcu**-*s*, 'falling.' In Greek *o*, and in Latin *u* (for *o*), corresponding to a *a* in *ka*, are often dropped; hence the Nom. Sing. ends in ξ for *κς*, and *x* for *cs*.

The English -*ing*, which is employed in forming *Abstract Nouns*, and has gradually taken the place of the active participle instead of -*nd* for *udh* = 1. gr. a. *nt*, is probably formed from this suffix by inserting the nasal; e. g. *king*, for *kin*-**ing**, 'powerful,' is an adjective, unless it be an appellative from the root *jan*, meaning 'producer.' The same form in *heal*-**ing** is used both as an *Abstract* and as a *Participle*.

The suffix *ka* also forms secondary derivatives, with *i* or *u* inserted after consonant stems, e. g. *mádra*-**ka**, 'of Madra land;' *haimanti*-**ká**, 'winterly;' gr. πολεμι-κό-ς, 'warlike;' ἀστυ-κό-ς, 'city-like;' l. *urbi*-**cu**-s, adj. 'city;' *hosti*-**cu**-s, 'hostile.' In Gothic this formative, which by the law of development should be *gha*, appears as *ga*. That the aspirate was pronounced originally appears from the fact that in some of these words the formative is -*ha*. The final vowel is dropped, as usual before *s* of the Nom. Sing. The vowel inserted before *ga* has different forms, e. g. *steina*-**ha**, 'stony;' *móda*-**ga**, 'angry,' 'moody;' *gréda*-**ga**, 'greedy;' *mahtei*-**ga**, 'mighty;' *handu*-**ga**, 'handy.' As the sound of the guttural aspirate is lost in English, the consonant is not generally preserved in writing, but is represented here by *y* as in many other cases. The English words corresponding to the above Gothic ones end in *y*, and that this is for the aspirate appears from the fact that *g*, which is the regular substitute in German for English *gh* is preserved in the same derivatives; for *stein*-**ig**, *muth*-**ig**, *mächt*-**ig** have the same relation in this respect to e. *ston*-**y**, *mood*-**y**, *might*-**y**, as *Tag* has to e. *day*.

Sometimes *s* is prefixed to *ka*, e. g. gr. παιδ-ίσκο-ς, 'little boy;' στεφαν-ίσκο-ς, 'wreath.' In Gothic the final vowel is dropped before the sign of the Nom. Sing., e.g. *barn*-**isk**-*s*. The *s* has prevented the usual development of the consonant. Hence we have *sk* instead of *sgh*. In English the two combine to form the sound *sh*, and in German *sch*. In both these languages the termination is extensively used, e. g. a. *child*-**ish**, ger. *kind*-**isch**.

TU.

283. In Sanskrit *-tu* (sometimes *-thu*) forms *Abstracts*. From the abstracts in *tu* the *Infinitive* is derived. The form *thu* is illustrated in *vama*-**thu**-*s*, though the corresponding word in Latin, *vomi*-**tu**-*s*, 'vomiting,' has not the aspirate. The regular form in Gothic would have the aspirate. It occurs as *th* in some instances, as *t* in others where the preceding consonant prevents the aspiration, and in many cases as *d*, which may have been pronounced *dh*, e. g. *dau*-**thu**-*s*, 'death;' *lus*-**tu**-*s*, 'lust.' In these instances the English words have the same consonants, i. e. *dea*-**th**, *lus*-**t**. go. *vrató*-**du**-*s*, 'travelling.'

Nomina agentis and *Appellatives* are also formed by *-tu*, e. g. s. *bâ*-**tú**-*s*, 'sun' (shiner); *tán*-**tu**-*s*, 'wire' (drawn out); *jîvấ'*-**tu**-*s*, 'life;' gr. μάρ-τυ-*s*, 'witness;' l. *principâ*-**tu**-*s*, 'princedom;' go. *hlif*-**tu**-*s*, 'theft' (lifting, gr. κλέπ-τω); *skil*-**du**-*s*, 'shield' (coverer). The English word has *sh* for *sk*, and preserves the formative consonant *d*.

TANA.

284. The suffix *tana* is probably formed by a combination of *ta* and *na*. It is affixed to adverbs of time to form *Adjectives*, e. g. s. *hyas*-**tána**-*s*, 'of yesterday;' *śvás*-**tana**-*s*, 'of to-morrow.' The Latin forms are *terno*, with *r* inserted, *tino*, and *tĭno*, e. g. *hes*-**ternu**-*s*, 'of yesterday;' *cras*-**tinu**-*s*, 'of to-morrow;' *vesper*-**tinu**-*s*, 'of evening.' This *r* appears also in the Germanic languages, *ges*-**tern** in German being an adverb of time, e. *yes*-**ter** having lost the *n* but preserved the adjective meaning in *yes*-**ter**-*day*. The *n* is also lost in Gothic *gis*-**tra**, but preserved in Anglo-Saxon *gistran*.

SYA.

285. The suffix *sya* is used to form *Adjectives*, e. g. a. *manu*-**shyâ**-*s*, in German *men*-**sch**, 'man,' from Manû. Either from this or with a primitive *r*, we have the Latin *â-rio*, denoting *persons* occupied with a matter, or what belongs to a thing, e. g. *tabell-â*-**riu**-*s*, 'letter-carrier;' *ar-â*-**riu**-*s*, 'coppersmith,' etc. In Gothic -*a*-*rja*, e. g. *sôk-a*-**rja**, 'seeker;' *vull-a*-**rja**, 'fuller.' In English the *r*, with the preceding vowel when needed, is preserved in a similar sense: *bake*-**r**, *farm*-**er**. The Latin *i* and Gothic *y* (j) are preserved in English as *y* in such words as denote the *place* where things are produced, and which correspond to such Latin neuters as *pomâ*-**riu**-*m*, 'orchard' (lit. apple ground), e. g. e. *bake*-**ry**, *shrubbe*-**ry**; unless these are imitations of the French, such as *boucherie*, 'butchery.'

b) COMPOUNDS.

286. Verbs and nouns are compounded with words of the same or of other parts of speech.

Verbal Compounds.

Verbs are usually combined with *prepositions*, and rarely with any other words. The prepositions in Sanskrit are accented. In Greek the compound follows the general rule of verbal accentuation, e. g. s. **ápa-kramati,** 'he goes away;' **prá-**dravati, 'he runs away;' gr. ἀπο-βαίνει, προ-βαίνει; l. **ab-**it (in which b is irregularly for p); **pro-**cedit; go. **af-**gangith, **fra-**létith; e. **under-**go, **over-**run.

The preposition and verb are sometimes separated even in the oldest literature; e. g. sam-indh denotes 'kindle,' and **sam** agnim indhaté nárah, 'men kindle fire.' So also, in Homer, κατείβω denotes 'shed,' and is used in the same sense with the preposition combined or separate, e. g. Od. xxi. 86, τί νυ δάκρυ κατείβετον, 'why ever are you shedding tears;' Il. xvi. 11, τῇ (κούρῃ) ἴκελος....κατὰ δάκρυον εἴβεις, 'you are shedding tears like a girl.'

This separation of the preposition is the general practice in the analytical method of modern languages. In German the separable prepositions are sometimes connected with the verb, but more frequently separated, and sometimes placed after the verb, e. g. er geht **ab,** 'he goes off;' **ab**gehen and **ab-**zu-gehen, 'to go off.' In English some compounds have the preposition immediately connected with the verb, but in a sense different from that which the word has when the preposition is separate, e. g. he **under**goes and he goes **under;** in these cases, however, the preposition is prefixed to the verb in all its parts. The general practice is to place the preposition after the verb, as in the above instances. So also he goes **over** the bridge; but in Latin, fines Helvetiorum **trans**ire (Cæs.), 'to go over the boundaries of the Helvetii.' In Latin the preposition is often used in both ways, both separate and combined, in the same sentence, e. g. Lucr. vi. 668, **per**que mare ac terras **per**currere, 'and (over)run both over sea and land.' *Inseparable* prepositions are generally retained in composition, even in modern languages, e.g. e. be-*hold*, for-*give*; ger. be-*halten*, ver-*geben*.

287. *Other words besides prepositions* are sometimes combined with *verbs*, e. g. s. kuṅḍalî-*karômi*, 'I make into a ring;' êkî-*bhavâmi*, 'I become one.' gr. δακρυχέων seems to imply the existence of a δακρυ-χέω, 'I shed tears,' and νουνεχόντως of a νουνέχω, 'I have sense.' In Latin there are several, e. g. **signi**-*fico*, 'I make a sign' (e. signify), from *signum*; **bene**-*dico*, 'I speak well of,' from *bene*. In Greek and Gothic the words which seem to be compounds of this kind are generally *denominatives*, e. g. gr. τοκογλυφέω, from τοκογλύφος; go. *veit-vódja*, from *veit-vód-s*.

Nominal Compounds.

288. When two *nouns* are combined together, if the first word has a vowel stem, the vowel is either preserved in its original state, or altered, or dropped; e. g. s. lôka-*pálá-s*, 'guardian of the world;' bhû-*dhará-s*, 'bearer of the earth;' gr. σκιά-γράφο-ς, 'shadow-painter;' νίκη-φόρο-ς, 'victorious;' l. albo-*galêrus*, 'white cap;' mero-*bibus*, 'drinker of unmixed wine;' go. guda-*faurhts*, 'god-fearing;' veina-*gards*, 'vineyard;' midja-*sveipeins*, 'deluge;' handu-*vaurhts*, 'hand-wrought.'

In the following the stem-vowel is changed, e. g. s. priya-*bhâryâ*, 'beloved wife,' from priyâ; gr. ἡμερο-δρόμο-ς, 'day-runner,' from ἡμέρά; l. lâni-*ger*, 'bearing wool,' from lâna; go. andi-*laus*, 'end-less,' from andja. This change generally makes the stem-vowel lighter, but in a few instances it becomes heavier, e. g. γεω–

γράφο-s, 'geographer,' for γεο-, as in other compounds.

When the first part has a consonant stem, the two words are usually connected by a short vowel. It is, however, not used in Sanskrit, e. g. *mandayát-sakha-s*, 'rejoicing friends;' *kshayád-vira-s*, 'ruling men.' In Greek o or ι is employed, e. g. παντ-ο-βίης, 'overpowering all;' αἰγ-ί-ποδες, 'goat-footed.' In Latin *i* is used, e. g. *noct-i-color*, 'colour of night.' Sometimes the first word is considerably abbreviated, e. g. *op-(er)i-fex*, 'worker;' *horr(or)-i-ficus*, 'horrifying.' The Gothic has but few consonant stems, and no connecting vowel.

Stems ending in *s*, both in Greek and Latin, sometimes omit the connecting vowel, e. g. σακεσ-φόρο-s, 'shield-bearer;' μυσ-κέλανδρον (for the Gen. μυ-ός is for μυσ-ος), l. *mus-cerda*.

On the other hand, a connecting vowel is sometimes used in Greek even after vowel stems, e. g. ἰχθυ-ο-φάγο-s, 'fish-eater;' φυσι-ο-λόγο-s, 'naturalist.'

In some cases the *final consonant is dropped*. *n* is thus omitted in a. *rája-putrá-s*, 'king's son,' from rájan; l. *homi-cida*, 'homicide,' from homo, Gen. homin-is; go. *smakka-bagms*, 'fig-tree,' from smakkan. In Greek ν is preserved, e. g. παν-δήμο-s, 'of all the people;' but τ is omitted from ματ, which sometimes becomes μο, e. g. ὀνομά-κλυτο-s, 'celebrated.' σπερμο-φόρο-s, 'seed-bearer,' is perhaps for σπερμ(ατ)-ο-φορο-s.

289. Both Zend and Greek furnish instances of the *Nominative* case being employed in the first part of a compound, e. g. z. **daivô**-*dáta*, 'made of God,' ô being = a. *as*; gr. θεός-δοτο-s, 'given of God.'

The *Genitive* occurs in the first part of compounds in both Greek and Gothic, e. g. gr. νεώς-οικοι, like

r

ger. *schiff-s-häuser*, 'ship-sheds;' οὐδενός-ωρα, 'fit for nothing;' go. **baurg-s-**vaddjus, 'city wall.'

290. A classification of compounds is made by Sanskrit grammarians which it may be useful here to introduce. They are arranged in six classes.

1. Copulative Compounds.

291. Two or more *Substantives* are united together, with a common termination. Their union serves the same purpose in regard to meaning as connecting them together by a conjunction. Some of them have a plural (or dual) termination, and others a neuter singular, e.g. a *súrya-chandramásâu*, 'sun-(and)-moon;' *pitárámátaráu*, 'father-(and)-mother;' *agni-váyu-ravibhyás*, 'fire-air-(and)-sun.' There is no limit to the number of words which may be thus combined together. Those compounds which have a neuter singular ending consist of words denoting inferior objects, e. g. *hastapâdam*, 'hands-(and)-feet;' gr. νυχθήμερον, 'night-(and)-day;' βατραχο-μυο in βατραχομυο-μαχία, 'the war of frog-(and)-mouse.' l. *suovitaurilia* has a neuter plural ending, and consists of three substantives thus combined together, su-ovi-tauri-lia, which is also abbreviated to *solitaurilia*, 'the solemnities during which were sacrificed a pig-sheep-(and)-bull.'

Adjectives are also thus combined, though less frequently, e. g. *vṛtta-pína*, 'round-(and)-thick;' gr. λευκο-μέλας, 'white-(and)-black.'

2. Possessive Compounds.

292. *Possessive Compounds* express the possession of what is denoted by the several parts of the compound.

They are sometimes appellatives, but most generally adjectives. The first member may belong to any part of speech except verb, conjunction, or interjection. The last must be a substantive, which undergoes no change except in the expression for gender, to adapt it as an *adjective* for all three. The accent is in Sanskrit upon the first member, as it would be in a separate state. In Greek it follows the general rule, being placed on the third quantity (short syllable) from the end.

The first part is most frequently an *adjective* or participle, e. g. s. **chā'ru**-*lóchana-s*, 'with beautiful eyes;' gr. λευκό-πτερο-ς, 'with white wings;' l. **atri**-*color*, 'of a black colour;' go. **hrainja**-*hairts*, 'with a pure heart;' e. **pure**-*heart-ed*. The form of the passive participle is used in English, as if derived from a verb.

The first part is a *substantive* in s. **bā'la**-*putra-s*, 'with a child as son;' gr. βου-κέφαλο-ς, 'with an ox's head;' l. **angui**-*comu-s*, 'with snakes for hair;' e. **pig**-*head-ed*.

The first part is a *pronoun* in s. **mād**-*vidha-s*, 'of my sort;' gr. αὐτο-θάνατο-ς, 'having death from oneself,' i. e. 'suicidal.'

The following have a *numeral* in the first part: s. **chátush**-*pād*, 'with four feet;' gr. δι-πόταμο-ς, 'with two rivers,' said of Thebes; l. **bi**-*corpor*, 'with two bodies,' applied to the Centaurs; go. **ha**-*ihs*, 'with one eye;' e. **two**-*head-ed*.

The following have an *adverb* in the first part: s.**táthā**-*vidha-s*, 'of such a sort;' gr. ἀεί-καρπο-ς, 'ever with fruit.'

The following have a *privative* in the first part: s. **a**-*malá-s*, 'without a spot;' gr. ἄ-φοβο-ς, 'without fear;' l. **in**-*somni-s*, 'without sleep.' In s. and gr. the *n* is preserved only before vowels, as in the English article *an*, but before consonants also in Latin, as the article in German: *ein Kopf*, 'a head.' Similar compounds are formed in English by affixing *less*, i.e. *fear-less*, *spot-less*.

The following have a *preposition* in the first part: s. **apa**-*bhí-s*, 'without fear;' **sá**-*káma-s*, 'with desire;' gr. ἀπό-κληρο-ς, 'without a share;' σύν-θρονο-ς, 'with the same throne;' l. **ab**-*normi-s*, 'without rule;' **con**-*color*, 'of like colour;' go. **af**-*gud-s*, 'without God;' **ga**-*gud-s*, 'with God,' 'godly.'

3. *Determinative Compounds.*

293. The first member, as in the previous class, may be any part of speech but verb, conjunction, or interjection. The last member is a noun. The most usual combination is an *adjective followed by a noun.* The first part modifies or *determines* the meaning of the second. The accent in Sanskrit is usually at the end of the word; in Greek it follows the general rule of being on the third quantity (short syllable) from the end, e. g. s. **divya**-*kusumú-s*, 'a heavenly flower;' **ghána**-*zyáma-s*, 'black as a cloud;' **zyéna**-*patwá*, 'with a falcon's flight;' gr. ἰσό-πεδο-ν, 'an even plain;' ἡμί-κενο-ς, 'half empty;' μεγαλό-μισθο-ς, 'with great pay;' l. **semi**-*mortuu-s*, 'half dead;' **decem**-*viri*, 'ten men;' **in**-*imicu-s*, 'enemy;' go. **junga**-*lauth-s*, 'a young man;' **anda**-*vaurd-s*, 'answer;' **ufar**-*gudja*, 'high priest;' e. **high**-*priest*, **half**-*way*, **in**-*road*; proper names, **White**-*field*, **Broad**-*head*.

4. *Dependent Compounds.*

294. The first member is *dependent* upon the second, and expresses the meanings of the case-forms in words uncompounded. In English the relation of the first to the second member has to be rendered generally by a preposition. The accent is on the first member in Sanskrit and in Greek when possible. *Genitive* relation: z. **zantu**-*paiti-s*, 'lord *of* the city;' gr. οἰκό-πεδο-ν, ' floor *of* the house;' l. **auri**-*fodina*, 'a mine *of* gold;' go. **aurti**-*gard-s*, 'a garden *of* vegetables' (e. *orchard*). *Accusative*: s. **arin**-*damá-s*, 'subduing enemies;' gr. ἱππό-δαμο-s, 'subduing horses;' l. **ovi**-*par-u-s*, 'bringing forth eggs.' *Instrumental*: s. **páti**-*jushthá*, 'beloved *by* a husband;' gr. χειροποίητο-s, 'made *by* hand;' go. **handu**-*vaurhts*, 'made *by* hand;' e. **hand**-*wrought*. *Dative*: s. **pitṛ́**-*sadṛ́za-s*, 'like (*to*) the father.' *Ablative*: s. **nabhas**-*chyutá-s*, 'fallen *from* heaven.' *Locative*: s. **nāu**-*sthá-s*, 'standing *in* a ship.'

None of the other languages has so great a variety and abundance of this class of compounds as the Sanskrit. The English language has preserved less facility in forming compounds than the German. It supplies their place by foreign words, or by using prepositions. Such forms as the following express the meaning of dependent compounds, i.e. **gold**-*mine* = a mine *of* gold, **door**-*keeper* = keeper *of* a door, **spring**-*water* = water *from* a spring, **reading**-*room* = a room *for* reading, **finger**-*post* = a post *with* a finger; and in proper names: *Hilton* (hill-town) = a town *on* a hill, *Johnson* = son *of* John, *Whetstone* = a stone *for* whetting, *Cartwright* = a maker *of* carts.

5. *Collective Compounds.*

295. *Collective Compounds* consist of a *numeral* for the first member and a *substantive* for the last, with an oxytone accent in Sanskrit, and an accent according with the general rule in Greek. These compounds end as neuters in -*a-m* or feminines in -*í* in Sanskrit, as neuters in -*m* or *u-m* in Latin, and as feminines in -*ia* in Greek. Some add in s. -*ya-m*, gr. -*ω-ν*, l. -*iu-m*, e.g. s. **tri**-*guṇá-m* or **trâi**-*gun-ya-m*, 'three qualities;' **tri**-*lókí*, 'three worlds;' gr. τετρα-όδ-ιο-ν, 'four ways;' τετρα-νυκτ-*ία*, 'four nights;' L. **bi**-*duu-m*, 'two days;' **bi**-*noct-iu-m*, 'two nights.' In English a few such compounds occur, e.g. **twi**-*light* = two lights; **se**'*nnight* = seven nights (a week); **fort**-*night* = fourteen nights.

6. Adverbial Compounds.

296. These consist of a *preposition*, the *negative particle*, or an *adverb* as the first member, and a *substantive* as the second. The accent is as in the fifth class; e.g. s. **praty**-*ahá-m*, 'daily' (for the day, *per diem*); **a**-*sanzayá-m*, 'without doubt;' **yathá**-*zraddhá-m*, 'according to belief;' gr. ἀντι-βίην, 'violently' (in return); L **præ**-*modu-m*, 'beyond measure.' Such adverbial compounds as gr. σή-μερο-ν, l. **ho**-*die*, e. **to**-*day*, have a *pronoun* as the first member.

XII. INDECLINABLE WORDS.

297. *Indeclinable* words are such as undergo no change of form, though many of them are themselves special forms of inflected words. Particular cases of nouns often assume the character of indeclinable words, especially those cases which have gone out of general use, such as the instrumental, ablative, and locative. The imperative mood of many verbs is also thus employed as conjunctions. We shall notice only a few such instances as illustrate the identity or the analogy of the methods resorted to in different languages. The complete analysis and enumeration of indeclinable words belongs to special grammar.

1. ADVERBS.

298. *Adverbs* are formed in a variety of ways, but are usually either *abbreviations* of words belonging to other parts of speech or particular *cases* of nouns, or are formed by special *suffixes*.

a) *Abbreviations.*

a. *sadyás,* 'immediately,' abbreviated from sa *divas,* 'this day;' ger. *heu-te,* 'to-day,' in which *te* is abbreviated from *Tag.*

b) *Cases of Nouns.*

Of particular *cases* there are a. Acc. Neut. *âshú,* 'quickly;' Instr. Sing. *dákshinéna,* 'southwards'

(lit. by the right hand); Plur. *uchchâ'is*, 'on high;'
Dat. *áhnáya*, 'soon' (lit. to the day); Ablat. *páżchát*,
'afterwards,' 'westward' (lit. from behind); Genit.
chirásya, 'at length' (lit. of long); Loc. *práhņé*, 'in
the forenoon.'

In Greek, Acc. Sing. μέγα, Pl. μεγάλα, 'greatly;'
Abl. Sing. the adverbs in -ως (for ατ) generally; ευθέως,
'quickly;' Gen. ὁμοῦ, 'altogether.'

In Latin, Acc. *multum*, 'much;' Abl. *multo*, unless
this form was originally Dative, i. e. Locative, 'in much;'
Loc. *nové* = novo + i, as the a. *návé* = nava + i, 'newly.'
The forms in -ê are by some regarded as for -ed, and
therefore Ablatives, after the analogy of *facillumed* in
the Senatusconsulto de Bach.

In Gothic, Acc. *filu*, 'much;' Abl. *wha-thrô*, 'from
whence;' Gen. *allis*, 'wholly.' In English the case-
sign is generally lost, as in *yesterday* as compared with
Gothic *gistradagi-s*, where *s* is the Gen. sign.

c) Adverbial Suffixes.

Several special *suffixes* are used in forming adverbs.

Adverbs of *place* are formed by adding *-tra* to pronouns : s. *tá*-**tra**, 'there;' gr. *h*-3a, the *r* being dropped
after perhaps having caused the aspiration of the dental.
In Latin *ci*-**tra**, 'on this side.' In Gothic *thra* was
used in the same way, as is seen in the Abl. *tha*-**thrô**,
'*from* there.'

In English and modern languages generally, adverbs
are formed from adjectives by adding another word,
e. g. *wise*-**ly** from *wise*, by adding *ly* (for like);
other-**wise** by adding *wise* (for ways) to *other*. Adverbs
are also formed by prefixing prepositions to nouns, e. g.
aground, afloat, anew, for 'on ground,' etc.

2. CONJUNCTIONS.

299. *Conjunctions* are indeclinable words which grammatically connect together single words or phrases or sentences, e. g. white *and* black, a white horse *and* a black horse, this horse is white *and* that is black. The formation of *Conjunctions* illustrates the operation of the same general mental laws, in the fact that throughout the Indo-European languages they are mostly derived from the pronominal stems; but the independence of action in the different branches of the one family is also shown in the fact that conjunctions which are to have the same meaning and to be employed in the same way are derived from different pronominal stems. This circumstance also makes it probable that many at least of the conjunctions were brought into general use only after the various tribes, which formed different languages out of the common stock of words, had separated from one another.

Thus, for instance, the following words correspond in meaning and construction, though derived from different stems: a. *yat, yáthá,* gr. ὅτι, ὡς, ἵνα, from the stem of the relative pronoun; l. *quod, ut,* the first and perhaps also the second being from the stem of the interrogative pronoun; go. *thatei,* e. *that,* ger. *dass* (for dats), from the demonstrative pronoun. It is evident that these were not *derived* one from another; it is also probable that they did not coexist as conjunctions in the same original language, but that their employment gradually arose after the languages had acquired a distinct individuality. When a sentence, i. e. a combination of words containing a finite verb, is to sustain the relation of a nominative or of an objective to another verb, this relation is expressed by interposing the conjunction *that*. To make the sentence *he is good* an objective to *I know*, they are thus arranged: I know *that* he is good = he is good, I know that. So also, to make the sentence *this is a pleasant country* the subject or nominative to *is well known*, they are thus arranged: it is well known *that* this is a pleasant country = this is a pleasant country, that is well known. The neuter pronoun *it* has to be placed at the beginning to intimate that the subject will be expressed after its verb.

Again, s. *tu*, gr. δί, are from the demonstrative stem *ta*; gr. ἀλ-λά from the demonstrative stem *ana*; l. *se-d* the ablative case of the reflexive stem, meaning 'but.' In English *only* for *only*, used as a conjunction, may be also from the pronominal stem *ana*, like the above Greek word.

The conditional conjunction, meaning 'if,' is s. *ya-di*, go. *ja-ba* (= ya-va), *i-ba*, e. *if*, ger. *ob*. The suffix in the Germanic languages differs from that in Sanskrit. In both English and German the pronominal root and the formative suffix are each reduced to a single letter. In Anglo-Saxon the sound *y* is represented by the letter *g*, and this conjunction is therefore written *gif*. It is thus easily confounded with the imperative of the verb 'to give.' The Germanic suffix is the exact representative of that which appears in Sanskrit as *apa*, and in Latin as *pe*, e. g. s. *yádyapi* = yadi + api, 'although,' 'even if;' L. *quippe* = quid + pe. It is not connected with the stem of the relative pronoun in Latin, but with the accusative singular neuter, and the meaning consequently differs from that in the other languages. In the Greek word δ-κα there is the stem of the relative pronoun, and possibly also the same suffix as in the Gothic *ja-ba*, though both its form and meaning suggest doubts on this point.

3. PREPOSITIONS.

300. The *Prepositions* also have evidently the same origin in different languages, though they have in particular instances acquired some variety of meaning and application.

They appear to be generally formed from pronominal stems, as s. *á-ti* from *a*, *ú-pa* from *u*, etc., and to be employed primarily to denote the relation of substantives (i. e. things) in regard to place, e. g. a bridge *over* a river, a mine *under* ground, an army *before* the town, a house *behind* the church, etc. From this use they are extended by analogy to express other meanings.

Of the same origin, and similar in meaning, are,
s. *ápa*, ' from ;' gr. ἀπό, l. *ab* (for *ap*), go. *af*, e. *of*.

s. *úpa*, ' near ;' gr. ὑπό, ' near,' and ' under ;' l. *sub* ; go. *uf*, ' under ;' e. *off*.

s. *upari*, ' over ;' gr. ὑπέρ, l. *super*, go. *ufar*, e. *over*, ger. *über*.

The Germanic preposition, go. *út*, e. *out*, ger. *aus* (for *auts*, o. ger. *âz=âts*), appears to have no exact representative in the Asiatic languages. The Sanskrit *ut*, ' up,' ' upwards,' with which it is compared by Bopp, differs from it in everything. s. *ut* has a short vowel, go. *út* long. It has the consonant *t*, which the Gothic would require to be *d*, and the meanings are quite different.

s. *prá-*, ' before ;' gr. πρό, l. *pró*, go. *fra*, e. *fore*.

s. *práti*, ' towards ;' gr. προτί (hence ποτί and πρός for προτ). The Latin forms are irregular, e. g. *por* in *por-rigo*, etc. e. *forth* has the same change of *or* for *ro* as in Latin.

s. sâkâm, 'with;' gr. ξύν (for σκυν), and then σύν; l. cum = s. kam.

The Zend furnishes a connecting link with a preposition extensively used in the European languages: z. maḍ, 'with;' gr. μετά, go. mith, e. with, s. s. both mid (for midh) and with, ger. mit (for mid). The English has changed m to w, and the German writes, as it usually pronounces, t for final d.

A verbal root, s. tṛ or tar, seems to be employed in s. tirás, 'across;' l. trans, go. thairh, e. through (thorough), ger. durch.

INDEX.

	SECT.		SECT.
Ablative Singular	148	Conjunctions	292
Accusative Singular	142–3	Conjunctive Mood	241–2
— Plural	160–1	Consonants:	
Adjectives	174–9	Anglo-Saxon	78–80
Adverbial Compounds	296	Gothic	70–2
Adverbs	298	Greek	62
Alphabetical Characters:		Latin	64–5
Anglo-Saxon	26–7	Sanskrit	36–45
Gothic	24–5	Zend	48–52
Greek	21	— Transmutation of	91–104
Latin	22–3	Constituent Parts of Verbs	209
Sanskrit	17–19	Copulative Compounds	291
Zend	20		
Anunâsika	33	Dative Sing. of Nouns	145, 7
Anuswâra	33	— — Pronouns	146, 7
Aorist Tense	233	— and Ablative Plural	163–4
Aspirated Consonants	86	Demonstrative Pronouns	204–6
Augment	232	Denominative Verbs	250
		Dependent Compounds	296
Cardinal Numerals	181–95	Derivative Adjective Pronouns	207
Cases of Nouns	139	— Nouns	251–85
Causal Verbs	247	Desiderative Verbs	248
Cerebral Consonants	84	Determinative Compounds	293
Chinese Language	110	Dual: Nom. Acc. Voc.	170–1
Classes of Sanskrit Verbs	114–29	— Instr. Dat. Abl.	172
Collective Compounds	295	— Gen. Loc.	173
Comparison of Adjectives	174–8		
Compounds	286–96	First Person Dual	216
Verbal	286–7	— — Plural	215
Nominal	288–9	— — Singular	214
Conditional Mood	244–5	Future Tense	240 a
Conjugations	224–7		
— of Sanskrit Verbs	115		

334 INDEX

	SECT.
Genitive Dual	173
— Plural	165-7
— Singular	149-50
Gerunds : s. *tvá*	262
ya	267
Guna	116
Half-Vowels	87
Anglo-Saxon	81
Gothic	73
Greek	62
Latin	64-5
Sanskrit	42
Zend	53-6
Imperative Mood	243
Imperfect Tense	231
Indeclinable Words	297-300
Infinitive : a. *tum*; ger. -*an*,	
-*en*; gr. εμεναι	262
— v. *sé*; gr. σαι; L. *se, re*	263
— Gothic	264
— Greek	265
Instrumental Dual	172
— Plural	162
— Singular	144
Intensive Verbs	240
Interrogative Pronouns	206
Letters divided into Three Classes	90-1
Locative Dual	173
— Plural	168-9
— Singular	151-5
— Names of Places in	153
Middle Voice	211-2
Moods :	
Potential, Optative, Conjunctive	241-2
Imperative	243
Conditional	244-5
Nasal Consonants	87
Nominal Stems	132

	SECT.
Nominative Dual	170-1
— Plural	158-9
— Singular	140-1
Numeral Adverbs	198
Numerals	180-98
Optative Mood	241-2
Ordinal Numerals	179, 196-7
Original Vowel Sounds	30
Palatal Consonants	85
Participles :	
Active Future	254
— Perfect	251a
— Present	251
Middle Fut. Perf. Pres.	252
Passive Future	253, 267-9
— Perfect	258-9
— Present	252, 263-6
Passive Voice	246
— Participles	252-3, 258-9, 263, 266-9
Perfect Tense	236-9
Persons of Verbs	213-22
Pluperfect Tense	240
Possessive Compounds	292
Potential Mood	241-2
Prepositions	300
Present Tense	230
Pronominal Adverbs	208
Pronouns of the First and Second Persons	199-202
— — — Third Person	203-8
Reduplication	237
Relative Pronouns	205
Roots	105-30
Monosyllabic	106-8
Predicative and Demonstrative, Verbal and Pronominal	113
List of	130
— employed as Stems	271
Second Person Dual	219
— — Plural	218
— — Singular	217

	SECT.		SECT.
Semitic Languages	. 109	Transmutation of Consonants	93–104
Sibilants	. 88		
Anglo-Saxon	. 82		
Gothic	. 74	Verbs	209–50
Greek	. 62	Visarga	. 33
Latin	64–5	Vocative Singular	156–7
Sanskrit	. 43–4	Voices of Verbs	. 210
Zend	. 57–8	Vowels:	
Stems	131–8	Anglo-Saxon	. 76–7
Nominal	132–8	Gothic	. 68–9
Strong and Weak	. 137	Greek	. 62
Syllabic Augment	. 231	Latin	. 64–5
		Sanskrit	. 32–5
Temporal Augment	. 231	Zend	. 47
Tenses, Formation of	228–9	Vriddhi	. 116
Third Person Dual	. 222		
— — Plural	. 221	Weight of Personal Endings 223	
— — Singular	. 220	— — Vowels	. 35

WHITE AND RIDDLE'S NEW LARGE LATIN-ENGLISH DICTIONARY.

Now ready, in One thick Volume, imperial 8vo. price 42s. cloth, comprising 2,128 pages,

A NEW

LATIN-ENGLISH DICTIONARY.

By the Rev. J. T. WHITE, M.A.
Of Corpus Christi College, Oxford;
AND
The Rev. J. E. RIDDLE, M.A.
Of St. Edmund Hall, Oxford.

Founded on the larger Dictionary of Freund, revised by himself.

*** Each copy of this work is provided with duplicate title-pages for the purpose of binding it in two volumes, at the option of the possessor; but an inconvenient thickness in the single volume has been prevented by its being printed on a peculiar paper of slight substance but unusual strength of texture. An ABRIDGMENT of this Dictionary, for the use of SCHOOLS, is at the present time in course of preparation.

Select Critical Opinions.

"WE were prepared to find in a volume of the bulk of this Dictionary many misplaced quantities and erroneous references. A long search has enabled us to find not more than two or three—a remarkable proof of the accuracy and care with which the work has been got up. Henceforward no scholar's library will be complete without a copy of this work, which, for completeness, accuracy, and scholarship, is greatly superior to any similar work in existence."
EDUCATIONAL TIMES.

"THIS is the third Latin Dictionary based upon Freund's *Wörterbuch* which has been offered to the English public. It differs from the two preceding editions, in being one-third larger, and twice as costly. .... At the same time, it is right to state that this Dictionary, which is the reverse of a hasty compilation, has a decided advantage over the other two in point of completeness and perfection. So vast an amount of additional labour by various hands has been bestowed upon it, that, though Andrews's translation of Freund is the basis on which it is founded, only a few of the shorter

articles in that work are found here without alteration or addition. Hence it is fairly entitled to be considered in a great measure a new production.... We may safely say that whatever can be effected by time, labour, scholarship, care, and expense, has been done to render this Dictionary a new and complete thesaurus of the language, worthy of the great originals by Forcellini and Freund, from which it is derived.... We must not omit to mention, that part of the additional matter supplied by the present editor consists of the explanation of words used by the Christian Fathers and in the Latin Vulgate, which will be a valuable aid to theological students."
ATHENÆUM.

"It is true that to the labours of Continental scholars we owe, in the first instance, this book — immeasurably the best Latin-English Dictionary which has been as yet published in Great Britain; as we owe the foundation of Liddell and Scott's excellent Lexicon to the labours of Passow. But Messrs. White and Riddle may, like Messrs. Liddell and Scott in the case of their Greek Lexicon, fairly claim that the work before us is now their own. The painful toil of years has been expended upon the correction and enlargement of Dr. Andrews's work; a work which, though undoubtedly possessed of very considerable merits, needed in nearly every page the correction and revision of a competent scholar.... The surviving editor says: 'From the principles on which this Dictionary has been constructed, it will be seen that Dr. Freund's Dictionary has been so thoroughly rewritten and enlarged as to entitle this to the character of a new work.' This claim is a thoroughly just one — well earned by the great amount of classical knowledge as well as intellectual and physical energy which has been expended on the two thousand closely printed pages before us. We have no hesitation in saying that the work, considered as a contribution to the knowledge of the Latin tongue, is at least equal to what the *first* edition of Liddell and Scott's Lexicon was in its department.... We must now take our leave of the editor of this admirable Dictionary. He has produced a work worthy in every way to stand side by side with Liddell and Scott's Greek Lexicon — *a work immeasurably superior to any English-Latin Dictionary now in existence, and which, in a great measure, wipes off the reproach so often cast in the teeth of English scholars, that they are dependent on the Continent for their dictionaries and works of reference.* Such flaws as we have been able to discover are of a very insignificant character; altogether excusable in a work of such a size and nature. We need only add the expression of our hope that both editor and publishers will receive a substantial reward for the labour and enterprise which have produced at last a really good Latin Dictionary." CRITIC.

"In this Dictionary we recognise both a decided, and substantially an English, success, worthy of the present advanced state of scholarship; a Dictionary condensing, in our judgment, the *maximum* of orderly, sound, and extensive scholarship into the *minimum* of space..... The great merit of the Dictionary is in the treatment of the words themselves. It would seem an obvious thing to occur to lexicographers, that the multiplicity of meanings attached to any given word would throw light upon one another if traced in the regular order of their connexion; and that an arrangement of the several constructions of the word in order, syntactically considered, would at least simplify the labour of a student who used their lexicons. Yet these considerations have only prevailed in our dictionaries by slow and painful steps. Mr. White, inheriting and improving upon the work of his predecessors, has produced a very successful result in both points.... As far as we have been able to test the work, this part seems admirably executed. A glance enables any student to take in the meanings and usages of a word, completely digested in order; and with a sufficient intimation also, either in terms or by symbols, or in the authors quoted, respecting the date of the word, whether old Latin, classical, or post-classical. The alphabetical accounts of each letter also, at the head of the department belonging to the letter, appear thoroughly done..... On the whole, we have in this volume the Liddell and Scott of the Latin language; the generally trustworthy repertory of the results of modern philological science, applied to the accumulated stores of German, enriched by English, Latin scholarship, and digested into a brief and pregnant manual, upon well-considered principles, and with a rigorous attempt at precision and accuracy; and all this, combined with the practical merits of a good type and paper, and a handy size." GUARDIAN.

"WE should imagine that the labour and attention which this work has received cannot fail to secure it a position as *facile princeps* among all our Latin Dictionaries for many generations to come. In compiling a dictionary the skill of the printer is an essential help to the lexicographer, and the typographical arrangements of this work are of the most admirable kind—a most important feature in the merit of the book. The whole of the type is remarkable for its clearness, and the printing appears to be accomplished with the most faithful accuracy. As regards the more scholar-like resources of the work, the names of the editors to whom it has been entrusted will of itself furnish a sufficient warranty; and even a cursory examination of its pages will show not only the amount of verbal learning which has been bestowed in enriching its pages, but also the philological acuteness with which the various meanings of the several words are deduced and harmonised..... The result, as we have said, is eminently satisfactory. A Latin Dictionary has been produced which is hardly more voluminous than Ainsworth's, while it has even more learning and better arrangement than Facciolati's. The project reflects the highest credit on the publishers under whose auspices it has been carried out." JOHN BULL.

"THIS Dictionary is based upon the work of Freund, but with considerable additions and modifications, and promises to be of extensive utility. It is a compactly printed volume of rather more than two thousand pages, and approaches far nearer to being a *Thesaurus totius Latinatis* than Forcellini's or any other work with which we are acquainted. It is, in fact, the joint production of Dr. Freund and the two English editors..... A principal feature in the arrangement of this Dictionary is that the original meaning of a word, ascertained, if possible, from its etymology, is always placed first, and then the secondary and derived meanings—an arrangement natural enough, but followed with little strictness in the older lexicons. The derivative meanings are distinguished into those which are merely metonymic—that is, where the general sense is individualised or specialised—and those which are figurative..... The Dictionary is greatly swelled in bulk, but certainly as much in utility, by the introduction of the words to be found in ecclesiastical writers and in the Vulgate. Hitherto these must have been sought in Ducange, the only book in which they were at all likely to be found. The list of the names of authors quoted prefixed to the work includes most of the Latin writers of the sixth century, and we even find amongst them the names of John of Salisbury in the twelfth, and Alexander ab Alexandro in the fifteenth century. Proper names of persons and places are also incorporated in the body of the work. The obsolete and provincial words found in Festus and Varro are of course included. The addition of the patristic Latinity is a decided advantage.... The quotations of passages are given at considerable length, sufficient to enable the reader to judge for himself of the manner in which a word is applied. The small but clear type of the work makes it possible to include a vast amount of quotation. On the whole, we may pronounce this Dictionary to be a monument of solid scholarship and conscientious labour. It will doubtless take the first rank among works of the kind." PARTHENON.

'THE object of this Dictionary is to supply the advanced student in Latin with a sufficient guide through the successive stages of the language from its earliest monuments to the period of its decline. We feel warranted in saying that Messrs. White and Riddle have attained that object with a much higher degree of success than any of their precursors, whether English or American, in the same field. The honest labour which has been bestowed by both gentlemen—particularly by Mr. White—on the performance of their task has rendered their Dictionary at once the most useful to the student and the most creditable to English scholarship. In the first place, it is in all respects more accurate and more complete than its predecessors. In the second place, it has classified with unexampled minuteness the quotations from the Latin authors according to the principles of syntax. In the third place, it gives, in considerable fulness, the proper names with their various inflections and with their adjectival forms—an advantage which no habitual reader of the classics will hold lightly. And, lastly, it has introduced, to a very large amount, the explanation of words found in *Ecclesiastical Writers* and in the *Vulgate*. In a word, it will be found a decidedly more convenient and trustworthy auxiliary to the study of Latin than has yet been placed within the reach of our colleges and schools."

EDINBURGH EVENING COURANT.

"THE classification of quotations according to the principles of syntax, though adopted to some extent by Dr. Freund, has been carried much further in the new Dictionary. Its authors have aimed at effecting this in every case. It must be conceded, therefore, that they have improved on Dr. Freund, for if the system is a good one, it is worth while to act upon it always....Among other additions, a number of words belonging to ecclesiastical Latin have been introduced, so that the student of the Vulgate or Latin Fathers will find what he wants in this Dictionary as well as the classical scholar."

SPECTATOR.

London: LONGMAN, GREEN, and CO., Ludgate Hill.

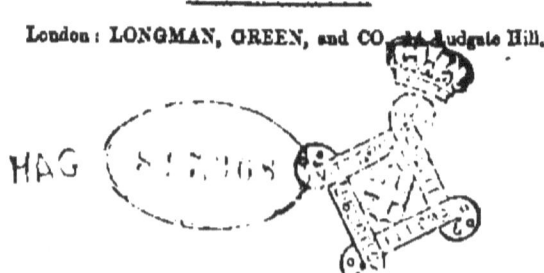

GENERAL LIST OF WORKS

PUBLISHED BY

MESSRS. LONGMAN, GREEN, AND CO.

39 PATERNOSTER ROW, LONDON.

THE CAPITAL OF THE TYCOON: A Narrative of a Three Years' Residence in Japan. By Sir RUTHERFORD ALCOCK, K.C.B., Her Majesty's Envoy Extraordinary and Minister Plenipotentiary in Japan. 2 vols. 8vo with Maps and above 100 Illustrations.

SIR JOHN ELIOT: a Biography. By JOHN FORSTER. With Two Portraits, from original Paintings at Port Eliot. [*Just ready.*]

HISTORY OF THE REFORMATION IN EUROPE IN THE TIME OF CALVIN. By J. H. MERLE D'AUBIGNÉ, D.D., President of the Theological School of Geneva, and Vice-President of the Société Evangélique; Author of *History of the Reformation of the Sixteenth Century.* VOLS. I. and II. 8vo

THE PENTATEUCH AND BOOK OF JOSHUA, Critically Examined. PART I. The Pentateuch Examined as an Historical Narrative. By the Right Rev. JOHN WILLIAM COLENSO, D.D., BISHOP OF NATAL. Second Edition, revised. 8vo 6s. PART II. *The Age and Authorship of the Pentateuch Considered,* is nearly ready.

THE STORY OF A SIBERIAN EXILE. By M. RUFIN PIOTROWSKI. Followed by a Narrative of Recent Events in Poland. Translated from the French. Post 8vo 7s 6d

REMINISCENCES OF THE LIFE AND CHARACTER OF COUNT CAVOUR. By WILLIAM DE LA RIVE. Translated from the French by EDWARD ROMILLY. 8vo 8s 6d

JEFFERSON AND THE AMERICAN DEMOCRACY: An Historical Study. By CORNELIS DE WITT. Translated, with the Author's permission, by R. S. H. CHURCH. 8vo 14s

DEMOCRACY IN AMERICA. By ALEXIS DE TOCQUEVILLE. Translated by HENRY REEVE, Esq. New Edition, with an Introductory Notice by the Translator. 2 vols. 8vo 21s

AUTOBIOGRAPHY OF THE EMPEROR CHARLES V. Recently Discovered in the Portuguese Language by Baron Kervyn de Lettenhove, Member of the Royal Academy of Belgium. Translated by LEONARD FRANCIS SIMPSON, M.R.S.L. Post 8vo 6s 6d

THE LAW OF NATIONS CONSIDERED AS INDEPENDENT POLITICAL COMMUNITIES. By TRAVERS TWISS, D.C.L., Regius Professor of Civil Law in the University of Oxford, and one of Her Majesty's Counsel. PART I. *The Right and Duties of Nations in Time of Peace.* 8vo 12s

Part II., *The Right and Duties of Nations in Time of War*, is in preparation.

THE CONSTITUTIONAL HISTORY OF ENGLAND, since the Accession of George III. 1760—1860. By THOMAS ERSKINE MAY, C.B. In Two Volumes. Vol. I. 8vo 15s Vol. II. just ready.

H.R.H. THE PRINCE CONSORT'S FARMS; An Agricultural Memoir. By JOHN CHALMERS MORTON. Dedicated, by permission, to H.M. the QUEEN. With 40 Illustrations on Wood, comprising Maps of Estates, Plans, Vignette Sketches, and Views in Perspective of Farm Buildings and Cottages. 4to 32s 6d

THE HISTORY OF ENGLAND, from the Accession of James II. By the Right Hon. LORD MACAULAY. Library Edition. 5 vols. 8vo £4

LORD MACAULAY'S HISTORY OF ENGLAND, from the Accession of James II. New Edition, revised and corrected, with Portrait and brief Memoir. 8 vols. post 8vo 48s

THE HISTORY OF FRANCE. (An entirely new Work, in Four Volumes.) By EYRE EVANS CROWE, Author of the 'History of France,' in the *Cabinet Cyclopædia.* 8vo VOL. I. 14s; VOL. II. 15s

₊ The THIRD VOLUME is just ready.

A HISTORY OF THE ROMANS UNDER THE EMPIRE. By the Rev. CHARLES MERIVALE, B.D., late Fellow of St. John's College, Cambridge. 7 vols. 8vo with Maps, £5 6s

By the same Author,

THE FALL OF THE ROMAN REPUBLIC: A Short History of the Last Century of the Commonwealth. 12mo 7s 6d

A CRITICAL HISTORY OF THE LANGUAGE AND 'LITERATURE OF ANCIENT GREECE. By WILLIAM MURE, M.P., of Caldwell. 5 vols. 8vo £3 9s

THE HISTORY OF GREECE. By the Right Rev. the LORD BISHOP OF ST. DAVID'S (the Rev. Connop Thirlwall). 8 vols. 8vo with Maps, £3; an Edition in 8 vols. fcp 8vo 28s

HISTORICAL AND CHRONOLOGICAL ENCYCLOPEDIA, presenting in a brief and convenient form Chronological Notices of all the Great Events of Universal History; including Treaties, Alliances, Wars, Battles, &c.; Incidents in the Lives of Great and Distinguished Men and their Works; Scientific and Geographical Discoveries; Mechanical Inventions, and Social, Domestic, and Economical Improvements. By B. B. WOODWARD, F.S.A., Librarian to the Queen. 8vo [*In the press.*

THE ANGLO-SAXON HOME; a History of the Domestic Institutions and Customs of England, from the Fifth to the Eleventh Century. By JOHN THRUPP. 8vo 12s

LIVES OF THE QUEENS OF ENGLAND. By AGNES STRICKLAND. Dedicated, by permission, to Her Majesty; embellished with Portraits of every Queen. 8 vols. post 8vo 60s

LIVES OF THE PRINCESSES OF ENGLAND. By Mrs. MARY ANNE EVERETT GREEN. With numerous Portraits, 6 vols. post 8vo 63s

LORD BACON'S WORKS. A New Edition, collected and edited by R. L. ELLIS, M.A.; J. SPEDDING, M.A.; and D. D. Heath, Esq. Vols. I. to V., comprising the Division of *Philosophical Works*. 5 vols. 8vo £4 6s Vols. VI. and VII., comprising the Division of *Literary and Professional Works*. 2 vols. 8vo £1 16s

THE LETTERS AND LIFE OF FRANCIS BACON, including all his Occasional Works and Writings not already printed among his *Philosophical, Literary*, or *Professional Works*. Collected and chronologically arranged, with a Commentary, biographical and historical, by J. SPEDDING, Trin. Coll. Cam. Vols. I. and II. 8vo 24s

MEMOIR OF THE LIFE OF SIR M. I. BRUNEL, Civil Engineer, &c. By RICHARD BEAMISH, F.R.S. *Second Edition*, revised; with a Portrait, and 16 Illustrations. 8vo 14s

LIFE OF ROBERT STEPHENSON, F.R.S., late President of the Institution of Civil Engineers. By JOHN CORDY JEAFFRESON, Barrister-at-Law; and WILLIAM POLE, Member of the Institution of Civil Engineers. With Portrait and Illustrations. 2 vols. 8vo [*In the press.*

THE LIFE OF SIR PHILIP SIDNEY, By the Rev. JULIUS LLOYD, M.A. Post 8vo 7s 6d

THE ROLL OF THE ROYAL COLLEGE OF PHYSICIANS OF LONDON; compiled from the Annals of the College, and from other Authentic Sources. By WILLIAM MUNK, M.D., Fellow of the College, &c. Vols. I. and II. 8vo 12s each.

THE HISTORY OF MEDICINE: Comprising a Narrative of its Progress, from the Earliest Ages to the Present Time, and of the Delusions incidental to its advance from Empiricism to the dignity of a Science. By EDWARD MERYON, M.D., F.G.S., Fellow of the Royal College of Physicians, &c. Vol. I. 8vo 12s 6d

MATERIALS FOR A HISTORY OF OIL PAINTING. By Sir CHARLES L. EASTLAKE, R.A. 8vo 16s

BIOGRAPHICAL SKETCHES. By NASSAU W. SENIOR. Comprising Biographical Sketches connected with the French Revolution, Legal Biographical Sketches, and Miscellaneous Biographical Sketches. Post 8vo

HALF-HOUR LECTURES ON THE HISTORY AND PRACTICE of the FINE and ORNAMENTAL ARTS. By WILLIAM B. SCOTT, Head Master of the Government School of Design, Newcastle-on-Tyne. 16mo with 50 Woodcuts, 8s 6d

SAVONAROLA AND HIS TIMES. By PASQUALE VILLARI, Professor of History in the University of Pisa; accompanied by new Documents. Translated from the Italian by LEONARD HORNER, Esq., F.R.S., with the co-operation of the Author. 8vo [*Nearly ready.*

THE LIFE OF WILLIAM WARBURTON, D.D., Lord Bishop of Gloucester from 1760 to 1779; with Remarks on his Works. By the Rev. JOHN SELBY WATSON, M.A., M.R.S.L. 8vo with Portrait, 18s

By the same Author.

LIFE OF RICHARD PORSON, M.A., Professor of Greek in the University of Cambridge from 1791 to 1808. With Portrait and 2 Facsimiles. 8vo 14s

BIOGRAPHIES OF DISTINGUISHED SCIENTIFIC MEN. By FRANÇOIS ARAGO. Translated by Admiral W. H. SMYTH, D.C.L., F.R.S., &c.; the Rev. B. POWELL, M.A.; and R. GRANT, M.A., F.R.A.S. 8vo 18s

By the same Author.

METEOROLOGICAL ESSAYS. With an Introduction by Baron HUMBOLDT. Translated under the superintendence of Major-General E. SABINE, R.A., V.P.R.S. 8vo 18s

POPULAR ASTRONOMY. Translated and edited by Admiral W. H. SMYTH, D.C.L., F.R.S.; and R. GRANT, M.A., F.R.A.S. With 25 Plates and 358 Woodcuts. 2 vols. 8vo £2 5s

TREATISE ON COMETS, from the above, price 5s

LIFE OF THE DUKE OF WELLINGTON, partly from the French of M. BRIALMONT; partly from Original Documents. By the Rev. G. R. GLEIG, M.A., Chaplain-General to H.M. Forces. *New Edition,* in One Volume, with PLANS, MAPS, and a PORTRAIT. 8vo 15s

MEMOIRS OF SIR HENRY HAVELOCK, Major-General, K.C.B. By JOHN CLARK MARSHMAN. With Portrait, Map, and 2 Plans. 8vo price 12s 6d

MEMOIRS OF ADMIRAL PARRY, THE ARCTIC NAVIGATOR. By his Son, the Rev. E. PARRY, M.A. Eighth Edition; with Portrait and coloured Chart. Fcp 8vo 5s

VICISSITUDES OF FAMILIES. By Sir BERNARD BURKE, Ulster King of Arms. FIRST, SECOND, and THIRD SERIES. 3 vols. crown 8vo price 12s 6d each

GREEK HISTORY FROM THEMISTOCLES TO ALEXANDER, in a Series of Lives from Plutarch. Revised and arranged by A. H. CLOUGH, sometime Fellow of Oriel College, Oxford. With 44 Woodcuts. Fcp 8vo 6s

TALES FROM GREEK MYTHOLOGY. By the Rev. G. W. Cox, M.A., late Scholar of Trinity College, Oxford. Square 16mo price 3s 6d

By the same Author.

TALES OF THE GODS AND HEROES. With 6 Landscape Illustrations from Drawings by the Author. Fcp 8vo 5s

THE TALE OF THE GREAT PERSIAN WAR, from the Histories of *Herodotus*. With 12 Woodcuts. Fcp 8vo 7s 6d

A DICTIONARY OF ROMAN AND GREEK ANTIQUITIES, with nearly 2,000 Wood Engravings, representing Objects from the Antique, illustrative of the Industrial Arts and Social Life of the Greeks and Romans. Being the Second Edition of the *Illustrated Companion to the Latin Dictionary and Greek Lexicon*. By ANTHONY RICH, Jun., B.A. Post 8vo 12s 6d

ANCIENT HISTORY OF EGYPT, ASSYRIA, AND BABYLONIA. By ELIZABETH M. SEWELL, Author of 'Amy Herbert,' &c. With Two Maps. Fcp 8vo 6s

By the same Author.

HISTORY OF THE EARLY CHURCH, from the First Preaching of the Gospel to the Council of Nicæa, A.D. 325. *Second Edition.* Fcp 8vo 4s 6d

MEMOIR OF THE REV. SYDNEY SMITH. By his Daughter, LADY HOLLAND. With a Selection from his Letters, edited by Mrs. AUSTIN. 2 vols. 8vo 28s

THOMAS MOORE'S MEMOIRS, JOURNAL, AND CORRESPONDENCE. People's Edition. With 8 Portraits and 2 Vignettes. Edited and abridged from the First Edition by the Right Hon. EARL RUSSELL. Square crown 8vo 12s 6d

SPEECHES OF THE RIGHT HON. LORD MACAULAY. Corrected by HIMSELF. *New Edition.* 8vo 12s

LORD MACAULAY'S SPEECHES ON PARLIAMENTARY REFORM IN 1831 AND 1832. Reprinted in the TRAVELLER'S LIBRARY. 16mo 1s

SOUTHEY'S LIFE OF WESLEY, AND RISE AND PROGRESS OF METHODISM. Fourth Edition, with Notes and Additions. Edited by the Rev. C. C. SOUTHEY, M.A. 2 vols. crown 8vo 12s

THE HISTORY OF WESLEYAN METHODISM. By GEORGE SMITH, F.A.S., Member of the Royal Asiatic Society, &c. 3 vols. crown 8vo 31s 6d

THE VOYAGE AND SHIPWRECK OF ST. PAUL: With Dissertations on the Life and Writings of St. Luke, and the Ships and Navigation of the Ancients. By JAMES SMITH, of Jordanhill, Esq., F.R.S. *Second Edition*; with Charts, &c. Crown 8vo 8s 6d

THE LIFE AND EPISTLES OF ST. PAUL. By the Rev. W. J. CONYBEARE, M.A., late Fellow of Trinity College, Cambridge; and the Rev. J. S. HOWSON, D.D., Principal of the Collegiate Institution, Liverpool. *People's Edition*, condensed; with 46 Illustrations and Maps. 2 vols. crown 8vo 12s

CONYBEARE AND HOWSON'S LIFE AND EPISTLES OF ST. PAUL. The Intermediate Edition, thoroughly revised; with a Selection of Maps, Plates, and Wood Engravings. 2 vols. square crown 8vo price 31s 6d

CONYBEARE AND HOWSON'S LIFE AND EPISTLES OF ST. PAUL. The Library Edition, corrected and reprinted; with all the Original Plates, Maps, Wood Engravings, and other Illustrations. 2 vols. 4to 48s

THE GENTILE AND THE JEW IN THE COURTS OF THE TEMPLE OF CHRIST. An Introduction to the History of Christianity. From the German of Professor DÖLLINGER, by the Rev. N. DARNELL, M.A., late Fellow of New College, Oxford. 2 vols. 8vo 21s

PORT-ROYAL; A Contribution to the History of Religion and Literature in France. By CHARLES BEARD, B.A. 2 vols. post 8vo price 24s

HIPPOLYTUS AND HIS AGE; or, the Beginnings and Prospects of Christianity. By C. C. J. BUNSEN, D.D., D.C.L., D. Ph. 2 vols. 8vo 30s

By the same Author.

OUTLINES OF THE PHILOSOPHY OF UNIVERSAL HISTORY, applied to Language and Religion: Containing an Account of the Alphabetical Conferences. 2 vols. 8vo 33s

ANALECTA ANTE-NICÆNA. 3 vols. 8vo 42s

EGYPT'S PLACE IN UNIVERSAL HISTORY: An Historical Investigation, in Five Books. Translated from the German by C. H. COTTRELL, M.A. With many Illustrations. 4 vols. 8vo £5 8s Vol. V., completing the work, is in preparation.

A NEW LATIN-ENGLISH DICTIONARY. By the Rev. J. T. WHITE, M.A., of Corpus Christi College, Oxford; and the Rev. J. E. RIDDLE, M.A., of St. Edmund Hall, Oxford. Imperial 8vo 42s

A GREEK-ENGLISH LEXICON. Compiled by HENRY GEO. LIDDELL, D.D., Dean of Christ Church; and ROBERT SCOTT, D.D., Master of Balliol. *Fifth Edition*, revised and augmented. Crown 4to price 31s 6d

A LEXICON, GREEK AND ENGLISH, abridged from LIDDELL and SCOTT's *Greek-English Lexicon*. Ninth Edition, revised and compared throughout with the Original. Square 12mo 7s 6d

PUBLISHED BY MESSRS. LONGMAN AND CO.　　7

A NEW ENGLISH-GREEK LEXICON, containing all the Greek Words used by Writers of good authority. By CHARLES DUKE YONGE, B.A. *Second Edition*, thoroughly revised. 4to 21*s*

A DICTIONARY OF THE ENGLISH LANGUAGE. By R. G. LATHAM, M.A., M.D., F.R.S., late Fellow of King's College, Cambridge. Founded on that of Dr. SAMUEL JOHNSON, as edited by the Rev. H. T. TODD, M.A., with numerous Emendations and Additions. 2 vols. 4to in course of publication in Thirty Monthly Parts, price 3*s* each.

THESAURUS OF ENGLISH WORDS AND PHRASES, classified and arranged so as to facilitate the Expression of Ideas, and assist in Literary Composition. By P. M. ROGET, M.D., F.R.S., &c. *Twelfth Edition*, revised and improved. Crown 8vo 10*s* 6*d*

A PRACTICAL DICTIONARY OF THE FRENCH AND ENGLISH LANGUAGES. By LÉON CONTANSEAU, lately Professor of the French Language and Literature in the Royal Indian Military College, Addiscombe (now dissolved); and Examiner for Military Appointments. *Sixth Edition*, with Corrections. Post 8vo 10*s* 6*d*

By the same Author.

A POCKET DICTIONARY OF THE FRENCH AND ENGLISH LANGUAGES; being a careful abridgment of the above, preserving all the most useful features of the original work, condensed into a pocket volume for the convenience of Tourists, Travellers, and English Readers or Students to whom portability of size is a requisite. Square 18mo 5*s*

LECTURES ON THE SCIENCE OF LANGUAGE, delivered at the Royal Institution of Great Britain. By MAX MÜLLER, M.A., Fellow of All Souls College, Oxford. *Third Edition*, revised. 8vo 12*s*

THE STUDENT'S HANDBOOK OF COMPARATIVE GRAMMAR, applied to the Sanskrit, Zend, Greek, Latin, Gothic, Anglo-Saxon, and English Languages. By the Rev. THOMAS CLARK, M.A. Crown 8vo price 7*s* 6*d*

THE DEBATER: A Series of Complete Debates, Outlines of Debates, and Questions for Discussion; with ample References to the best Sources of Information. By F. ROWTON. Fcp 8vo 6*s*

THE ENGLISH LANGUAGE. By R. G. LATHAM, M.A., M.D., F.R.S., late Fellow of King's College, Cambridge. *Fifth Edition*, revised and enlarged. 8vo 18*s*

By the same Author.

HANDBOOK OF THE ENGLISH LANGUAGE, for the Use of Students of the Universities and Higher Classes of Schools. *Fourth Edition*. Crown 8vo 7*s* 6*d*

ELEMENTS OF COMPARATIVE PHILOLOGY. 8vo 21*s*

MANUAL OF ENGLISH LITERATURE, HISTORICAL AND CRITICAL; with a Chapter on English Metres. For the use of Schools and Colleges. By THOMAS ARNOLD, B.A., Professor of English Literature, Cath. Univ. Ireland. Post 8vo 10*s* 6*d*

ON TRANSLATING HOMER: Three Lectures given at Oxford. By MATTHEW ARNOLD, M.A., Professor of Poetry in the University of Oxford, and formerly Fellow of Oriel College. Crown 8vo 3s 6d—Mr. ARNOLD's *Last Words on Translating Homer*, price 3s 6d

JERUSALEM: A Sketch of the City and Temple, from the Earliest Times to the Siege by Titus. By THOMAS LEWIN, M.A. With Map and Illustrations. 8vo 10s

PEAKS, PASSES, AND GLACIERS; a Series of Excursions by Members of the Alpine Club. Edited by J. BALL, M.R.I.A., F.L.S. Fourth Edition; with Maps, Illustrations, and Woodcuts. Square crown 8vo 21s—TRAVELLERS' EDITION, condensed, 16mo 5s 6d

SECOND SERIES OF PEAKS, PASSES, AND GLACIERS. Edited by E. S. KENNEDY, M.A., F.R.G.S., President of the Alpine Club. With 1 DOUBLE MAP and 10 Single Maps by E. WELLER, F.R.G.S.; and 51 Illustrations on Wood by E. WHYMPER and G. PEARSON. 2 vols. square crown 8vo 42s

NINETEEN MAPS OF THE ALPINE DISTRICTS: from the First and Second Series of *Peaks, Passes, and Glaciers*. Square crown 8vo price 7s 6d

MOUNTAINEERING IN 1861; a Vacation Tour. By JOHN TYNDALL, F.R.S., Professor of Natural Philosophy in the Royal Institution of Great Britain. Square crown 8vo with 2 Views, 7s 6d

A SUMMER TOUR IN THE GRISONS AND ITALIAN VALLEYS OF THE BERNINA. By Mrs. HENRY FRESHFIELD. With 2 coloured Maps and 4 Views. Post 8vo 10s 6d

By the same Author.

ALPINE BYWAYS; or, Light Leaves gathered in 1859 and 1860. With 8 Illustrations and 4 Route Maps. Post 8vo 10s 6d

A LADY'S TOUR ROUND MONTE ROSA; including Visits to the Italian Valleys of Anzasca, Mastalone, Camasco, Sesia, Lys, Challant, Aosta, and Cogne. With Map and Illustrations. Post 8vo 14s

THE ALPS; or, Sketches of Life and Nature in the Mountains. By Baron H. VON BERLEPSCH. Translated by the Rev. LESLIE STEPHEN, M.A. With 17 Tinted Illustrations, 8vo 15s

THEBES, ITS TOMBS AND THEIR TENANTS, Ancient and Modern; including a Record of Excavations in the Necropolis. By A. HENRY RHIND, F.S.A. With 17 Illustrations, including a Map. Royal 8vo 16s

LETTERS FROM ITALY AND SWITZERLAND. By FELIX MENDELSSOHN-BARTHOLDY. Translated from the German by LADY WALLACE. *Second Edition*, revised. Post 8vo 9s 6d

PUBLISHED BY MESSRS. LONGMAN AND CO. 9

A GUIDE TO THE PYRENEES; especially intended for the use of Mountaineers. By CHARLES PACKE. With Frontispiece and 3 Maps. Fcp 8vo 6s

The MAP of the *Central Pyrenees*, separately, price 2s 6d

HERZEGOVINA; or, Omer Pacha and the Christian Rebels: With a Brief Account of Servia, its Social, Political, and Financial Condition. By Lieut. G. ARBUTHNOT, R.H.A., F.R.G.S. Post 8vo, Frontispiece and Map, 10s 6d

CANADA AND THE CRIMEA; or, Sketches of a Soldier's Life, from the Journals and Correspondence of the late Major RANKEN, R.E. Edited by his Brother, W. B. RANKEN. *Second Edition*. Post 8vo, with Portrait, price 7s 6d

NOTES ON MEXICO IN 1861 AND 1862, Politically and Socially considered. By CHARLES LEMPRIERE, D.C.L., of the Inner Temple, and Law Fellow of St. John's College, Oxford. With Map and 10 Woodcuts. Post 8vo 12s 6d

EXPLORATIONS IN LABRADOR, the Country of the Montagnais and Nasquapee Indians. By HENRY YOULE HIND, M.A., F.R.G.S., Professor of Chemistry and Geology in the University of Trinity College, Toronto. 2 vols. *[Just ready.*

By the same Author.

NARRATIVE OF THE CANADIAN RED RIVER EXPLORING EXPEDITION OF 1857; and of the ASSINNIBOINE AND SASKATCHEWAN EXPLORING EXPEDITION OF 1858. With several Coloured Maps and Plans, numerous Woodcuts, and 20 Chromoxylographic Engravings. 2 vols. 8vo 42s

HAWAII; the Past, Present, and Future of its Island-kingdom: An Historical Account of the Sandwich Islands (Polynesia). By MANLEY HOPKINS, Hawaiian Consul-General. Post 8vo, Map and Illustrations, price 12s 6d

WILD LIFE ON THE FJELDS OF NORWAY. By FRANCIS M. WYNDHAM. With Maps and Woodcuts. Post 8vo 10s 6d

THE LAKE REGIONS OF CENTRAL AFRICA: A Picture of Exploration. By RICHARD F. BURTON, Captain H.M. Indian Army. 2 vols. 8vo, Map and Illustrations, 31s 6d

By the same Author.

FIRST FOOTSTEPS IN EAST AFRICA; or, An Exploration of Harar. With Maps and coloured Illustrations. 8vo 18s

PERSONAL NARRATIVE OF A PILGRIMAGE TO EL MEDINAH and MECCAH. *Second Edition*; with numerous Illustrations. 2 vols. crown 8vo 24s

THE CITY OF THE SAINTS; and Across the Rocky Mountains to California. *Second Edition*; with Maps and Illustrations. 8vo 18s

THE AFRICANS AT HOME: A Popular Description of Africa and the Africans, condensed from the Accounts of African Travellers from the time of Mungo Park to the Present Day. By the Rev. R. M. MACBRAIR, M.A. Fcp 8vo, Map and 70 Woodcuts, 7s 6d

LOWER BRITTANY AND THE BIBLE; its Priests and People: with Notes on Religious and Civil Liberty in France. By JAMES BROMFIELD, Author of 'Brittany and the Bible,' &c. Post 8vo 9s

SOCIAL LIFE AND MANNERS IN AUSTRALIA; Being the Notes of Eight Years' Experience. By a RESIDENT. Post 8vo 6s

IMPRESSIONS OF ROME, FLORENCE, AND TURIN. By the Author of *Amy Herbert*. Crown 8vo 7s 6d

AN AGRICULTURAL TOUR IN BELGIUM, HOLLAND, AND ON THE RHINE; With Practical Notes on the Peculiarities of Flemish Husbandry. By ROBERT SCOTT BURN. Post 8vo with 43 Woodcuts, 7s

A WEEK AT THE LAND'S END. By J. T. BLIGHT; assisted by E. H. RODD, R. Q. COUCH, and J. RALFS. With Map and 96 Woodcuts by the Author. Fcp 8vo 6s 6d

VISITS TO REMARKABLE PLACES: Old Halls, Battle-Fields, and Scenes illustrative of Striking Passages in English History and Poetry. By WILLIAM HOWITT. With about 80 Wood Engravings. 2 vols. square crown 8vo 25s

By the same Author.

THE RURAL LIFE OF ENGLAND. Cheaper Edition. With Woodcuts by Bewick and Williams. Medium 8vo 12s 6d

ESSAYS ON SCIENTIFIC AND OTHER SUBJECTS, contributed to the *Edinburgh* and *Quarterly Reviews*. By Sir HENRY HOLLAND, Bart., M.D., F.R.S., Physician-in-Ordinary to the Queen. *Second Edition*. 8vo 14s

By the same Author.

MEDICAL NOTES AND REFLECTIONS. *Third Edition*, revised, with some Additions. 8vo 18s

CHAPTERS ON MENTAL PHYSIOLOGY; founded chiefly on Chapters contained in *Medical Notes and Reflections*. *Second Edition*. Post 8vo 8s 6d

PSYCHOLOGICAL INQUIRIES: in a Series of Essays intended to illustrate the Influence of the Physical Organisation on the Mental Faculties. By Sir BENJAMIN C. BRODIE, Bart., &c. Fcp 8vo 5s. PART II. Essays intended to illustrate some Points in the Physical and Moral History of Man. Fcp 8vo 5s

PUBLISHED BY MESSRS. LONGMAN AND CO.   11

AN INTRODUCTION TO MENTAL PHILOSOPHY, on the Inductive Method. By J. D. MORELL, M.A., LL.D. 8vo 12s

By the same Author.

ELEMENTS OF PSYCHOLOGY: Part I., containing the Analysis of the Intellectual Powers. Post 8vo 7s 6d

OUTLINE OF THE NECESSARY LAWS OF THOUGHT: A Treatise on Pure and Applied Logic. By the Most Rev. WILLIAM THOMSON, D.D., Lord Archbishop of York. *Fifth Edition.* Post 8vo 5s 6d

THE CYCLOPÆDIA OF ANATOMY AND PHYSIOLOGY. Edited by ROBERT B. TODD, M.D., F.R.S. Assisted in the various departments by nearly all the most eminent Cultivators of Physiological Science of the present age. 5 vols. 8vo with 2,853 Woodcuts, price £6 6s

A DICTIONARY OF PRACTICAL MEDICINE: Comprising General Pathology, the Nature and Treatment of Diseases, Morbid Structures, and the Disorders especially Incidental to Climates, to Sex, and to the different Epochs of Life. By JAMES COPLAND, M.D., F.R.S. 3 vols. 8vo price £5 11s

HEAT CONSIDERED AS A MODE OF MOTION: A Course of Lectures delivered at the Royal Institution of Great Britain. By JOHN TYNDALL, F.R.S., Professor of Natural Philosophy in the Royal Institution. Crown 8vo with Illustrations.   [*Just ready.*

THE COMPARATIVE ANATOMY AND PHYSIOLOGY OF THE VERTEBRATE ANIMALS. By RICHARD OWEN, F.R.S., D.C.L., Superintendent of the Natural History Department, British Museum, &c. With upwards of 1,200 Wood Engravings. 8vo   [*Nearly ready.*

VAN DER HOEVEN'S HANDBOOK OF ZOOLOGY. Translated from the Second Dutch Edition. By the Rev. WILLIAM CLARK, M.D., F.R.S., &c. 2 vols. 8vo. with 24 Plates of Figures, price 60s cloth; or separately, Vol. I. *Invertebrata*, 30s; and Vol. II. *Vertebrata*, 30s

THE EARTH AND ITS MECHANISM; an Account of the various Proofs of the Rotation of the Earth; with a Description of the Instruments used in the Experimental Demonstrations; also the Theory of Foucault's Pendulum and Gyroscope. By HENRY WORMS, F.R.A.S., F.G.S. 8vo with 31 Woodcuts, price 10s 6d

VOLCANOS, the Character of their Phenomena; their Share in the Structure and Composition of the Surface of the Globe; and their Relation to its Internal Forces; including a Descriptive Catalogue of Volcanos and Volcanic Formations. By G. POULETT SCROPE, M.P., F.R.S., F.G.S. *Second Edition*, with Map and Illustrations. 8vo 15s

A MANUAL OF CHEMISTRY, Descriptive and Theoretical. By WILLIAM ODLING, M.B., F.R.S., Secretary to the Chemical Society, and Professor of Practical Chemistry in Guy's Hospital. Part I. 8vo 9s

A DICTIONARY OF CHEMISTRY, founded on that of the late Dr. URE. By HENRY WATTS, B.A., F.C.S., Editor of the *Quarterly Journal of the Chemical Society*. To be published in Monthly Parts, uniform with the New Edition of Dr. URE's *Dictionary of Arts, Manufactures, and Mines*, recently completed.

HANDBOOK OF CHEMICAL ANALYSIS, adapted to the Unitary System of Notation. Based on the 4th Edition of Dr. H. Wills' *Anleitung zur chemischen Analyse*. By F. T. CONINGTON, M.A., F.C.S. Post 8vo price 7s 6d

CONINGTON'S TABLES OF QUALITATIVE ANALYSIS, to accompany in use his Handbook of *Chemical Analysis*. Post 8vo 2s 6d

A HANDBOOK OF VOLUMETRICAL ANALYSIS. By ROBERT H. SCOTT, M.A., T.C.D., Secretary of the Geological Society of Dublin. Post 8vo 4s 6d

A TREATISE ON ELECTRICITY, in Theory and Practice. By A. DE LA RIVE, Professor in the Academy of Geneva. Translated for the Author by C. V. WALKER, F.R.S. With Illustrations. 3 vols. 8vo price £3 13s

AN ESSAY ON CLASSIFICATION [The Mutual Relation of Organised Beings]. By LOUIS AGASSIZ. 8vo 12s

A DICTIONARY OF SCIENCE, LITERATURE, AND ART: Comprising the History, Description, and Scientific Principles of every Branch of Human Knowledge. Edited by W. T. BRANDE, F.R.S.L. and M. The Fourth Edition, revised and corrected. 8vo [*In the press.*

THE CORRELATION OF PHYSICAL FORCES. By W. R. GROVE, Q.C., M.A., V.P.R.S., Corresponding Member of the Academies of Rome, Turin, &c. Fourth Edition. 8vo 7s 6d

THE ELEMENTS OF PHYSICS. By C. F. PESCHEL, Principal of the Royal Military College, Dresden. Translated from the German, with Notes, by E. WEST. 3 vols. fcp 8vo 21s

PHILLIPS'S ELEMENTARY INTRODUCTION TO MINERALOGY. A New Edition, with extensive Alterations and Additions by H. J. BROOKE, F.R.S., F.G.S.; and W. H. MILLER, M.A., F.G.S. With numerous Woodcuts. Post 8vo 16s

A GLOSSARY OF MINERALOGY. By HENRY WILLIAM BRISTOW, F.G.S., of the Geological Survey of Great Britain. With 486 Figures on Wood. Crown 8vo 12s

ELEMENTS OF MATERIA MEDICA AND THERAPEUTICS. By JONATHAN PEREIRA, M.D. F.R.S. *Third Edition*, enlarged and improved from the Author's Materials. By A. S. TAYLOR, M.D., and G. O. REES, M.D. With numerous Woodcuts. VOL. I. 8vo 28s; VOL. II. PART II. 21s; VOL. II. PART II. 26s

OUTLINES OF ASTRONOMY. By Sir J. F. W. Herschel, Bart., M.A. *Fifth Edition*, revised and corrected. With Plates and Woodcuts. 8vo 18s

By the same Author.

ESSAYS FROM THE EDINBURGH AND QUARTERLY REVIEWS, with Addresses and other Pieces. 8vo 18s

CELESTIAL OBJECTS FOR COMMON TELESCOPES. By the Rev. T. W. Webb, M.A., F.R.A.S. With Woodcuts and Map of the Moon. 16mo 7s

A GUIDE TO GEOLOGY. By John Phillips, M.A., F.R.S., F.G.S., &c. Fourth Edition. With 4 Plates. Fcp 8vo 5s

THE LAW OF STORMS considered in connexion with the ordinary Movements of the Atmosphere. By H. W. Dove, F.R.S., Member of the Academies of Moscow, Munich, St. Petersburg, &c. Second Edition, translated, with the Author's sanction, by R. H. Scott, M.A., Trin. Coll. Dublin. With Diagrams and Charts. 8vo 10s 6d

THE WEATHER-BOOK; A Manual of Practical Meteorology. By Rear-Admiral Robert FitzRoy, R.N. With 16 Diagrams on Wood. 8vo 15s

ON THE STRENGTH OF MATERIALS; Containing various original and useful Formulae, specially applied to Tubular Bridges, Wrought-Iron and Cast-Iron Beams, &c. By Thomas Tate, F.R.A.S. 8vo 5s 6d

MANUAL OF THE SUB-KINGDOM COELENTERATA. By J. Reay Greene, B.A., M.R.I.A. Being the Second of a New Series of Manuals of the *Experimental and Natural Sciences*; edited by the Rev. J. A. Galbraith, M.A., and the Rev. S. Haughton, M.A., F.R.S., Fellows of Trinity College, Dublin. With 39 Woodcuts. Fcp 8vo 5s

By the same Author and Editors.

MANUAL OF PROTOZOA; With a General Introduction on the Principles of Zoology, and 16 Woodcuts; Being the First Manual of the Series. Fcp 8vo 2s

THE SEA AND ITS LIVING WONDERS. By Dr. George Hartwig. Translated by the Author from the Fourth German Edition; and embellished with numerous Illustrations from Original Designs. 8vo 18s

By the same Author.

THE TROPICAL WORLD: a Popular Scientific Account of the Natural History of the Animal and Vegetable Kingdoms in the Equatorial Regions. With 8 Chromoxylographs and 172 Woodcut Illustrations. 8vo 21s

FOREST CREATURES. By Charles Boner, Author of 'Chamois Hunting in the Mountains of Bavaria,' &c. With 18 Illustrations from Drawings by Guido Hammer. Post 8vo 10s 6d

SKETCHES OF THE NATURAL HISTORY OF CEYLON; With Narratives and Anecdotes Illustrative of the Habits and Instincts of the Mammalia, Birds, Reptiles, Fishes, Insects, &c., including a Monograph of the Elephant. By Sir J. Emerson Tennent, M.C.S., LL.D., &c. With 82 Illustrations on Wood. Post 8vo 12s 6d

By the same Author.

CEYLON; An Account of the Island, Physical, Historical, and Topographical; with Notices of its Natural History, Antiquities, and Productions. Fifth Edition; with Maps, Plans, and Charts, and 90 Wood Engravings. 2 vols. 8vo £2 10s

MARVELS AND MYSTERIES OF INSTINCT; or, Curiosities of Animal Life. By G. Garratt. Third Edition, revised and enlarged. Fcp. 8vo 7s.

KIRBY AND SPENCE'S INTRODUCTION TO ENTOMOLOGY; or, Elements of the Natural History of Insects: Comprising an Account of Noxious and Useful Insects, of their Metamorphoses, Food, Stratagems, Habitations, Societies, Motions, Noises, Hybernation, Instinct, &c. Seventh Edition. Crown 8vo 5s

YOUATT'S WORK ON THE HORSE; Comprising also a Treatise on Draught. With numerous Woodcut Illustrations, chiefly from Designs by W. Harvey. New Edition, revised and enlarged by E. N. Gabriel, M.R.C.S., C.V.B. 8vo 10s 6d

By the same Author.

THE DOG. A New Edition; with numerous Engravings, from Designs by W. Harvey. 8vo 6s

THE DOG IN HEALTH AND DISEASE: Comprising the Natural History, Zoological Classification, and Varieties of the Dog, as well as the various modes of Breaking and Using him. By Stonehenge. With 70 Wood Engravings. Square crown 8vo 15s

By the same Author.

THE GREYHOUND: A Treatise on the Art of Breeding, Rearing, and Training Greyhounds for Public Running. With many Illustrations. Square crown 8vo 21s

THE ENCYCLOPÆDIA OF RURAL SPORTS; A Complete Account, Historical, Practical, and Descriptive, of Hunting, Shooting, Fishing, Racing, &c. By D. P. Blaine. With above 600 Woodcut Illustrations, including 20 from Designs by John Leech. 8vo 42s

COL. HAWKER'S INSTRUCTIONS TO YOUNG SPORTSMEN in all that relates to Guns and Shooting. 11th Edition, revised by the Author's Son. With Portrait and Illustrations. Square crown 8vo 18s

THE DEAD SHOT, or Sportsman's Complete Guide; a Treatise on the Use of the Gun, with Lessons in the Art of Shooting Game of all kinds; Dog-breaking, Pigeon-shooting, &c. By Marksman. Third Edition; with 6 Plates. Fcp 8vo 5s

THE FLY-FISHER'S ENTOMOLOGY. By ALFRED RONALDS. With coloured Representations of the Natural and Artificial Insect. Sixth Edition, revised by an experienced Fly-Fisher; with 20 new coloured Plates. 8vo 14s

THE CHASE OF THE WILD RED DEER in the Counties of Devon and Somerset. With an APPENDIX descriptive of Remarkable Runs and Incidents connected with the Chase, from the year 1780 to the year 1860. By C. P. COLLYNS, Esq. With a Map and numerous Illustrations. Square crown 8vo 16s

THE HORSE'S FOOT, AND HOW TO KEEP IT SOUND. Eighth Edition; with an Appendix on Shoeing and Hunters. 12 Plates and 12 Woodcuts. By W. MILES, Esq. Imperial 8vo 12s 6d

Two Casts or Models of Off Fore Feet—No. 1, Shod for All Purposes; No. 2, Shod with Leather, on Mr. Miles's plan—may be had, price 3s each.

By the same Author.

A PLAIN TREATISE ON HORSE-SHOEING. With Plates and Woodcuts. New Edition, Post 8vo 2s

HINTS ON ETIQUETTE AND THE USAGES OF SOCIETY; With a Glance at Bad Habits. New Edition, revised (with Additions). By a LADY of RANK. Fcp 8vo 2s 6d

SHORT WHIST; its Rise, Progress, and Laws: with Observations to make anyone a Whist-player. Containing also the Laws of Picquet, Cassino, Écarté, Cribbage, Backgammon. By Major A. Fcp 8vo 3s

TALPA; or, the Chronicles of a Clay Farm: an Agricultural Fragment. By C. W. HOSKYNS, Esq. With 24 Woodcuts from Designs by G. CRUIKSHANK. 16mo 5s 6d

THE SAILING-BOAT: A Treatise on English and Foreign Boats, with Historical Descriptions; also Practical Directions for the Rigging, Sailing, and Management of Boats, and other Nautical Information. By H. C. FOLKARD, Author of *The Wildfowl*, &c. Third Edition, enlarged; with numerous Illustrations. [*Just ready.*

ATHLETIC AND GYMNASTIC EXERCISES: Comprising 114 Exercises and Feats of Agility. With a Description of the requisite Apparatus, and 64 Woodcuts. By JOHN H. HOWARD. 16mo 7s 6d

THE LABORATORY OF CHEMICAL WONDERS: A Scientific Mélange for the Instruction and Entertainment of Young People. By G. W. S. PIESSE, Analytical Chemist. Crown 8vo 5s 6d

By the same Author.

CHEMICAL, NATURAL, AND PHYSICAL MAGIC, for the Instruction and Entertainment of Juveniles during the Holiday Vacation. With 30 Woodcuts and an Invisible Portrait. Fcp 8vo 3s 6d

THE ART OF PERFUMERY; being the History and Theory of Odours, and the Methods of Extracting the Aromas of Plants, &c. Third Edition; with numerous additional Recipes and Analyses, and 53 Woodcuts. Crown 8vo 10s 6d

16　　　GENERAL LIST OF NEW WORKS

THE CRICKET FIELD; or, the History and the Science of the Game of Cricket. By the Rev. J. PYCROFT, B.A., Trin. Coll. Oxon. *Fourth Edition*; with 2 Plates. Fcp 8vo 5s

By the same Author.

THE CRICKET TUTOR; a Treatise exclusively Practical, dedicated to the Captains of Elevens in Public Schools. 18mo 1s

THE WARDEN: a Novel. By ANTHONY TROLLOPE. New and cheaper Edition. Crown 8vo 3s 6d

By the same Author.

BARCHESTER TOWERS: A Sequel to the *Warden*. New and cheaper Edition. Crown 8vo 5s

ELLICE: A Tale. By L. N. COMYN. Post 8vo 9s 6d

THE LAST OF THE OLD SQUIRES: A Sketch. By the Rev. J. W. WARTER, B.D., Vicar of West Tarring, Sussex. *Second Edition*. Fcp. 8vo 4s 6d

THE ROMANCE OF A DULL LIFE. Second Edition, revised. Post 8vo 9s 6d

By the same Author.

MORNING CLOUDS. Second and cheaper Edition, revised throughout. Fcp 8vo 5s

THE AFTERNOON OF LIFE. Second and cheaper Edition, revised throughout. Fcp 8vo 5s

PROBLEMS IN HUMAN NATURE. Post 8vo 6s

THE TALES AND STORIES OF THE AUTHOR OF AMY HERBERT. New and cheaper Edition, in 10 vols. crown 8vo price £1 14s 6d boards; or each work separately, complete in a single volume.

AMY HERBERT	2s 6d	IVORS	2s 6d
GERTRUDE	2s 6d	KATHERINE ASHTON ..	2s 6d
The EARL'S DAUGHTER.	2s 6d	MARGARET PERCIVAL .	5s 0d
EXPERIENCE of LIFE	2s 6d	LANETON PARSONAGE .	4s 6d
CLEVE HALL	3s 6d	URSULA	4s 6d

*** Each work may be had separately in cloth, with gilt edges, at One Shilling per volume extra.

SUNSETS AND SUNSHINE; or, Varied Aspects of Life. By ERSKINE NEALE, M.A., Vicar of Exning, and Chaplain to the Earl of Huntingdon. Post 8vo 9s 6d

MY LIFE, AND WHAT SHALL I DO WITH IT? A Question for Young Gentlewomen. By an OLD MAID. *Fourth Edition*. Fcp 8vo 6s

DEACONESSES: An Essay on the Official Help of Women in Parochial Work and in Charitable Institutions. By the Rev. J. S. HOWSON, D.D., Principal of the Collegiate Institution, Liverpool. Fcp 8vo 5s

ESSAYS IN ECCLESIASTICAL BIOGRAPHY. By the Right Hon. Sir JAMES STEPHEN, LL.D. Fourth Edition, with a Biographical Notice of the Author, by his Son. 8vo 14s

By the same Author.

LECTURES ON THE HISTORY OF FRANCE. Third Edition. 2 vols. 8vo 24s

CRITICAL AND HISTORICAL ESSAYS contributed to The Edinburgh Review. By the Right Hon. Lord MACAULAY. Four Editions, as follows:—

1. A LIBRARY EDITION (the *Tenth*), 3 vols. 8vo 36s
2. Complete in ONE VOLUME, with Portrait and Vignette. Square crown 8vo 21s
3. Another NEW EDITION, in 3 vols. fcp 8vo 21s
4. The PEOPLE'S EDITION, in 2 vols. crown 8vo 8s

LORD MACAULAY'S MISCELLANEOUS WRITINGS: comprising his Contributions to *Knight's Quarterly Magazine*, Articles contributed to the Edinburgh Review not included in his *Critical and Historical Essays*, Biographies written for the *Encyclopædia Britannica*. Miscellaneous Poems and Inscriptions. 2 vols. 8vo with Portrait, 21s

THE REV. SYDNEY SMITH'S MISCELLANEOUS WORKS: Including his Contributions to the Edinburgh Review. Four Editions, viz.

1. A LIBRARY EDITION (the *Fourth*). In 3 vols. 8vo with Portrait, 36s
2. Complete in ONE VOLUME, with Portrait and Vignette. Square crown 8vo 21s
3. Another NEW EDITION, in 3 vols. fcp 8vo 21s
4. The PEOPLE'S EDITION, in 2 vols. crown 8vo 8s

By the same Author.

ELEMENTARY SKETCHES OF MORAL PHILOSOPHY, delivered at the Royal Institution. Fcp 8vo 7s

THE WIT AND WISDOM OF THE REV. SYDNEY SMITH: A Selection of the most memorable Passages in his Writings and Conversation. 16mo 7s 6d

ESSAYS SELECTED FROM CONTRIBUTIONS TO THE *Edinburgh Review*. By HENRY ROGERS. Second Edition. 3 vols. fcp 8vo 21s

By the same Author.

THE ECLIPSE OF FAITH; or, A Visit to a Religious Sceptic. Tenth Edition. Fcp 8vo 5s

DEFENCE OF THE ECLIPSE OF FAITH, by its Author: Being a Rejoinder to Professor Newman's *Reply*. Fcp 8vo 3s 6d

SELECTIONS FROM THE CORRESPONDENCE OF R. E. H. GREYSON, Esq. Edited by the Author of *The Eclipse of Faith*. Crown 8vo 7s 6d

ESSAYS AND REVIEWS. By the Rev. W. Temple, D.D., Rev. R. Williams, B.D., Rev. B. Powell, M.A., the Rev. H. B. Wilson, B.D., C. W. Goodwin, M.A., Rev. M. Pattison, B.D., and Rev. B. Jowett, M.A. Fcp 8vo 5s

ESSAYS AND REVIEWS. *Ninth Edition,* in 8vo price 10s 6d

REVELATION AND SCIENCE, in respect to Bunsen's *Biblical Researches,* the Evidences of Christianity, and the Mosaic Cosmogony. With an Examination of certain Statements put forth by the remaining Authors of *Essays and Reviews.* By the Rev. B. W. Savile, M.A. 8vo price 10s 6d

THE HISTORY OF THE SUPERNATURAL IN ALL AGES AND NATIONS, IN ALL CHURCHES, CHRISTIAN AND PAGAN: Demonstrating a Universal Faith. By William Howitt, Author of *Colonisation and Christianity.* 2 vols. post 8vo [*Nearly ready.*

THE MISSION AND EXTENSION OF THE CHURCH AT HOME, considered in Eight Lectures, preached before the University of Oxford in the year 1861, at the Lecture founded by the late Rev. J. Hampton, M.A. By J. Sandford, D.D., Archdeacon of Coventry. 8vo price 12s

PHYSICO-PROPHETICAL ESSAYS ON THE LOCALITY OF THE ETERNAL INHERITANCE; its Nature and Character; the Resurrection Body; the Mutual Recognition of Glorified Saints. By the Rev. W. Lister, F.G.S. Crown 8vo 6s 6d

BISHOP JEREMY TAYLOR'S ENTIRE WORKS: With Life by Bishop Heber. Revised and corrected by the Rev. C. P. Eden, Fellow of Oriel College, Oxford. 10 vols. 8vo £5 5s

MOSHEIM'S ECCLESIASTICAL HISTORY. The Rev. Dr. Murdock's Literal Translation from the Latin, as edited, with Additional Notes, by Henry Soames, M.A. *Third Revised Edition,* carefully re-edited and brought down to the Present Time by the Rev. William Stubbs, M.A., Vicar of Navestock, and Librarian to the Archbishop of Canterbury. 5 vols. 8vo [*In the press.*

PASSING THOUGHTS ON RELIGION. By the Author of *Amy Herbert.* New Edition. Fcp 8vo 5s

By the same Author.

SELF-EXAMINATION BEFORE CONFIRMATION: With Devotions and Directions for Confirmation-Day. 32mo 1s 6d

READINGS FOR A MONTH PREPARATORY TO CONFIRMATION; Compiled from the Works of Writers of the Early and of the English Church. Fcp 8vo 4s

READINGS FOR EVERY DAY IN LENT; Compiled from the Writings of Bishop Jeremy Taylor. Fcp 8vo 5s

A COURSE OF ENGLISH READING, adapted to every taste and capacity; or, How and What to Read: With Literary Anecdotes. By the Rev. J. PYCROFT, B.A., Trin. Coll. Oxon. Fcp 8vo 5s

LEGENDS OF THE SAINTS AND MARTYRS, as represented in Christian Art. By Mrs. JAMESON. Third Edition, revised; with 17 Etchings and 180 Woodcuts. 2 vols. square crown 8vo 31s 6d

By the same Author.

LEGENDS OF THE MONASTIC ORDERS, as represented in Christian Art. New and improved Edition, being the Third; with many Etchings and Woodcuts. Square crown 8vo [*Nearly ready.*

LEGENDS OF THE MADONNA, as represented in Christian Art. Second Edition, enlarged; with 27 Etchings and 165 Woodcuts. Square crown 8vo 28s

THE HISTORY OF OUR LORD AND OF HIS PRECURSOR JOHN THE BAPTIST; with the Personages and Typical Subjects of the Old Testament as represented in Christian Art. Square crown 8vo with many Etchings and Woodcuts [*In the press.*

CATS' AND FARLIE'S BOOK OF EMBLEMS: Moral Emblems, with Aphorisms, Adages, and Proverbs of all Nations: Comprising 60 circular Vignettes, 60 Tail-pieces, and a Frontispiece composed from their works by J. LEIGHTON, F.S.A., and engraved on Wood. The Text translated and edited, with Additions, by R. PIGOT. Imperial 8vo 31s 6d

BUNYAN'S PILGRIM'S PROGRESS: With 126 Illustrations on Steel and Wood, from original Designs by C. Bennett; and a Preface by the Rev. C. KINGSLEY. Fcp 4to 21s

THEOLOGIA GERMANICA: Translated by SUSANNA WINKWORTH. With a Preface by the Rev. C. KINGSLEY; and a Letter by Baron BUNSEN. Fcp 8vo 5s

LYRA GERMANICA, Translated from the German by CATHERINE WINKWORTH. FIRST SERIES, Hymns for the Sundays and Chief Festivals of the Christian Year. SECOND SERIES, the Christian Life. Fcp 8vo price 5s each series.

HYMNS FROM LYRA GERMANICA. 18mo 1s

LYRA GERMANICA. FIRST SERIES, as above, translated by C. WINKWORTH. With Illustrations from Original Designs by John Leighton, F.S.A., engraved on Wood under his superintendence. Fcp 4to 21s

THE CHORALE-BOOK FOR ENGLAND; A Complete Hymn-Book for Public and Private Worship, in accordance with the Services and Festivals of the Church of England: The Hymns from the *Lyra Germanica* and other Sources, translated from the German by C. WINKWORTH; the Tunes, from the Sacred Music of the Lutheran, Latin, and other Churches, for Four Voices, with Historical Notes, &c., compiled and edited by W. S. BENNETT, Professor of Music in the University of Cambridge, and by OTTO GOLDSCHMIDT. Fcp 4to price 10s 6d cloth, or 18s half-bound in morocco.

HYMNOLOGIA CHRISTIANA: Psalms and Hymns for the Christian Seasons. Selected and Contributed by Philhymnic Friends; and Edited by BENJAMIN HALL KENNEDY, D.D., Prebendary of Lichfield. Crown 8vo [Just ready.

LYRA SACRA; Being a Collection of Hymns, Ancient and Modern Odes, and Fragments of Sacred Poetry; compiled and edited, with a Preface, by the Rev. B. W. SAVILE, M.A. Fcp 8vo 5s

LYRA DOMESTICA: Christian Songs for Domestic Edification. Translated from the *Psaltery and Harp* of C. J. P. SPITTA. By RICHARD MASSIE. Fcp 8vo 4s 6d

THE WIFE'S MANUAL; or, Prayers, Thoughts, and Songs on Several Occasions of a Matron's Life. By the Rev. W. CALVERT, M.A. Ornamented in the style of *Queen Elizabeth's Prayer Book*. Crown 8vo price 10s 6d

HORNE'S INTRODUCTION TO THE CRITICAL STUDY AND KNOWLEDGE OF THE HOLY SCRIPTURES. Eleventh Edition, revised throughout, and brought up to the existing state of Biblical Knowledge. Edited by the Rev. T. H. HORNE, D.D., the Author, the Rev. JOHN AYRE, M.A., and S. P. TREGELLES, LL.D.; or with the Second Volume, on the *Old Testament*, edited by S. DAVIDSON, D.D. and LL.D. With 4 Maps and 22 Woodcuts and Facsimiles. 4 vols. 8vo price £3 13s 6d

HORNE'S COMPENDIOUS INTRODUCTION TO THE STUDY OF THE BIBLE. *Tenth Edition*, carefully re-edited by the Rev. JOHN AYRE, M.A., of Gonville and Caius College, Cambridge. With 3 Maps and 6 Illustrations. Post 8vo 9s

THE TREASURY OF BIBLE KNOWLEDGE: Comprising a Summary of the Evidences of Christianity; the Principles of Biblical Criticism; the History, Chronology, and Geography of the Scriptures; an Account of the Formation of the Canon; separate Introductions to the several Books of the Bible, &c. By the Rev. JOHN AYRE, M.A. Fcp 8vo with Maps, Engravings on Steel, and numerous Woodcuts; uniform with *Maunder's Treasuries*. [Nearly ready.

INSTRUCTIONS IN THE DOCTRINE AND PRACTICE OF CHRISTIANITY. Intended chiefly as an Introduction to Confirmation. By the Right Rev. G. E. L. COTTON, D.D., BISHOP of CALCUTTA. 18mo price 2s 6d

BOWDLER'S FAMILY SHAKSPEARE; in which nothing is *added* to the Original Text, but those words and expressions are *omitted* which cannot with propriety be read aloud. Cheaper Genuine Edition, complete in 1 vol. large type, with 36 Woodcut Illustrations, price 14s Or, with the same ILLUSTRATIONS, in 6 volumes for the pocket, price 5s each.

GOLDSMITH'S POETICAL WORKS. Edited by BOLTON CORNEY, Esq. Illustrated with numerous Wood Engravings, from Designs by Members of the Etching Club. Square crown 8vo 21s

MOORE'S IRISH MELODIES. With 161 Designs on Steel by DANIEL MACLISE, R.A., and the whole of the Text of the Songs engraved by BECKER. Super-royal 8vo 31s 6d

TENNIEL'S EDITION OF MOORE'S LALLA ROOKH. With 68 Woodcut Illustrations, from Original Drawings, and 5 Initial Pages of Persian Designs by T. Sulman, Jun. Fcp 4to 21s

MOORE'S POETICAL WORKS. People's Edition, complete in One Volume, large type, with Portrait after Phillips. Square crown 8vo price 12s 6d

POETICAL WORKS OF LETITIA ELIZABETH LANDON (L.E.L.) Comprising the *Improvisatrice*, the *Venetian Bracelet*, the *Golden Violet*, the *Troubadour*, and Poetical Remains. New Edition; with 2 Vignettes. 2 vols. 16mo 10s

LAYS OF ANCIENT ROME; with *Ivry* and the *Armada*. By the Right Hon. Lord MACAULAY. 16mo 4s 6d

LORD MACAULAY'S LAYS OF ANCIENT ROME. With Illustrations, Original and from the Antique, drawn on Wood by G. Scharf. Fcp 4to 21s

POEMS. By MATTHEW ARNOLD. FIRST SERIES, Third Edition. Fcp 8vo 5s 6d SECOND SERIES, 5s

By the same Author.

MEROPE: A Tragedy. With a Preface and an Historical Introduction. Fcp 8vo 5s

SOUTHEY'S POETICAL WORKS; with all the Author's last Introductions and Notes. *Library Edition*, with Portrait and Vignette. Medium 8vo 21s; in 10 vols. fcp 8vo with Portrait and 19 Vignettes, 35s

By the same Author.

THE DOCTOR, &c. Complete in One Volume. Edited by the Rev. J. W. WARTER, B.D. With Portrait, Vignette, Bust, and coloured Plate. Square crown 8vo 12s 6d

CALDERON'S THREE DRAMAS: *Love the Greatest Enchantment, The Sorceries of Sin,* and *The Devotion of the Cross,* attempted in English Assonante and other Imitative Verse, by D. F. MACCARTHY, M.R.I.A., with Notes, and the Spanish Text. Fcp 4to 15s

A SURVEY OF HUMAN PROGRESS TOWARDS HIGHER CIVILISATION: a Progress as little perceived by the multitude in any age, as is the growing of a tree by the children who sport under its shade. By NEIL ARNOTT, M.D., F.R.S., &c. 8vo price 4s 6d

COLONISATION AND COLONIES: Being a Series of Lectures delivered before the University of Oxford in 1839, '40, and '41. By HERMAN MERIVALE, M.A., Professor of Political Economy. Second Edition, with Notes and Additions. 8vo 18s

C. M. WILLICH'S POPULAR TABLES for Ascertaining the Value of Lifehold, Leasehold, and Church Property, Renewal Fines, &c.; the Public Funds; Annual Average Price and Interest on Consols from 1731 to 1861; Chemical, Geographical, Astronomical, Trigonometrical Tables, &c. &c. *Fifth Edition*, enlarged. Post 8vo 10s

THOMSON'S TABLES OF INTEREST, at Three, Four, Four and a-Half, and Five per Cent., from One Pound to Ten Thousand, and from 1 to 365 Days. 12mo 3s 6d

A DICTIONARY, PRACTICAL, THEORETICAL, AND HISTORICAL, of Commerce and Commercial Navigation. By J. R. M'CULLOCH, Esq. Illustrated with Maps and Plans. New Edition, containing much additional information. 8vo 50s

By the same Author.

A DICTIONARY, GEOGRAPHICAL, STATISTICAL, AND HISTORICAL, of the various Countries, Places, and principal Natural Objects in the World. New Edition, revised; with 6 Maps. 2 vols. 8vo 63s

A MANUAL OF GEOGRAPHY, Physical, Industrial, and Political. By WILLIAM HUGHES, F.R.G.S., &c., Professor of Geography in Queen's College, London. New and thoroughly revised Edition; with 6 coloured Maps. Fcp 8vo 7s 6d

Or, in Two Parts: PART I. Europe, 3s 6d; PART II. Asia, Africa, America, Australasia, and Polynesia, 4s

By the same Author.

THE GEOGRAPHY OF BRITISH HISTORY; a Geographical Description of the British Islands at successive Periods, from the Earliest Times to the Present Day; with a Sketch of the commencement of Colonisation on the part of the English Nation. With 6 full-coloured Maps. Fcp 8vo 8s 6d

A NEW BRITISH GAZETTEER; or, Topographical Dictionary of the British Islands and Narrow Seas: Comprising concise Descriptions of about 60,000 Places, Seats, Natural Features, and Objects of Note, founded on the best Authorities. By J. A. SHARP. 2 vols. 8vo £2 16s

A NEW DICTIONARY OF GEOGRAPHY, Descriptive, Physical, Statistical, and Historical: Forming a complete General Gazetteer of the World. By A. K. JOHNSTON, F.R.S.E., &c. *Second Edition*, revised. In One Volume of 1,360 pages, comprising about 50,000 Names of Places. 8vo 30s

AN ENCYCLOPÆDIA OF CIVIL ENGINEERING, Historical, Theoretical, and Practical. Illustrated by upwards of 3,000 Woodcuts. By E. CRESY, C.E. *Second Edition*, revised and extended. 8vo 42s

THE ENGINEER'S HANDBOOK; explaining the Principles which should guide the Young Engineer in the Construction of Machinery, with the necessary Rules, Proportions, and Tables. By C. S. LOWNDES, Engineer. Post 8vo 5s

USEFUL INFORMATION FOR ENGINEERS: Being a First Series of Lectures delivered before the Working Engineers of Yorkshire and Lancashire. By W. FAIRBAIRN, LL.D., F.R.S., F.G.S. With Plates and Woodcuts. Crown 8vo 10s 6d

SECOND SERIES: Containing Experimental Researches on the Collapse of Boiler Flues and the Strength of Materials, and Lectures on subjects connected with Mechanical Engineering, &c. With Plates and Woodcuts. Crown 8vo 10s 6d

By the same Author.

A TREATISE ON MILLS AND MILLWORK. Vol. I. on the principles of Mechanism and on Prime Movers. With Plates and Woodcuts. 8vo 16s

AN ENCYCLOPÆDIA OF ARCHITECTURE, Historical, Theoretical, and Practical. By JOSEPH GWILT. With more than 1,000 Wood Engravings, from Designs by J. S. Gwilt. 8vo 42s

LOUDON'S ENCYCLOPÆDIA of Cottage, Farm, and Villa Architecture and Furniture. New Edition, edited by Mrs. LOUDON; with more than 2,000 Woodcuts. 8vo 63s

THE ELEMENTS OF MECHANISM, designed for Students of Applied Mechanics. By T. M. GOODEVE, M.A., Professor of Natural Philosophy in King's College, London. With 206 Figures on Wood. Post 8vo 6s 6d

URE'S DICTIONARY OF ARTS, MANUFACTURES, AND MINES. Fifth Edition, re-written and enlarged; with nearly 2,000 Wood Engravings. Edited by ROBERT HUNT, F.R.S., F.S.S., Keeper of Mining Records, &c., assisted by numerous gentlemen eminent in Science and connected with the Arts and Manufactures. 3 vols. 8vo £4

AN ENCYCLOPÆDIA OF DOMESTIC ECONOMY: Comprising such subjects as are most immediately connected with Housekeeping. By THOS. WEBSTER; assisted by Mrs. PARKES. With nearly 1,000 Woodcuts. 8vo 31s 6d

MODERN COOKERY FOR PRIVATE FAMILIES, reduced to a System of Easy Practice in a Series of carefully-tested Receipts, in which the Principles of Baron Liebig and other eminent Writers have been as much as possible applied and explained. By ELIZA ACTON. Newly revised and enlarged Edition; with 8 Plates, comprising 27 Figures, and 150 Woodcuts. Fcp 8vo 7s 6d

A PRACTICAL TREATISE ON BREWING, based on Chemical and Economical Principles. With Formulæ for Public Brewers, and Instructions for Private Families. By W. BLACK. 8vo price 10s 6d

ON FOOD AND ITS DIGESTION: Being an Introduction to Dietetics. By W. BRINTON, M.D., Physician to St. Thomas's Hospital, &c. With 48 Woodcuts. Post 8vo 12s

HINTS TO MOTHERS ON THE MANAGEMENT OF THEIR HEALTH DURING THE PERIOD OF PREGNANCY AND IN THE LYING-IN ROOM. By T. BULL, M.D. Fcp 8vo 5s

THE MATERNAL MANAGEMENT OF CHILDREN IN HEALTH AND DISEASE. Fcp 8vo 5s

LECTURES ON THE DISEASES OF INFANCY AND CHILDHOOD. By CHARLES WEST, M.D., &c. *Fourth Edition*, carefully revised throughout; with numerous additional Cases, and a copious INDEX. 8vo 14s

THE PATENTEE'S MANUAL: A Treatise on the Law and Practice of Letters Patent, especially intended for the use of Patentees and Inventors. By J. JOHNSON and J. H. JOHNSON, Esqrs. Post 8vo 7s 6d

THE PRACTICAL DRAUGHTSMAN'S BOOK OF INDUSTRIAL DESIGN. By W. JOHNSON, Assoc. Inst. C.E. *Second Edition*, enlarged; comprising 500 Pages of Letterpress, 210 Quarto Plates, and numerous Woodcuts. 4to 28s 6d

THE PRACTICAL MECHANIC'S JOURNAL: An Illustrated Record of Mechanical and Engineering Science, and Epitome of Patent Inventions. 4to price 1s monthly. VOLS. I. to XV. price 14s each, in cloth.

THE PRACTICAL MECHANIC'S JOURNAL RECORD OF THE INTERNATIONAL EXHIBITION OF 1862. A full and elaborate Illustrated Account of the Exhibition, contributed by 42 Writers of eminence in the Departments of Science and Art. In One Volume, comprising 630 Pages of Letterpress, illustrated by 20 Plate Engravings and 200 Woodcuts. 4to price 2s 6d cloth.

COLLIERIES AND COLLIERS; A Handbook of the Law and leading Cases relating thereto. By J. C. FOWLER, Barrister-at-Law; Stipendiary Magistrate for the District of Merthyr Tydfil and Aberdare. Fcp 8vo 6s

THE THEORY OF WAR ILLUSTRATED by numerous Examples from History. By Lieut.-Col. MACDOUGALL, late Superintendent of the Staff College. *Third Edition*, with 10 Plans. Post 8vo price 10s 6d

PROJECTILE WEAPONS OF WAR AND EXPLOSIVE COMPOUNDS. By J. SCOFFERN, M.B. Lond. late Professor of Chemistry in the Aldersgate School of Medicine. *Fourth Edition*. Post 8vo with Woodcuts, 9s 6d

SUPPLEMENT, containing New Resources of Warfare, price 2s

A MANUAL FOR NAVAL CADETS. By JOHN M'NEIL BOYD, late Captain R.N. Published with the Sanction and Approval of the Lords Commissioners of the Admiralty. *Second Edition*; with 240 Woodcuts, 7 coloured Plates of Signals, &c., and 11 coloured Plates of Flags. Post 8vo 12s 6d

PROJECTION AND CALCULATION OF THE SPHERE. For Young Sea Officers; being a complete Initiation into Nautical Astronomy. By S. M. Saxby, R.N., Principal Instructor of Naval Engineers, H.M. Steam Reserve. With 77 Diagrams. Post 8vo 5s

By the same Author.

THE STUDY OF STEAM AND THE MARINE ENGINE. For Young Sea Officers in H.M. Navy, the Merchant Navy, &c.; being a complete Initiation into a knowledge of Principles and their Application to Practice. Post 8vo with 87 Diagrams, 5s 6d

A TREATISE ON THE STEAM ENGINE, in its various Applications to Mines, Mills, Steam Navigation, Railways, and Agriculture. With Theoretical Investigations respecting the Motive Power of Heat and the Proportions of Steam Engines; Tables of the Right Dimensions of every Part; and Practical Instructions for the Manufacture and Management of every species of Engine in actual use. By JOHN BOURNE, C.E. Fifth Edition; with 37 Plates and 546 Woodcuts (200 new in this Edition). 4to 42s

By the same Author.

A CATECHISM OF THE STEAM ENGINE, in its various Applications to Mines, Mills, Steam Navigation, Railways, and Agriculture; with Practical Instructions for the Manufacture and Management of Engines of every class. New Edition, with 60 Woodcuts. Fcp 8vo 6s

HANDBOOK OF FARM LABOUR: Comprising Labour Statistics; Steam, Water, Wind; Horse Power; Hand Power; Cost of Farm Operations; Monthly Calendar; APPENDIX on Boarding Agricultural Labourers, &c.; and INDEX. By JOHN CHALMERS MORTON, Editor of the *Agricultural Gazette*, &c. 16mo 1s 6d

By the same Author.

HANDBOOK OF DAIRY HUSBANDRY; Comprising Dairy Statistics; Food of the Cow; Choice and Treatment of the Cow; Milk; Butter; Cheese; General Management of a Dairy Farm; Monthly Calendar of Daily Operations; APPENDIX of Statistics; and INDEX. 16mo 1s 6d

CONVERSATIONS ON NATURAL PHILOSOPHY, in which the Elements of that Science are familiarly explained. By JANE MARCET. 14th Edition; with 24 Plates. Fcp 8vo 10s 6d

By the same Author.

CONVERSATIONS ON CHEMISTRY, in which the Elements of that Science are familiarly explained and illustrated. A thoroughly revised Edition. 2 vols. fcp 8vo 14s

CONVERSATIONS ON LAND AND WATER. Revised Edition, with a Coloured Map, showing the comparative Altitude of Mountains. Fcp 8vo 5s 6d

CONVERSATIONS ON POLITICAL ECONOMY. Fcp 8vo 7s 6d

BAYLDON'S ART OF VALUING RENTS AND TILLAGES, and Claims of Tenants upon Quitting Farms, at both Michaelmas and Lady-Day. Seventh Edition, enlarged. 8vo 10s 6d

AN ENCYCLOPÆDIA OF AGRICULTURE; Comprising the Theory and Practice of the Valuation, Transfer, Laying-out, Improvement, and Management of Landed Property, and of the Cultivation and Economy of the Animal and Vegetable Productions of Agriculture. By J. C. LOUDON. With 1,100 Woodcuts. 8vo 31s 6d

By the same Author.

AN ENCYCLOPÆDIA OF GARDENING; Comprising the Theory and Practice of Horticulture, Floriculture, Arboriculture, and Landscape Gardening. Corrected and improved by Mrs. LOUDON. With 1,000 Woodcuts. 8vo 31s 6d

AN ENCYCLOPÆDIA OF TREES AND SHRUBS; Containing the Hardy Trees and Shrubs of Great Britain, Native and Foreign, Scientifically and Popularly Described. With 2,000 Woodcuts. 8vo 50s

AN ENCYCLOPÆDIA OF PLANTS; Comprising the Specific Character, Description, Culture, History, Application in the Arts, and every other desirable Particular respecting all the Plants found in Great Britain. Corrected by Mrs. LOUDON. With upwards of 12,000 Woodcuts. 8vo £3 13s 6d

THE CABINET LAWYER; A Popular Digest of the Laws of England, Civil and Criminal: Comprising also a Dictionary of Law Terms, Maxims, Statutes, and much other useful Legal Information. 19th Edition, extended by the Author; with the Statutes and Legal Decisions to *Michaelmas Term*, 24 and 25 Victoria. Fcp 8vo 10s 6d

THE EXECUTOR'S GUIDE. By J. C. HUDSON. New and enlarged Edition, revised by the Author. Fcp 8vo 6s

By the same Author.

PLAIN DIRECTIONS FOR MAKING WILLS IN CONFORMITY WITH THE LAW. New Edition, corrected and revised by the Author. Fcp 8vo 2s 6d

THE BRITISH FLORA; Comprising the Phænogamous or Flowering Plants, and the Ferns. 6th Edition, with Additions and Corrections; and numerous Figures engraved on 12 Plates. By Sir W. J. HOOKER, K.H., &c.; and G. A. WALKER-ARNOTT, LL.D., F.L.S. 12mo 14s; with the Plates coloured, 21s

BRYOLOGIA BRITANNICA; Containing the Mosses of Great Britain and Ireland systematically arranged and described according to the method of *Bruch* and *Schimper*; with 61 Illustrative Plates. By WILLIAM WILSON. 8vo 42s; or with the Plates coloured, price £4 4s

HISTORY OF THE BRITISH FRESH-WATER ALGÆ. Including Descriptions of the Desmideæ and Diatomaceæ. By A. H. HASSALL, M.D. With 100 Plates of Figures. 2 vols. 8vo £1 15s

By the same Author.

ADULTERATIONS DETECTED; or, Plain Instructions for the Discovery of Frauds in Food and Medicine. By ARTHUR HILL HASSALL, M.D. Lond., Analyst of *The Lancet* Sanitary Commission. With 225 Woodcuts. Crown 8vo 17s 6d

CORDON-TRAINING OF FRUIT TREES, Diagonal, Vertical, Spiral, Horizontal, adapted to the Orchard-House and Open-Air Culture. By Rev. T. COLLINGS BREHAUT. Fcp 8vo with Woodcuts, 2s 6d

THE THEORY AND PRACTICE OF HORTICULTURE; or, An Attempt to Explain the Principal Operations of Gardening upon Physiological Grounds. By J. LINDLEY, M.D., F.R.S., F.L.S. With 98 Woodcuts. 8vo 21s

By the same Author.

AN INTRODUCTION TO BOTANY. New Edition, revised and enlarged; with 6 Plates and many Woodcuts. 2 vols. 8vo 24s

THE ROSE AMATEUR'S GUIDE: Containing ample Descriptions of all the fine leading Varieties of Roses, regularly classed in their respective Families; their History and Mode of Culture. By THOMAS RIVERS. Seventh Edition. Fcp 8vo 4s

THE GARDENERS' ANNUAL FOR 1863. Edited by the Rev. S. REYNOLDS HOLE. With a coloured Frontispiece by JOHN LEECH. Fcp. 8vo 2s 6d

THE TREASURY OF NATURAL HISTORY; or, Popular Dictionary of Zoology: in which the Characteristics that distinguish the different Classes, Genera, and Species are combined with a variety of interesting Information illustrative of the Habits, Instincts, and General Economy of the Animal Kingdom. By SAMUEL MAUNDER. With above 900 accurate Woodcuts. Fcp 8vo 10s

By the same Author.

THE SCIENTIFIC AND LITERARY TREASURY: A Popular Encyclopædia of Science and the Belles-Lettres; including all branches of Science, and every subject connected with Literature and Art. Fcp 8vo 10s

THE TREASURY OF GEOGRAPHY, Physical, Historical, Descriptive, and Political; containing a succinct Account of every Country in the World. Completed by WILLIAM HUGHES, F.R.G.S. With 7 Maps and 16 Plates. Fcp 8vo 10s

THE HISTORICAL TREASURY: Comprising a General Introductory Outline of Universal History, Ancient and Modern, and a Series of Separate Histories of every principal Nation. Fcp 8vo 10s

THE BIOGRAPHICAL TREASURY: Consisting of Memoirs, Sketches, and Brief Notices of above 12,000 Eminent Persons of All Ages and Nations. 12th Edition. Fcp 8vo 10s

THE TREASURY OF KNOWLEDGE AND LIBRARY OF REFERENCE: Comprising an English Dictionary and Grammar, a Universal Gazetteer, a Classical Dictionary, a Chronology, a Law Dictionary, a Synopsis of the Peerage, useful Tables, &c. Fcp 8vo 10s

Uniform with the above.

THE TREASURY OF BOTANY. By Dr. J. LINDLEY. [*In the press.*

THE TREASURY OF BIBLE KNOWLEDGE. By Rev. J. AYRE, M.A. [*In the press.*

GRADUATED SERIES OF ENGLISH READING-BOOKS.

In 5 vols. fcp 8vo price 10s cloth, each of which Volumes may be had separately as below.

THE GRADUATED SERIES
OF
FIVE READING-LESSON BOOKS
WITH EXPLANATORY NOTES;

Adapted, as a Progressive Course of Reading, for all Classes of English Schools and Families.

Edited by J. S. LAURIE,

Editor of the *Shilling Entertaining Library*, &c.

	s.	d.
FIRST BOOK, 192 Pages, *Sixth Edition*	1	0
SECOND BOOK, 236 Pages, *Fifth Edition*	1	6
THIRD BOOK, 312 Pages, *Sixth Edition*	2	0
FOURTH BOOK, 440 Pages, *Sixth Edition*	2	6
FIFTH BOOK, 496 Pages, *Second Edition*	3	0

THIS is an entirely new series of Reading-Books, carefully adapted throughout to the requirements of modern education. The Five Books are arranged each in corresponding sections, on a metal and uniform scheme of progressive, yet constantly varied selections. BOOK I. consists of rhymes and fireside stories, fables and parables, and short simple tales, all within the comprehension of children who have mastered the first steps in reading. BOOK II. contains miscellanies, tales of adventure, imaginative and real, anecdotes in natural history, and ballad poetry—all preliminary to the Third Book. BOOK III. comprises literary selections in prose and verse, descriptive travel, natural history (with reference to the previous section), and narratives of English history. BOOK IV. to which the Third Book is introductory, is a further extension of the same general plan, with the addition of a division on the more popular branches of Natural Science and Physics, sequentially arranged. BOOK V., which completes the course, forms a further advance and a completion of the general plan, and aims at answering the practical purposes of a Class-book of later English Literature.

By the same Author.

FIRST STEPS to READING: being an Introduction to the Graduated Series of English Reading-Books. Fcp 8vo PART I. price 3d. PART II. price 6d sewed; or complete, price 10d cloth. Or the whole conspicuously printed in bold type for CLASS TEACHING, on a Set of Broadside Sheets, price 4s 6d, or price 7s the Set of BROADSIDES mounted on 15 Cardboards, or 8s 6d with convenient IRON FRAME; the IRON FRAME, separately, price 2s 6d

LAURIE'S ENTERTAINING LIBRARY.

In course of publication, in Quarterly Volumes, from January 1863, each volume in square 16mo, with Six full-page Illustrations, price One Shilling cloth, or Ninepence sewed,

THE
SHILLING ENTERTAINING LIBRARY,

Adapted to the requirements of School Libraries, Families, and Working Men.

By J. S. LAURIE,

Editor of the *Graduated Series of Reading-Lesson Books*, &c.

The First Three Volumes are now ready, viz.

ROBINSON CRUSOE. | **GULLIVER'S TRAVELS.**
CHRISTMAS TALES.

The object of the ENTERTAINING LIBRARY is to provide the young and, generally speaking, the less educated portion of the community with books which they will find readable. Many similar projects have been started, and have failed. The Proprietors of the present LIBRARY believe that these failures are to be ascribed to a fundamental deficiency which, with proper attention and care, may be fully supplied.

In undertakings of this kind too little allowance has been made for what may almost be termed the repulsiveness of a book to the untutored mind. Children freed from irksome tasks, and working men wearied with a hard day's toil, cannot possibly be induced to read until they find out what a wealth of entertainment is concealed under the hard, ungraceful forms of typography. Nothing appears more certain than that they will not read at all, unless materials are placed before them which are calculated to arouse their interest and enchain their attention.

The practical problem to be solved would seem to be to furnish a selection of works which will appeal to that dominant principle in the human breast, the love of pleasure. The aim of the Editor of the ENTERTAINING LIBRARY is to provide an ample and varied repast for the gratification of this instinct. The concentration of his efforts upon this single point will give the present series of books its distinctive character.

A glance at the sources upon which he has already drawn will, it is believed, convince those who are acquainted with English literature, that such volumes as the ENTERTAINING LIBRARY promises to contain will necessarily tend to enlarge the intellectual views, and to direct and strengthen the moral sentiments of every reader. But the prime end kept in view will be to afford, in a wide and liberal sense, pleasure and amusement; and to this end whatever bears more directly upon the practical utilities of life will invariably be held subordinate.

It is proper to state that the Editor assumes the right of adapting the original text so as to suit his purpose. Grammatical constructions which are too involved and difficult will be simplified; modern words and idioms will be substituted for such as have become obsolete or nearly obsolete; and in all cases passages which are unsuitable to the young will be expunged.

Care will be taken to adorn each of the volumes with a number of striking illustrations. The illustrations to the three volumes now ready are drawn by Mr. Wanderbrock, a rising artist, whose merit has been acknowledged by competent judges.

Special attention will be paid to the binding of the volumes. They will be prepared for being well thumbed. The type, also, in which they will be printed will be of the clearest and distinctest kind that can be procured.

Volumes preparing for Publication Quarterly, uniform with the above three:

SANDFORD and MERTON | **HISTORY of the PLAGUE**
[On March 31.] | **The VICAR of WAKEFIELD**
The PILGRIM'S PROGRESS | **CITIZEN of the WORLD**
EVENINGS AT HOME | **SWISS FAMILY ROBINSON**

AND OTHER WORKS.

INDEX.

Acton's Cookery-Book 22	Chorale-Book (The) for England 19
Afternoon of Life 14	Clark's Comparative Grammar 7
Agassiz on Classification 19	Clough's Lives from Plutarch 4
Alcock's Japan 1	Colenso on the Pentateuch 3
Arago's Scientific Biographies 4	Collyns on Stag-Hunting 19
Arago's Meteorological Essays 4	Conwy's Ellice, a Tale 16
Arago's Popular Astronomy 4	Covington's Chemical Analysis 12
Arago's Treatise on Comets 4	Contanseau's French Dictionary 7
Arbuthnot's Herzegovina 9	Conybeare and Howson's St. Paul 6
Arnott's Manual of English Literature 7	Copland's Dictionary of Medicine ... 11
Arnold's Poems 17	Cotton's Instructions in Christianity .. 19
Arnold's Merope 21	Cox's Tales from Greek Mythology .. 5
Arnold on Translating Homer 6	Cox's Tale of the Great Persian War 5
Arnott on Progress 21	Cox's Tales of the Gods and Heroes .. 5
Autobiography of Charles V 1	Cresy's Encyclopædia of Civil Engineering 12
Ayre's Treasury of Bible Knowledge .. 20	
Bacon's Life, by Spedding 2	Cricket Field (The) 14
Bacon's Works 2	Cricket Tutor (The) 14
Bayldon's Rents and Tillages 26	Crowe's History of France 2
Beard's Port-Royal 16	
Berlepsch's Alps 8	D'Aubigné's Calvin 1
Black on Brewing 25	Dead Shot (The) 14
Blaine's Encyclopædia of Rural Sports 14	De la Rive's Reminiscences of Cavour 1
Blight's Land's End 10	De la Rive's Electricity 12
Boner's Forest Creatures 13	De Tocqueville on Democracy 1
Bourne on the Steam Engine 25	De Witt's Jefferson 1
Bowen's Catechism of dittto 25	Dollinger's Gentile and Jew 6
Boutlier's Family Shakespeare 20	Dove's Law of Storms 12
Boyd's Naval Cadet's Manual 24	Eastlake on Oil Painting 8
Brande's Dictionary of Science 12	Eclipse of Faith (The) 17
Bréhaut on Cordon-Training 27	Defence of ditto 17
Brodie's Psychological Inquiries 10	Essays and Reviews 19
Bristow on Food 23	
Bristow's Glossary of Mineralogy 12	Fairbairn's Information for Engineers 23
Brownfield's Brittany and the Bible .. 10	Fairbairn's Treatise on Millwork 23
Brunel's Life, by Beamish 3	FitzRoy's Weather Book 13
Bull's Hints to Mothers 24	Falkland's Sailing Boat 14
Bull on Management of Children 24	Forster's Life of Eliot 1
Bunsen's Hippolytus 6	Fowler's Collieries 24
Bunsen's Outlines of Universal History 6	Freshfield's Alpine Byways 8
Bunsen's Analecta Ante-Nicæna 6	Freshfield's Tour in the Grisons 8
Bunsen's Ancient Egypt 6	
Bunyan's Pilgrim's Progress illustrated 19	Garrett's Marvels of Instinct 14
Burke's Vicissitudes of Families 4	Goldsmith's Poems, illustrated 20
Burn's Agricultural Tour in Belgium 16	Goodeve's Elements of Mechanism .. 12
Burton's Lake Regions of Central Africa 9	Green's English Princesses 3
Burton's Footsteps in East Africa 9	Greene's Manual of Coelenterata 13
Burton's Medina and Mecca 9	Greene's Manual of Protozoa 13
Burton's City of the Saints 9	Gresson's Correspondence 17
	Grove on Physical Forces 12
Cabinet Lawyer (The) 25	Gwilt's Encyclopædia of Architecture 11
Calderon's Dramas, by MacCarthy ... 17	
Calvert's Wife's Manual 20	Hartwig's Sea 13
Cats' and Farlie's Emblems 19	Hartwig's Tropical World 13

NEW WORKS PUBLISHED BY LONGMAN AND CO.   31

Hassall's Freshwater Algæ 16
Hassall's Adulterations Detected 16
Havelock's Life, by Marshman 4
Hawker on Guns and Shooting 16
Herschel's Outlines of Astronomy 12
Herschel's Essays 12
Hind's American Exploring Expedition 9
Hind's Labrador 9
Hints on Etiquette 13
Hole's Gardeners' Annual 17
Holland's Essays 10
Holland's Medical Notes 10
Holland on Mental Physiology 10
Hooker's British Flora 20
Hopkins's Hawaii 9
Horne's Introduction to the Scriptures 20
Horne's Compendium of ditto 20
Hoskyns' Talpa 15
Howard's Athletic Exercises 15
Howitt's History of the Supernatural 10
Howitt's Remarkable Places 10
Howitt's Rural Life of England 10
Hudson's Descoverers 16
Hudson's Directions for Making Wills 20
Hudson's Executor's Guide 20
Hughes's Geography of History 27
Hughes's Manual of Geography 27

Jameson's Saints and Martyrs 19
Jameson's Monastic Orders 19
Jameson's Legends of the Madonna .. 19
Jameson's Legends of the Saviour ... 19
Johnson's Dictionary by Latham 7
Johnson's Patentee's Manual 24
Johnson's Book of Industrial Designs 24
Johnston's Geographical Dictionary ... 12

Kennedy's Hymnologia 20
Kirby and Spence's Entomology 14

L. E. L's. Poetical Works 21
Lady's Tour round Monte Rosa 6
Latham's Comparative Philology 7
Latham's English Language 7
Latham's Handbook of ditto 7
Laurie's Entertaining Library 20
Laurie's Graduated Reading Books .. 12
Lempriere's Notes on Mexico 9
Liddell and Scott's Greek Lexicons .. 6
Lindley's Horticulture 27
Lindley's Introduction to Botany 27
Lindley's Treasury of Botany 27
Lister's Physico-Prophetical Essays .. 18
Lewis's Jerusalem 6
London's Encyclopædia of Cottage Architecture 22
London's Encyclopædia of Agriculture 22

London's Encyclopædia of Gardening 22
London's Encyclopædia of Trees and Shrubs 22
London's Encyclopædia of Plants 22
London's Engineer's Handbook 22
Lyra Domestica 20
Lyra Germanica 19
Lyra Sacra 20

Macaulay's England 3
Macaulay's Essays 17
Macaulay's Miscellaneous Writings .. 17
Macaulay's Lays of Ancient Rome ... 21
Macaulay's Speeches 5
MacBrair's Africans 10
MacDougall's Theory of War 14
M'Culloch's Commercial Dictionary .. 12
M'Culloch's Geographical Dictionary.. 12
Marcet's Land and Water 16
Marcet's Political Economy 23
Marcet's Conversations on Natural Philosophy 23
Marcet's Conversations on Chemistry 23
Maunder's Biographical Treasury ... 27
Maunder's Geographical Treasury ... 27
Maunder's Historical Treasury 27
Maunder's Natural History 27
Maunder's Scientific and Literary Treasury 27
Maunder's Treasury of Knowledge ... 27
May's England 2
Memoir of Sydney Smith 6
Memoirs, &c. of Thomas Moore 6
Mendelssohn's Letters 6
Merivale's Romans under the Empire 2
Merivale's Fall of the Roman Republic 3
Merivale's (H.) Lectures on Colonization 21
Meryon's History of Medicine 3
Miles on Horse's Foot 16
Miles on Shoeing Horses 16
Moore's Lalla Rookh 21
Moore's Irish Melodies 21
Moore's Poetical Works 21
Morell's Mental Philosophy 11
Morell's Elements of Psychology 11
Morning Clouds 16
Morton's Royal Farms 9
Morton's Dairy Husbandry 25
Morton's Farm Labour 25
Moshaim's Ecclesiastical History 16
Müller's Lectures on Language 7
Munk's College of Physicians 3
Mure's Language and Literature of Greece 3
My Life, and What shall I do with it? 16
Funk's Sunsets and Sunshine 16

NEW WORKS PUBLISHED BY LONGMAN AND CO.

Odling's Chemistry 11
Owen's Anatomy 11
Parks's Guide to the Pyrenees 5
Parry's Memoirs..................... 4
Peaks, Passes, and Glaciers........... 5
Pereira's Materia Medica............. 12
Pischel's Elements of Physics........ 12
Phillips's Guide to Geology........... 10
Phillips's Introduction to Mineralogy.. 12
Piesse's Art of Perfumery............ 13
Piesse's Chemical Wonders.......... 15
Piesse's Chemical and Natural Magic 13
Piotrowski's Siberian Exile........... 1
Powers's Life by Nasmon 4
Practical Mechanic's Journal......... 24
Problems in Human Nature 16
Pycroft's English Reading........... 19

Ranke's Canada and the Crimea 5
Record of International Exhibition .. 24
Rhind's Thebes 5
Rich's Roman and Greek Antiquities 3
Rivers's Rose Amateur's Guide...... 27
Rogers's Essays 17
Roget's English Thesaurus 7
Romance of a Dull Life 18
Ronald's Fly-Fisher................. 15
Rowton's Debater 7

Sandford's Bampton Lectures 19
Savile on Revelation and Science 16
Scaby on Projection of Sphere 25
Scaby on Study of Steam............ 22
Scoffern on Projectiles 24
Scott's Lectures on the Fine Arts ... 4
Scott's Volumetrical Analysis 4
Scrope on Volcanos 11
Senior's Biographical Sketches........ 3
Sewell's Ancient History 5
Sewell's Early Church 5
Sewell's Passing Thoughts on Religion 18
Sewell's Self-Examination for Confirmation 18
Sewell's Readings for Confirmation.. 18
Sewell's Readings for Lent........... 18
Sewell's Impressions of Rome, &c.... 19
Sewell's Stories and Tales 18
Sharp's British Gazetteer............ 11
Short Whist....................... 15
Sidney's (Sir P.) Life, by Lloyd...... 3
Smith's (J.) St. Paul's Shipwreck ... 4
Smith's (G.) Wesleyan Methodism... 3
Social Life in Australia.............. 16
Southey's Poetical Works............ 21

Southey's Doctor................... 21
Stephen's Essays.................... 17
Stephen's Lectures on the History of France......................... 17
Stephenson's Life, by Jeaffreson and Pole......................... 6
'Stonehenge' on the Dog........... 16
'Stonehenge' on the Greyhound..... 16
Strickland's Queens of England 3
Sydney Smith's Works............... 17
Sydney Smith's Moral Philosophy.... 17

Tate on Strength of Materials....... 13
Taylor's (Jeremy) Works............. 20
Tennent's Ceylon 14
Tennent's Natural History of Ceylon 14
Theologia Germanica............... 19
Thirlwall's Greece.................. 2
Thomson's Interest Tables 23
Thomson's Laws of Thought........ 11
Thrupp's Anglo-Saxon Home....... 5
Todd's Cyclopaedia of Anatomy and Physiology 11
Trollope's Warden 18
Trollope's Barchester Towers........ 18
Twiss's Law of Nations 9
Tyndall on Heat 11
Tyndall's Mountaineering........... 5

Ure's Dictionary of Arts, Manufactures, and Mines 23

Van Der Hoeven's Handbook of Zoology........................ 11
Villari's History of Savonarola 4

Warburton's Life, by Watson 4
Warter's Last of the Old Squires ... 18
Watts's Dictionary of Chemistry..... 12
Webb's Celestial Objects 12
Webster and Parkes's Domestic Economy 23
Wellington's Life, by Gleig 4
Wesley's Life, by Southey 5
West on Children's Diseases 6
White and Riddle's Latin Dictionary 8
Wilson's Bryologia Britannica........ 28
Willich's Popular Tables 22
Wit and Wisdom of Sydney Smith .. 17
Woodward's Chronological and Historical Encyclopaedia 8
Worms on the Earth's Motion 11
Wyndham's Norway 5

Yonge's English-Greek Lexicon 7
Youatt on the Horse 16
Youatt on the Dog 16

[January 1863.

www.ingramcontent.com/pod-product-compliance
Lightning Source LLC
Chambersburg PA
CBHW030403230426
43664CB00007BB/727